Remittance Markets in Africa

Remittance Markets in Africa

Sanket Mohapatra and
Dilip Ratha

Editors

THE WORLD BANK
Washington, D.C.

ISBN: 978-0-8213-8475-6
eISBN: 978-0-8213-8553-1
DOI: 10.1596/978-0-8213-8475-6

Library of Congress Cataloging-in-Publication Data
Remittance markets in Africa / Sanket Mohapatra and Dilip Ratha, editors.
    p. cm.
  Includes bibliographical references and index.
  ISBN 978-0-8213-8475-6—ISBN 978-0-8213-8553-1 (electronic)
1. Emigrant remittances—Africa, Sub-Saharan. 2. Economic development—Finance—Africa, Sub-Saharan. 3. Africa, Sub-Saharan—Emigration and immigration—Economic aspects. 4. Africa, Sub-Saharan—Economic conditions. 5. Financial services industry—Africa, Sub-Saharan. 6. Africans—Economic aspects—Europe, Western. 7. Immigrants—Economic aspects—Europe, Western. I. Mohapatra, Sanket, 1975- II. Ratha, Dilip.
  HG3982.R46 2011
  332.450869120967—dc22

                                                                              2011013215

Cover illustration: Diana Ong/SuperStock/by Getty Images
Cover design: Drew Fasick

Contents

Foreword   *xv*
Acknowledgments   *xvii*
Abbreviations   *xix*

PART I   **Overview**   **1**

Chapter 1   **Migrant Remittances in Africa: An Overview**   **3**
                    Sanket Mohapatra and Dilip Ratha

                    Recent Remittance Trends in Africa   6
                    Macroeconomic Impacts of Remittances   11
                    Impact on Households   16
                    Remittance Markets in Africa   26
                    Policies for Leveraging Remittances
                         for Development   38
                    Overview of Remittance Market Surveys
                         in Africa and Two Remittance-Source Countries   42
                    Annex 1.1   50
                    Annex 1.2   51
                    Notes   54
                    References   59

PART II   **Remittance Markets in Remittance-Receiving**
              Countries   **71**

Chapter 2   **Burkina Faso**   **73**
              Yiriyibin Bambio

              Remittance and Migration Trends   74
              Characteristics of the Remittance Industry   77
              The Regulatory and Business Environment   81
              Conclusions and Recommendations   86
              Annex 2.1   87
              Notes   88
              References   88

Chapter 3   **Cape Verde**   **91**
              Georgiana Pop

              Remittance and Emigration Trends   91
              Characteristics of the Remittance Industry   96
              Access to Other Financial Services   100
              The Regulatory and Business Environment   100
              Remittance Costs and Identification Requirements   103
              Conclusions and Recommendations   106
              Annex 3.A Financial Sector Development
                  in Cape Verde   109
              Notes   110
              References   110

Chapter 4   **Ethiopia**   **113**
              Alemayehu Geda and Jacqueline Irving

              Recent Migration Trends   114
              Remittance Sources and Trends   114
              Characteristics of the Remittance Industry   116
              The Regulatory and Business Environment   124
              Remittance Costs   126
              Customer Identification Requirements   127
              Conclusions and Policy Implications   127
              Annex 4.1 Banks and MTOs Interviewed
                  for the Study of the Ethiopian
                  Remittance Services Industry   130

| | Notes | 130 |
| | References | 131 |

Chapter 5   **Ghana**   **133**
Peter Quartey

Remittance and Migration Trends	133
Characteristics of the Remittance Industry	138
The Regulatory and Business Environment	145
Conclusions and Recommendations	149
Notes	151
References	152

Chapter 6   **Kenya**   **155**
Rose W. Ngugi

Remittance and Migration Trends	156
Characteristics of the Remittance Industry	158
The Regulatory and Business Environment	172
Conclusions and Recommendations	178
Notes	182
References	182

Chapter 7   **Nigeria**   **185**
Chukwuma Agu

Remittance and Emigration Trends	187
Characteristics of the Remittance Industry	190
The Regulatory and Business Environment	199
Conclusions and Recommendations	210
Notes	216
References	217

Chapter 8   **Senegal**   **221**
Fatou Cisse

Remittance Trends and Their Economic Significance	222
Characteristics of the Remittance Industry in Senegal	229
The Regulatory and Business Environment	235
Conclusion	238

	Notes	239
	References	239
Chapter 9	**Uganda**	**243**
	Rose W. Ngugi and Edward Sennoga	
	Trends and Uses of Remittances	245
	Characteristics of the Remittance Industry	247
	Emerging Products: Mobile Money Transfers	256
	Transport Service for Domestic Remittances	258
	Remittances and Access to Financial Services	259
	Regulatory and Business Environment	260
	Remittance Costs and Identification	
	Requirements	262
	Conclusion	266
	Recommendations	267
	Notes	268
	References	268
PART III	**Remittance Markets in Remittance-Source Countries**	**271**
Chapter 10	**France**	**273**
	Frederic Ponsot	
	Remittance and Migration Trends	273
	Characteristics of the Remittance Industry	278
	The Regulatory and Business Environment	295
	Conclusions and Recommendations	302
	Annex 10.1	308
	Acknowledgments	310
	Notes	311
	References	315
Chapter 11	**United Kingdom**	**317**
	Leon Isaacs	
	Migration and Remittance Trends	317
	Characteristics of the Remittance Industry	320
	The Regulatory and Business Environment	329

Conclusions and Recommendations 340
Annex 11.1 Country-Specific Pricing Grids 344
Notes 345
References 346

Contributors 347

Boxes
2.1 Remittances and Poverty Reduction in Burkina Faso 74
2.2 Remittances from Côte d'Ivoire 77
2.3 The Financial System in Burkina Faso 82
3.1 The Central Bank's Regulatory and
Supervisory Role 101
4.1 The Ethiopian Financial Sector 117
4.2 Case Study: Birritu Express 120
5.1 Informal RSP Case Study: A Shoe Seller at
Madina Market, Accra 144
5.2 The Financial Sector in Ghana 146
6.1 The M-PESA Money Transfer System 162
6.2 Transport Industry and Money Transfer
Services in Kenya 164
6.3 *Hawala:* The Somali Community-Based
Remittance System 165
6.4 The Financial Sector in Kenya 171
7.1 Geographic Nuances of Nigerian Migration
and Remittances 188
7.2 Recharge Cards for Domestic and International
Remittances: The MTN Model 192
7.3 The Financial System in Nigeria 193
7.4 NIPOST's Potential to Revolutionize the
Nigerian Remittance Market 197
7.5 The Plague of Fraud in Remittance and
Other Electronic Fund Transfers 211
9.1 Financial Institutions in Uganda 248
9.2 SACCOs and MFIs as Providers of Domestic and
Cross-Border Remittance Services 254
9.3 The Transport Sector as a Provider of Remittance
Services in Uganda and in East Africa 258
10.1 French Banks and Sub-Saharan Migrants 282
10.2 The BdE Experience: Developing Agent Networks 283

10.3	Loro/Nostro Accounts Enable African Banks to Collect Deposits in France	293
10.4	Telemedia and Tagattitude: New Channels for Micropayments to Mali	294
10.5	RSP Remittance Ceilings	302
11.1	Case Study: A Formal Remittance Service Provider Coping with Global Financial Crisis	319
11.2	Case Study: A Shipping Company as Informal RSP	323
11.3	Case Study: An Arab RSP with a Large Branch Network in the United Kingdom	324
11.4	Case Study: A Competitive Small Formal RSP	326
11.5	The EU Payment Services Directive	330

Figures

1.1	Remittances and Other Resource Flows to Africa, 1990–2010	7
1.2	Sources of Remittances to Africa and All Developing Regions in 2010	10
1.3	Stability of Resource Flows to Africa, 1990–2008, by Source	12
1.4	External Debt as a Share of Exports from, and Remittances to, Selected Countries	13
1.5	Shares of Remittance Recipients in Top Two Consumption Quintiles, Selected Countries	18
1.6	Average Annual Remittance to Selected Countries, by Source	19
1.7	Secondary and Tertiary Educational Attainment of Remittance Recipient and Nonrecipient Households, Selected Countries	22
1.8	Household Bank Accounts in Selected African Countries, by Remittance Status	25
1.9	Cost of Sending Remittances	27
1.10	South-South Remittance Costs in Sub-Saharan Africa	28
1.11	Banking Networks and Costs, by Region	29
1.12	Factors Inhibiting Use of Formal Remittance Channels	30
1.13	Formal and Informal Remittance Channels in Africa	33
1.14	Average M-PESA Transaction Size, March 2007–March 2009	35
1.15	Top Remittance Areas Needing Attention in Sub-Saharan Africa	39

2.1	Migrant Remittance Flows to Burkina Faso, WAEMU, and ECOWAS, 1974–2010	75
2.2	Obstacles to Providing Formal Remittance Services	83
2.A.1	Remittance Sources and Destinations, WAEMU vs. Non-WAEMU Countries	87
2.A.2	Inward and Outward Remittances among WAEMU Countries	88
3.1	Composition of External Financing for Cape Verde, 1995 and 2007	92
3.2	Share of 2007 Remittances to Cape Verde by Country of Origin	94
3.3	Cape Verdean Overseas Disapora, 2000	96
4.1	Remittance Flows to Ethiopia, 1990–2009	116
5.1	Remittance Transmission Channels in Ghana	135
5.2	Destinations of Ghanaian Emigrants	136
5.3	Sources of Remittance Inflows to Ghana through Banks, 2007	139
5.4	RSP Types in Ghana	141
5.5	Partnership Benefits to RSP Firms	142
5.6	RSP Remittance Instruments	143
5.7	Perceptions of Competition from Informal RSPs	148
6.1	RSP Partnership Benefits	168
6.2	Remittance Instruments Used by RSPs	169
7.1	Foreign Direct Investment and Remittances in Nigeria, 2005–09	186
7.2	Peak Remittance Periods in Nigeria	189
7.3	RSP Perceptions of Laws and Regulations as Obstacles to Remittance Business	201
7.4	RSP Perceptions of Barriers to Remittance Business, by Type	202
7.5	Perceptions of Informal RSPs as Competitors	206
8.1	Volume of Migrant Workers' Remittances to Senegal, 2001–10	222
8.2	Share of GDP from Migrant Workers' Remittances, 2001–09	223
8.3	Comparison of Remittance Flows to Senegal, 1995–2010, by Source	226
8.4	Regional Coverage of Bank Branches in Senegal, 2009	231
8.5	MTO Remittance Market Shares in Senegal, 2009	232

8.6	RSP Firms' Perceptions of Laws and Regulations as Obstacles to Providing Remittance Services in Senegal	236
10.1	Migrants in France, 2007, by Region of Origin	274
10.2	Migrant Remittance Outflows from France, 1999–2007	275
10.3	Comparisons of 2005 GDP Per Capita, by Region	278
10.4	Distribution of Interviewed RSPs, by Type	280
10.5	Distribution of Formal Remittance Flows, by Channel	292
10.A.1	Formal Sector RSP Categories Identified in the Catalog	308
10.A.2	Categories of Formal Sector RSPs Interviewed	309
10.A.3	Formal Sector Market Shares, by RSP Type	310
11.1	Average Fees and Foreign Exchange Charges for Remittances to Africa	320
11.2	Prices to Send £100, by African Corridor	335
11.3	Prices to Send £250, by African Corridor	336
11.4	Comparison Remittance Fees to Africa over Three Waves of Data	336
11.5	Costs to Send Remittances to Africa and South Asia	337
11.6	U.K. Remittances Customer Charter	342

Tables

1.1	Remittances and Other Resource Flows to Africa, 1990–2010	8
1.2	Securitization Potential for Sub-Saharan Africa, 2009	14
1.3	Use of Remittances by Recipient Households in Selected African Countries, by Source	20
1.4	Food Security Strategies and Remittances in Ethiopian Households	24
1A.1	Household Access to Information and Communication Technology in Selected African Countries, by Remittance Status	50
1A.2	Formal and Informal Remittance Channels, Select African Countries	51
2.1	RSP Types and Coverage in Burkina Faso	79
2.2	Money Transfer Instruments Offered by RSPs	80
2.3	Rates to Send $200 in Burkina Faso, by RSP type	84
3.1	International Remittance Flows to and from Cape Verde, 2001–10	93
3.2	RSP Branches in Cape Verde	97

3.3	Business Partnerships for Remittance Services	97
3.4	Remittance Products, by RSP	99
3.5	Fees for Remittances to Cape Verde, by MTO	105
4.1	Branches of Primary Remittance Service Providers in Ethiopia	118
4.2	Remittance Instruments in Ethiopia, by RSP Type	121
4.A1	Ethiopia RSPs Interviewed	130
5.1	Uses of Migrant Remittances in Ghana	135
5.2	RSP Perceptions of Laws and Regulations as Entry Barriers	147
6.1	Remittance Inflows to Kenya	157
6.2	Kenyan RSP Survey Sample Distribution	159
6.3	Financial Services Coverage in Kenya, 2007	161
6.4	Remittance Charges in Kenya, by RSP Type	177
7.1	Branches and Coverage of Primary RSPs in Nigeria	191
7.2	Average Fees for Domestic Remittances in Nigeria	207
7.3	Bank Fees for Outward International Remittances in Nigeria, 2007–08	208
8.1	Remittance Transfers by Use in Senegal, 2008	224
8.2	Impact of Remittances on Poverty Rates, by Location	225
8.3	Sources of Remittances to Senegal, 2008, by Location	225
8.4	Principal Destinations of Senegalese International Migrants, 2008	228
8.5	Volume and Market Share of Remittance Transfers in Senegal, by Method	230
9.1	Remittance Trends in Uganda	245
9.2	Participation of RSPs and Services Provided by RSPs in Uganda, 2008	249
9.3	Remittance Charges for Sending U.S. Currency, 2008	263
10.1	Growth of Immigrant Population in France, 1999–2005, by Region of Origin	276
10.2	Remittance Market from France to Selected North African and Sub-Saharan Countries	277
10.3	Remittance Channels Used by Senegalese Migrants in France	281
10.4	Transfer Channels from France to Mali, Senegal, and Comoros	281

10.5	Community-Based RSP Chain of Operations and Main Actors, by Role	287
10.6	Estimate of Total French Remittance Market from Average Transfer and Propensity Data (Model 1)	290
10.7	Estimate of the French Remittance Market from AfDB Country Data (Model 2)	290
10.8	Remittances from France to Selected Sub-Saharan African Countries	291
10.9	Main RSP Types and Coverage of Selected Remittance Corridors	297
10.10	Remittance Charges of African CBIP Partners, 2009	300
10.11	Charges to Send €150 through Selected RSPs	301
10.12	MTO Charges to Send €150 from Selected Countries	301
10.A.1	Extrapolated Data	310
10.A.2	Repartition of Extrapolated Data, by Destination Country	311
11.1	Average Fee and Foreign Exchange Charges	334
11.2	Fee Comparison for Remittances to Africa, 2008 vs. 2007	335
11.A.1.1	Remittance Pricing, by African Corridor	346

Foreword

A substantive literature suggests that migration generates benefits for migrants, the host societies, and the countries of origin. The economic benefits for the countries of origin are realized primarily through the receipt of remittances. These large and stable resource flows remained relatively resilient during the global financial crisis compared to steep declines in private capital flows, and they have quickly recovered to the precrisis levels. African countries are estimated to have received $40 billion in officially recorded flows in 2010, but the true size is believed to be far larger. Remittances are associated with reduction in poverty, improved education and health outcomes, and increased availability of funds for small business investments. Remittances represent a positive and relatively noncontroversial outcome of migration.

Despite the importance of remittances, the official data on remittance flows to Africa are weak, and remittance markets in Africa remain underdeveloped. Informal remittance channels continue to dominate cross-border and domestic remittance flows in the region. The cost of sending remittances to Africa continues to remain significantly higher than those in more mature migration corridors, such as between Mexico and the United States.

This volume brings together studies of remittance markets in eight Sub-Saharan African countries and two key destinations for African migrants outside the African continent. It provides an overview of the remittance markets, and the policy and institutional environments in both sending and receiving countries. Based on primary surveys of remittance service providers about the types of remittance services, barriers to entry and exit, legal and regulatory environment, remittance costs, and innovative technologies, the chapters of this volume provide a unique window into the functioning of remittance markets in this region.

These country studies served as background material for a joint flagship report of the African Development Bank and the World Bank, *Leveraging Migration for Africa: Remittances, Skills, and Investments*, released in March 2011. Reflecting the objective of the project to build local capacity in African countries, the country studies were prepared primarily by local researchers and institutions in Africa, France, and the United Kingdom. The chapter authors presented preliminary findings during a workshop conducted at the African Development Bank in Tunis (March 16–17, 2009) and final findings at the World Bank in Washington, D.C. (March 18, 2010). The country studies were then peer reviewed.

As discussed in the volume, measures to reduce remittance fees, increase market competition and consumer protection, increase the involvement of post offices and other non-bank institutions, and encourage the extension of mobile money transfer services to cross-border remittances will benefit the ultimate clients, the people of Africa. I hope that the findings of this volume will motivate more research, improved data collection, and policy action in the area of migrant remittances in Africa.

Hans Timmer
Director
Development Prospects Group
The World Bank

Acknowledgments

This volume represents a companion volume to *Leveraging Migration for Africa: Remittances, Skills, and Investments*, a flagship report of the Africa Migration Project. Most of the country studies of remittance markets included in this volume are authored by local researchers and practitioners located in the countries. This volume has benefited from the guidance and direction of Hans Timmer.

This report benefited from the comments and suggestions of participants at a workshop at the African Development Bank in Tunis on March 16–17, 2009: Ernest Addison, Chukwuma Agu, David Olusanya Ajakaiye, Gisèle Aubut, Yiriyibin Bambio, Mohamed Bourenane, Fatou Cissé, Marie-Laure de-Bergh, Julie Fortin, Mandla Sizwe Gantsho, Patrick Giraud, Jacqueline Irving, Leon Isaacs, David Asiimwe Kihangire, Sarah Lahmani, Pedro de Lima, Sam Lugaraba, Albertine A. H. Lipou Massala, Henriette B. Mampuya, Subha Nagarajan, Stefan Nalletamby, Léonce Ndikumana, Rose Ngugi, Kerry Nelson, Caglar Ozden, John Page, Marc Petzoldt, Sonia Plaza, Aruma Oteh, Peter Quartey, Neil Ruiz, Carlotta Saporito, Sara Johansson De Silva, Simon Turner, and Rosemary Vargas-Lundius.

We are grateful to Neil Ruiz for coordinating the financial and administrative aspects of the survey implementation, and to Sonia Plaza for useful suggestions. Mirafe Marcos and Deepak Mishra provided help in facilitating interviews in Addis Ababa. Special thanks to Antonio C. David for his contribution during the initial phase of the project to develop a harmonized survey questionnaire, identifying relevant country contacts, and for his participation in a mission to several African countries. Tola Oni and Ani Silwal provided research assistance at various stages of the project.

This report was made possible with the financial support for the Africa Migration Project by the African Development Bank; Canadian International Development Agency (CIDA); U.K. Department for International Development (DFID); Ministry of Immigration, Integration, Asylum and Solidarity Development, France; Ministry of Foreign Affairs, Denmark; International Fund for Agricultural Development (IFAD); and Swedish International Development Cooperation Agency (Sida), and the World Bank.

Book design, editing, and production were coordinated by Mary Fisk, Steven McGroarty, and Denise Bergeron of the World Bank Office of the Publisher. We are especially grateful to Mary Fisk for her consistent support, good humor, and patience through the process of editing this volume. We are thankful to Stephen McGroarty and Santiago Pombo-Bejarano for their support during the publication process.

Sanket Mohapatra
Dilip Ratha
Editors

Abbreviations

AfDB	African Development Bank
AML	anti-money-laundering (regulations)
AML-CFT	anti-money-laundering and combating the financing of terrorism
ATM	automated teller machine
BCEAO	Central Bank of West African States (Banque Centrale des États de l'Afrique de l'Ouest)
BACB	Agricultural and Commercial Bank of Burkina Faso
BCA	Atlantic Commercial Bank (Banco Comercial do Atlântico) (Cape Verde)
BCB	Commercial Bank of Burkina Faso
BCN	Cape Verde Business Bank (Banco Caboverdiano de Negócios)
BCV	Bank of Cape Verde
BdE	Banque d'Escompte (France)
BIA	Inter-Atlantic Bank (Banco Interatlântico) (Cape Verde)
BIB	International Bank of Burkina Faso
BIM	Banque Internationale pour le Mali
BOFID	Banks and Other Financial Institutions Decree (Nigeria)

CBAO	Banking Company of West Africa (Compagnie Bancaire de l'Afrique Occidentale) (Senegal)
CBIP	Company of International Banks in Paris (Compagnie de Banques Internationales de Paris)
CCK	Communication Commission of Kenya
CECV	Savings Bank of Cape Verde (Caixa Economica de Cabo Verde)
CVEsc	Cape Verde escudo
DMA	Developing Markets Associates Ltd
DMB	deposit money bank
ECOWAS	Economic Community of West African States
EEA	European Economic Area
EFCC	Economic and Financial Crimes Commission (Nigeria)
EFT	electronic funds transfer
EML	electronic money license
FATF	Financial Action Task Force (Nigeria)
FDI	foreign direct investment
FSA	Financial Services Authority (United Kingdom)
GDP	gross domestic product
GLSS	Ghana Living Standards Survey
GSM	Global System for Mobile Communications
HMRC	Her Majesty's Revenue and Customs (United Kingdom)
IMF	International Monetary Fund
INSEE	French National Institute for Statistics and Economic Studies (Institut National de la Statistique et des Études Économiques)
K Sh	Kenyan shilling
KYC	know-your-customer (regulations)
MECSEF	Mutual Savings and Loan of Senegalese France (La Mutuelle d'Epargne et de Crédit des Sénégalais de France)
MEF	Ministry of Economy and Finance (Burkina Faso)
MFI	microfinance institution
MoFED	Ministry of Finance and Economic Development (Ethiopia)
MSB	money service business
MTO	money transfer operator

NBE	National Bank of Ethiopia
NIPOST	Nigerian Postal Service
ODA	official development assistance
PE	payment establishment
PI	payment institution
POS	point of sale
PSD	Payment Services Directive
RSP	remittance service provider
RTGS	real time gross settlement (funds transfer systems)
SACCO	savings and credit cooperative organization
SEPA	Single Euro Payments Area
SFDP	Société Financière de Paiement (joint venture of Western Union and La Banque Postale)
SG	Société Générale (France)
SONAPOST	national postal service (Burkina Faso)
SWIFT	Society for Worldwide Interbank Financial Telecommunication
UKMTA	U.K. Money Transmitters Association
VAT	value added tax
WAEMU	West African Economic and Monetary Union

Note: All monetary amounts are U.S. dollars unless otherwise indicated.

PART I

Overview

CHAPTER 1

Migrant Remittances in Africa: An Overview

Sanket Mohapatra and Dilip Ratha

Remittances are often said to be the most tangible and least controversial link between migration and development (Russell 1992; Ratha 2007). Remittance flows to developing countries have increased substantially during the past decade to reach $325 billion in 2010 (World Bank 2011). Remittances sent by 31 million international African migrants reached nearly $40 billion in 2010, equivalent to 2.6 percent of Africa's gross domestic product (GDP).

The data on African migration and remittance flows, however, are likely to be understated because of the scale of undocumented migration within the African continent, the prevalence of informal remittance channels within the region, and the relatively weak official data in many African countries (World Bank 2006). The true size of remittance flows to Africa, including unrecorded flows through formal and informal channels, is believed to be significantly larger than the official data. After foreign direct investment (FDI), recorded remittances are the African continent's largest source of foreign inflows.

Remittance receipts generate large benefits for the countries of origin in Africa. The review of the literature and evidence presented in this chapter suggests that remittances tend to be stable, and often counter-cyclical, compared to other private flows and help to sustain consumption and investment during economic downturns. Cross-country analysis and evidence from household surveys show that remittance receipts are associated with reductions in poverty, increased household resources devoted to investment, and improved health and education outcomes. Migrant remittances help smooth household consumption and act as a form of insurance for African households facing shocks to their income and livelihood caused by drought, famine, and other natural disasters. The securitization of future remittance flows—the use of hard currency remittances as collateral to raise financing—can increase the access of African banks and firms to international capital markets and can be used to fund longer-term development and infrastructure projects.

In spite of the size, stability, and development implications of these financial flows, this chapter suggests that remittance markets in Africa remain relatively underdeveloped. Africa has arguably the largest share of cross-border remittances flowing through informal channels, and significantly higher remittance costs, compared with other, more mature remittance corridors (for example, from the United States to Mexico and from the Persian Gulf to South Asia). African migrants—especially those residing in other African countries—and recipient households often have limited access to formal remittance and banking services. A large share of international remittances to Africa is channeled through a few large international money transfer agencies, which sometimes work in exclusive partnership with African banks and post offices.

The broader business and operating environment for provision of remittance services is relatively weak in many African countries. At the same time, the rapid adoption of innovative money transfer and branchless-banking technologies is transforming the landscape for domestic or within-country remittances and potentially broader financial services in Africa. However, the adoption of these technologies for cross-border transfers has been limited so far, in part because of concerns about money laundering and terrorist financing related to cross-border money transfers.

This volume represents an effort to better understand the current state and issues in remittance markets in Africa and in selected remittance-source countries. It brings together studies of remittance markets for eight Sub-Saharan African countries and in two key migrant-destination countries outside the African continent conducted as part of the Africa Migration Project in 2008–10. These studies served as background material for a joint regional report of the African Development Bank (AfDB) and the World Bank titled *Leveraging Migration for Africa: Remittances, Skills, and Investments* (AfDB and World Bank 2011).

The surveys of remittance service providers (RSPs) were implemented by primarily country-based researchers and institutions between 2008 and 2009. The country studies cover recent migration and remittance trends, business environments, services provided to remittance senders and receivers, remittance costs, and innovations in the remittance market-place. Collectively, these studies provide a unique perspective of RSPs about their business and operating environment, regulations governing remittance transfers, and innovations in remittance technologies across a wide range of African countries.

In general, the country studies reflect the state of the remittance markets in Africa and migrant-destination countries at the time of the surveys. Given the rapidly changing and dynamic nature of remittance markets in Africa, some of the key facts and trends (such as volumes of remittances received, subscribers of mobile money-transfer services, and recent regulatory changes) have been updated to reflect the latest information available. Many findings of the country studies—especially the discussions of market structure and policy issues—are equally or even more relevant today in view of the increasing awareness of migrant remittances as a source of development financing for recipient countries and the international efforts targeted at reducing the cost of international remittances.

This overview chapter outlines the implications of remittances for Africa's development and the related policy issues. It sets out the context for better understanding the importance of effective functioning of remittance markets for the livelihood strategies of African households. The chapter also shows how migrant remittances serve essential consumption needs and act as an insurance against adverse shocks; contribute to the future productivity of Africans by providing funds for nutrition, education, and health; and improve their access to formal banking services and information and communication technology. In addition, it briefly discusses the implications of remittances for growth, sovereign creditworthiness, and external financing. The chapter's conclusion provides a bridge to the remainder of the volume and summarizes the 10 remittance-market country studies.

The overview chapter and country studies paint a nuanced picture of not only the opportunities, but also the many obstacles still to be overcome in the quest for providing affordable and transparent remittance and broader financial services to the poorest in Africa. The cost of sending remittances to Africa, and especially within Africa, is the highest among developing countries. The market for cross-border remittances in Africa continues to be characterized by a high degree of informality, lack of effective competition, exchange controls on outward transfers, and often-exclusive partnerships of international money transfer companies with local banks and post offices that contribute to high costs and restrict market entry and competition. At the same time, the widespread adoption of mobile money transfers for domestic remittances represents a success story of how Africa has effectively leapfrogged the technology frontier to design and deliver technology solutions targeting the poorest.

This rest of the overview is organized as follows. We first discuss recent trends and prospects for migration and remittances in Africa. Next, we examine the implications of remittances for growth and access to external finance of African countries. The section on implication of remittances for the welfare of African households draws on the literature and recent household surveys. The subsequent section reviews remittance costs, competition, legal and regulatory environments, and technological innovations in African remittance markets. We then discuss recent policy initiatives and outline some policy options for better leveraging remittances for Africa's development. The final section summarizes the studies of eight remittance markets in Sub-Saharan Africa (chapters 2–9 of this volume) and two key destination countries of African migrants: France and the United Kingdom (chapters 10–11 of this volume).

Recent Remittance Trends in Africa

Migrant remittances have become an important source of external finance for the African continent. Officially recorded remittance flows to Africa, as shown in figure 1.1, are estimated to have increased from $9.1 billion in 1990 to nearly $40 billion in 2010 (divided roughly equally between North Africa and Sub-Saharan Africa). The true size of remittances, including unrecorded flows, is believed to be significantly higher. Remittances to Africa equaled 2.6 percent of GDP in 2009, higher than the average of 1.9 percent of GDP for all developing countries.

Recorded remittance flows to the African continent are several times larger than official aid to North Africa (3.3 percent versus 0.6 percent of GDP) and almost 60 percent of the size of official aid flows to Sub-Saharan Africa, as table 1.1 shows. For many low-income African countries, remittances exceed private investment flows and represent a lifeline to the poor.

A few countries account for a substantial share of remittances to Sub-Saharan Africa and North Africa. Nigeria's $10 billion equaled about half

Figure 1.1   Remittances and Other Resource Flows to Africa, 1990–2010

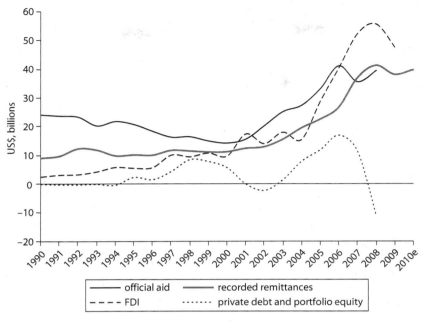

Sources: World Bank 2010c and Bank staff calculations.
Note: FDI = foreign direct investment. 2010e = estimated amount.

of all officially recorded remittances to Sub-Saharan Africa in 2010. Other large remittance recipients in Sub-Saharan Africa, in order of importance, include Sudan, Kenya, Senegal, South Africa, and Uganda.

As a share of GDP, however, the largest recipients are Lesotho (28.5 percent), Togo (10.7 percent), Cape Verde (9.4 percent), Senegal (9.3 percent), and The Gambia (8.2 percent). In North Africa, the Arab Republic of Egypt and Morocco—the two largest recipients in North Africa in terms of both U.S. dollar–denominated flows and share of GDP—account for three-quarters of flows to North Africa region, followed by Algeria and Tunisia.

These estimates of remittance inflows, based on data officially reported in the International Monetary Fund (IMF) balance of payments statistics (IMF 2010a), are likely well below the actual volume of remittance flows to Africa. The remittance inflows data reported by country authorities themselves are often higher than the IMF figures. For example, Ghana's central bank reported $1.6 billion in remittance inflows in

Table 1.1 Remittances and Other Resource Flows to Africa, 1990–2010

US$ billions, except where otherwise indicated

Region/resource flow	1990	1995	2000	2005	2007	2008	2009	2010e	2009[a] (% of GDP)
Sub-Saharan Africa									
Migrant remittances	1.9	3.2	4.6	9.4	18.6	21.4	20.6	21.5	2.2
Official aid	16.9	17.8	12.1	30.8	32.6	36.0	..	..	3.7
Foreign direct investment	1.2	4.4	6.7	18.1	28.7	37.0	30.2	..	3.2
Private debt and portfolio equity flows	0.6	2.5	4.9	10.6	15.6	−6.5	12.3	..	1.3
North Africa									
Migrant remittances	7.2	7.0	6.6	13.1	18.3	19.8	17.5	18.2	3.3
Official aid	7.2	3.0	2.2	2.5	3.0	3.5	..	..	0.6
Foreign direct investment	1.1	0.9	2.8	9.9	22.5	21.6	14.9	..	2.9
Private debt and portfolio equity flows	−0.1	0.0	1.2	1.7	−3.6	−0.4	−0.5	..	−0.1
All Africa									
Migrant remittances	9.1	10.2	11.3	22.5	36.9	41.2	38.1	39.7	2.6
Official aid	24.1	20.7	14.3	33.2	35.6	39.5	..	..	2.6
Foreign direct investment	2.4	5.3	9.5	28.0	51.1	58.6	45.1	..	3.1
Private debt and portfolio equity flows	0.5	2.5	6.2	12.3	12.0	−6.8	11.8	..	0.8

Source: World Bank 2010c and authors' calculations.

Note: .. = negligible; FDI = foreign direct investment. GDP = gross domestic product; e= estimated.

a. Data for official aid is for 2008.

2009—more than 10 times the $114 million reported in the IMF balance of payments statistics. Ethiopia reported more than $700—about twice the $353 million reported by the IMF. These discrepancies are in part related to the misreporting of migrant remittances with other types of current transfers, such as transfers to nongovernmental organizations and embassies and payments related to small-value trade transactions. In addition, only about half of Sub-Saharan African countries report remittance data with any regularity (Irving, Mohapatra, and Ratha 2010). And some countries—such as the Central African Republic, the Democratic Republic of Congo, Somalia, and Zimbabwe, all of which are believed to receive significant remittance flows—report no remittance data at all. Even fewer Sub-Saharan African countries report monthly or quarterly data on remittances.[1]

Remittance flows through money transfer companies are often captured indirectly (in the reporting of partner banks, for example), but the independent operations of such firms may not be fully captured. Cross-border flows through other institutions (such as post offices, savings cooperatives, and microfinance institutions) and emerging channels (such as mobile money transfer services) are not captured in most Sub-Saharan African countries.

Surveys of migrants and remittance recipients and other secondary sources suggest that informal remittance flows, which are not included in the IMF estimates, could be equal to or exceed official figures for Sub-Saharan Africa (Page and Plaza 2006; IFAD 2009). Central banks in some African countries, such as Uganda, are making efforts to estimate these informal flows—through, for example, foreign exchange transactions data and surveys of remittance-receiving households—but these efforts appear to be limited to a few countries.

Data on the sources of remittance flows to Sub-Saharan Africa are not available for most countries in the region. Official data on intraregional migration and in particular on remittance flows within the region are often outdated or in many cases simply not available. However, estimates based on bilateral migration stocks, incomes in destination countries, and incomes in countries of origin indicate that the top sources of remittances for Sub-Saharan Africa, as shown in figure 1.2, are the European Union (EU)-15 countries (41 percent of inflows) and the United States (28 percent) (Ratha and Shaw 2007; World Bank 2011). The remaining sources are other developing countries, primarily in Africa (13 percent); the Gulf Cooperation Council (GCC) countries (9 percent), and other high-income countries

Figure 1.2   Sources of Remittances to Africa and All Developing Regions in 2010

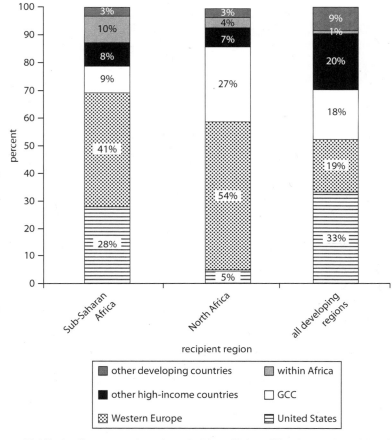

Sources: World Bank staff estimates, updating the methodology of Ratha and Shaw (2007) and using bilateral migration data from World Bank 2011 and economic data from World Bank 2010c.
Note: GCC = Gulf Cooperation Council.

(8 percent). North African countries are even more dependent on remittances from Western Europe (54 percent) and the GCC countries (27 percent).

Although intraregional migration is more important in Sub-Saharan Africa than in any other developing region, with more than two-thirds of emigrants from Sub-Saharan African countries within the region, however, intraregional remittances are estimated to be much smaller than remittances from outside the region. These estimated remittances are smaller primarily because the incomes of cross-border migrants within Africa are significantly lower than the incomes of African migrants in Europe, the United States, and the Gulf.

Macroeconomic Impacts of Remittances

Remittances tend to behave countercyclically and thus act as a form of insurance for origin countries against macroeconomic shock. Remittances rose during the financial crises in Mexico in 1995 and in Indonesia and Thailand in 1998 (Ratha 2007) and have increased with natural disasters and political conflicts (Yang and Choi 2007; Yang 2008a; Clarke and Wallsten 2004; Mohapatra, Joseph, and Ratha 2009).

Remittances thus behave very differently from most other private-source flows, which tend to be procyclical (Ratha 2003; Chami, Hakura, and Montiel 2009; Frankel 2011). This is largely because most remittances involve transactions among members of the same household, and thus are less driven by profit-seeking motives than private resource flows. Remittances are also less at the mercy of changes in the priorities of official aid donors and their fiscal situations (World Bank 2006). But remittances can be procyclical when they are sent for investment purposes, usually in middle-income countries (Sayan 2006; Lueth and Ruiz-Arranz 2008).[2]

In Sub-Saharan Africa, where private capital flows have fluctuated considerably from year to year, remittances were more stable than both FDI and private debt and equity flows (Gupta, Pattillo, and Wagh 2009; Singh, Haacker, and Lee 2009), as shown in figure 1.3.

Impact of Global Financial Crisis

Analysis of the impact of the global financial crisis of 2008–09 on remittance flows is difficult because of the lack of timely and reliable data in most African countries. Remittance flows to Sub-Saharan Africa are estimated to have declined by a modest 3.7 percent in 2009 (Ratha, Mohapatra, and Silwal 2010; table 1.1). The decline in North African countries was more severe, in part because most North African migrants live in Europe, where GDP fell sharply in 2009.[3] Flows to North Africa are estimated to have fallen by 11.1 percent in 2009.

Remittance flows to Sub-Saharan Africa appear to have been less affected than those to North Africa because the remittance sources are more diversified, as seen in figure 1.2. Remittance flows to Egypt, the largest recipient in the North African region, declined by 18 percent in 2009; flows to Morocco, the second-largest recipient, declined

Figure 1.3   Stability of Resource Flows to Africa, 1990–2008, by Source

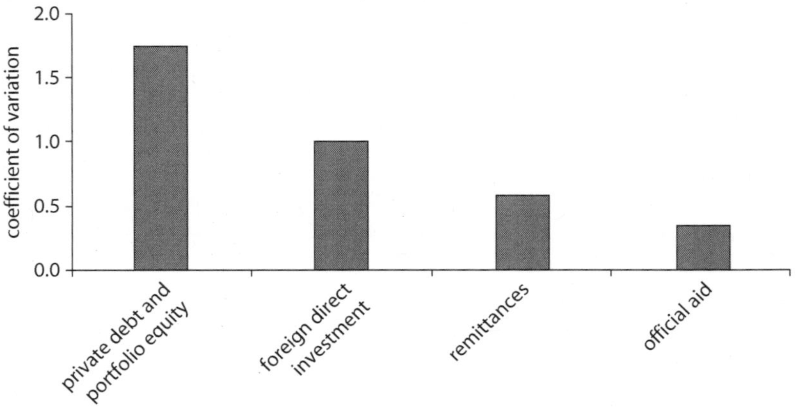

Source: World Bank 2010a.

9 percent. In Sub-Saharan Africa, flows to Kenya remained flat in 2009, and they declined by 6 percent in Cape Verde and by 9 percent in Ethiopia.

Remittance flows to Africa are estimated to have registered a quick recovery, rising by 4 percent in 2010. In the medium term, an uncertain economic recovery, high unemployment rates, and possible moves toward tightening immigration restrictions in destination countries (which likely would be aimed at migrants from outside the EU) could restrain the growth of remittance inflows to Africa. The implications of the widespread protests and crisis in North Africa and the Middle East in early 2011 were not clear as of the time of writing this chapter.

Remittances and Countries' Creditworthiness
Remittance inflows can improve sovereign creditworthiness by increasing the level and stability of foreign exchange receipts (Ratha 2007; Avendaño, Gaillard, and Nieto-Parra 2009). Remittances also help stabilize the current account by reducing the volatility of overall capital flows (Chami and others 2008). Remittances can reduce the probability of current account reversals, especially when they exceed 3 percent of GDP (Bugamelli and Paterno 2009).

Appropriately accounting for remittances can improve evaluations of African countries' external debt sustainability and creditworthiness. Remittances are now being factored into sovereign ratings in middle-income countries and debt sustainability analysis in low-income countries (IMF 2010b).[4] But fewer than half of African countries have a sovereign rating from one of the three major rating agencies (Ratha, Mohapatra, and Plaza 2009). Obtaining a sovereign rating—and improving the sovereign rating in those African countries that have one (after appropriately accounting for remittances)—will translate into improved market access for subsovereign entities, such as African banks and firms, whose foreign currency borrowing is typically subject to the country's "sovereign ceiling" (Borensztein, Cowan, and Valenzuela 2007; Ratha, De, and Mohapatra 2011).[5]

Including remittances in the calculation of the debt-to-exports ratio, as shown in figure 1.4, can provide a more accurate evaluation of debt sustainability and the amount of fiscal adjustment that may be needed to place debt on a sustainable path (World Bank 2006; Abdih and others 2009; IMF and World Bank 2009).[6] Including remittances in creditworthiness analysis using the shadow ratings model of Ratha, De, and Mohapatra (2011) suggests that the creditworthiness of remittance-recipient countries would improve by one to three notches. The poor quality of remittance data in many African countries makes it difficult to assess the extent of improvement in sovereign creditworthiness that

Figure 1.4   External Debt as a Share of Exports from, and Remittances to, Selected Countries

percentage of value of exports and received remittances

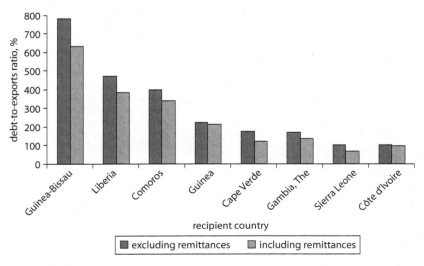

would result from the inclusion of remittances in the Africa region, however.

The securitization of future remittance flows (and other future receivables) can help African countries to use future remittances as collateral to raise additional financing from international capital markets and to reduce interest costs and lengthen the maturity of bonds for financing development projects such as low-income housing or power and water supply (Ratha 2005; Ketkar and Ratha 2009a, 2009b).[7] Banks in several African countries, aided by the African Export-Import Bank, have used remittance securitization to raise international financing at lower cost and longer maturities.

In 1996, the African Export-Import Bank coarranged the first future-flow securitization by a Sub-Saharan African country: a $40 million medium-term loan in favor of a development bank in Ghana, backed by its Western Union remittance receivables (Afreximbank 2005; Rutten and Oramah 2006). In 2001, it arranged a $50 million remittance-backed syndicated note issuance facility for a Nigerian entity using Moneygram receivables. In 2004, it coarranged a $40 million remittance-backed syndicated term loan facility to an Ethiopian bank using its Western Union receivables (Afreximbank 2005). Updated estimates using the methodology used by Ratha, Mohapatra, and Plaza (2009) suggest that the potential for securitization of remittances and other future receivables is $35 billion annually for Sub-Saharan Africa, as shown in table 1.2.

A low level of domestic financial development; extensive use of informal remittance channels; a lack of banking relationships with banks abroad; and the high fixed costs of legal, investment banking, and credit-rating services—especially in poor African countries with few large

Table 1.2   Securitization Potential for Sub-Saharan Africa, 2009
US$, billions

	Receivable	Securitization potential
Fuel exports	91.1	18.2
Agricultural raw materials exports	6.7	1.3
Ores and metals exports	37.7	7.5
Travel services	19.0	3.8
Remittances	20.6	4.1
Total	175.0	35.0

Source: Authors' estimates of securitization potential, based on the methodology of Ratha, Mohapatra, and Plaza (2009) and data from World Bank 2010c.

entities—make the use of securitization instruments difficult for Sub-Saharan countries (Ketkar and Ratha 2009a). The viability of securitization of future remittance flows can be facilitated by introducing a securitization law and improving flows through formal channels. Bilateral and multilateral donors can play a role in facilitating securitization—building, for example, on the United Nations Development Programme's partnership with Standard & Poor's to help African countries obtain sovereign ratings, which act as a ceiling for private sector borrowings.[8] There are risks to taking on foreign currency debt, however, and remittance securitization needs to be accompanied by prudent debt management and sound macroeconomic policies.

Remittances can affect economic growth in a positive manner by raising consumption and investment expenditures; by increasing expenditures on health, education, and nutrition that contribute to long-term productivity (discussed further in the next section); and by improving the stability of consumption and output at both the household and macroeconomic level (Chami, Hakura, and Montiel 2009). These benefits in turn increase the supply of investment from both domestic and foreign sources by increasing financial intermediation (Aggarwal, Demirgüç-Kunt, and Martinez Peria 2006; see Gupta, Pattillo, and Wagh 2009 for evidence for Sub-Saharan Africa), which can ultimately contribute to higher growth (Rajan and Zingales 1998; see Ghirmay 2004 and Akinlo and Egbetunde 2010 for Sub-Saharan Africa).[9]

Large inflows of remittances can cause the real exchange rate to appreciate ("Dutch disease"), which can impair growth if tradeable production imparts external benefits such as economies of scale and learning effects (World Bank 2006; Acosta, Lartey, and Mandelman 2009; Gupta, Pattillo, and Wagh 2009). But remittances do not appear to have had a significant impact on competitiveness for developing countries on average (Rajan and Subramanian 2005).[10] And there is little evidence of this effect for Africa, apart from some small countries such as Cape Verde, where remittance inflows are nearly 10 percent of GDP (Bourdet and Falck 2006).

In principle, large remittance receipts may also reduce the labor supply (Lucas 1987; Azam and Gubert 2006; Bussolo and Medvedev 2007; Chami and others 2008). There is little evidence of this phenomenon, however, and choices by some individuals to work less would be unlikely to have a significant impact on output in African countries with high levels of underemployment. Some experts argue that the additional income from remittances can reduce pressure to improve the quality of policies and institutions by making recipients less dependent on government benefits (Abdih and others 2008) or by providing sufficient foreign exchange to ease governments' concerns over structural rigidities. Others, however, find that remittances have a positive impact on growth in countries with higher-quality political and economic policies and institutions (Catrinescu and others 2009).[11]

The complexity of the growth process and the well-known problems of cross-country growth regressions make it difficult to determine whether remittances increase growth rates. In economies in which the financial system is underdeveloped, remittances may alleviate liquidity and credit constraints and help finance small-business investments, thereby effectively acting as a substitute for financial development. Giuliano and Ruiz-Arranz (2009) find evidence that the impact of remittances on growth is stronger when the level of financial development is weaker. Regression analysis suggests that remittances have the greatest impact on growth when the share of the broad money supply (M2) in GDP (an indicator of financial development) is below 28 percent, as it is in most African economies.

Impact on Households

Remittances can help reduce poverty, raise household investment, and increase access to health and education services. This section reviews the literature on the development implications of remittances from several developing regions, including Africa. It also looks at recent evidence collected through the Africa Migration Project surveys of the characteristics of households that receive remittances from outside Africa, within Africa, and within the same country (see Plaza, Navarrete, and Ratha, 2011). Although it can be difficult to separate the effects of remittances from the overall effect of migration in empirical studies (McKenzie and Sasin 2007), it is well established that the primary economic benefit of migration to recipient households is the receipt of remittances (World Bank 2006).[12] The findings regarding households receiving remittances in origin countries complement information about the characteristics of remittance senders in destination countries (World Bank 2006; Bollard, McKenzie, and Morten 2010).

Remittances can reduce poverty by directly augmenting the incomes of poor recipient households and increasing aggregate demand, thereby increasing employment and wages of the poor. Cross-country regressions generally find that remittances have reduced the share of poor people in the population (Adams and Page 2003, 2005). Econometric analyses suggest that remittances have reduced poverty in Africa. Anyanwu and Erhijakpor (2010) find that a 10 percent increase in official international remittances as a share of GDP led to a 2.9 percent decline in the share of people living in poverty in a sample of 33 African countries for 1990–2005, with similar declines observed for the depth and severity of poverty (see also Ajayi and others 2009). Gupta, Pattillo, and Wagh (2009) find that the impact of remittances on poverty in Africa, although positive, was smaller than for other developing countries, a result they attribute to the possibility that poverty can itself cause increased migration and hence greater remittances.

Studies of Burkina Faso (Lachaud 1999; Wouterse 2010); Ghana (Quartey and Blankson 2004; Adams 2006; Adams, Cuecuecha, and Page 2008a); Lesotho (Gustafsson and Makonnen 1993); Morocco (Sorensen 2004); and Nigeria (Odozia, Awoyemia, and Omonona 2010) conclude that remittances are associated with a reduction in the share of people in poverty—and, in some cases, the depth and severity of poverty as well. A substantial part of remittances in Mali is saved for unexpected events, thus serving as insurance for entire households (Ponsot and Obegi 2010). Food security in rural areas of Nigeria improved considerably with an increase in remittances (Babatunde and Martinetti 2010).

The evidence about the implications of remittances for inequality is less clear because it is not possible to observe the counterfactual incomes in the absence of migration (World Bank 2006; Ratha 2007). Households that receive remittances, especially from outside the African continent, may be richer to begin with in order to have the resources needed for migration, but they may also have higher incomes because of migration and the receipt of remittances. As figure 1.5 illustrates, recent household surveys conducted as part of the Africa Migration Project and an earlier survey in Ghana find that more than half of households in Burkina Faso, Ghana, and Nigeria, and 30 percent of households in Senegal receiving remittances from outside Africa are in the top two consumption quintiles.

As figure 1.6 illustrates, remittances from outside Africa tend to be much larger, on average, than remittances from other African countries or domestic sources.

A recent study on the characteristics of African remittance senders based on microdata of more than 12,000 African migrants in nine Organisation for Economic Co-operation and Development (OECD) countries (Bollard, McKenzie, and Morten 2010) complements the findings from surveys of remittance-recipient households. The destination-country data suggest that Africans remit twice as much on average as

Figure 1.5   Shares of Remittance Recipients in Top Two Consumption Quintiles, Selected Countries

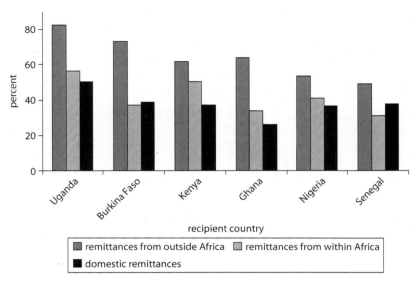

Source: Authors' calculations, based on household surveys conducted in Burkina Faso, Kenya, Nigeria, Senegal, and Uganda in 2009 as part of the Africa Migration Project and Ghana Living Standards Survey in 2005–06.

migrants from other developing countries. The average annual remittance sent by African migrant households in the OECD is $1,268—more than the average annual per capita income of African countries.[13] Africans also tend to remit more often, and African migrants from poorer African countries are more likely to remit than those from richer African countries.[14] Male African migrants in the OECD send larger amounts on average than females ($1,446 compared with $878 for females) partly because of their higher earnings but also because they are more likely to have spouses back home.

The evidence from other regions suggests that a significant part of remittances is spent on housing investment and the purchase of land, particularly in situations where other investment assets are not available.[15] The evidence for Africa on the uses of remittances for investment and entrepreneurship is somewhat limited. In Egypt, overseas savings are associated with a higher likelihood of entrepreneurship (and thus investment) among return migrants (McCormick and Wahba 2001, 2003). In 1997, Osili (2004) conducted a survey of 112 Nigerian migrant households in Chicago and a matched sample of 61 families in Nigeria. She found that one-third of remittances were spent on housing investment in the preceding year and

Figure 1.6   Average Annual Remittance to Selected Countries, by Source

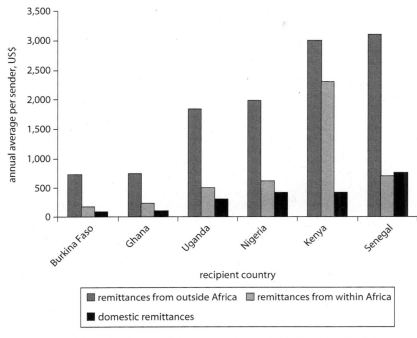

Source: Authors' calculations based on household surveys conducted in Burkina Faso, Kenya, Nigeria, Senegal, and Uganda in 2009 as part of the Africa Migration Project and Ghana Living Standards Survey in 2005–06.

that migrants' housing investment was responsive to changes in macro-economic conditions such as inflation, the real exchange rate, and political stability.

Recent household surveys conducted as part of the Africa Migration Project and an earlier survey in Ghana find that a significant portion of international remittances are spent on land purchases, building a house, business, improving the farm, agricultural equipment, and other investments, (as a share of total remittances, investment in these items represented 36.4 percent in Burkina Faso, 55.3 percent in Kenya, 57.0 percent in Nigeria, 15.5 percent in Senegal, and 20.2 percent in Uganda, as table 1.3 shows). A substantial share of within-Africa remittances were also used for these purposes in Kenya (47 percent), Nigeria (40 percent), and in Uganda and Burkina Faso (19 percent each). The share of domestic remittances devoted to these purposes was much lower in all of the countries surveyed, with the exception of Nigeria and Kenya.

Remittances may increase educational expenditures by helping finance schooling and reducing the need for child labor. But the absence of an

Table 1.3 Use of Remittances by Recipient Households in Selected African Countries, by Source

percentage of total remittances

Use	Burkina Faso Outside Africa	Within Africa	Domestic	Kenya Outside Africa	Within Africa	Domestic	Nigeria Outside Africa	Within Africa	Domestic	Senegal Outside Africa	Within Africa	Domestic	Uganda Outside Africa	Within Africa	Domestic
New-house construction	25.7	10.1	2.6	11.2	27.5	1.3	5.8	0.0	0.1	7.0	0.7	0.0	2.5	1.6	0.4
Food	23.5	34.9	48.7	12.8	14.5	29.7	10.1	20.1	1.0	52.6	72.6	81.9	7.6	9.7	12.4
Education	12.4	5.9	9.4	9.6	22.9	20.5	22.1	19.6	4.5	3.6	2.3	4.6	12.7	14.5	20.2
Health	11.3	10.1	12.5	7.3	5.8	7.0	5.1	12.0	10.6	10.7	7.3	2.9	6.3	14.5	24.8
Business	10.4	2.6	2.4	3.9	8.4	13.0	21.7	20.1	11.1	1.3	5.7	0.2	7.6	9.7	2.1
Clothing	5.0	0.7	0.7	..	..	..	..	..	..	..	..	..	..	..	..
Marriage/funeral	2.1	3.9	3.1	0.9	1.7	2.0	0.4	1.0	0.7	2.9	2.4	1.1	7.6	6.5	1.7
Rent (house, land)	1.4	0.6	1.7	5.7	0.4	7.4	4.4	4.9	0.8	1.0	0.0	2.2	5.1	8.1	4.5
House rebuilding	0.3	1.0	1.2	5.3	3.1	1.3	4.7	3.2	7.0	4.2	0.7	0.1	6.3	3.2	2.1
Cars or trucks	0.1	0.0	0.1	1.3	1.0	0.4	0.0	0.0	0.5	0.2	0.0	0.0	2.5	0.0	0.0
Land purchase	0.0	1.4	0.1	8.4	7.0	1.3	24.8	16.6	18.2	3.0	0.0	0.0	3.8	4.8	2.1
Farm improvement[a]	0.0	3.9	1.1	2.3	0.4	4.4	..	..	..	..	..	..	..	..	..
Investment	..	24.2	..	24.2	0.6	4.7	..	..	..	..	..	..	..	..	..
Other	7.7	24.9	16.3	7.2	6.6	6.9	0.8	2.6	3.5	13.5	8.3	6.9	38.0	27.4	29.8

Source: Authors' calculations based on household surveys conducted in Burkina Faso, Kenya, Nigeria, Senegal, South Africa, and Uganda in 2009 as part of the Africa Migration Project and Ghana Living Standards Survey in 2005–06.

Note: .. = negligible or missing.

a. Includes agricultural equipment.

adult household member may put pressure on children to perform additional household chores or work on the family farm, reducing time for education. Evidence from other regions suggests that remittances can contribute to better school attendance, higher school enrollment rates, and additional years in school, especially for females.[16]

The paucity of household survey data means that the evidence on the impact of remittances on educational outcomes in Africa is relatively weak. In Egypt, children of remittance-receiving households were more likely than other children to enroll in university, and girls ages 15–17 in remittance-receiving households performed less domestic work and were more likely to be in school than other girls the same age (Elbadawi and Roushdy 2009). Remittance-receiving households in Ghana invested more in education than did other households (Adams, Cuecuecha, and Page 2008b).

Recent household surveys for Burkina Faso, Nigeria, Senegal, and Uganda conducted as part of the Africa Migration Project and an earlier survey in Ghana show that education was the second-highest use of remittances from outside Africa in Nigeria and Uganda, the third-highest in Burkina Faso, and the fourth-highest in Kenya, as seen in table 1.3. Households that receive international remittances have substantially more household members who have completed secondary and tertiary education than do other households, as figure 1.7 illustrates.

In Kenya and Uganda, households devote 15 percent or more of domestic and intraregional remittances to education; Nigerian households devote 20 percent of intra-Africa remittances to education. Although the amounts spent were much smaller than those from remittances from outside Africa, these figures indicate that a significant share of all sources of remittances goes to education. Although these findings do not control for the possible endogeneity of remittance-receiving status, they nevertheless suggest that remittances may help raise the level of resources devoted to education.

Remittances can contribute to better health outcomes by enabling household members to purchase more food and health care services and perhaps by increasing information about health practices. A cross-country analysis of 56 developing countries found that higher remittances per capita were associated with greater access to private treatment for fever and diarrhea and that remittances complemented foreign health aid in poor countries (Drabo and Ebeke 2010). A cross-country analysis of 84 countries (46 countries with quintile-level data) found that remittances reduced overall child mortality but tended to

Figure 1.7   Secondary and Tertiary Educational Attainment of Remittance Recipient and Nonrecipient Households, Selected Countries

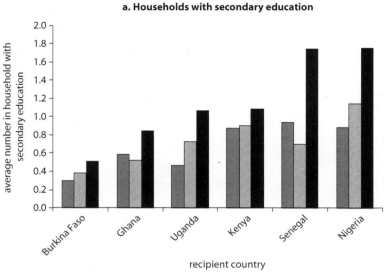

a. Households with secondary education

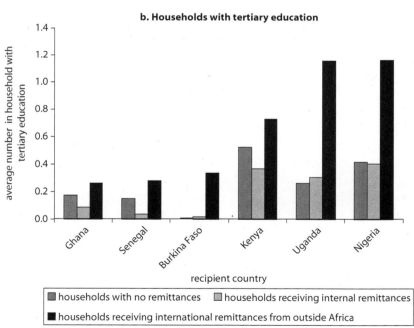

b. Households with tertiary education

households with no remittances   households receiving internal remittances
households receiving international remittances from outside Africa

Source: Africa Migration Project Household surveys in Burkina Faso, Kenya, Nigeria, Senegal, and Uganda in 2009 and Ghana Living Standards Survey in 2005–06.

be more effective in reducing mortality among children from the richest households than from the poorest households (Chauvet, Gubert, and Mesplé-Somps 2009).[17]

The evidence on the impact of remittances on health outcomes is rather sparse for Africa. Evidence from the household surveys above indicates that households dedicate 5–12 percent of remittances from outside Africa to health care, as seen in table 1.3. A similar share of within-Africa and domestic remittances is devoted to health expenditures, but the amounts spent are much lower because of the smaller average size of these remittances. Among households in Ghana that receive remittances from outside and within Africa, households headed by women spend more on health care than do households headed by men (Guzmán, Morrison, and Sjöblom 2007). In rural Mali, households receiving remittances increased demand for health services and were more likely to seek modern care (Birdsall and Chuhan 1986). A recent study using panel data for 1993–2004 for the KwaZulu-Natal province in South Africa finds that remittance-receiving households spent a larger budget share on food and health expenditures and that remittances enabled poorer households to access better-quality medical care (Nagarajan 2009).

Migration enables households to diversify their sources of income and thus reduce their vulnerability to risks such as drought, famine, and other natural disasters.[18] Migration and remittances have been a part of coping mechanisms adopted by African households facing shocks to incomes and livelihoods (Block and Webb 2001). During droughts in Botswana, families at risk of losing cattle and those relying on crops for their sustenance tended to receive more remittances than other families (Lucas and Stark 1985). Ethiopian households that receive international remittances were less likely than other households to sell their productive assets, such as livestock, to cope with food shortages (Mohapatra, Joseph, and Ratha 2009), as table 1.4 shows. Remittances in Ghana helped smooth the household consumption of rural farmers (Quartey and Blankson 2004; Quartey 2006).

In rural Mali, remittances responded positively to shocks suffered by recipient households (Gubert 2002, 2007). Surveys in the Senegal River Valley in Mali and in Senegal suggest that migration acts as an intrahousehold risk-diversification strategy, with remittances a contingent flow that supports family consumption in case of an adverse shock (Azam and Gubert 2005, 2006). Similar mechanisms for sharing risk through interhousehold transfers of cattle have been observed for East African pastoralists (Huysentruyt, Barrett, and McPeak 2009).

Table 1.4   Food Security Strategies and Remittances in Ethiopian Households
percentage of households using strategy to cope with food shortages

Food security strategy	Households not receiving remittances	Households receiving domestic remittances	Households receiving international remittances
Food aid	42.3	55.9	0.0
Sale of livestock and livestock products	40.5	3.9	0.0
Sale of other agricultural products	18.2	3.7	0.0
Sale of household assets	4.1	4.6	11.5
From own cash	10.3	5.3	31.3
Others	15.6	33.0	48.9

Source: Mohapatra, Joseph, and Ratha 2009.
Note: Column totals add up to more than 100 percent because households reported more than one response.

Remittances can also enable recipient households to build stronger and more resilient housing. Mohapatra, Joseph, and Ratha (2009) find that remittance-receiving households in Burkina Faso and Ghana were more likely to have a concrete house, after controlling for the possible endogeneity of the remittance-receiving status by using propensity score-matching methods.

Remittances can play an important role in improving access to information and communication technology. A household survey conducted as part of the Africa Migration Project shows that in Burkina Faso, 66 percent of international remittance recipients have access to a mobile phone compared with 41 percent of nonrecipients (as shown in annex 1.1, table 1A.1).[19] These households also have significantly higher ownership of radios (66 percent versus 39 percent), televisions (41 percent versus 9 percent), and computers (14 percent versus 2 percent). Households in Ghana, Nigeria, Senegal, and Uganda receiving international remittances also report having higher rates of access to mobile phones, radios, televisions, and computers.

Remittances are often the only relationship that many poor people have with the formal financial system. If remittances are received through banks or other financial intermediaries (such as microfinance institutions or savings cooperatives), there is a high likelihood that some part of the remittance will be saved (Aggarwal, Demirgüç-Kunt, and Martinez Peria 2006; Gupta, Pattillo, and Wagh 2009). Even if remittances are received through money transfer companies or informal providers, recipients may save the remittance in some type of financial institution rather than put it under the mattress. The steady stream of remittance receipts can also be used as a factor in evaluating the creditworthiness of recipients for microloans, consumer loans, and small-business loans (sought, for example, to purchase agricultural equipment) (Ratha 2007). Remittances also play a role in smoothing the income stream of poor households that face high income volatility and shocks. This reduced income volatility can make them more attractive borrowers.

Data from recent household surveys conducted as part of the Africa Migration Project and an earlier survey in Ghana reveal that households that receive international remittances typically have better access to financial services, such as bank accounts, as figure 1.8 shows. Households receiving domestic remittances tend to be worse off in terms of financial access than households receiving international remittances, in part

Figure 1.8   Household Bank Accounts in Selected African Countries, by Remittance Status

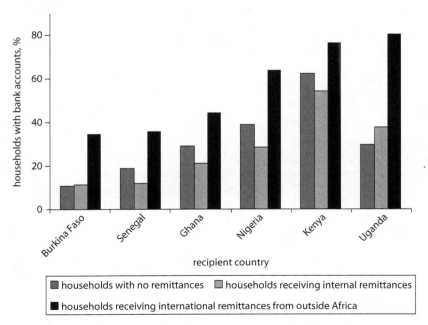

Source: Authors' calculations based on household surveys conducted in Burkina Faso, Kenya, Nigeria, Senegal, and Uganda in 2009 as part of the Africa Migration Project and Ghana Living Standards Survey in 2005–06.

because households that send out domestic migrants tend to be poorer. There are some notable exceptions, such as Kenya, where the widespread use of mobile money transfers and the ability to save using mobile phones has effectively substituted for formal banking services (see next section for a detailed discussion).

Remittance Markets in Africa

Remittance markets in Africa remain relatively underdeveloped in terms of their financial infrastructure and the regulatory environment. Surveys of African households and RSPs conducted in the context of the Africa Migration Project indicate three broad patterns:

• Intraregional (south-south) and domestic remittances are sent overwhelmingly through informal channels. They are hand carried during visits home, sent through transport companies, or sent through informal *hawala* channels, in part because of limited access to and the high cost of formal financial (banking) services relative to average per capita incomes in African countries (Pendleton and others 2006; Tevera and Chikanda 2009; Bracking and Sachikonye 2008).

• A large share of remittances from outside Africa is channeled through a few large international money transfer agencies, which often work de facto or de jure in exclusive partnership with African banks and post offices (IFAD 2009).

• The rapid adoption of innovative mobile-money transfer and branchless-banking technologies is transforming the landscape for remittances and broader financial services in Africa (Morawczynski and Pickens 2009; Aker and Mbiti 2010). Although the adoption of these innovative technologies has been limited mostly to domestic money transfers (in part because of concerns about money laundering and terrorist financing related to cross-border remittances), the technologies have the potential to vastly improve access to both remittances and broader financial services, including low-cost savings and credit products, for African migrants and remittance recipients.

The cost of sending remittances to Sub-Saharan Africa and within Africa, however, is the highest among all developing regions, as shown in figure 1.9. In mature corridors such as those between the United States

Figure 1.9   Cost of Sending Remittances

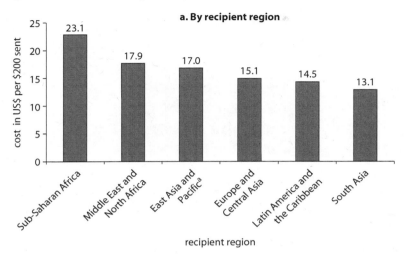

a. By recipient region

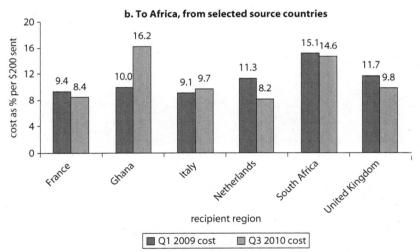

b. To Africa, from selected source countries

Source: Authors' calculations based on data from World Bank 2010b.
Note: Remittance cost includes fees and foreign exchange commissions.
a. Excludes Pacific Islands.

and Mexico, remittance costs can be as low as $5 per transaction; between the Persian Gulf and South Asia, the cost can be as low as $1.[20]

Data for select intra-African remittance corridors suggests that the cost of sending remittances ranges from 5 percent to 15 percent of the amount sent, as shown in figure 1.10. Large parallel market premiums

Figure 1.10   South-South Remittance Costs in Sub-Saharan Africa

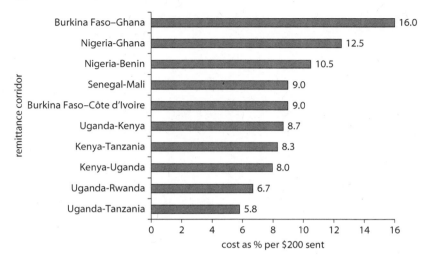

Source: Authors' calculations based on surveys of selected remittance service providers conducted at end of 2008.

between official and parallel market exchange rates in many African countries imply that the true cost is likely to be larger.

Surveys of RSPs in Africa suggest that the high costs of remittances in Africa is in part caused by exclusivity agreements between banks and international money transfer companies (IFAD 2009; Irving, Mohapatra, and Ratha 2010). Other studies show that such exclusive partnerships keep costs high for migrants and reduce the amounts sent, thereby limiting the development impact of remittances (Ratha and Riedberg 2005; World Bank 2006). Several African countries, including Ethiopia, Nigeria, and Rwanda, have taken steps to eliminate these partnerships in recent years.

These high remittance costs are also related to the low level of financial development in Africa (Aggarwal, Demirgüç-Kunt, and Martinez Peria 2006; Beck and Martinez-Peria 2009) and the small number of firms handling remittance transfers (IFAD 2009, Orozco 2009).[21] The cost of banking services tends to be high relative to income levels in African countries, and the reach of banks outside of urban areas is limited (Demirgüç-Kunt, Beck, and Honohan 2008).[22] For example, the average fee to open a savings account is 28 percent of the average African's annual income—compared with less than 1 percent in countries in Latin America and the Caribbean, as shown in figure 1.11. The number of bank

Figure 1.11   Banking Networks and Costs, by Region

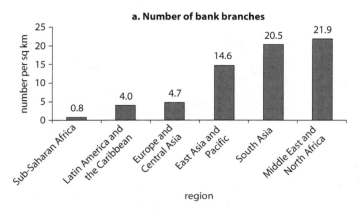

a. Number of bank branches

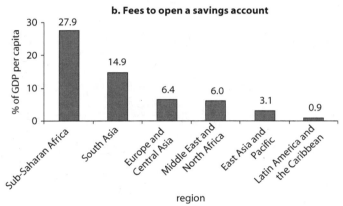

b. Fees to open a savings account

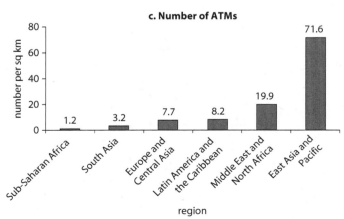

c. Number of ATMs

Source: Authors' calculations based on data from Demirgüç-Kunt, Beck, and Honohan 2008.
Note: GDP = gross domestic product. ATM = automatic teller machine. sq km = square kilometer.

branches and automatic teller machines (ATMs) per square kilometer is lower in Sub-Saharan Africa than in any other developing region.

High remittance costs represent an unnecessary burden on African migrants. In a recent survey, almost 70 percent of central banks in Sub-Saharan Africa cited high costs as the most important factor inhibiting the use of formal remittance channels (Irving, Mohapatra, and Ratha 2010), as figure 1.12 shows. Evidence based on surveys and field experiments suggests that remittance flows respond to reductions in costs (Gibson, McKenzie, and Rohorua 2006; Martinez, Aycinena, and Yang 2010). Reducing remittance costs can lead to increases in the remittances sent by migrants, in turn increasing the resources available to recipient African households.

Issues in Remittance Source Countries

Surveys and interviews of RSPs in key migrant destination countries (France, the United Kingdom, and the United States) reveal that African

Figure 1.12   Factors Inhibiting Use of Formal Remittance Channels

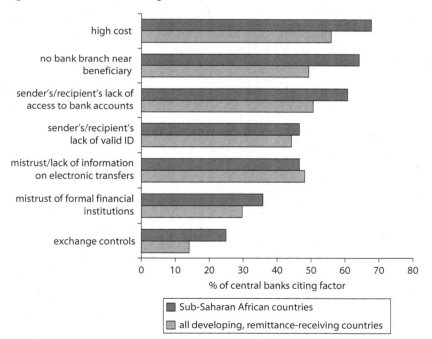

Source: Irving, Mohapatra, and Ratha 2010.

migrants' lack of access to formal financial services and required identi-fication, exclusive partnerships, and regulations related to anti-money-laundering and combating the financing of terrorism (AML/CFT) also raise the costs of transferring money to Africa.[23] Most transfers from des-tination countries outside Africa are sent as cash through money transfer companies or through banks that are acting as agents of money-transfer companies, rather than potentially cheaper account-to-account and cash-to-account transfers because (a) remittance senders lack access to banking facilities, perhaps due to inadequate identification requirements; (b) banking services are too costly in the remittance-source countries and in recipient countries in Africa; and (c) African banks lack branches or representative offices in the destination countries, and vice-versa. Some West African banks have representative offices in France and operate through partnerships with French banks (see chapter 10) but the range of services provided appears to be small. Many West African migrants in France appear to prefer to send money through friends, relatives, or even community groups.

Exclusivity partnerships are also found in some remittance-source countries. The French postal service has an exclusive partnership with Western Union (see chapter 10). Although documented remittance costs are among the lowest for France-Africa corridors, such partnerships can limit competition and the access of migrants to alternative RSPs. U.S. reg-ulations aimed at AML/CFT implemented after September 11, 2001, have made it more difficult for smaller RSPs to access banking and settlement facilities for the transfer of remittances to Africa. Mainstream U.S. banks appear to be wary of having money transfer operators—particularly from East Africa and other African subregions—as clients.

Regulations in destination countries could encourage greater trans-parency in remittance markets. For example, the United States is requir-ing the disclosure of prices and exchange rate commissions by remittance providers, establishing error resolution mechanisms for consumers, and encouraging access by low-income consumers. Although the U.S. govern-ment has recently undertaken these and other measures to reduce remit-tance costs, improve consumer protections related to remittances, and leverage remittances for improving financing of infrastructure projects (such as the BRIDGE initiative discussed earlier), differences in legal and regulatory frameworks, compliance requirements, and institutions gov-erning remittances across the U.S states make the exercise of implement-ing national-level policies on remittances challenging (Andreassen 2006). There is need for a national-level institutional focal point for remittances in the United States. A similar initiative to improve transparency, competition, and consumer protection in remittance markets is under way in Europe under the EU's Payment Services Directive (see chapter 11).

Remittance Channels in Africa

The high cost and limited reach of formal channels, along with the informal and seasonal character of African migration, results in the large role that informal channels (money carried during visits, sent through friends and relatives, sent through the *hawala* system, through settlement of small trade transactions, and carried by buses and transport companies) play in African remittances. Some estimates suggest that the prevalence of informal transfers is the highest in Africa among all developing regions (Page and Plaza 2006; Ratha and Shaw 2007). Surveys conducted in Southern Africa in 2004–05 found that carrying remittances by hand during visits home accounted for about half of remittance transfers in southern Africa: remittances carried by hand and sent through friends and relatives accounted for 68 percent of remittances in Botswana, 88 percent in Lesotho, 73 percent in Swaziland, and 46 percent in Zimbabwe (Pendleton and others 2006; Tevera and Chikanda 2009; see also Bracking and Sachikonye 2008 for evidence from Zimbabwe on the increasing reliance on informal channels during a period of hyperinflation).[24]

Recent household surveys conducted in the context of the Africa Migration Project in 2009 and an earlier survey in Ghana show some country variation in the importance of informal channels. The share of households receiving within-Africa remittances through informal channels was 60 percent or more in Burkina Faso, Ghana, and Senegal, as shown in figure 1.13 and annex table 1A.2. Among migrants in South Africa sending remittances to other African countries, mostly within the Southern African region, the share of those using informal channels was close to 80 percent. The share of households receiving within-Africa remittances that used informal channels was only 24 percent in Kenya (the only country of the five with extensive reliance on transfers through mobile phones—24 percent of within-Africa remittances); 33 percent in Nigeria, where banks are more widely used than in the other countries; and 44 percent in Uganda with money transfer operators and banks accounting for the remaining half.

Informal channels were even more prevalent for domestic money transfers (95 percent for Burkina Faso, 94 percent in Ghana, 95 percent

Figure 1.13   Formal and Informal Remittance Channels in Africa

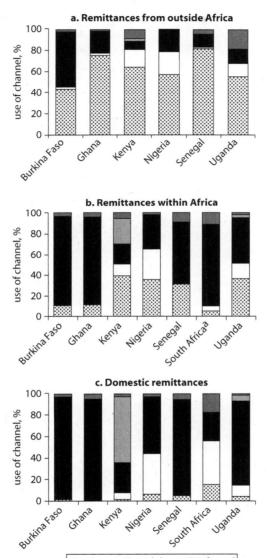

a. Remittances from outside Africa

use of channel, %

Burkina Faso, Ghana, Kenya, Nigeria, Senegal, Uganda

b. Remittances within Africa

use of channel, %

Burkina Faso, Ghana, Kenya, Nigeria, Senegal, South Africa[a], Uganda

c. Domestic remittances

use of channel, %

Burkina Faso, Ghana, Kenya, Nigeria, Senegal, South Africa, Uganda

other   mobile   informal
bank   MTO

Source: Africa Migration Project Household surveys in Burkina Faso, Kenya, Nigeria, Senegal, South Africa, and Uganda in 2009, and Ghana Living Standards Survey in 2005–06.
Note: MTO = money transfer operator.
a. Channels used for remittances sent from South Africa to other African countries.

in Senegal, and 78 percent for Uganda), also shown in figure 1.13 and annex table 1A.2). In relatively prosperous South Africa, informal remittance channels account for only a quarter of domestic remittances, in part because of a well-developed financial system and recent efforts to improve financial inclusion, such as the introduction of the Mzansi scheme, where South African banks provide basic, low-cost banking accounts; banks in South Africa now account for 41 percent of domestic remittances and money transfer companies for 16 percent. Similarly, in Nigeria, which has a better banking infrastructure than most other African countries, banks accounted for more than one-third (37 percent) and money transfer companies for 6 percent.

The most prominent exception to the view of domestic remittances in Africa being sent through mostly informal channels is Kenya, where nearly two-thirds (62 percent) of domestic remittance transfers were conducted through mobile phones at the time of the household survey in late 2009, as figure 1.13 shows. The next section recounts the transformation of the domestic remittance landscape in Kenya since the introduction of the M-PESA mobile money service in early 2007. Uganda has also seen the introduction of mobile money transfers, with 5 percent of domestic remittances conducted by mobile phones at the time of the survey in the second half of 2009. This share is likely to have increased subsequent to the survey.

Formal channels for both remittances from outside Africa and within the region were heavily dominated by money-transfer companies (mostly Western Union). In particular, only about 2 percent of households receiving remittances from outside Africa use banks, although the share is slightly higher in Kenya (16.2 percent), Nigeria (22.3 percent), and Uganda (12.5 percent). The role of other intermediaries—including post offices, microfinance institutions, savings and credit cooperatives, and new technologies such as Internet transfers and mobile money transfers—is even more limited for international remittances from outside Africa. By contrast, the share of households using informal channels for remittances from outside Africa was less than 21 percent in five of the six countries surveyed on receipt of remittances (the exception was 52 percent in Burkina Faso).

Mobile Money Services for Domestic Remittances

The availability of the M-PESA mobile money service has brought about a profound change in the types of domestic remittance channels used by Kenyans in the relatively short time span since its introduction in March

2007 (Pulver, Jack, and Suri 2009; Joseph 2010; Mas and Radcliffe 2010). Surveys by Kenya's Financial Sector Deepening (FSD) found that the most commonly used means of sending money within Kenya in 2006 were by hand (58 percent), bus (27 percent), post office and money order (24 percent), direct deposit (11 percent), and money-transfer service (9 percent). By 2008, M-PESA had come to dominate domestic remittances, with 47 percent of Kenyans using this service, while the share of remittances sent by hand and by transport companies decreased to 32 percent and 9 percent, respectively. Reliance on mobile-phone transfers dramatically reduced the need for domestic migrants to travel home to deliver money by hand or send it by bus or transport company.

The use of mobile phones to transfer money has also enabled recipients to send smaller amounts of money but more often (and collectively more), in response to lower costs because of the greater accessibility of M-PESA agents. As figure 1.14 illustrates, the average transaction size decreased by 30 percent between March 2007 and March 2009 from 3,300 Kenya shillings (about $41 at prevailing exchange rates) to 2,300 Kenya shillings (about $29) (Morawczynski and Pickens 2009; Pulver, Jack, and Suri 2009).

Mobile money-transfer services are now increasingly used for savings. More than one-fifth (21 percent) of respondents in the 2008 FSD survey reported using electronic money (e-money) on their mobile phones for storing or saving money for everyday use and for emergencies. Safaricom,

Figure 1.14   Average M-PESA Transaction Size, March 2007–March 2009

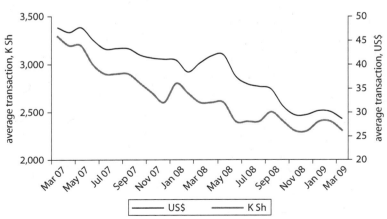

Source: Pulver, Jack, and Suri 2009.
Note: K Sh = Kenya shillings.

in partnership with Kenya's Equity Bank, recently launched a mobile savings account, "M-Kesho," that provides access to interest-bearing savings accounts and access to the ATM network of Equity Bank. Other firms such as Zain are now competing with M-PESA in Kenya to provide similar services. In neighboring Uganda, Zain and MTN's mobile money services have more than a million users (*Business Daily Africa* 2010).

Similar mobile money-transfer and mobile banking services have expanded to other countries and subregions in Africa. The mobile operator Zain, with operations in 15 African countries and 42 million subscribers, offers Zain Zap, a mobile remittance service that, in addition to money transfers, also offers services such as payments for bills and groceries (*Economist* 2010).[25] Orange Money offers mobile money transfers in a number of West African countries, including Côte d'Ivoire, Madagascar, Mali, and Senegal.[26] In Benin in West Africa, mobile operator MTN and Ecobank have launched a service that allows users to open accounts and to transfer, deposit, and withdraw money. In Sierra Leone, Splash mobile money service was introduced in September 2009 and gained more than 150,000 clients within a year (*Awareness Times* 2010). In South Africa, Wizzit offers person-to-person mobile money-transfer services and works in partnership with the mainstream ABSA Bank and the South African post office to provide banking facilities, including access to point-of-sale devices and debit cards that can be used at ATMs.[27]

Mobile money technologies are being mostly used for domestic money transfers in Africa and other regions, but their use for cross-border remittances is still nascent (see CGAP and Dalberg 2010 for some examples). This is in part because of concerns related to money laundering using cross-border transfers but also because of insufficient maturity of branchless-banking infrastructure on the receiving end and lack of customer awareness and trust in new services (Bold 2010).

Some telecommunications firms that operate across countries are starting to offer cross-border remittances in certain subregions. In East Africa, for example, Zain Zap (in partnership with CitiBank and Standard Chartered Bank) allows its customers to send money to any bank in Kenya, Tanzania, and Uganda and to receive money from any bank account in the world. In West Africa, where members of the West African Economic and Monetary Union have a common central bank and similar monetary regulations, cross-border mobile money-transfer services do not appear to be functional. Mobile money transfers being piloted in partnership with international money transfer companies (for example, from the United Kingdom and the United States to M-PESA mobile money accounts in

Kenya) are almost identical to cash-based remittances for the remittance sender and have a similar cost structure, with the difference that the remittance is deposited into the mobile money account of the recipient.

Even within this limited scope, the deposit of cross-border remittances directly into the mobile money account of the recipient has potentially significant advantages over traditional cash-based money transfer services. It increases the reach of remittance services because the recipient can withdraw the remittance at domestic money transfer outlets. In Kenya, for example, the international RSP can piggyback on the vast network of M-PESA agents, greatly reducing, if not eliminating, the need to build a costly network for distribution of international remittances or to form alliances with banks or post offices. For the recipient, receiving remittances directly into a mobile money account obviates the need to travel to the nearest town or outlet of the money transfer operator to receive cash.

Money transfers through mobile phones raise the issue of whether telecommunications or banking regulators should regulate these services. Kenya's M-PESA was allowed to operate with little regulatory oversight and few reporting requirements in its initial years. Regulators appear to be learning how to deal with this innovation. There is considerable variation in the experience of countries with mobile money services in Africa and other regions.[28] Regulatory "forbearance" may allow new technologies to scale up rapidly, but it can expose the financial system to systemic risk if the volume of transactions flowing through the mobile money transfer system is large and the deposits are stored in one or two financial institutions. The issue of how to regulate and create a level playing field between mobile network operators and banks is becoming more important as banks enter the mobile money space. Another issue is how to replicate the Kenyan example in other African countries where telecommunications infrastructure is less developed and operators are state monopolies.

Developing a robust and efficient regulatory framework that provides clear guidelines, expands permitted points of service (such as retail agents), reduces reporting requirements for small-value cross-border transactions, and eliminates requirements for proof of legal residence to set up a bank account can facilitate mobile money transfers (Maimbo, Saranga, and Strychacz 2010). Learning from the experiences of countries such as Brazil and the Philippines can help African countries come up with innovative regulatory solutions.[29] Some pilot projects are attempting to bridge the divide between community-based pooled remittances and the use of Internet and mobile technologies. Some service providers are attempting to use Internet-based technologies to transfer remittances from France to villages in Mali, West Africa (see chapter 10).

Postal Services' Role in Improving Access to Remittances and other Financial Services

Post offices typically have strong networks in both urban and rural areas, with significant potential to reach poor populations. They also have the right business model of serving the poor. While commercial banks are inaccessible to the poorest in many countries, post offices are typically more familiar and more accessible. In a recent study, Clotteau and Anson (2011) of the Universal Postal Union estimate that more than 80 percent of post offices in Sub-Saharan Africa are located outside the three largest cities, in areas where more than 80 percent of people in the country live. This stands in sharp contrast to the mainstream commercial banks that are usually concentrated in the largest cities in Africa. This provides postal networks a unique opportunity to become key players in both international and domestic remittances—and to bring the unbanked into the formal financial system.

However, posts in Africa face operational risks in handling cash, inadequate training, and outdated information technology systems (Clotteau and Anson 2011).[30] For very small remittances, the application of anti-money-laundering regulations is not proportional to the risk raised by such transactions and hinders the reduction of remittance fees. Also, most post offices are not connected to national clearing and settlement systems, which considerably limits their efficiency. Furthermore, a number of posts are prevented from collecting savings, which is a natural complement to remittance services. And most postal operators are government public corporations or government departments. Perhaps most important, exclusivity arrangements of some post offices in Africa with international money-transfer companies prevent effective competition in the remittances market. These agreements can also include offices that are not providing any remittance service or where the partner of the post will never deploy the service. Last, in some instances, the post is regulated by the postal regulator for international money orders and by the financial regulator for account-based services.

Policies for Leveraging Remittances for Development

This section outlines policies to improve the quality of data on remittances; reduce costs and improve transparency in remittance markets;

encourage innovative money-transfer technologies; use remittances to improve access to capital markets; and cope with large remittance inflows.

As shown in figure 1.15, most central banks in remittance-receiving countries in Sub-Saharan Africa cited *better statistics on migration and remittances* and *improved delivery to remote areas* as the top issues needing attention to promote more efficient and secure transfer and delivery of migrant remittances (Irving, Mohapatra, and Ratha 2010).

Data collection on remittances is also receiving attention from the international community: the G-8 Global Remittances Working Group lists improving remittance data collection as one of its four thematic areas (World Bank 2009). African central banks and statistical agencies can improve data collection by expanding the reporting of remittances from banks to nonbank providers of remittance services (such as money-transfer companies, post offices, savings cooperatives, and microfinance institutions); using surveys of migrants and recipient households to estimate remittance flows through formal and informal channels; and asking labor ministries and embassies in destination countries to provide estimates of remittance flows and the associated costs paid by migrants (see also IMF 2009 for further recommendations).

Policies designed to increase financial sector development—for example, by encouraging greater competition among banks and by promoting alternative providers such as microfinance institutions, credit cooperatives,

Figure 1.15   Top Remittance Areas Needing Attention in Sub-Saharan Africa

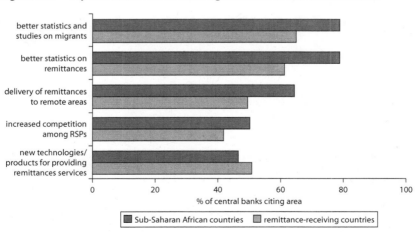

Source: Irving, Mohapatra, and Ratha 2010.
Note: RSP = remittance service provider.

and postal savings banks—are likely to have a beneficial impact on the market for remittances.

Increasing the role of African post offices in remittances can be facilitated by several policy measures. African post offices can partner with destination-country post offices, banks, and money-transfer companies to extend existing domestic money-order facilities to international remittances. Better coordination among the various regulating entities should be promoted to ensure better consumer protection. Other measures include inclusion of financial services in the definition of universal service of post offices; connecting post offices to high-speed Internet and creating integrated management information systems; encouraging basic savings accounts where remittances can be paid, small savings deposited, and payments processed; and integrating new technologies into their operations. Some mobile money-transfer operators, such as Wizzit in South Africa and M-PESA in Kenya, are actively working with post offices and postal savings banks as their agents.[31] A clear policy recommendation for post offices in Africa to more effectively participate in remittances is to eliminate exclusive partnerships and encourage African post offices to partner with more money-transfer companies (and even banks). This will put downward pressure on costs. This recommendation has already led to policy changes in some African countries[32] and has been implemented by the Central Bank of Nigeria and by Rwandan authorities.

African rural banks, savings cooperatives, and microfinance institutions can also play a similar role in improving access to formal remittance (and financial) services. Money transfers can act as an entry point for providing remittance senders and unbanked recipients in rural areas other financial products and services such as deposits, savings, and credit facilities. Measures to encourage the participation of savings and credit cooperatives, rural banks, and microfinance institutions in providing remittance services will help to improve financial access. A similar recommendation—to eliminate exclusive partnerships and allow multiple partnerships for sending and delivering remittances—also applies to rural banks and microfinance institutions.

Disseminating information about remittance channels and the costs of sending money to Africa would increase transparency and competition in the remittance industry, thus encouraging lower prices and new entrants while fostering the increased use of formal channels. Following the success of a U.K. remittance price database, France, Germany, Italy, the Netherlands, New Zealand, and Norway have commissioned websites that provide information on available channels. The World Bank has launched a Remittance Prices Worldwide database with over 150 remittance corridors (World Bank 2010b).

In addition to national and global price databases, information on remittance channels and costs should also be provided in published form (for example, pamphlets) to emigrants at airports before departure, during predeparture orientation and training, and at embassies and associations in destination countries to reach migrants without access to the Internet. It can also be made available through central banks, labor ministries, foreign employment bureaus, and recruitment associations in origin countries.

Measures that would encourage the expansion of mobile phones to cross-border remittances include (a) harmonizing banking and telecommunications regulations to enable mainstream African banks to participate in mobile money transfers and for telecommunications firms to offer microdeposit and savings accounts; (b) simplifying AML/CFT regulations for small-value transfers; and (c) ensuring that mobile distribution networks are open to multiple international RSPs instead of becoming exclusive partnerships between an international money transfer operator (MTO) and country-based mobile money services. Also, the implications of such exclusive partnerships for the price structure of mobile money services should be examined; the price of mobile money services appears to be similar to that charged for sending cash remittances, despite the fact that reliance on mobile-phone transfers reduces the need to build a costly distribution network.

Policy makers in Sub-Saharan Africa should be more alert to "Dutch disease" in countries where remittances inflows are large compared with the size of the economy, where supply constraints are a significant hindrance to the expansion of the nontradeable sector, and where a significant portion of remittances are spent on domestic goods, especially nontradeables (Gupta, Pattillo, and Wagh 2009). Countries should adjust to large remittance inflows that are likely to be permanent by maintaining market-based exchange-rate policies, taking steps to support the production of tradeables that might be harmed due to exchange rate overvaluation (for example, through infrastructure investments), and reducing labor and product market rigidities that impair competitiveness. Large inflows that are likely to be temporary can be sterilized, although the cost of sterilization can be high. Meanwhile, the resulting rise in domestic interest rates can attract more capital inflows, placing further pressure on the exchange rate (Fajnzylber and Lopez 2007). It can be difficult to distinguish between temporary and permanent levels of remittance inflows, although because remittances tend to be relatively stable, "Dutch disease" effects are of less concern than for natural resource windfalls and other cyclical flows.

Overview of Remittance Market Surveys in Africa and Two Remittance-Source Countries

This section provides an overview of the studies—presented in the remainder of this volume—of remittance markets in African countries and in key destination countries of African migrants. These country studies are based on primary surveys of a wide range of RSPs, including commercial and state-owned banks, MTOs, exchange bureaus, post offices, savings and credit cooperatives, microfinance institutions, telecommunication companies, retail stores, travel agencies, and informal providers such as transport companies. Similar issues of cost, competition, and regulatory environment are examined from the perspective of the providers, but the focus is on (a) understanding the regulatory, market, and institutional constraints in the sending of remittances, and (b) discussion of recent policy initiatives to improve transparency, consumer protection, and competition in remittance markets in the sending countries.

Chapters 2–9 present the findings of remittance market studies of the following Sub-Saharan African countries: Burkina Faso, Cape Verde, Ethiopia, Ghana, Kenya, Nigeria, Senegal, and Uganda. Chapters 10–11 present studies of remittance markets in two key remittance-source countries outside the African continent: France and the United Kingdom. Summarized below are some of the policy-relevant findings of each country study.

Yiriyibin Bambio in chapter 2 discusses the remittance market in *Burkina Faso*—a major source of intraregional migrants in the West Africa subregion. An estimated 1.6 million recorded emigrants live outside the country, with large numbers going to Côte d'Ivoire, Niger, and Mali within the subregion and to Italy and France outside the region (World Bank 2011). Despite the large volume of migration, Burkina Faso received only $43 million in officially recorded remittances in 2010 (less than 1 percent of GDP) mainly because of the prevalence of informal channels. The study finds that the remittance industry in Burkina Faso operates within the broader regional regulatory environment of the West African Monetary Union. Although formal remittance channels (such as Western Union, Moneygram, and MoneyExpress) are faster and more secure, they are also more expensive for the customer and do not adequately reach rural areas, which often lack electricity and computer access.

The Burkina Faso survey also found that although remittance firms do not consider regulations (centered on anti-money-laundering, tax policy, and exchange controls) to constitute a significant barrier to entry, they do consider regulations to be significant impediments to business activities. There are also inefficiencies in the clearing and settlement system and lack of adequately trained staff, which can create difficulties in compliance and in fulfilling Know-Your-Customer (KYC) requirements. As a consequence, remittance costs remain high, and informal providers continue to coexist with formal providers. However, some Burkinabè banks are active in the destination countries of migrants (for example, in Côte d'Ivoire and Italy) and facilitate the transfer of funds and savings of Burkinabè migration back to their home country.

Recommendations to improve the efficiency of remittance markets include developing prepaid cards and mobile money transfer; encouraging Burkinabè banks with branches or representative offices in destination countries to provide savings, investment, and money transfer products to Burkinabè migrants; dialoguing with migrant communities to understand their money transfer and investment needs; creating more transparency in the clearing and settlement system of banks with their agents and sub-agents; and training to improve the KYC compliance of nonbank money transfer operators.

In chapter 3, Georgiana Pop provides an overview of the remittance market in **Cape Verde**, a small country with the highest emigration rate in Africa at 38 percent of the population (World Bank 2011). Cape Verde received $144 million in remittances in 2010, about 9 percent of its GDP. Around two-thirds of families in Cape Verde receive money from abroad, mainly from Portugal, France, the United States, and the Netherlands. The survey finds that the industry is dominated by four private banks and one exchange office; two banks in partnership with MTOs such as Western Union and MoneyGram account for more than 90 percent of the market. However, there significant inefficiencies, with banks lacking significant branch networks in rural areas and the country lacking microfinance institutions.

Although the banks in Cape Verde provide a range of deposits, saving products, loans, credit cards, and mortgages, which can contribute to financial deepening, fees for sending domestic and international outward remittances are high relative to the incomes of the poor, which limits their access to such services. The RSPs perceive the regulatory and business environment as favorable to conducting a remittance business, and they comply with minimum capital requirements and regulations on reporting requirements for suspicious activities and large currency transactions. Access to finance for banks and nonfinancial institutions, in terms of availability, costs, and competition from the informal sector, are perceived as moderate obstacles to doing business by 60 percent of RSPs.

Some specific recommendations to improve the efficiency of remittances in Cape Verde include requiring RSPs to report outward and inward remittance flows separately (instead of a net flow); improving statistics on intra-African and within-country remittance flows; better estimating the size of the informal remittance market; setting up microfinance institutions and new money-transfer technologies, such as prepaid cards or mobile-phone banking; encouraging the entry of nonbank providers to stimulate competition and help to reduce overall transaction fees; and developing diaspora bonds, the securitization of remittances to leverage migration and remittances for investment, and financial products targeted at migrants.

Alemayehu Geda and Jacqueline Irving find in chapter 4 that, despite the contribution of remittances to *Ethiopia's* external financing position, there are many barriers in the effective delivery of remittances. A low level of financial intermediation and the lack of a modern national clearing and settlement system are seen as challenges. Most Ethiopian banks are concentrated in the major cities, and the bank branch and ATM networks are very limited, with little coverage of rural areas. Ethiopia also appears to be behind other East African countries such as Kenya and Uganda in the development and use of mobile money transfers and in providing remittance-linked financial services. This is partly because of Ethiopia's relatively underdeveloped financial system and a weak telecommunications infrastructure. Most remittances appear to be either consumed or invested in real estate, which offers higher returns than savings deposits and other financial instruments in a high-inflation environment.

Policy recommendations for improving the remittance market in Ethiopia include expediting the process for obtaining a license; facilitating entry of new players; establishing a national real-time gross settlement funds-transfer system; introducing more competition and reducing barriers to entry in the telecom sector to encourage firms to use mobile money transfer services; granting post offices and MFIs access to clearing and settlement systems to expand access to rural areas and increase competition; and frequently updating the information on available remittance channels and costs to assist Ethiopian migrants.

Peter Quartey finds in chapter 5 that **Ghana's** regulatory environment governing remittances services is generally effective and that current laws and regulations do not present major challenges to RSPs' business operations. However, banks have gained a progressively larger share of the remittance market in Ghana because of the introduction of universal banking, the population's greater trust in banks than in nonbank financial institutions, and the banks' extensive presence in rural areas.

The establishment of a National Switch (E-Zwich) as a common payment platform will enable the integration of existing bank switches and reduce costs of money transfers. An E-Zwich debit card has been introduced on a pilot basis for payments of salaries and other government assistance, and it is expected that financial institutions will launch a product that will enable remittance recipients to access money transfers through the card. There is currently little adoption of mobile money transfers in Ghana, but high mobile-phone penetration suggests potential for development of this sector. Similarly, the completion of a fiber-optic backbone and fall in Internet costs could encourage people to use Internet transfers.

Financial sector reforms have made it easier for institutions to engage in remittance services. However, informal remittance services, such as hand carrying, sending through friends and relatives, and incorrect invoicing of cross-border trade transactions, continue to be significant. Because inward remittances can be paid out only in local currency, while outward remittances are not permitted, informal firms have an opportunity to thrive.

Rose W. Ngugi summarizes of the remittance market in chapter 6 on **Kenya**, which has been in the spotlight for its rapid adoption of mobile money transfers; the largest provider, M-PESA, acquired more than 12 million customers within four years of its launch in early 2007. The study finds that although Kenya has a diverse range of RSPs, the role of informal channels (such as transport companies) has declined with the increasing popularity of mobile money. And while the cost of maintaining an account is prohibitive and constrains the demand for other financial services for remittance clients, mobile money transfer services in recent years have provided banking services in partnership with banks, including savings accounts and bank account management through the mobile phone service.

The cost of international remittances is significantly high across the various providers, and the rate charged for sending $200 ranges between 8 percent and 18 percent for international transfers. The use of mobile money is mostly used for domestic remittances. Although there have been some pilot projects for international money transfers in partnership with international money transfer companies, the costs appear to be similar to conventional cash transfers, and the amounts transferred appear to be small compared to those sent through mobile phones.

Chukwuma Agu provides an overview in chapter 7 of the remittance market in **Nigeria**, the largest remittance recipient in the African continent. The study finds that remittances have outpaced FDI, official development assistance, and other inflows into the country, and are second only to oil exports as a foreign exchange earner for Nigeria. However, it also finds that the remittance market in Nigeria is not yet well managed.

International money transfer companies play a dominant role, with Nigerian banks acting as intermediaries and distributors of remittances. Remittance transfers are expensive—as high as 20 percent for inward remittances—and the instruments quite limited beyond cash-to-cash transfers. Remittance services are seldom linked to regular bank services in a way that could promote improved use of remittance funds or access to other services on account of regular transfers. Outward-bound remittances are highly regulated, and limits are placed on transactions, while internal remittances can be expensive except for account-to-account transfers within the same bank.

Even though recent reforms have regularized the activities of foreign exchange bureaus, they are not allowed to handle remittance transactions. The use of mobile money transfers and card-based remittances is small compared with other countries in East Africa. There continues to be a large informal sector. The official remittances data do not adequately differentiate between migrant remittances and other small-value transfers related to trade and other payments.

Recommendations to increase competition and reduce cost in Nigeria's remittance market include enforcing recent regulation to expunge exclusivity from contracts among RSPs; encouraging banks to open outlets in remittance-source countries; regulating maximum chargeable fees on international transfers; allowing foreign exchange bureaus and microfinance institutions to partner with foreign and local MTOs and banks to provide remittance services; empowering the Nigerian Postal Service (whose network spreads across the entire country and offers affordable tariffs) to compete on remittances services, improving rural areas' access to remittance services putting downward pressure on costs; encouraging use of mobile money transfers to enhance access to remittance services in rural areas and reduce associated costs; and improving data collection on remittances.

In chapter 8, Fatou Cisse finds that remittances have become the principal source of external financing for **Senegal**, far exceeding FDI, external borrowing, and foreign aid. The EU countries account for more than half the remittances sent to the country. Money transfer services, banks, and the post office make up the formal sector. Money transfer companies account for one-third of the remittance market—with one company accounting for more than 70 percent—and have high costs because of their monopoly status. Banks have only a small share in remittance transfers in Senegal for several reasons, including high cost, the distance of bank branches from residential areas (especially in rural areas), long service delivery delays, long wait times at branches, and sometimes unexpected and arbitrary commission charges upon receipt. Banks also often work in exclusive partnership with international MTOs. The post office, which has a large network and presence in rural areas, provides postal money orders for local transfers and works with several international MTOs to deliver international transfers.

Remittances sent through informal channels (by migrants themselves, by relatives and friends, or through intermediaries) remain prevalent, particularly among the poor, because of the proximity to recipients, simplicity of operations, lack of overhead costs, freedom from regulatory constraints, and low-cost products. However, the informal sector's share appears to have declined in recent years. Mobile money is a recent phenomenon in Senegal. A "Yoban'tel" service, launched jointly by Obopay and Société Générale de Banques au Sénégal in mid-2010 (after the survey), allows cash deposits into mobile accounts and a variety of bill payment options.

Rose W. Ngugi and Edward Sennoga find in chapter 9 that a key barrier to understanding remittances in **Uganda** is inadequate data collection and reporting. Ugandan banks find it difficult to separate migrant remittances from other small-value payments when reporting remittances to the central bank. Remittance costs for outward international remittances tend to be high. The nonformal providers include community-based and transport companies. Few financial services are offered to remittance transfer clients. Mobile telephone transfer services are gaining entry, but they have yet to make significant contributions to domestic remittances.

Frederic Ponsot examines in chapter 10 the remittance market in **France**, a key destination country for migrants from West Africa and North Africa. Two-fifths of an estimated 6.7 million immigrants in France are estimated to originate in the African continent (World Bank 2011). The largest African sources of immigrants in France are the North African countries (Algeria, Morocco, and Tunisia), followed by Senegal, Côte d'Ivoire, Mali, Cameroon, the Republic of Congo, and the Democratic Republic of Congo in Sub-Saharan Africa. Recorded remittance outflows from France were $5.2 billion in 2009, with a significant share going to Africa; however, the actual amounts, including flows through unrecorded channels, are likely to be higher.

The study finds that the remittance industry in France is dominated by banks, a few money transfer companies that are registered as financial institutions, and a partnership between La Banque Postale and Western Union. French banks do not appear to view African migrants as viable mass-market clients. Some African banks have representative offices in France that facilitate remittances, payments of pensions to retirees in their countries of origin (especially in North Africa), and investments. However, Sub-Saharan African banks have little presence in France, with a few exceptions (for example, banks from Burkina Faso and Senegal).

On the receiving side, the corridors in Africa are marked by weak financial infrastructure, and the informal sector plays a significant role in rural areas. However, the emergence of microfinance institutions and retail card-based payment systems (with the help of monetary authorities and international donors) have the potential to improve the delivery of remittances.

The chapter makes some concrete policy recommendations to improve the quality of remittance outflows data, including comparing these with remittance-recipient African countries, and discusses policies to increase competition and reduce costs, including eliminating exclusive partnerships; promoting payment institutions; reducing barriers to entry for money transfers; encouraging banks to partner with a variety of RSPs; clarifying regulations about the involvement of telecom operators in cross-border remittances to facilitate remittances from France to Africa through mobile phones; and improving the infrastructure for remittance payments, a key step toward bringing remittances into the formal financial system.

In chapter 11, Leon Isaacs summarizes the remittance market in the **United Kingdom**, a key destination country for migrants from East Africa and Southern Africa. Over one-sixth of immigrants (1.2 million) are estimated to be from Africa (World Bank 2011). The largest African-migrant countries of origin in the United Kingdom include South Africa, Kenya, Nigeria, Zimbabwe, Somalia, Ghana, and Uganda. Recorded remittance outflows from the United Kingdom were $3.7 billion in 2009, but the actual amounts, including flows through unrecorded channels, are likely to be much higher.

The study finds that a broad range of RSPs send money to Africa. Because of a "light touch" regulatory regime relative to other European countries, there are few barriers to entry of small RSPs to the U.K. remittance market. Average costs for sending remittances to Africa, however, tend to be higher than for sending to, for example, South Asia, but these costs have been declining over time. Most RSPs have now been registered as Payments Institutions, under the EU Payments Services Directive. Some services offer Internet-based transfers, and some (such as Mukuru) used to offer even transfers for goods and fuel in Zimbabwe because of the country's hyperinflation.

Recommendations to improve the efficiency of remittance flows from the United Kingdom to Africa include (a) establishing a dialogue between the money transfer companies and central banks of recipient countries in Africa; (b) broadening the types of businesses that can provide remittances, including nonbank financial institutions and retail businesses; (c) working with authorities to remove incentives to transfer through informal channels (by eliminating the parallel market premium between official and market rates through exchange liberalization); (d) increasing cost transparency by frequently updating, and increasing coverage of, available remittance price data; and (e) promoting financial literacy for African migrants.

Annex 1.1

Table 1A.1   Household Access to Information and Communication Technology in Selected African Countries, by Remittance Status

percentage of households with selected devices

Country and technology	Households receiving domestic remittances	Households receiving remittances from within Africa	Households receiving remittances from outside Africa	Households with no remittances
Burkina Faso				
Mobile phone	40.1	40.6	65.5	39.3
Radio	65.4	64.1	69.0	61.5
Television	7.8	6.9	41.4	8.7
Computer access	1.0	1.6	13.8	1.8
Observations	422	507	29	1,145
Ghana				
Mobile phone	9.1	14.6	45.4	19.6
Radio	48.2	31.4	47.3	49.9
Television	18.7	16.9	52.7	33.6
Computer access	0.5	0.0	3.3	2.4
Observations	367	33	133	8,105
Kenya				
Mobile phone	79.5	82.3	87.0	77.3
Radio	84.8	86.7	88.9	82.7
Television	50.4	56.6	76.2	52.2
Computer access	7.1	17.7	30.4	20.6
Observations	395	113	369	1,065
Nigeria				
Mobile phone	70.4	87.3	95.5	57.3
Radio	86.9	94.3	93.8	82.5
Television	54.2	75.8	93.8	48.8
Computer access	7.2	15.1	22.6	10.7
Observations	573	77	328	1,272
Senegal				
Mobile phone	72.8	82.3	97.5	75.2
Radio	76.3	66.9	95.1	75.9
Television	40.3	37.9	79.7	49.1
Internet access	1.6	0.9	9.6	6.6
Observations	320	163	460	1,010
Uganda				
Mobile phone	58.3	76.2	85.4	50.4
Radio	78.1	81.0	90.2	73.4
Television	19.4	28.6	59.8	25.7
Internet access	4.1	3.2	28.1	7.1
Observations	242	63	82	1,528

Sources: Authors' calculations based on results household surveys conducted in Burkina Faso, Kenya, Nigeria, Senegal, South Africa, and Uganda in 2009 as part of the Africa Migration Project and Ghana Living Standards Survey in 2005–06.

Annex 1.2

Table 1A.2   Formal and Informal Remittance Channels, Select African Countries
percentage of recipients (other than for South Africa)

a. Burkina Faso, 2009

Remittance channel	Remittances from outside Africa	Remittances from within Africa	Domestic remittances
Money transfer operator[a]	43.2	10.5	2.0
Postal money order	0.0	3.2	1.4
Received through banks	2.3	0.7	0.4
Through friend or relative	18.2	64.7	37.4
Courier, bus, transport, travel agency	0.0	3.0	5.8
Brought by hand during visit	34.1	15.2	49.5
Informal individual agents	0.0	2.5	1.9
ATM cards, Internet money transfers	0.0	0.0	0.2
Other	2.3	0.2	1.3
Total	**100.0**	**100.0**	**100.0**

Source: Africa Migration Project household survey in Burkina Faso in 2009.
a. Western Union, Moneygram, and others.

b. Ghana, 2005–06

Remittance channel	Remittances from outside Africa	Remittances from within Africa	Domestic remittances
Money transfer operator[a]	67.8	10.9	0.6
Fast money transfer	7.8	0.0	0.0
Bank account	2.2	0.0	0.6
Friend/relative	16.1	52.2	45.1
Brought home by migrant	4.4	32.6	49.0
Other	1.7	4.3	4.7
Total	**100.0**	**100.0**	**100.0**

Source: Ghana Living Standards Survey in 2005–06.
a. Western Union, Moneygram, and Vigo (Merchant Bank).

Table 1A.2   *(continued)*

c. Kenya, 2009

Remittance channel	Remittances from outside Africa	Remittances from within Africa	Domestic remittances
Money transfer operator[a]	64.0	38.6	1.5
Postal money order	1.4	1.5	1.1
Received through banks	17.2	11.4	6.3
Through friend or relative	3.8	9.1	6.5
Courier, bus, or travel agency	0.5	3.8	1.5
Brought by hand during visit	2.0	7.6	20.0
Informal individual agents	1.4	0.0	0.0
Foreign exchange bureau, credit union	6.3	1.5	0.6
Mobile phone	2.9	23.5	61.5
ATM cards, Internet money transfers	0.5	0.0	0.0
Other	0.0	0.0	0.8
Total	**100.0**	**100.0**	**100.0**

Source: Africa Migration Project household survey in Kenya in 2009.
a. Western Union, Moneygram, and others.

d. Nigeria, 2009

Remittance channel	Remittances from outside Africa	Remittances from within Africa	Domestic remittances
Money transfer operator[a]	57.1	35.2	6.3
Postal money order	0.0	1.1	0.0
Direct transfer to bank account	11.8	12.1	35.0
Bank as paying agent for MTO	10.5	17.6	2.6
Foreign exchange bureau	0.0	1.1	0.1
Credit union	0.0	0.0	0.2
Travel agency	0.0	0.0	0.4
Informal individual agents	2.5	4.4	4.1
Mobile phone/telecom service providers	0.0	0.0	0.4
Through friend or relative	12.8	15.4	21.2
Courier, bus, or other transport	0.0	0.0	0.5
Brought by hand during visit	5.4	13.2	27.7
Prepaid cards/ATM card	0.0	0.0	0.2
Internet money transfer	0.0	0.0	0.1
Other	0.0	0.0	1.2
Total	**100.0**	**100.0**	**100.0**

Source: Africa Migration Project household survey in Nigeria in 2009.
a. Western Union, Moneygram, and others.

Table 1A.2 *(continued)*

e. Senegal, 2009

Remittance channel	Remittances from outside Africa	Remittances within Africa	Domestic remittances
Money transfer operator[a]	81.5	30.8	4.9
Postal money order	2.5	6.3	3.4
Direct transfer to bank account	0.3	0.0	0.0
Bank as paying agent for MTO	1.5	0.0	0.1
Foreign exchange bureau	0.4	0.4	0.0
Credit union	0.7	0.0	0.0
Travel agency	0.0	0.0	0.0
Informal individual agents	1.9	4.3	3.4
Mobile phone/telecom service providers	0.0	0.0	0.6
Through friend or relative	10.1	41.1	37.3
Courier, bus, or other transport	0.0	0.6	11.8
Brought by hand during visit	0.5	14.2	36.7
Prepaid cards/ATM card	0.0	0.0	0.0
Internet money transfer	0.0	0.0	0.0
Other	0.4	2.2	1.9
Total	**100.0**	**100.0**	**100.0**

Source: Africa Migration Project household survey in Senegal in 2009.
a. Western Union, Moneygram, and others.

f. Uganda, 2009

Remittance channel	Remittances from outside Africa	Remittances within Africa	Domestic remittances
Money transfer operator[a]	55.4	36.3	4.2
Postal money order	2.7	0.0	0.2
Received through banks	12.5	15.0	10.8
Through friend or relative	8.9	21.3	27.4
Courier, bus, or other transport, travel agency	0.0	2.5	3.1
Brought back himself during visit	4.5	20.0	47.6
Informal individual agents	0.0	0.0	0.0
Foreign exchange bureau, credit union	13.4	1.3	0.9
Mobile phone	0.9	2.5	5.2
ATM cards, internet money transfers	0.9	0.0	0.0
Other	0.0	1.3	0.0
Total	**100.0**	**100.0**	**100.0**

Source: Africa Migration Project household survey in Uganda in 2009.
a. Western Union, Moneygram, and others.

Table 1A.2   *(continued)*

g. South Africa 2009 (% of remittance senders)

Remittance channel	Remittances sent to other countries within Africa	Domestic remittances
Money transfer operator[a]	4.6	15.8
Postal money order	6.1	6.7
Direct transfer to bank account	5.3	40.6
Foreign exchange bureau	0.8	0.6
Credit union	0.0	0.6
Travel agency	0.8	0.6
Other nonfinancial institution that provides remittance services	0.0	1.2
Mobile phone/telecom service providers	0.0	0.6
Through friend or relative	58.0	18.8
Courier, bus, or other transport	18.3	1.2
Brought back himself during visit	2.3	5.5
Prepaid cards/ATM card	2.3	2.4
Internet money transfer	0.0	1.8
Other	1.5	3.6
Total	**100.0**	**100.0**

Source: Africa Migration Project household survey of *immigrants* in South Africa in 2009.
a. Western Union, Moneygram, and others.

Notes

1. Some notable exceptions occur in Sub-Saharan Africa. For example, Cape Verde, Ethiopia, Kenya, and Nigeria collect and publish monthly data on remittances. Several North African countries, such as Egypt and Morocco, publish quarterly data.

2. Sayan (2006) finds that remittances are strongly countercyclical in poor countries, such as Bangladesh and India, but procyclical in middle-income countries, such as Jordan and Morocco. Lueth and Ruiz-Arranz (2008) find that remittances to Sri Lanka are positively correlated with oil prices—perhaps reflecting the economic situation of Sri Lankan migrants in destination countries in the Gulf—but tend to decline when the Sri Lankan currency weakens.

3. In the past, remittances did not appear to be affected by economic cycles in migrants' destination countries. Roache and Gradzka (2007) find that remittance flows to Latin America were relatively insensitive to business cycle fluctuations in the United States over the 1990–2007 period. Given the magnitude of the financial crisis that began in 2008, there is a strong possibility that it has affected the incomes of migrants and their ability to send money home.

4. The stability of remittances to the Philippines was an important factor in its ability to issue a $750 million bond despite the global financial crisis. Bangladesh was rated for the first time in April 2010, receiving a BB rating

from Standard & Poor's Investor Relations Service and a Ba3 from Moody's Investors Service, similar to the ratings of many emerging markets. The rating agencies cited the high share of remittance flows in GDP and the high growth rate as important factors in their rating decisions.

5. In developed countries, a firm's credit risk typically accounts for a large part of the information content of its ratings; in developing countries, the sovereign rating exerts significant influence on—and often acts as a ceiling for—the foreign currency ratings of firms and banks in the country (Borensztein, Cowan, and Valenzuela 2007; Ratha, De, and Mohapatra 2011).

6. The joint World Bank–IMF Low-Income Country Debt Sustainability Framework now allows for more explicit consideration of remittances in evaluating the ability of countries to repay external obligations and take on non-concessional borrowing from private creditors (IMF 2010b).

7. Banks in several developing countries—including Brazil, Egypt, El Salvador, Guatemala, Kazakhstan, Mexico, and Turkey—have been able to raise cheaper and longer-term financing (more than $15 billion since 2000) from international capital markets by securitizing future remittance flows (Ratha 2005, Ketkar and Ratha 2009a).

8. The United States, in partnership with the Inter-American Development Bank, launched the BRIDGE (Building Remittance Investments for Development, Growth and Entrepreneurship) initiative, which aims to securitize remittances for infrastructure projects in developing countries, starting with pilots in El Salvador and Honduras.

9. An empirical study of 109 countries for 1990–2003 shows that a well-developed financial sector can more effectively intermediate remittances with investment and that the impact of remittance inflows on exchange rate appreciation is smaller when the level of financial development is higher (Acosta, Baerg, and Mandelman 2009). Increased receipt of remittances is also associated with higher market capitalization, a key indicator of financial market development (Billmeier and Massa 2009). A higher sovereign rating as a result of remittances can translate into greater access of subsovereign entities to international capital markets, thereby increasing the level of investment in the economy.

10. Latin American countries receiving remittances have experienced some exchange rate appreciation (Fajnzylber and Lopez 2007; Amuedo-Dorantes and Pozo 2004), but Fajnzylber and Lopez (2007) find little or no impact of remittance flows on the exchange rate outside the Latin American region.

11. Empirical specifications that include remittances in cross-country growth regressions provide mixed results (Barajas and others 2009; Catrinescu and others 2009; Singh, Haacker, and Lee 2009). The lack of significance of remittances in some growth equations may reflect the fact their effects on human and physical capital are realized only over a long time period; that the effects are endogenous (that is, they rise with declines in output); or that official data

on remittances are of poor quality. Another factor accounting for the lack of significance may be omitted variables, such as policies and institutions (Catrinescu and others 2009), the level of financial development (Giuliano and Ruiz-Arranz 2009), and other indirect channels through which remittances can influence economic growth (Rao and Hassan 2009).

12. Other benefits include the transmission of knowledge, trade and investment linkages, fertility norms, and so on.

13. Only one-third of African migrant households in the OECD send remittances. The average remittance sent by migrant households that remit is $2,638 (Bollard, McKenzie, and Morten 2010).

14. The evidence on whether skilled or unskilled migrants send larger remittances is mixed. Some studies suggest that skilled migrants remit less because they are more likely to settle down in their host countries and eventually bring their families (Niimi and Ozden 2006; Faini 2007). Other studies, based on microdata, find a positive relationship between education and the amounts remitted (Bollard and others 2009; Clemens 2009). Some authors suggest that remittances sent by skilled migrants may exceed the cost of their training (Clemens 2009; Easterly and Nyarko 2009).

15. Taylor and Wyatt (1996) argue that the shadow value of remittances for overcoming risk and liquidity constraints is particularly important to households in the low- to middle-income range, which otherwise tend to be credit-constrained. Guatemalan households receiving remittances spend more at the margin on housing, even after controlling for the endogeneity of remittance-receiving status (Adams and Cuecuecha 2011). About one-fifth of the capital invested in 6,000 microenterprises in urban Mexico was financed by remittances (Woodruff and Zenteno 2001, 2007; see also Massey and Parrado 1998). In rural Pakistan, international remittances raise the propensity to invest in agricultural land (Adams 1998). Remittance-receiving households that benefited from an exchange rate shock spent more hours in self-employment and were more likely to start relatively capital-intensive entrepreneurial enterprises in the Philippines (Yang 2008b). Some recent studies (for example, Ashraf and others 2010) find that giving migrants more control over the uses of remittances can increase savings rates among both migrants and remittance recipients.

16. See Acosta, Fajnzylber, and López (2007); Acosta and others (2008); Ebeke (2010); Cox-Edwards and Ureta (2003); Hanson and Woodruff (2003); Lopez-Cordova (2005); Calero, Bedi, and Sparrow (2009); Amuedo-Dorantes, Georges, and Pozo (2010); Bredl (2011); Adams and Cuecuecha (2010); De and Ratha (2006); Mansuri (2007); Yang (2008b); Bansak and Chezum (2009). However, other studies have found a negative impact of migration on educational outcome. A recent study found

that living in a migrant-sending household in Mexico reduced the likelihood of children completing high school by 13–15 percent (McKenzie and Rapoport 2010).

17. Fajnzylber and Lopez (2007) find that in Guatemala and Nicaragua, children 1–5 in remittance-receiving households were more likely to be of above-average height and weight and to have had a doctor-assisted delivery. Studies of Mexico find that remittances were associated with lower infant mortality rates (Hildebrandt and McKenzie 2005; Lopez-Cordova 2005) and higher health care expenditures (Amuedo-Dorantes, Pozo, and Sainz 2007; Valero-Gil 2009). Kanaiaupuni and Donato (1999) find that infant mortality rates initially rose in Mexican villages with very high rates of migration to the United States but that remittances eventually reduced infant mortality rates.

18. In Ecuador, remittances helped keep children of remittance-receiving households in school when faced with adverse shocks (Calero, Bedi, and Sparrow 2009). Increased remittances helped smooth household consumption and compensate for the loss of assets after an earthquake in El Salvador in 2001 (Halliday 2006). Transfers from friends and relatives in the United States played an important role in reducing the distress caused in Haiti by Cyclone Jeanne in 2004 (Weiss-Fagan 2006) and after the devastating earthquake in 2010 (Ratha 2010). Remittance-receiving households in the Aceh region of Indonesia recovered more quickly than other households after the 2004 tsunami (Wu 2006). Migrant remittances were important factors in disaster recovery and reconstruction after a devastating earthquake in Pakistan in 2005 (Suleri and Savage 2006). In the Philippines, remittances helped compensate for the loss in income caused by adverse rainfall shocks (Yang and Choi 2007). In Thailand, domestic remittances increased in response to below-average rainfall in the recipients' region and to increases in medical expenses in recipient households (Miller and Paulson 2007).

19. Mohapatra, Joseph, and Ratha (2009) find that remittance-receiving households in Ghana are likely to have better access to communication equipment and mobile phones than households that do not receive any remittances, even after controlling for the possibility of self-selection of remittance-receiving households.

20. The World Bank's Remittance Prices Worldwide database provides average remittance costs through banks and nonbank intermediaries for more than 150 migration corridors. http://remittanceprices.worldbank.org.

21. Transfer costs tend to be lower when financial systems are more developed and exchange rates less volatile (Freund and Spatafora 2008). Beck and Martinez Peria (2009) find that remittance corridors with larger stocks of migrants, a larger number of RSPs, and greater banking competition have lower costs.

22. Access to "bank-like" institutions, such as microfinance institutions and savings and credit cooperatives, is also limited outside of urban areas (Demirgüç-
Kunt, Beck, and Honohan 2008).

23. Qualitative information was collected for the United States. Conducting a
survey in the United States proved infeasible because there is no national-
level institutional focal point; each state has a different legal and regulatory
framework, compliance requirements, and institutions governing remittances
(Andreassen 2006).

24. The Southern African Migration Project conducted national-level representative surveys on remittance flows and usage at the household level for five
countries belonging to the Southern African Development Community:
Botswana, Lesotho, Southern Mozambique, Swaziland, and Zimbabwe, with
a focus on intraregional transfers from South Africa and Botswana (Pendleton
and others 2006). While the use of informal channels is predominant in
remittances sent from South Africa to neighboring countries, among formal
channels used, TEBA Bank provides bank transfers for migrant mining workers in South Africa, accounting for about 16 percent of transfers to Botswana
and 8 percent for Swaziland.

25. The concept of mobile money transfers is being transferred from Africa to
other developing regions. India's Bharti Telecom, which recently acquired
Zain, has received approval from India's central bank to start mobile payments services in India. The "semiclosed wallet" will allow Bharti Airtel's customers in India to exchange physical cash for virtual money, which can then
be used to pay for goods and services up to Rs 5,000 (about $108) per trans-
action. It does not, however, allow cash withdrawals at present. See *Economic
Times* 2010.

26. http://allafrica.com/stories/201006071332.html.

27. http://www.wizzit.co.za.

28. In the Philippines, for example, regulators have imposed the same reporting
requirements on bank and nonbank mobile money providers (Dolan 2009).

29. The Philippines has been at the forefront of mobile money-transfer services
(World Bank 2006), while Brazil has considerable experience with "branchless
banking" using retail payment networks and point-of-sale devices deployed at
agents such as grocery stores (Pickens, Porteous, and Rotman 2009).

30. For example, in Sub-Saharan Africa in 2008, only 17 percent of post offices
were equipped with computers and had Internet access. A study led by the
Universal Postal Union in 2010 showed that only two African countries out
of 43 who answered a questionnaire had developed a cost-accounting system
(Clotteau and Anson 2011).

31. http://www.postbank.co.ke/.

32. World Bank and BIS-CPSS 2007.

References

Abdih, Yasser, Ralph Chami, Jihad Dagher, and Peter Montiel. 2008. "Remittances and Institutions: Are Remittances a Curse?" Working Paper 08/29, International Monetary Fund, Washington, DC.

Abdih, Yasser, Michael Gapen, Amine Mati, and Ralph Chami. 2009. "Fiscal Sustainability in Remittance-Dependent Economies." Working Paper 09/190, International Monetary Fund, Washington, DC.

Acosta, Pablo, Nicole Baerg, and Federico Mandelman. 2009. "Financial Development, Remittances, and Real Exchange Rate Appreciation." *Economic Review* (Federal Reserve Bank of Atlanta) 94 (1): 1–12.

Acosta, Pablo A., Cesar Calderon, Humberto López, and Pablo Fajnzylber. 2008. "What is the Impact of International Remittances on Poverty and Inequality in Latin America?" *World Development* 36 (1): 89–114.

Acosta, Pablo, Pablo Fajnzylber, and Humberto López. 2007. "The Impact of Remittances on Poverty and Human Capital: Evidence from Latin American Household Surveys." In *International Migration, Economic Development and Policy*, ed. Caglar Özden and Maurice Schiff, 59–98. New York: World Bank and Palgrave Macmillan.

Acosta, Pablo, Emmanuel Lartey, and Federico Mandelman. 2009. "Remittances and the Dutch Disease." *Journal of International Economics* 79(1): 102–16.

Adams, Richard H. 1998. "Remittances, Investment and Rural Asset Accumulation in Pakistan." *Economic Development and Cultural Change* 47 (1): 155–73.

———. 2006. "Remittances and Poverty in Ghana." Policy Research Working Paper 3838, World Bank, Washington, DC.

Adams, Richard H., and Alfredo Cuecuecha. 2010. "Remittances, Household Expenditure and Investment in Guatemala." *World Development*, 38 (11): 1626–1641.

Adams, Richard H., Alfredo Cuecuecha, and John Page. 2008a. "Remittances, Consumption and Investment in Ghana." Policy Research Working Paper 4515, World Bank, Washington, DC.

———. 2008b. "The Impact of Remittances on Poverty and Inequality in Ghana." Policy Research Working Paper 4732, World Bank, Washington, DC.

Adams, Richard H., and John Page. 2003. "International Migration, Remittances and Poverty in Developing Countries." Policy Research Working Paper 3179, World Bank, Washington, DC.

———. 2005. "Do International Migration and Remittances Reduce Poverty in Developing Countries?" *World Development* 33 (10): 1645–69.

AfDB (African Development Bank) and World Bank. 2011. *Leveraging Migration for Africa: Remittances, Skills, and Investments.* Washington, DC: World Bank.

Afreximbank (African Export-Import Bank). 2005. *Annual Report*. http://www
.afreximbank.com.

Aggarwal, Reena, Asli Demirgüç-Kunt, and Maria Soledad Martinez Peria. 2006.
"Do Workers' Remittances Promote Financial Development?" Policy Research
Working Paper 3957, World Bank, Washington, DC.

Ajayi, Michael A., Mukaila A. Ijaiya, Gafar T. Ijaiya, Raji A. Bello, Mufthau A. Ijaiya,
and Sidikat L. Adeyemi. 2009. "International Remittances and Well-Being in
Sub-Saharan Africa." *Journal of Economics and International Finance* 1 (3):
78–84.

Aker, Jenny C., and Isaac M. Mbiti. 2010. "Mobile Phones and Economic
Development in Africa." Working Paper 211, Center for Global Development,
Washington, DC.

Akinlo, Anthony E., and Tajudeen Egbetunde. 2010. "Financial Development and
Economic Growth: The Experience of 10 Sub-Saharan African Countries
Revisited." *The Review of Finance and Banking* 2 (1): 17–28.

Amuedo-Dorantes, Catalina, and Susan Pozo. 2004. "Workers' Remittances and the
Real Exchange Rate: A Paradox of Gifts." *World Development* 32 (8): 1407–17.

———. 2011. "New Evidence on the Role of Remittances on Health Care
Expenditures by Mexican Households." *Review of Economics of the Household*
9 (1): 69–98.

Amuedo-Dorantes, Catalina, Susan Pozo, and Tania Sainz. 2007. "Remittances and
Healthcare Expenditure Patterns of Populations in Origin Communities:
Evidence from Mexico." *Integration & Trade* 27 (July–December): 159–84.

Andreassen, Ole. 2006. "Remittance Service Providers in the United States: How
remittance firms operate and how they perceive their business environment."
Financial Sector Discussion Series, Payments Systems and Remittances, World
Bank, Washington DC. June.

Anyanwu, John C., and Andrew E. O. Erhijakpor. 2010. "Do International
Remittances Affect Poverty in Africa?" *African Development Review* 22
(1): 51–91.

Avendaño, Rolando, Norbert Gaillard, and Sebastián Nieto Parra. 2009. "Are
Workers' Remittances Relevant for Credit Rating Agencies?" Development
Center Working Paper 282, Organisation for Economic Co-operation and
Development, Paris.

Awareness Times (Sierra Leone). 2010. "In Sierra Leone, Over 150,000 Clients
Registered with Splash Mobile Money." September 16. http://news.sl/drwebsite/
publish/article_200516307.shtml.

Azam, Jean-Paul, and Flore Gubert. 2005. "Those in Kayes. The Impact of
Remittances on Their Recipients in Africa." *Revue Économique* 56 (6): 1331–58.

———. 2006. "Migrants' Remittances and the Household in Africa: A Review of
Evidence." *Journal of African Economies* 15 (AERC Supplement): 426–62.

Babatunde, Raphael O., and Enrica C. Martinetti. 2010. "Impact of Remittances on Food Security and Nutrition in Rural Nigeria." Unpublished manuscript, Center for International Cooperation and Development, University of Pavia, Italy.

Bansak, Cynthia, and Brian Chezum. 2009. "How Do Remittances Affect Human Capital Formation of School-Age Boys and Girls?" *American Economic Review* 99 (2): 145–48.

Barajas, Adolfo, Ralph Chami, Connel Fullenkamp, Michael Gapen, and Peter J. Montiel. 2009. "Do Workers' Remittances Promote Economic Growth?" Working Paper 09/153, International Monetary Fund, Washington, DC.

Beck, Thorsten, and Maria Soledad Martinez Peria. 2009. "What Explains the Cost of Remittances? An Examination Across 119 Country Corridors." Policy Research Working Paper 5072, World Bank, Washington, DC.

Billmeier, Andreas, and Isabella Massa. 2009. "What Drives Stock Market Development in Emerging Markets—Institutions, Remittances, or Natural Resources?" *Emerging Markets Review* 10 (1): 23–35.

Birdsall, Nancy, and Punam Chuhan. 1986. "Client Choice of Health Care Treatment in Rural Mali." Unpublished manuscript for the Health, Nutrition and Population Department, World Bank, Washington, DC.

Block, Steven, and Patrick Webb. 2001. "The Dynamics of Livelihood Diversification in Post-Famine Ethiopia." *Food Policy* 26 (4): 333–50.

Bold, Chris. 2010. "Borderless Branchless Banking." Technology Blog, Consultative Group to Assist the Poor (CGAP), Washington DC. December 14.

Bollard, Albert, David McKenzie, and Melanie Morten. 2010. "The Remitting Patterns of African Migrants in the OECD." *Journal of African Economies* 19 (5): 605–34.

Bollard, Albert, David McKenzie, Melanie Morten, and Hillel Rapoport. 2009. "Remittances and the Brain Drain Revisited: The Microdata Show that More Educated Migrants Remit More." Policy Research Working Paper 5113, World Bank, Washington, DC.

Borensztein, Eduardo, Kevin Cowan, and Patricio Valenzuela. 2007. "Sovereign Ceilings 'Lite'? The Impact of Sovereign Ratings on Corporate Ratings in Emerging Market Economies." Working Paper 07/75, International Monetary Fund, Washington, DC.

Bourdet, Yves, and Hans Falck. 2006. "Emigrants' Remittances and Dutch Disease in Cape Verde." *International Economic Journal* 20 (3): 267–84.

Bracking, Sarah, and Lloyd Sachikonye. 2008 "Remittances, Poverty Reduction and Informalization in Zimbabwe 2005–6: A Political Economy of Dispossession?" Brooks World Poverty Institute Working Paper 28, University of Manchester, U.K.

Bredl, Sebastian. 2011. "Migration, Remittances and Educational Outcomes: The Case of Haiti." *International Journal of Educational Development* 31 (2): 162–68.

Bugamelli, Matteo, and Francesco Paterno. 2009. "Do Workers' Remittances Reduce the Probability of Current Account Reversals?" *World Development* 37 (12): 1821–38.

Business Daily Africa. 2010. "Mobile Money Transforms Uganda." September 7. allafrica.com/stories/201009070007.html.

Bussolo, Maurizio, and Dennis Medvedev. 2007. "Do Remittances Have a Flip Side? A General Equilibrium Analysis of Remittances, Labor Supply Responses, and Policy Options for Jamaica." Policy Research Working Paper 4143, World Bank, Washington, DC.

Calero, Carla, Arjun S. Bedi, and Robert Sparrow. 2009 "Remittances, Liquidity Constraints and Human Capital Investments in Ecuador." *World Development* 37 (6): 1143–54.

Catrinescu, Natalia, Miguel Leon-Ledesma, Matloob Piracha, and Bryce Quillin. 2009. "Remittances, Institutions, and Economic Growth." *World Development* 37 (1): 81–92.

CGAP (Consultative Group to Assist the Poor) and Dalberg (Global Development Advisers). 2010. "Improving Access and Reducing Costs of International Remittances through Branchless Banking Solutions." Landscaping research by Dalberg for the CGAP Technology Program, CGAP, Washington, DC. http://www.cgap.org/gm/document-1.9.49049/Dalberg-CGAP_Int l_Remit_Branchless_Banking_Findings.pdf.

Chami, Ralph, Adolfo Barajas, Thomas Cosimano, Connel Fullenkamp, Michael Gapen, and Peter Montiel. 2008. "Macroeconomic Consequences of Remittances." Occasional Paper 259, International Monetary Fund, Washington, DC.

Chami, Ralph, Dalia Hakura, and Peter Montiel. 2009. "Remittances: An Automatic Stabilizer?" Working Paper 09/91, International Monetary Fund, Washington, DC.

Chauvet, Lisa, Flore Gubert, and Sandrine Mesplé-Somps. 2009. "Are Remittances More Effective than Aid to Reduce Child Mortality? An Empirical Assessment Using Inter- and Intra-Country Data." Développement Institutions & Mondialisation (DIAL) Working Paper DT/2009-11, DIAL, Paris.

Clarke, George, and Scott Wallsten. 2004. "Do Remittances Protect Households in Developing Countries against Shocks? Evidence from a Natural Disaster in Jamaica." Unpublished manuscript, World Bank, Washington, DC.

Clemens, Michael. 2009. "The Financial Effects of High-Skill Emigration: New Data on African Doctors Abroad." Presentation at the International Conference on Diaspora for Development, World Bank, Washington, DC, July 13–14. http://siteresources.worldbank.org/INTPROSPECTS/Resources/ 334934-1110315015165/Clemens.pdf.

Clotteau, Nils, and Jose Anson. 2011. "Role of Post Offices in Remittances and Financial Inclusion." Background note prepared for the Africa Migration

Project, Universal Postal Union, Berne, Switzerland. Migration and Development Brief 15, World Bank, Washington, DC.

Cox-Edwards, Alejandra, and Manuelita Ureta, M. 2003. "International Migration, Remittances and Schooling: Evidence from El Salvador." *Journal of Development Economics* 72 (2): 429–61.

De, Prabal, and Dilip Ratha. 2006. "Migration and Remittances in Sri Lanka." Unpublished manuscript, Development Prospects Group, World Bank, Washington, DC.

Demirgüç-Kunt, Asli, Thorsten Beck, and Patrick Honohan. 2008. "Finance for All? Policies and Pitfalls in Expanding Access." Policy Research Report, World Bank, Washington, DC.

Dolan, Jonathan. 2009. "Accelerating the Development of Mobile Money Ecosystems." Report on the Mobile Money Summit 2009, International Finance Corporation and Harvard Kennedy School, Cambridge, MA. http://www.hks.harvard.edu/m-rcbg/CSRI/publications/report_39 _mobile_money_january_09.pdf.

Drabo, Alassane, and Christian Ebeke. 2010. "Remittances, Public Health Spending and Foreign Aid in the Access to Health Care Services in Developing Countries." Working Paper E 2010.04, Central Extension Resources Development Institute (CERDI), Clermont-Ferrand, France.

Easterly, William, and Yaw Nyarko. 2009. "Is the Brain Drain Good for Africa?" In *Skilled Immigration Today: Prospects, Problems, and Policies*, ed. Jagdish Bhagwati and Gordon Hanson, 316–60. New York: Oxford University Press.

Ebeke, Christian H. 2010. "The Effect of Remittances on Child Labor: Cross-Country Evidence." *Economics Bulletin* 30 (1): 351–64.

Economic Times. 2010. "Bharti Gets RBI Nod for Mobile Money Services." September 17. http://economictimes.indiatimes.com/articleshow/6559841 .cms?prtpage=1.

Economist. 2010. "Low-Cost Bundle: India's Biggest Mobile Operator Makes a Fresh Attempt to Enter Africa." February 18. http://www.economist.com/ node/15546456?story_id=15546456.

Elbadawi, Asmaa, and Rania Roushdy. 2009. "Impact of International Migration and Remittances on Child Schooling and Child Work: The Case of Egypt." Paper for the World Bank's MENA International Migration Program funded by the European Commission, World Bank, Washington, DC.

Faini, Riccardo. 2007. "Remittances and the Brain Drain: Do More Skilled Migrants Remit More?" *The World Bank Economic Review* 21 (2): 177–91.

Fajnzylber, Pablo, and Humberto López. 2007. *Close to Home: The Development Impact of Remittances in Latin America.* Washington, DC: World Bank.

Frankel, Jeffrey. 2011. "Are Bilateral Remittances Countercyclical?" *Open Economies Review* 22 (1): 1–16 .

Freund, Caroline, and Nikola Spatafora. 2008. "Remittances, Transaction Costs, and Informality." *Journal of Development Economics* 86 (2): 356–66.

Ghirmay, Teame. 2004. "Financial Development and Economic Growth in Sub-Saharan African Countries: Evidence from Time Series Analysis." *African Development Review* 16 (3): 415–32.

Gibson, John, David McKenzie, and Halahingano Rohorua. 2006. "How Cost-Elastic Are Remittances? Evidence from Tongan Migrants in New Zealand." *Pacific Economic Bulletin* 21 (1): 112–28.

Giuliano, Paola, and Marta Ruiz-Arranz. 2009. "Remittances, Financial Development and Growth." *Journal of Development Economics* 90 (1): 144–52.

Gubert, Flore. 2002. "Do Migrants Insure Those who Stay Behind? Evidence from the Kayes Area (Western Mali)." *Oxford Development Studies* 30 (3): 267–287.

———. 2007. "Migration and Development: Mixed Evidence from Western Mali." *Development* 50 (4): 94–100.

Gupta, Sanjeev, Catherine A. Pattillo, and Smita Wagh. 2009. "Impact of Remittances on Poverty and Financial Development in Sub-Saharan Africa." *World Development* 37 (1): 104–15.

Gustafsson, Bjorn, and Negatu Makonnen. 1993. "Poverty and Remittances in Lesotho." *Journal of African Economies* 2 (1): 49–73.

Guzmán, Juan Carlos, Andrew R. Morrison, and Mirja Sjöblom. 2007. "The Impact of Remittances and Gender on Household Expenditure Patterns." In *The International Migration of Women*, ed. Maurice Schiff, Andrew R. Morrison, and Mirja Sjöblom, 125–52. Washington, DC: World Bank.

Halliday, Timothy. 2006. "Migration, Risk and Liquidity Constraints in El Salvador." *Economic Development and Cultural Change* 54 (4): 893–925.

Hanson, Gordon, and Christopher Woodruff. 2003. "Emigration and Educational Attainment in Mexico." Unpublished manuscript, University of California, San Diego.

Hildebrandt, Nicole, and David McKenzie. 2005. "The Effects of Migration on Child Health in Mexico." *Economia* 6 (1): 257–289.

Huysentruyt, Marieke, Christopher B. Barrett, and John G. McPeak. 2009. "Understanding Declining Mobility and Interhousehold Transfers among East African Pastoralists." *Economica* 76 (302): 315–36.

IFAD (International Fund for Agriculture and Development). 2009. "Sending Money Home to Africa: Remittance Markets, Enabling Environment and Prospects." Study report, IFAD, Rome.

IMF (International Monetary Fund). 2009. *International Transactions in Remittances: Guide for Compilers and Users*. Washington, DC: IMF.

———. 2010a. *Balance of Payments Statistics Yearbook 2010*. Washington, DC: IMF.

————. 2010b. "Staff Guidance Note on the Application of the Joint Bank-Fund Debt Sustainability Framework for Low-Income Countries." Guidance Note, IMF and World Bank staffs, Washington, DC.

IMF and World Bank. 2009. "A Review of Some Aspects of the Low-Income Country Debt Sustainability Framework." Policy Paper, IMF and World Bank, Washington, DC. http://www.imf.org/external/np/pp/eng/2009/080509a.pdf.

Irving, Jacqueline, Sanket Mohapatra, and Dilip Ratha. 2010. "Migrant Remittance Flows: Findings from a Global Survey of Central Banks." Working Paper 194, World Bank, Washington, DC.

Joseph, Michael. 2010. "Kenya's Telecom Revolution and Invention of Mobile Money." Presentation at the World Bank, Washington, DC, November 12.

Kanaiaupuni, Shawn M., and Katharine M. Donato. 1999. "Migradollars and Mortality: The Effects of Migration on Infant Survival in Mexico." *Demography* 36 (3): 339–53.

Ketkar, Suhas, and Dilip Ratha, eds. 2009a. *Innovative Financing for Development.* Washington, DC: World Bank.

————. 2009b. "New Paths to Funding." *Finance and Development*, International Monetary Fund.

Lachaud, Jean-Pierre. 1999. "Envoi de fonds, inegalite et pauvrete au Burkina Faso." Documents de travail 40, Groupe d'Economie du Développement de l'Université Montesquieu Bordeaux IV.

Lopez-Cordova, E. 2005. "Globalization, Migration and Development: The Role of Mexican Migrant Remittances." *Economia* 6 (1): 217–56.

Lucas, Robert E. B. 1987. "Emigration to South Africa's Mines." *American Economic Review* 77 (3): 313–30.

Lucas, Robert E. B., and Oded Stark. 1985. "Motivations to Remit: Evidence from Botswana." *Journal of Political Economy* 93 (5): 901–18.

Lueth, Erik, and Marta Ruiz-Arranz. 2008. "Determinants of Bilateral Remittance Flows." *The B.E Journal of Macroeconomics* 8 (1), Article 26.

Maimbo, Samuel, Tania Saranga, and Nicholas Strychacz. 2010. "Facilitating Cross-Border Mobile Banking in Southern Africa." *Economic Premise* No. 26, World Bank, Washington, DC.

Mansuri, Ghazala. 2007. "Does Work Migration Spur Investment in Origin Communities? Entrepreneurship, Schooling, and Child Health in Rural Pakistan." In *International Migration, Economic Development, and Policy*, ed. Çaglar Özden and Maurice Schiff, 99–140. Basingstoke, U.K.: Palgrave Macmillan.

Martinez, Claudia, Diego Aycinena, and Dean Yang. 2010. "The Impact of Remittance Fees on Remittance Flows: Evidence from a Field Experiment among Salvadoran Migrants." Unpublished manuscript, University of Michigan, Ann Arbor.

Mas, Ignacio, and Dan Radcliffe. 2010. "Mobile Payments Go Viral: M-PESA in Kenya." Working paper, Bill and Melinda Gates Foundation, Seattle.

Massey, Douglas, and Emilio A. Parrado. 1998. "International Migration and Business Formation in Mexico." *Social Science Quarterly* 79 (1): 1–20.

McCormick, Barry, and Jackline Wahba. 2001. "Overseas Work Experience, Savings and Entrepreneurship amongst Return Migrants to LDCs." *Scottish Journal of Political Economy* 48 (2):164–78.

———. 2003 "Return International Migration and Geographical Inequality: The Case of Egypt." *Journal of African Economies* 12 (4): 500–32.

McKenzie, David, and Hillel Rapoport. 2010. "Can Migration Reduce Educational Attainment? Evidence from Mexico." *Journal of Population Economics.* Published online: DOI No. 10.1007/s00148-010-0316-x. http://www.springerlink.com/content/95ht846m8m306517

McKenzie, David, and Marcin J. Sasin. 2007. "Migration, Remittances, Poverty, and Human Capital: Conceptual and Empirical Findings." Policy Research Working Paper 4272, World Bank, Washington, DC.

Miller, Douglas L., and Anna L. Paulson. 2007. "Risk Taking and the Quality of Informal Insurance: Gambling and Remittances in Thailand." Working Paper 2007-01, Federal Reserve Bank of Chicago.

Mohapatra, Sanket, George Joseph, and Dilip Ratha. 2009. "Remittances and Natural Disasters: Ex-Post Response and Contribution to Ex-Ante Preparedness." Policy Research Working Paper 4972, World Bank, Washington, DC.

Morawczynski, Olga, and Mark Pickens. 2009. "Poor People Using Mobile Financial Services: Observations on Customer Usage and Impact from M-PESA." Consultative Group to Assist the Poor (CGAP) Brief, CGAP, Washington, DC.

Nagarajan, Subha. 2009. "Migration, Remittances, and Household Health: Evidence from South Africa." Ph.D. dissertation, George Washington University, Washington, DC.

Niimi, Yoko, and Caglar Ozden. 2006. "Migration and Remittances: Causes and Linkages." Policy Research Working Paper 4087, World Bank, Washington, DC.

Odozia, John C., Timothy T. Awoyemia, and Bolarin T. Omonona. 2010. "Household Poverty and Inequality: The Implication of Migrants' Remittances in Nigeria." *Journal of Economic Policy Reform* 13 (2): 191–99.

Orozco, Manuel. 2009. "Emerging Markets for Rwanda: Remittance Transfers, Its Marketplace and Financial Intermediation." Report, Inter-American Dialogue, Washington, DC.

Osili, Una Okonkwo, 2004. "Migrants and Housing Investments: Theory and Evidence from Nigeria." *Economic Development and Cultural Change* 52 (4): 821–49.

Page, John, and Sonia Plaza. 2006. "Migration Remittances and Development: A Review of Global Evidence." *Journal of African Economies* 15 (Suppl. 2): 245–336.

Pendleton, Wade, Jonathan Crush, Eugene Campbell, Thuso Green, Hamilton Simelane, Daniel Tevera, and Fion de Vletter. 2006. "Migration, Remittances and Development in Southern Africa." Migration Policy Series 44, Southern African Migration Project, Cape Town, South Africa.

Pickens, Mark, David Porteous, and Sarah Rotman. 2009. "Scenarios for Branchless Banking in 2020." Consultative Group to Assist the Poor (CGAP) Focus Note 57, CGAP, Washington, DC. http://www.cgap.org/gm/document-1.9.40599/FN57.pdf.

Plaza, Sonia, Mario Navarrete, and Dilip Ratha. 2011. "Migration and Remittances Household Surveys: Methodological Issues and New Findings from Sub-Saharan Africa." Unpublished manuscript, Africa Migration Project, World Bank, Washington DC.

Ponsot, Frédéric, and Bruno Obegi. 2010 "Etude de capitalisation des initiatives et mécanismes en matière de transferts de fonds au Mali." Study conducted for Centre d'Information et de Gestion des Migrations (CIGEM), Mali.

Pulver, Caroline, William Jack, and Tavneed Suri. 2009. "The Performance and Impact of M-PESA: Preliminary Evidence from a Household Survey." Unpublished paper, FSD Kenya Trust, Nairobi. http://technology.cgap.org/technologyblog/wp-content/uploads/2009/10/fsd_june2009_caroline_pulver.pdf.

Quartey, Peter. 2006. "The Impact of Migrant Remittances on Household Welfare in Ghana." Research Paper 158, African Economic Research Consortium, Nairobi.

Quartey, Peter, and Theresa Blankson. 2004. "Do Migrant Remittances Minimize the Impact of Macro-Volatility on the Poor in Ghana?" Report for the Global Development Network, University of Ghana, Legon.

Rajan, Raghuram G., and Arvind Subramanian. 2005. "What Undermines Aid's Impact on Growth?" Working Paper 05/127, International Monetary Fund, Washington, DC.

Rajan, Raghuram G., and Luigi Zingales. 1998. "Financial Dependence and Growth." *The American Economic Review* 88 (3): 559–86.

Rao, Bhaskara, and Gazi Hassan. 2009. "A Panel Data Analysis of the Growth Effects of Remittances." Munich Personal RePEc Archive (MPRA) Working Paper 18021, Munich. http://mpra.ub.uni-muenchen.de/18021/1/MPRA_paper_18021.pdf.

Ratha, Dilip. 2003. "Workers' Remittances: An Important and Stable Source of External Development Finance." In *Global Development Finance: Striving for Stability in Development Finance*, 157–75. Washington, DC: World Bank.

————. 2005. "Leveraging Remittances for Capital Market Access." Unpublished manuscript, World Bank, Washington, DC.

————. 2007. "Leveraging Remittances for Development." *Policy Brief* (June), Migration Policy Institute, Washington, DC.

————. 2010. "Mobilize the Diaspora for the Reconstruction of Haiti." SSRC Feature: Haiti, Now and Next, Social Science Research Council, New York. http://www.ssrc.org/features/pages/haiti-now-and-next/1338/1438.

Ratha, Dilip, Prabal De, and Sanket Mohapatra. 2011. "Shadow Sovereign Ratings for Unrated Developing Countries." *World Development* 39(3): 295–307.

Ratha, Dilip, Sanket Mohapatra, and Sonia Plaza. 2009. "Beyond Aid: New Sources and Innovative Mechanisms for Financing Development in Sub-Saharan Africa." In *Innovative Financing for Development*, ed. Suhas Ketkar and Dilip Ratha, 143–83. Washington DC: World Bank.

Ratha, Dilip, Sanket Mohapatra, and Ani Silwal. 2010. "Outlook for Remittance Flows 2010–11: Remittance Flows to Developing Countries Remained Resilient in 2009, Expected to Recover in 2010–11." Migration and Development Brief 12, World Bank, Washington, DC. http://www.worldbank.org/prospects/migrationandremittances.

Ratha, Dilip, and Jan Riedberg. 2005. "On Reducing Remittance Costs." Unpublished manuscript, Development Research Group, World Bank, Washington, DC.

Ratha, Dilip, and William Shaw. 2007. "South-South Migration and Remittances." Development Prospects Group Working Paper 102, World Bank, Washington, DC.

Roache, Shaun K., and Ewa Gradzka. 2007. "Do Remittances to Latin America Depend on the U.S. Business Cycle?" Working Paper 07/273, International Monetary Fund, Washington, DC.

Russell, Sharon S. 1992. "Remittances from International Migration: A Review in Perspective." *World Development* 14 (6): 677–96.

Rutten, Lamon, and Okey Oramah. 2006. "Using Commoditized Revenue Flows to Leverage Access to International Finance; with a Special Focus on Migrant Remittances and Payment Flows." Study for the United Nations Conference on Trade and Development (UNCTAD) Secretariat UNCTAD/DITC/COM/2006/9, UNCTAD, Geneva.

Sayan, Serdar. 2006. "Business Cycles and Workers' Remittances: How Do Migrant Workers Respond to Cyclical Movements of GDP at Home?" Working Paper 06/52, International Monetary Fund, Washington, DC.

Singh, Raju J., Markus Haacker, and Kyung-woo Lee. 2009. "Determinants and Macroeconomic Impact of Remittances to Sub-Saharan Africa." Working Paper 09/216, International Monetary Fund, Washington, DC.

Sorensen, Ninna Nyberg. 2004. "Migrant Remittances as a Development Tool: The Case of Morocco." Working Paper 2, International Organization for Migration, Geneva. http://www.belgium.iom.int/pan-europeandialogue/documents/remittances_morocco.pdf.

Suleri, Abid Qaiyum, and Kevin Savage. 2006. "Remittances in Crises: A Case Study from Pakistan." Humanitarian Policy Group background paper, Overseas Development Institute, London. http://www.odi.org.uk/hpg/papers/BGPaper_RemittancesPakistan.pdf.

Taylor, J. Edward, and T. J. Wyatt. 1996. "The Shadow Value of Migrant Remittances, Income and Inequality in a Household-Farm Economy." *The Journal of Development Studies* 32 (6): 899–912.

Tevera, Daniel, and Abel Chikanda. 2009. "Migrant Remittances and Household Survival in Zimbabwe." Working Paper, Southern African Migration Project, Cape Town.

Valero-Gil, Jorge N. 2009. "Remittances and the Household's Expenditures on Health." *Journal of Business Strategies* 26 (1): 119–40.

Weiss-Fagan, Patricia. 2006. "Remittances in Crises: A Haiti Case Study." Humanitarian Policy Group background paper, Overseas Development Institute, London. http://www.odi.org.uk/hpg/papers/BG_Haiti_remittances.pdf.

Woodruff, Christopher, and Rene Zenteno. 2001. "Remittances and Microenterprises in Mexico." Working Paper, Graduate School of International Relations and Pacific Studies, University of California, San Diego.

———. 2007. "Migration Networks and Microenterprises in Mexico." *Journal of Development Economics* 82 (2): 509–28.

World Bank. 2006. *Global Economic Prospects 2006: Economic Implications of Remittances and Migration*. Washington, DC: World Bank.

———. 2009. Issue Brief on Migration and Remittances, Washington, DC: World Bank. (www.worldbank.org)

———. 2010a. Global Development Finance (database). World Bank, Washington, DC. http://data.worldbank.org/data-catalog/global-development-finance.

———. 2010b. Remittance Prices Worldwide (database). World Bank, Washington, DC. http://remittanceprices.worldbank.org.

———. 2010c. World Development Indicators (database). World Bank, Washington, DC. http://data.worldbank.org/data-catalog/world-development-indicators.

———. 2011. *Migration and Remittances Factbook 2011*. Washington, DC: World Bank.

Wouterse, F. 2010. "Remittances, Poverty, Inequality and Welfare: Evidence from the Central Plateau of Burkina Faso" *The Journal of Development Studies* 46 (4): 771–89.

Wu, Treena. 2006. "The Role of Remittances in Crisis: An Aceh Research Study." Humanitarian Policy Group background paper, Overseas Development Institute, London. http://www.odi.org.uk/hpg/papers/BG_Remittances_Aceh.pdf.

Yang, Dean. 2008a. "Coping With Disaster: The Impact of Hurricanes on International Financial Flows, 1970–2002." *The B.E. Journal of Economic Analysis and Policy* 8 (1): Article 13.

———. 2008b. "International Migration, Remittances and Household Investment: Evidence from Philippine Migrants' Exchange Rate Shocks." *The Economic Journal* 118 (528): 591–630.

Yang, Dean, and HwaJung Choi. 2007. "Are Remittances Insurance? Evidence from Rainfall Shocks in the Philippines." *The World Bank Economic Review* 21 (2): 219–48.

PART II

Remittance Markets in
Remittance-Receiving Countries

CHAPTER 2

Burkina Faso

Yiriyibin Bambio

The extent of migration is considerable in Burkina Faso. In 2011, the number of Burkinabè emigrants equaled an estimated 9.7 percent of the country's population, and immigrants to Burkina Faso made up 6.4 percent of the population (World Bank 2011). Consequently, remittances—the transfers of funds associated with internal or international migration—affect the country's development and per capita income (as discussed in box 2.1). The extent of the impact depends on the volume and the use of the transfers.

To increase understanding of the remittance market in Burkina Faso, the analysis in this chapter draws upon a 2008 survey of remittance service providers (RSPs). The results help explain the remittance industry's operations, potential, and limitations. Such an analysis can enhance the contribution of remittance flows to development by helping policy makers and institutions to analyze trends and the determinants of remittance flows. The principal focus is on RSP characteristics; regulation; and remittance costs, volumes, sources, and destinations. The literature so far has provided qualitative data about these aspects. However, little quantitative information about remittances is available, and the unrecorded flows are significant.

Box 2.1

Remittances and Poverty Reduction in Burkina Faso

Burkina Faso's development depends largely on emigration to neighboring countries. Transfers of funds to Burkina Faso—about half of which come from Côte d'Ivoire—significantly improve household living conditions, and the redistribution is especially expressed in the mobilization of social capital.

Remittances to Burkina Faso go to about one-third of the households, especially the poorest, who thereby profit the most from the international transfers. The increase in remittances substantially affects the well-being of rural households. Because remittances supplement home earnings, they reduce the headcount poverty of rural and urban households by 7.2 and 3.2 percentage points, respectively.

These results emphasize Burkina Faso's dependence on remittances in two ways: (a) in the short run, on households' living conditions and (b) in the long run, on the long-term capacity to accumulate physical and human capital from external resources.

Source: Lachaud 1999.

Remittance and Migration Trends

Annual remittance flows into Burkina Faso from 1974 to 2010 reached a maximum of $192 million in 1986 and subsequently declined gradually after 2000, to about $43 million in 2010. As figure 2.1 indicates, the lower levels (under $100 million) were recorded in 1984—the year following the August 4, 1983, military coup d'état—and resumed in 1994, when the CFA franc was devaluated. In Burkina Faso, migrant remittances are usually sent or received in CFA francs.

From 1994 to 1999, remittance flows stagnated throughout the West African Economic and Monetary Union (WAEMU)[1] zone, including Burkina Faso. Remittances then declined in 2000, after the beginning of the 1999 coup d'état in Côte d'Ivoire. A second stagnation, in 2002, followed the civil war in Côte d'Ivoire—an event that shaped the landscape of remittances to Burkina Faso over the past 10 years. Thus, the socioeconomic situation in Côte d'Ivoire is important to an analysis of migration in Burkina Faso. Moreover, since 1991, the growing economic importance of Nigeria has influenced the remittance trends in the Economic Community of West African States (ECOWAS)[2] relative to those in the WAEMU zone.

Figure 2.1   Migrant Remittance Flows to Burkina Faso, WAEMU, and ECOWAS, 1974–2010

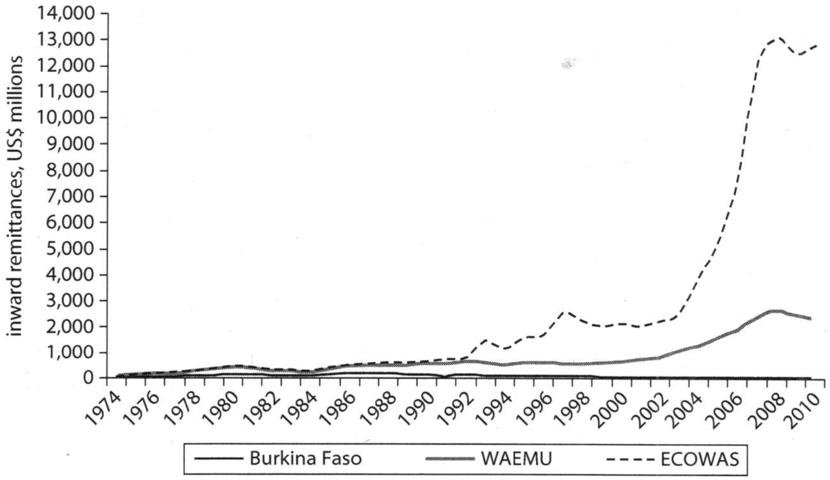

Source: IMF 2008.
Note: ECOWAS = Economic Community of West African States, WAEMU = West African Economic and Monetary Union.

The literature indicates that inward remittances to Burkina Faso are more important than outward remittances. The net inflows in 2010 represented about 0.5 percent of gross domestic product (GDP) in 2010 (World Bank 2011). Net inflows in the WAEMU zone were negative from 1974 through 1999 but have been positive since 2000. Conversely, the ECOWAS zone inflows have exceeded outflows since 1993.

Destinations of Migrants

By 2010, an estimated 1,576,400 Burkinabè were living in other countries, and Burkina Faso's immigrant population had reached 1,043,000 (World Bank 2011). Skilled emigration is low, and the emigration rate among the college-educated population was 2.6 percent in 2010.

Among the Sub-Saharan Africa region's countries, Burkina Faso ranks second in total number of emigrants (World Bank 2011). Their principal destination is Côte d'Ivoire, where 50 percent of the immigrants are Burkinabè. Migration flows in the Burkina Faso–Côte d'Ivoire corridor are the most significant not only in West Africa (Konseiga 2005b), but also throughout Sub-Saharan Africa. Thus, in terms of emigration from one African country to another, Burkina Faso has the largest diaspora (Lindley 2008).

In 1960, 56.6 percent of the emigrants from Burkina Faso moved to Côte d'Ivoire, 31.3 percent to Ghana, and 3.9 percent to Mali (Somé 1991). In 1985, 91 percent of migrants went to Côte d'Ivoire and 8.8 percent to Ghana. Between 1988 and 1992, emigrants from Burkina Faso divided their destinations as follows: 85.4 percent to Côte d'Ivoire, 4.3 percent to Niger, 3.3 percent to Mali, 5.5 percent to other African countries, and 0.6 percent to other continents entirely (Konseiga 2005b). Today, the top 10 destination countries for Burkinabè emigrants (in order of total numbers) are Côte d'Ivoire, Mali, Italy, Benin, Nigeria, France, Gabon, Germany, and the United States (Ratha and Xu 2008).

Internal migration in Burkina Faso represents nearly 30 percent of all migration flows (Konseiga 2005a), usually representing a drift from migrants' homelands because of difficult living conditions in the rural areas, where most of the poor live. Seasonal migration is principally a survival strategy in regions where natural resources are scarce (Konseiga 2005a).

Remittance Volumes, Sources, and Destinations

Partial data from SNC-Finances and some bank agencies show that, with 30 percent of the total transfers, Côte d'Ivoire is the principal source of Burkina Faso migrant remittance transfers (box 2.2). The WAEMU countries, as a whole, represent nearly one-third of remittance sources and approximately 40 percent of migrant destinations. The migrant and remittance flows to and from certain destinations such as Mali, Senegal, and Togo are determined by the respective importance or transit activities of those countries' nationals in Burkina Faso.

Seasonal variations in the volume of remittance transfers also have been observed. Transfers tend to grow at the beginning and in the last quarter of each year—a variation that seems related to festivals and the start of the new school year.

According to the 2008 survey responses, RSPs' average net profit from the provision of remittance services in 2007 was €20,298. Over 2004–07, the annual inward international remittances processed by the firms in the sample averaged about €3.5 million, from about 336,972 transactions. At the same time, the firms' annual outward international remittances averaged €1.2 million, from 219,358 transactions.

According to the survey, the total estimated size of the inward international remittance market in Burkina Faso was €33.3 million from

Box 2.2

Remittances from Côte d'Ivoire

In the 1990s, remittances to Burkina Faso were 6 percent of GDP. Although these remittances have proved difficult to quantify, the World Bank estimated that, in 1990, Burkinabè sent home a total of $140 million. In 1994, exports totaled $216 million and imports stood at $344 million, demonstrating the significance of remittances to the country's income and expenditure accounts. However, the 1999 turmoil in Côte d'Ivoire, the primary source of remittances, led to the occasional expulsion of Burkinabè from that country. As a result, annual remittances fell to $67 million (2.5 percent of GDP) by the end of the decade.

Returning migrants do not always send remittances home or bring money back to invest, except for the Fulani ethnic group, who may invest in herds, or the Lobi, who may invest in more livestock for trading. Mossi migrants do remit money, but returnees also tend to bring money back personally or even use it to buy goods such as sunglasses, umbrellas, and clothes to impress those at home. Therefore, it may be questionable whether the Mossi economy experienced an impact from the accumulation of capital and investment.

Source: Kress 2006.

formal channels and €3.8 million from informal channels in 2007. The annual inward domestic remittances by firms during the past three years averaged €2.9 million, from 83,202 transactions per year. The total outward internal remittances per sample firm over the same period averaged €3.7 million per year, from 108,812 transactions.

The total estimated size of the domestic formal remittance market is €7.9 million and the informal market, €3.05 million. The survey respondents, many of whom did not seem well informed, had widely underestimated this market to be about half of its actual size.

Characteristics of the Remittance Industry

The 2008 RSP survey revealed that the remittance industry in Burkina Faso comprises several types of formal and informal firms that operate primarily in urban zones. The instruments and products used in remittance transactions are weakly diversified. Partnership and agreement characteristics differ depending on the money operator and whether the

RSP is a formal or informal provider. The sample size for this survey was 32 firms, of which 23 percent are informal providers.

Types and Coverage of Remittance Firms

The national postal service (Société Nationale des Postes, or SONAPOST) pioneered money transfer services in Burkina Faso, but Western Union (the country's most important money transfer operator [MTO]) introduced electronic transfers. Its principal competitors are MoneyGram and Money Express. Money transfer services in Burkina Faso were initially supplied by the banks in partnership with these MTOs. However, since 2003, nonbank firms can also provide these services with authorization from the Ministry of Economy and Finance (MEF). As a result, about 100 firms are now active in the RSP market.

The formal sector comprises 11 banks and about 60 private nonbank firms (table 2.1). The most important nonbank firms are SNC-Finances and SONAPOST. Most of these nonbank firms not only supply remittance services, but also engage in other activities. The formal money transfer sector operates mainly in urban and semiurban zones. Rural branches represent only 11 percent of their coverage. The informal sector includes about 30 firms, operating principally within the transportation sector.

The informal sector has developed considerably during the past decade. It is generally associated with companies that transport passengers or goods and is intensively involved in the rural zone. Money sending and receiving conditions are simplified, with low tariffs relative to the formal sector. Informal firms are particularly active in the domestic transfer market. However, these channels are less secure than the formal ones. Because informal providers are survey averse, the survey could capture little information about them.

Partnerships and Agreements with Money Transfer Operators

Each non-MTO formal firm operates, directly or indirectly, in partnership with an international MTO that provides and manages the electronic transfer system. The partnership between a commercial bank and MTO is exclusive; each bank is contractually required to work with only one MTO for remittance services. A formal firm benefits from the partnership primarily by receiving a portion of the commission on remittance payments or receipts.

As MTOs, two formal nonbank firms—SNC-Finances and SONAPOST—provide their own money transfer services as bank agents. However, these arrangements are also exclusive.

Table 2.1   RSP Types and Coverage in Burkina Faso

				Interviewed firms		
RSP type	Total number of RSPs	Number of RSP survey respondents	Average number of branches[a]	Average number of rural branches[a]	Share of branches in rural areas(%)[a]	Market share (%)[b]
Firms specializing in money transfers	11	7	5.6	0.7	13	32
Currency exchanges	7	5	1	0	0	—
Private commercial banks	11	1	4	0	0	20
SONAPOST	1	1	89	64	72	—
Other nonfinancial institutions	37	10	1.4	0	0	12
Savings and loans	2	0	—	—	—	—
Courier, bus, and other transport services	34	8	4.3	0.6	15	1
Microfinance institutions	1	0	—	—	—	—
Total	**104**	**32**	**3.1**	**0.3**	**11**	**45**

Source: Author's compilation from 2008 RSP survey in Burkina Faso.
Note: Data are from 32 RSP survey respondents.
a. Among survey respondents.
b. Market share of each RSP type extrapolated from survey responses.
— = not available.

The informal transfer service providers operate independently, without partnerships with either banks or MTOs.

Remittance Instruments

The RSPs' money transfer instruments are not well diversified. The MTOs in Burkina Faso primarily use electronic funds transfer instruments. SONAPOST uses the TELIMAN[3] system, which transfers money within Burkina Faso by mobile phone but is not available for SONAPOST's international remittance service. Similarly, SNC-Finances has tried to operate in semirural areas by using mobile phones in tellers' offices for a modest fee.

Newer instruments, such as credit cards, have emerged recently: the Visa card of the International Bank of Burkina (BIB) and the Nasuba card of the Regional Bank of Solidarity. However, they are not yet commonly used. Generally, the money is sent and received in cash and in the local currency (CFA francs), and the remittance sender pays the fees. Many transfer agencies supply manual exchange services to facilitate transfer operations.

The 2008 RSP survey found that none of the informal RSPs uses modern electronic instruments for remittance transactions, as table 2.2 shows. Instead, as passenger or goods transportation firms that carry funds physically to destinations, they prefer to pay the recipients by check to avoid security problems.

Access to Other Financial Services

Money transfer serves as an entry point for other formal financial products—an emerging strategy to cope with remittance problems throughout the Burkinabè diaspora.

In the 2008 RSP survey, four commercial banks in Burkina Faso reported providing other financial services geared specifically to senders and recipients of remittances. BIB and Coris Bank have tried to facilitate the remittance services for Burkinabè in Côte d'Ivoire because migrants send about $2 million per month to Burkina Faso through this corridor. The Commercial Bank of Burkina (BCB) and the Agricultural and Commercial Bank of Burkina (BACB) have adopted the same strategy in Italy with more success.

Table 2.2   Money Transfer Instruments Offered by RSPs

	Electronic funds transfer		Manual funds transfer		
RSP type	Number of formal firms	Number of informal firms	Number of formal firms	Number of informal firms	Total
Private commercial banks	1	0	0	0	1
SONAPOST	1	0	0	0	1
Firms specializing in money transfers	7	0	0	0	7
Currency exchanges	5	0	0	0	5
Other nonfinancial institutions	10	0	0	0	10
Courier, bus, and other transport services	1	0	0	7	8
Total	**25**	**0**	**0**	**7**	**32**

Source: Author's compilation from 2008 RSP survey in Burkina Faso.
Note: Data are from 32 RSP survey respondents.

The Burkinabè diaspora in Italy is important and has one of the most significant impacts on local development. These banks also provide money-sending or -receiving migrants with credit privileges (checking and savings accounts, mortgages, consumer loans, and microfinance loans) and insurance. BACB created a VIP (very important person) teller counter especially for Burkinabè migrants in Italy to facilitate their bank transactions when they are in Burkina Faso. Moreover, this bank often goes on missions to Italy to encourage the Burkinabè there to bring their money back into Burkina Faso.

Coris Bank also created a teller counter in the Agricultural Bank of Côte d'Ivoire. Unfortunately, there were some collaboration problems, so Coris plans to establish a filial branch in Côte d'Ivoire. One of the firms interviewed in the RSP survey has proposed to create a regional bank of diaspora to deal more productively with migrant remittance flows and their impact on development.

The Regulatory and Business Environment

The money transfer industry in Burkina Faso, operating under laws and regulations, faces some related impediments to creating and conducting a remittance business. These factors might create a preference for informal providers within the highly competitive RSP industry.

Obstacles to Business

The principal barriers to entry for the formal, nonbank RSPs in Burkina Faso are banking approval and capital requirements, as bill guarantees. The guarantees are high and the certification process complex. Each firm must be registered with the Central Bank of West African States (Banque Centrale des États de l'Afrique de l'Ouest, or BCEAO) and the MEF, as box 2.3 notes, and must respect the transfer laws and regulatory requirements. These regulatory constraints have less effect on firm creation than on remittance activities. The regulations mainly concern money laundering, tax policy, and exchange control.

Each money transfer service provider also must file a suspicious-activity report with the central bank (BCEAO), the regulatory authority in Burkina Faso. Suspicion arises more about the frequency of transactions per customer than about the amounts. In addition, the average minimum capital requirement for money transfer firms to operate in Burkina Faso is €15,221. Each RSP is also required to charge a value added tax (VAT) on each transaction.

Box 2.3

The Financial System in Burkina Faso

The Burkina Faso financial sector comprises 11 banks and 5 financial establishments. BCEAO—which is also the central bank for WAEMU—administers the conditions for bank creation, banking supervision, credit control, and regulation. Thus, the authorization for the creation of a financial firm is guaranteed by the MEF and approved by the central bank. The principal conditions for approval are the name of the firm, legal status, minimum capital, adequate resources given the objectives, quality of the shareholders, managerial experience, and viability of the operation.[4]

Results from the RSP survey indicate that the main obstacles when providing formal remittance services in Burkina Faso are lack of access to clearing and settlement systems and the anti-money-laundering requirements, as figure 2.2 illustrates. Many bank agencies have said that they did not know how this system works. Limitations in access to capital and finance further constrain money transfer activities.

Generally, the RSPs consider laws and regulations to be major obstacles and access to financing, a moderate obstacle. However, they did not consider corruption among government officials to be a significant impediment to business activities.

Competitive Factors

The Burkina Faso market has become increasingly competitive because the demand for remittance services exceeds supply. The formal remittance sector is more competitive than the informal sector, particularly among the three principal international MTOs: Western Union, MoneyGram, and Money Express, which have different coverage areas.

The formal RSP sector in general, however, considers the informal sector (which has significant market share) to be a strong and unfair competitor. Although RSPs are not well informed about their own market shares in the remittance service industry, about half of the formal firms surveyed consider the informal sector to be a severe obstacle to their money transfer business.

The informal sector's principal advantage is its ability to impose lower tariffs on customers and to offer its services in rural areas, which formal

Figure 2.2   Obstacles to Providing Formal Remittance Services
% of survey respondents

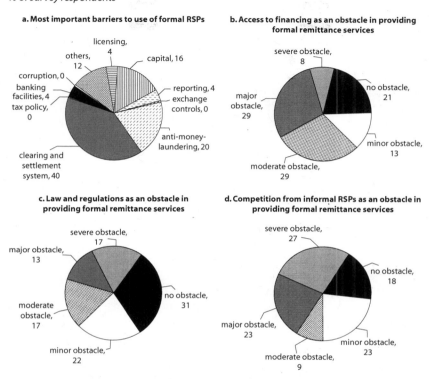

a. Most important barriers to use of formal RSPs

licensing, 4
others, 12
capital, 16
corruption, 0
banking facilities, 4
tax policy, 0
reporting, 4
exchange controls, 0
anti-money-laundering, 20
clearing and settlement system, 40

b. Access to financing as an obstacle in providing formal remittance services

severe obstacle, 8
no obstacle, 21
major obstacle, 29
minor obstacle, 13
moderate obstacle, 29

c. Law and regulations as an obstacle in providing formal remittance services

severe obstacle, 17
major obstacle, 13
no obstacle, 31
moderate obstacle, 17
minor obstacle, 22

d. Competition from informal RSPs as an obstacle in providing formal remittance services

severe obstacle, 27
no obstacle, 18
major obstacle, 23
minor obstacle, 23
moderate obstacle, 9

Source: Author's compilation from 2008 RSP survey in Burkina Faso.
Note: Data are from 32 RSP survey respondents.

RSPs have difficulty reaching. The informal sector's primary disadvantages are that its remittance services are riskier and slower than formal remittance services, whose electronic instruments enable rapid service and more efficient response to emergencies.

The entry barriers in the formal sector and the obstacles to increasing the supply of formal remittance services are likely to support the emergence and the development of informal RSPs. In the formal sector, the anti-money-laundering regulations, exchange controls, and tax policies are restrictive and thus badly perceived in a business environment hampered by weak professional skills. In fact, many currency exchanges operate partially in the informal sector to escape the constraints of regulatory exchange controls.

Remittance Fees, Customer Protection, and Identification Requirements

Each international operator is free to determine its remittance service fees, grievance procedures, and customer identification requirements without interference from the central bank or regulatory authorities. However, all the partners of each operator charge identical fees to money senders. The leading MTOs have similar commercial strategies.

Remittance service fees. Each operator establishes remittance rates based on the amount sent and the destination. Only narrow cost differences separate the MTOs in the WAEMU zone. For example, the fee to send CFAF 100,000 (about $200) within the WAEMU area is CFAF 10,620 through Western Union and CFAF 8,555 through MoneyGram.[5] This difference is greater to destinations outside the WAEMU zone. Those costs did not change substantially between 2007 and 2008, except in Côte d'Ivoire, where Western Union slightly reduced its remittance rates.

International transfers of $200, on average, are 14 percent more expensive than domestic transfers, as table 2.3 indicates. This international-domestic rate difference is greatest among firms specializing in money transfers, currency exchanges, and other nonfinancial institutions; the difference is less for remittances through SONAPOST and is particularly small among private banks.

Table 2.3   Rates to Send $200 in Burkina Faso, by RSP type

RSP type	Domestic transfer cost (US$)	Share of domestic transfer amount (%)	International transfer cost (US$)	Share of international transfer amount (%)
Private commercial banks	14.4	7.2	14.6	7.3
SONAPOST	12.6	6.3	15.2	7.6
Firms specializing in money transfers	15.6	7.8	20.0	10.0
Currency exchanges	15.2	7.6	20.0	10.0
Other nonfinancial institutions	15.2	7.6	20.0	10.0
Courier, bus, and other transport services[a]	5.2	2.6	..	..
Average rate	**12.6**	**6.3**	**14.6**	**7.3**

Source: Author's compilation from 2008 RSP survey in Burkina Faso.
Note: The sample remittance of $200 is equivalent to about CFAF 100,000.
.. = negligible.
a. The informal sector operates mostly domestically; international remittance services are negligible by comparison.

The informal sector deals heavily in internal transfers, and its rates are only about 40 percent of what the formal RSPs would charge, as table 2.3 also shows. For example, the cost of sending CFAF 100,000 within Burkina Faso is CFAF 7,552 through Western Union and less than CFAF 3,000, on average, through informal channels.

Customer grievance procedures. Complaints about remittances not being received or delivered are rare. According to the survey responses, few remittance transactions go unclaimed each month. Among the 32 surveyed firms, 4 percent reported at least one unclaimed transaction per month, and another 2 percent reported two unclaimed transactions per month.

If the remittance is not delivered as promised, the customer's main option is to talk to the agent. However, most of the nonbank remittance firms do not have customer service centers specifically charged with addressing customer grievances or disputes.

The private banks and SONAPOST reported only moderate customer grievance-solving issues. Those RSPs have systems for addressing customer grievances, generally within one week at the most. However, more than 47 percent of RSPs lack a system to handle consumer grievances, and agents often fulfill many functions within the same firm. For instance, the checkout assistant might also be an accountant or a sales representative with responsibility for helping any aggrieved customers.

Thirty-five percent of all RSP survey respondents said they solve customer grievances within one week, and only 29 percent of the specialized money transfer firms state that it takes a full week. In the informal sector, the grievance-resolution period varies more widely, but it appears to be longer on average than in the formal sector.

Identification and other reporting requirements. Banks and other financial institutions, including all money transfer agencies, require an identification document to send or receive funds—not only to prevent theft or fraud, but also to comply with know-your-customer (KYC) policies in general and AML-CFT (Anti-Money-Laundering–Combating the Financing of Terrorism) reporting requirements in particular. The accepted forms of identification are typically the national identity card, passport, military professional card, consular card, or refugee card. Employment certificates or proof-of-residence documents are not accepted because they do not sufficiently identify the customer if a transfer issue arises. Presumably, these criteria do not limit the access of poor households to transfer services.

In addition, as a safeguard against suspicious transactions, the sender must specify how recipients will use the remittances. Remittances appear to be used mostly to purchase food and medicines and for housing and utilities and seldom for land, kerosene or petrol, school fees, or trade.

No commission or fee is charged to the receiver of remittances from abroad, which are not directly received in foreign currency but in the local currency. However, the sender can exchange funds for foreign currency, in which case the receiver has to pay fees or a commission. In general, there is no limit on the amount that customers can receive, but a limit can sometimes depend on the firm's liquidity level.

Conclusions and Recommendations

In summary, the scope of migration and remittances is important for Burkina Faso, which is an emigration country. The primary destination of migrants from Burkina Faso is Côte d'Ivoire, which is also the principal source of migrant remittances and significantly influences remittance inflows.

The regulatory requirements for remittance transfers center principally on tax policy, exchange controls, and AML laws. Although regulations do not constitute a significant barrier to the establishment of remittance service firms, formal sector RSPs do consider them to be significant impediments to business activities that, as a result, encourage migrants to use informal providers. Other significant obstacles to the formal RSPs' business are competition from informal providers and limitations on or lack of access to capital and finance.

In the formal sector, electronic money transfers are the preferred remittance instruments, and the principal MTOs in Burkina Faso are Western Union, MoneyGram, and Money Express. Although formal remittance services are quicker and more secure than informal sector services—which operate through manual transfer of funds—formal channels are more expensive for the customer and are less efficient in underserved rural areas.

Other findings of the RSP survey included the following:

- The clearing and settlement system between commercial banks and their agencies is not fully transparent.
- The prevalence of unskilled staff in most of the RSP firms makes operations inefficient; in many cases, the KYC requirements are not satisfied.
- Although the customer identification requirements and other regulations have been simplified, remittance fees remain high.

The analysis in this chapter leads to several evidence-based recommendations for reducing the cost and increasing remittance flows through formal channels:

- *Develop money transfer instruments such as prepaid cards or mobile-phone transfers.* The use of mobile phones as a transfer instrument could help formal firms to better cover rural areas that lack electricity or computer access, thus reducing competition from the informal sector.
- *Give Burkinabè migrants incentives to transfer savings to Burkina Faso bank accounts.* Banks such as BIB or BCB have already implemented this strategy in Côte d'Ivoire and Italy (although the implementation has encountered some problems in Côte d'Ivoire because of the political crisis). Dialogue with migrant communities in their resident countries about their money transfer and investment needs could help banks to propose attractive savings and investment products in Burkina Faso.
- *Clarify the banks' clearing and settlement systems with their agencies to build trust and encourage transparency.*
- *Develop training and workshops to enhance the quality of KYC performance by MTOs among nonbank providers.*

Annex 2.1

Figure 2.A.1   Remittance Sources and Destinations, WAEMU vs. Non-WAEMU Countries

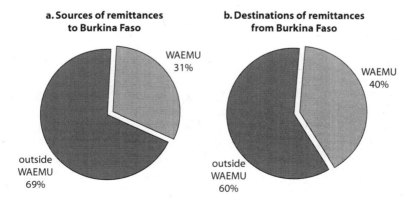

a. Sources of remittances to Burkina Faso

WAEMU 31%

outside WAEMU 69%

b. Destinations of remittances from Burkina Faso

WAEMU 40%

outside WAEMU 60%

Source: WAEMU.
Note: WAEMU = West African Economic and Monetary Union; Non-WAEMU = worldwide.

Figure 2.A.2   Inward and Outward Remittances among WAEMU Countries

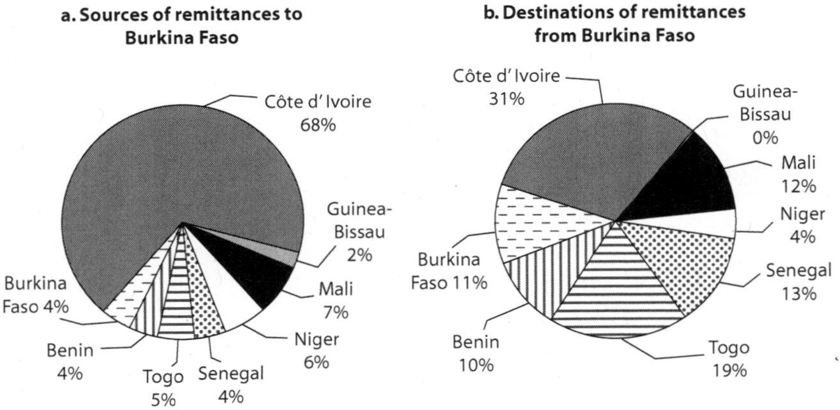

a. Sources of remittances to
Burkina Faso

Côte d'Ivoire
68%

Guinea-Bissau
2%

Burkina
Faso 4%

Mali
7%

Benin
4%

Niger
6%

Togo
5%

Senegal
4%

b. Destinations of remittances
from Burkina Faso

Côte d'Ivoire
31%

Guinea-Bissau
0%

Mali
12%

Niger
4%

Burkina
Faso 11%

Senegal
13%

Benin
10%

Togo
19%

Source: WAEMU.

Notes

1. The West African Economic and Monetary Union (WAEMU) in French is Union Economique et Monétaire Ouest Africaine (UEMOA). The member countries of WAEMU are Benin, Burkina Faso, Côte d'Ivoire, Guinea-Bissau, Mali, Niger, Senegal, and Togo.

2. The member countries of ECOWAS are Benin, Burkina Faso, Cape Verde, Côte d'Ivoire, The Gambia, Ghana, Guinea, Guinea-Bissau, Liberia, Mali, Niger, Nigeria, Senegal, Sierra Leone, and Togo.

3. *Teliman* means "quickness" in dioula, a local language.

4. Approval conditions are from the BCEAO Web site: http://www.bceao.int/.

5. All formal remittance fees are taxed at 18 percent.

References

IMF (International Monetary Fund). 2008. *Balance of Payments Statistics Yearbook.* Washington, DC: IMF.

Konseiga, Adama. 2005a. "Household Migration Decisions as Survival Strategy: The Case of Burkina Faso." Discussion Paper 1819, Institute for the Study of Labor, Bonn, Germany. http://ssrn.com/abstract=840768.

———. 2005b. "New Patterns of Migration in West Africa." *Stichproben (Vienna Journal of African Studies)* 8: 23–46. http://www.univie.ac.at/ecco/stichproben/Nr8_Konseiga.pdf.

Kress, Brad. 2006. "Burkina Faso: Testing the Tradition of Circular Migration."
    Country profile, Centre for Research into Economic and Social Trends,
    Migration Policy Institute, Washington, DC. http://www.migrationinformation
    .org/Profiles/display.cfm?ID=399.

Lachaud, Jean-Pierre. 1999. "Envois de fonds, inégalité et pauvreté au Burkina
    Faso." Working paper, Centre d'économie et développement Université
    Montesquieu-Bordeaux IV, France. http://ged.u-bordeaux4.fr/ceddt40.pdf.

Lindley, Anna. 2008. "African Remittances and Progress: Opportunities and
    Challenges." Análisis del Real Instituto 52, Real Instituto Elcano, Madrid.

Somé, P. 1991. "Emigration from Burkina Faso from 1960 to 1985: Analysis of
    Demographic and Socioeconomic Consequences." *Pop Sahel* 1991 (16):
    13–8.

World Bank. 2011. *Migration and Remittances Factbook 2011*, 2nd ed. Washington,
    DC: World Bank.

CHAPTER 3

Cape Verde

Georgiana Pop

Remittances sent by international migrants are perceived to enhance the development prospects of low- and middle-income economies, maintain their macroeconomic stability, mitigate the impact of exogenous shocks, and reduce poverty because of the increasing volumes and more stable trends relative to other external flows.[1]

The remittance inflows to Sub-Saharan Africa have been modest compared with those to other developing regions. Remittance flows to Sub-Saharan Africa quadrupled from US$4.6 billion in 2000, to US$21.5 billion in 2010 (World Bank 2011). However, Sub-Saharan Africa attracted only 6.6 percent of total remittances to developing countries in 2010. In many African countries (such as Cape Verde, Lesotho, Mauritius, Nigeria, Swaziland, and Togo), remittances are similar in size to or have outpaced official development assistance (Gupta, Patillo, and Wagh 2009; World Bank 2011).

Remittance and Emigration Trends

Cape Verde is one of the top recipients of remittances in Sub-Saharan Africa, receiving high inflows relative to other small island economies that depend heavily on remittances, including the Dominican Republic,

Grenada, and Jamaica. The official data show that 192,000 Cape Verdeans live abroad, more than one-third of the country's resident population of about 500,000 (World Bank 2011); however, anecdotal evidence suggests that the number of Cape Verdean emigrants exceeds the the country's resident population. As a result, Cape Verde has benefited from significant external financing from its diaspora, which has made remittance flows less volatile than other foreign capital inflows (from foreign direct investment and official development assistance). However, remittances have been declining as a share of total foreign financing—from 46 percent in 1995 to 19 percent in 2007 (IMF 2008), as figure 3.1 shows.

Remittance Volumes and Economic Impact

International remittance flows to Cape Verde increased at an average annual rate of 10 percent in the past 20 years, helping to finance the nation's current account deficit (IMF 2008). The macroeconomic stability devolving from a credible exchange rate peg, the relaxation of foreign exchange controls on the purchase and sale of foreign currencies, and financial sector development encouraged remittance inflows through formal channels. An International Monetary Fund study showed that emigrant deposits did not appear to be affected by events in the source countries,

Figure 3.1   Composition of External Financing for Cape Verde, 1995 and 2007

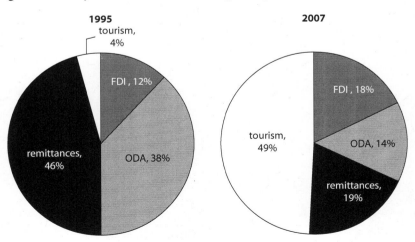

Source: IMF 2008.
Note: FDI = foreign direct investment. ODA = official development assistance.

such as the introduction of the euro or the events of September 11, 2001, in the United States (IMF 2008).

Remittances represented around 9.3 percent of the Cape Verdean gross domestic product (GDP) in 2007, second to Lesotho among African countries, and higher than the averages of 2.6 percent in Sub-Saharan Africa and 2 percent in all developing countries. Remittances are an important source of foreign exchange, and they support the fixed exchange rate policy through an increase in international reserves. Remittances have accounted for 40 percent, on average, of export earnings in Cape Verde since 2000, and net accumulation of nonresident deposits was around 4 percent of GDP in 2004, or 40 percent of the total bank deposits (IMF 2005). This has stimulated financial sector development and investment, particularly in real estate. The annual growth rate of nonresident deposits has slowed down, but is still around 6 percent (IMF 2008b).

Official remittance figures shown in table 3.1 tend to be underestimated because they do not include transfers through informal channels, such as the amounts that emigrants bring home during their visits to Cape Verde.

Although remittance inflows reached US$155 million in 2008 (World Bank 2011), they appear to have declined in 2009–10 because of the effect of the global financial crisis on Cape Verdean migrants' employments and incomes.

Remittances also have increasingly become procyclical. In the 1980s, remittances to Cape Verde were driven mainly by altruism, but after the mid-1990s the remittance flows became more investment driven (IMF 2008).[2] Although they continue to be a reliable source of foreign investment, their growth has slowed, in part because robust economic growth in Cape Verde and increase in incomes of Cape Verdeans have relieved pressures on emigrants to supplement their relatives' incomes directly through remittances.

Table 3.1   International Remittance Flows to and from Cape Verde, 2001–10
US$, millions

Remittance flows	2003	2004	2005	2006	2007	2008	2009	2010e
Inward[a]	109	113	137	137	139	155	145	144
Outward	7	12	5	6	6	10	10	—

Source: World Bank 2011.
Note: e = estimated; — = not available.
a. 9 percent of GDP in 2009.

Regarding remittance sources, around two-thirds of families receive money from abroad—the highest proportions coming (in order of percentage) from Portugal, France, the United States, and the Netherlands as shown in figure 3.2. Empirical evidence shows that remittances from the United States are markedly procyclical, indicating that investment drivers are increasingly replacing the consumption-smoothing considerations. Meanwhile, the flows from the European countries seem to be largely driven by altruism (IMF 2008). The highest shares of remittance receipts tend to be absorbed by the residents of the island of São Vincente (around 20 percent) and the capital city, Praia (around 17 percent), and are mainly used to fund construction and education.

Typically, inward remittances are normally disbursed in the local currency, the Cape Verde escudo (CVEsc), based on the current exchange rate. Interviews with remittance service providers (RSPs) in Cape Verde

Figure 3.2   Share of 2007 Remittances to Cape Verde by Country of Origin

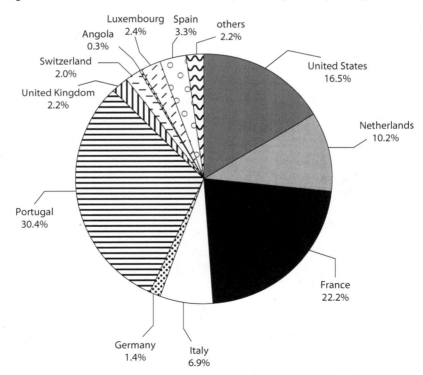

Source: Central Bank of Cape Verde 2008.

suggest that inward remittance flows are seasonal. Spikes are observed from June to August and from December to January, as remittance inflows aim to support increased consumption associated with summer and winter holidays.

Despite exceptionally high remittance amounts, evidence about the loss in external competitiveness from an appreciation of the exchange rate as a result of these large remittance inflows, or the so-called "Dutch disease," is weak. Although there is some evidence that an appreciating effective real exchange rate could be attributed to the Dutch disease (Bourdet and Falck 2004), the exchange rate in Cape Verde has been generally in line with fundamental goods while the wages in the nontradable sector do not seem to have an impact on the tradable sector wages (IMF 2008). This is mainly because the nontradable sector is shallow and most of the tradable sector wages are concentrated in the tourism sector (IMF 2008).

Destinations of Migrants

Cape Verde is one of the few countries that have experienced large-scale emigration. As of 2010, 192,000 Cape Verdeans lived abroad, representing around 37.5 percent of the population (World Bank 2011). The top migrant destination countries in Africa (from highest to lowest percentages of Cape Verde emigrants) are Angola, Senegal, Mozambique, and Nigeria. The main destinations outside Africa (also in order of migrants' preference) are the United States, Portugal, Angola, France, Senegal, Argentina, the Netherlands, Italy, Spain, and Luxembourg (IMF 2008; see figure 3.3).

Interestingly, although the largest share of the overseas diaspora lives in the United States (53 percent of the total), those emigrants supply only 16.5 percent of the remittances. One explanation may be that the Cape Verdeans living in the United States are often fourth- and fifth-generation U.S. residents, with decreasing identification as Cape Verdeans. Although the disapora in Portugal and France is smaller (totaling around 21 percent), the remittance flows originating in these two countries collectively account for more than 52 percent of total remittances.

Emigration of skilled workers is the predominant trend. Cape Verde ranks among the top-10 middle-income economies in the emigration of skilled workers, with an emigration rate of college-educated people as high as 67.5 percent (World Bank 2011). It is also the largest source country of educated emigrants, physicians, and nurses from Sub-Saharan Africa.

Figure 3.3   Cape Verdean Overseas Disapora, 2000
destinations of Cape Verdean emigrants, by %

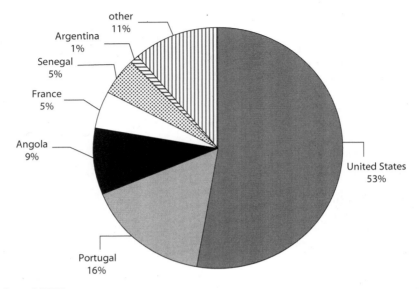

Source: IMF 2008.

Characteristics of the Remittance Industry

This section describes the characteristics of the remittance industry in Cape Verde. It relies on a survey and interviews with Cape Verdean RSPs conducted in 2008.

RSP Firm Types and Coverage

Among the formal RSPs that facilitate the transfers, five financial institutions—four private banks and one exchange office—dominate the industry: Banco Comercial do Atlântico (BCA), Caixa Económica de Cabo Verde (CECV), Banco Interatlântico (BIA), Banco Caboverdiano de Negócios (BCN), and Cotacâmbios.

CECV and BCA have the most extensive network—with 33 and 27 total branches, respectively—covering both urban (including the capital city, Praia) and rural areas. Both CECV and BCA have branches in the islands of Santiago, São Vincente, Santo Antâo, Sal, Fogo, and Boa Vista. The third- and fourth-largest RSPs are BCN and BIA, respectively. The smallest of the five—the exchange office, Cotacâmbios—has four branches in Praia.

In the rural areas, however, only CECV and BCN have branches, as table 3.2 indicates. Moreover, there are no microfinance institutions to facilitate remittances in the rural areas.

Two banks facilitated about 92 percent of the reported inward international remittance volume in 2007: BCA and CECV, which processed US$76.3 million (62 percent) and US$37.2 million (30 percent), respectively.[3] BCN facilitated US$0.95 million in 2007 (1 percent) and Cotacâmbios, US$1.0 million (1 percent). BIA, the fifth major RSP, did not provide 2005–07 data on its inward remittance volumes.

Partnerships and Agreements with Money Transfer Operators

The four major banks are independent firms, and the exchange office is a branch of an international group, Cotacâmbios Portugal (part of the Group Cota). All five facilitate remittance services to their clients through partnerships with foreign banks, money transfer operators (MTOs), and telecommunications service providers.

The banks usually partner with international MTOs for remittance services. The primary MTOs, as table 3.3 shows, are Western Union and

Table 3.2   RSP Branches in Cape Verde

RSP	Total branches	Urban branches	Rural branches
CECV	33	25	8
BCA	27	27	0
BCN	13	11	2
BIA	6	6	0
Cotacâmbios	4	4	0

Source: Survey of RSPs in Cape Verde.

Table 3.3   Business Partnerships for Remittance Services

RSP	MTO	Correspondent banks[a]
BCA	Western Union	√
CECV	Western Union	√
BCN	—	√
BIA	MoneyGram International	√
Cotacâmbios	Western Union	—

Source: RSP survey in Cape Verde.
Note: — = Not avilable. √ = bank provides inward remittance services but it may not offer account-to-account transfers for outward international or domestic remittances.

MoneyGram International. Typically, those partnerships are exclusive; for example, if a bank signs a partnership with Western Union for money transfer operations, it cannot enter a partnership with MoneyGram. However, other types of money transfer services (such as account-to-account transfers) involving foreign correspondent banks do not exclude partnerships with Western Union or MoneyGram.

The partnerships with MTOs and correspondent banks include various profit-sharing arrangements. The significant remittance inflows also generate indirect benefits to the RSPs, such as enhancing their capacity and supporting their financial consolidation. Most commonly, these financial institutions benefit from full access to payment infrastructures and distribution networks (particularly in the countries from which remittances originate); access to foreign exchange; and commissions (about 20 percent) charged on remittance payments and receipts.

Other institutions, such as Correios de Cabo Verde (Post Office of Cape Verde), also provide remittance services through Western Union, but data on these inward remittance flows are not available. Overall remittance inflows might be higher than reported because some of the statistics include inflows processed only through formal channels (for example, Western Union). Inflows through informal channels or person-to-person transfers are not captured. This trend confirms the overall assumption that remittance inflows may be underreported in Cape Verde.

Remittance Products

Remittance products are well developed in Cape Verde, and all RSPs offer a wide range of services—mainly electronic cash transfers and account-to-account transfers. In addition, as table 3.4 shows, some banks (such as BCA, BIA, and BCN) offer other remittance products, including bank drafts, checks, money orders, prepaid cards for use at designated retailers, prepaid debit cards, and money transfers transmitted by cellular phone.

The settlement system and customer services are effective, and they facilitate the processing of remittance inflows. In the case of electronic cash transfers (using MTOs such as Western Union or MoneyGram), the settlement of international remittance transactions is instantaneous. In the case of international account-to-account transfers, the remittance recipients in Cape Verde normally receive the amounts due within two working days from the transfer date.

Banks do not require customers of remittance services to open an account, thus eliminating their monthly fees for account maintenance. The remittance sender pays all the fees due for the money transfers.

Table 3.4 Remittance Products, by RSP

RSP	Electronic cash transfers	Account-to-account transfers	Bank drafts	Checks	Money orders	Prepaid cards for use at designated retailers	Prepaid debit cards	Money transfers through cellular phones
BCA	✓	✓	✓	✓	✓			
CECV	✓	✓						
BCN	✓	✓		✓	✓	✓	✓	
BIA	✓	✓		✓	✓	✓	✓	
Cotacâmbios	✓	✓						✓

Source: RSP survey in Cape Verde.

Furthermore, all financial institutions designate one or two staff members to deal with customer grievances, particularly when remittances are not delivered on time or at all. The most common way to address such complaints is by talking to the sending agents. Among the Cape Verde RSPs, customer complaints vary in frequency between once a week and once every two or three months—in some cases, as seldom as once every five months. The customer service is effective because grievances are handled relatively quickly (within one week, often in as little as two days) to resolve customers' complaints about remittances not being received or delivered.

Access to Other Financial Services

Most of the banks providing remittance services in Cape Verde also extend other financial services to remittance receivers and senders, irrespective of whether they are regular banking customers or not. The most common products offered to remittance receivers are deposits, savings products, small and large consumer loans, business loans, educational and vehicle loans, credit cards, and mortgages (however, nonresidents cannot benefit from mortgages). Remittance senders, too, may have access to deposits, savings accounts, business loans, and mortgages.

By facilitating remittances, the banks can also potentially enlarge their customer bases and financial revenues. By developing customized services for remittance receivers and senders, the banks may help to formalize remittance flows, reduce remittance costs, and increase the scope for investment in Cape Verde.

The Regulatory and Business Environment

All the RSPs who participated in the survey perceive the regulatory and business environment as conducive to remittance service operations. Sixty percent of the respondents perceive the laws and regulations governing remittances, collectively, as a minor obstacle. The remaining 40 percent do not consider laws and regulations to be an obstacle at all.

The Central Bank of Cape Verde is responsible for the regulation and supervision of commercial banks, offshore banks, and nonfinancial institutions. All commercial banks are subject to standard regulatory requirements (as described in box 3.1), an annual on-site examination, and regular monthly reporting. BCA, CECV, BCN, BIA, and Cotacâmbios are registered with the central bank to provide remittance services as well as any other banking or financial services.

Box 3.1

The Central Bank's Regulatory and Supervisory Role

The Central Bank of Cape Verde (CBCV) is responsible for the regulation and supervision of commercial banks, offshore banks, and non-bank financial institutions. The law governing the central bank was revised in 2002 to clarify the bank's overriding policy objectives and to bring the law in line with international practices. Among the main revisions were the following:

- Cash advances to the government may never exceed 5 percent of the current revenue collected in the preceding year. Any overdraft account of this kind must be in balance at the end of each year.
- The central bank's independence and accountability was explicitly stated in the law.
- The admissible operations using domestic monetary policy instruments were streamlined.
- Best practices for safeguarding the central bank's capital ("top-up" rules), determining net income, and distributing net profits were introduced.

Under this law, the central bank may provide liquidity support for commercial banks—in particular, by granting short-term credit to commercial banks with the collateral of marketable government securities. Furthermore, to bridge temporary liquidity shortages, it may act as a lender of last resort, but any lending of this type is limited to three times the borrowing entity's capital and carries a penalty rate of interest determined on a case-by-case basis. The central bank also can issue temporary emergency rules to govern the volume of credit and interest rates applicable to commercial banking operations.

As the regulations of the banking and financial sectors have improved, the central bank has been implementing measures to reinforce its operational and oversight responsibilities by training its staff and modernizing computer systems and internal controls. A framework for internal controls for the commercial banks for anti-money-laundering is part of on-site inspection. The anti-money-laundering legislation (2002) and the accompanying regulations (2003) complete the legal framework. The banks now must comply with a series of prudential regulations, including the following:

- Equity stakes in firms not supervised by the central bank may not exceed certain limits.

(continued)

Box 3.1 *(continued)*

- Equity and loans exceeding 10 percent of the bank's capital are considered high risk.
- Exposure to any client may not exceed 25 percent of the institution's capital, and the amount of high-risk obligations may not exceed eight times the bank's capital.
- The minimum capital requirement for a bank is CVEsc 300 million, and the risk-weighted capital adequacy ratio is 10 percent.
- Banks are obliged to set up provisions for overdue loans, general credit risks, retirement pensions, survivors' benefits, and capital losses on securities and other instruments. (Nonperforming loans are divided into five groups—up to 3 months, 6 months, 12 months, 36 months, and more than 36 months—with nonperforming loans secured by collateral requiring lower provisioning.)

Source: IMF 2005.

Among the reporting requirements, banks and nonfinancial institutions must comply with reporting requirements in case of suspicious activities and large currency transactions. They have to notify the central bank of all currency transactions exceeding CVEsc 1 million (approximately US$12,412)[4] as well as all suspicious activities they might detect.

To handle foreign exchange transactions, all these banks and institutions must establish partnerships with correspondent banks, and they may order cross-border transfers freely because the central bank sets no maximum fee or charge for such transfers, nor does it limit foreign exchange holdings or remittance inflows.

The mandatory minimum capital requirement to operate in the banking and financial market is CVEsc 300 million (approximately US$3.7 million). The minimum capital for the exchange offices is CVEsc 35 million (approximately US$434,000 at the time of the survey in 2008). Some banks also indicated that they must comply with a net worth requirement of 10 percent of net results above the minimum capital and a requirement that 5 percent of deposits be in the national currency.

Entry and Other Barriers to Provision of Remittance Services

Although laws and regulations do not seem to significantly affect the remittance industry, the RSPs differ in their perceptions of the main barriers to entry when starting a remittance-related business. Half of the respondents consider the following to be moderate to major barriers: banking license requirements, access to financial infrastructure (payment systems), minimum capital requirements, and access to capital and finance. One respondent considered competition to be a major barrier to entry.

Among the lesser barriers to entry, 75 percent of the respondents perceived access to distribution networks as a minor barrier, and they unanimously considered corruption to be the least important barrier.

In particular, 60 percent of respondents consider capital requirements, anti-money-laundering requirements, and exchange controls to be moderate barriers to providing remittance-related services. Sixty percent also consider license requirements and lack of access to clearing and settlement systems to be minor obstacles. Finally, tax policy, lack of access to banking facilities, and government corruption are perceived as the least important barriers to running remittance-related operations.

Remittance Costs and Identification Requirements

Remittance fees for transfers outside and within Cape Verde do not vary significantly across RSPs. Typically, the fee to send money abroad or within the country ranges between CVEsc 1,500 and CVEsc 2,100 (approximately US$20 to US$28)[5] for money transfer operators' services, irrespective of the remittance corridor—a scant increase from previous years. For example, BCA reported fixed fees of CVEsc 1,900 (approximately US$24.00)[6] in 2007 and CVEsc 2,000 (approximately US$26.60) in 2008.

The fee for account-to-account transfers at some banks is also fixed at CVEsc 2,500 (approximately US$31). These costs are higher than those to remit from the United States to Mexico or to other Latin American countries through credit unions, which is about US$10 for up to US$300 in remittances (Maimbo and Ratha 2005; World Bank 2006).

The average foreign exchange commission charged by some banks is 0.018 percent for all major remittance corridors. However, because most inflows come from European countries, this commission does not apply to transactions involving an exchange from euro to CVEsc because the exchange rate between the two currencies is fixed. Typically, for receipt of remittances from abroad, banks do not charge any fee for transfers through money transfer operators, but they do charge CVEsc 500 (approximately US$6) for account-to-account transfers. Nevertheless, these costs may be prohibitive for the less wealthy population, thereby fueling the development of informal remittance networks.

Remittance fees are also fixed for destination countries in Africa. People send money from Cape Verde to other African countries primarily through these corridors:

- Northern Africa: Algeria and Morocco
- Western Africa: Burkina Faso, The Gambia, Ghana, Guinea, Guinea-Bissau, Nigeria, Senegal, Sierra Leone, and Togo
- West-central Africa: Cameroon, Gabon, and São Tomé and Príncipe
- Southern and southwest Africa: Angola, Namibia, South Africa, and Swaziland
- Eastern Africa: Uganda.

The growing demand to send remittances from developed financial markets to Cape Verde boosted the development of money transfer services and customized programs in the source countries. In the United States, major commercial banks such as Citizens Bank and Wells Fargo view remittance services as a way to attract a significant number of the unbanked population to their mainstream financial products. In an arrangement with banks in Cape Verde, for example, Citizens Bank offers Cape Verdean migrants a remittance facility that is cheaper than Western Union. In its three years of operations, this program has made more than 1,000 formerly unbanked Cape Verdean migrants customers of Citizens Bank. However, most of such programs require the migrant to open a bank account and are thus unlikely to appeal to undocumented workers (IMF 2008).

The cost of sending money from developed countries to Cape Verde is relatively high, especially for poor migrants. Transferring money to Cape Verde through Western Union and MoneyGram is slightly more expensive than through other operators or services. Fees range between US$10.00 and US$18.60 to send US$100 through MoneyGram International, and the fees for the high-volume corridors (such as France, Portugal, and the United States) are lower than those for low-volume corridors (such as the United Kingdom). These fees through Western Union and MoneyGram are also lower than fees they charge to send money *from* Cape Verde (see table 3.5).

Nevertheless, such fees may be prohibitive for poor migrants who send home only a few hundred dollars per transaction and may encourage the use of informal channels to facilitate such transfers. These channels charge, on average, 14.3 percent, confirming the generally high transaction costs for Sub-Saharan Africa.[7] Moreover, fees to send remittances from the United Kingdom to Cape Verde and other countries, either within or outside Africa, do not differ substantially.

Table 3.5 Fees for Remittances to Cape Verde, by MTO

Originating country	France	Portugal	United Kingdom	United States	Transfer speed
Remittance amount	**€100**	**€100**	**£100**	**US$100**	
MoneyGram International	€8[a]	€12[b]	£12[c]	US$10	instant
Western Union	€10[d]	n.a.	£14[e]	US$12	instant
Currencies direct (account-to-account via cell phone, online, telephone)	n.a.	n.a.	£0	n.a.	1–2 days
Money Line UK (cash to cash via agent branch, cell phone, telephone)	n.a.	n.a.	£10[f]	n.a.	24 hours
Coinstar Money Transfer (cash to cash via agent)	n.a.	n.a.	£4[g]	n.a.	instant
ePay (upload to MTO account online)	n.a.	n.a.	£0	n.a.	5 days
Sole Provider International (upload to ATM card account, online)	n.a.	n.a.	n.a.	US$3	instant
iKobo (prepaid credit card via FedEx, online)	n.a.	n.a.	n.a.	US$8	n.a.

Sources: Western Union, www.westernunion.com. Money Gram International, www.moneygram.com. SendMoneyHome, www.sendmoneyhome.org. iKobo, www.ikobo.com.

Note: ATM = automated teller machine. n.a. = not applicable.

a. Approximately US$11.50, at an exchange rate (2008) of €1 = US$1.44.
b. Approximately US$17.30, at an exchange rate (2008) of €1 = US$1.44.
c. Approximately US$18.60, at an exchange rate (2008) of £1 = US$1.55.
d. Approximately US$14.40, at an exchange rate (2008) of €1 = US$1.44.
e. Approximately US$21.70, at an exchange rate (2008) of £1 = US$1.55.
f. Approximately US$15.50, at an exchange rate (2008) of £1 = US$1.55.
g. Approximately US$6.20, at an exchange rate (2008) of £1 = US$1.55.

Typically, to disburse or send remittances outside or within Cape Verde, all RSPs require official identification documents—either a national passport or national identification card—regardless of whether the customers hold an account with the respective banks. Driver's licenses or utility bills are rarely accepted as identification documents. Only Cotacâmbios reported accepting these two types of identification documents. Letters from the village head or local authorities are not accepted.

Because poor populations or those living in rural areas may not always possess national identification cards or national passports, their access to remittance services and, implicitly, to additional sources of revenue may be limited.

Conclusions and Recommendations

As one of the few countries in Africa that have experienced large-scale emigration, as a share of its population, Cape Verde is among the top recipients of remittances (as a share of its GDP) in Africa.

Summary of findings

However, official statistics often fail to capture informal remittance inflows, including person-to-person transfers, often used for remittances to rural areas and poor segments of the population. In addition, estimates of the volume of remittances sent from other African countries are not easily available.

Four private banks and one exchange office are Cape Verde's primary RSPs. However, the industry is highly concentrated: Among the five primary RSPs, two banks (BCA and CECV) facilitated around 92 percent of the inward remittance flows in 2007.

Rural areas in Cape Verde remain underserved. Only two banks (CECV and BCN) even have branches in the rural areas. Moreover, no microfinance institutions exist that might facilitate remittances in the rural areas.

The RSPs have established partnerships to facilitate the transfer of remittances—most commonly with MTOs, such as Western Union and MoneyGram International, and with foreign correspondent banks. All RSPs offer one or more of the most common remittance products: electronic cash transfers, account-to-account transfers, bank drafts, checks, money orders, prepaid debit cards or cards for use at designated retailers, and money transfers through cellular phones.

Overall, the remittance settlement system and customer services appear to be effective, and remittance recipients may benefit from a relatively wide range of financial products, including deposits, saving products, loans, credit cards, and mortgages. High remittance levels enhance the RSPs' capacity and support their financial consolidation, confirming the overall effect of remittances on financial deepening documented in various studies (including Gupta, Pattillo, and Wagh 2009).

The RSPs' fees for sending remittances abroad and within the country do not vary significantly, but they are high—and the high fees especially limit the poor population's access to such services. Similarly, the cost of sending money from developed countries to Cape Verde is relatively high, especially for poor migrants. Transferring money from France, Portugal, or the United States through Western Union and MoneyGram appears to be slightly more expensive than through other operators or services. However, fees to send money through high-remittance-volume corridors are lower than fees for low-volume corridors, as observed in other countries.

All RSPs perceive the regulatory and business environment as favorable to conducting a remittance business. There is a mandatory minimum capital requirement to operate in the banking and financial market. Banks and nonfinancial institutions also must comply with the existing regulations on reporting requirements for suspicious activities and large currency transactions. However, laws and regulations do not seem to significantly affect the remittance industry. Most of the RSPs perceive insufficient access to finance for banks and nonfinancial institutions—in terms of availability, costs, and competition from informal sector—as moderate obstacles to doing business.

Recommendations

For better leveraging of the impact of remittances on development in Cape Verde, specific actions are recommended in three areas: data collection, remittance transaction costs, and investment and financial products.

Improve data collection. RSPs can take the following actions to improve data collection on remittance flows and, hence, to increase the accuracy of national remittance volume estimates and forecasts:

- Streamline statistics on both inward and outward remittance flows (remittances that Cape Verde emigrants send home and those sent by immigrants living in Cape Verde) by keeping separate books for inward remittances from Cape Verdeans abroad and outward volumes remitted by immigrants.

- Track the within-country remittance flows, and in particular, improve knowledge of the flows remitted into rural areas and to poor segments of the population.
- Improve data collection on remittance flows for the intra-African corridors.

Reduce transaction costs, and increase access of the poor. Steps to increase access of the poor to remittance services and to reduce remittance costs include:

- Improve access to remittance services in rural areas by encouraging entry of microfinance institutions to reach poor populations.
- Encourage the use of new money-transfer technologies such as pre-paid cards or mobile phones, which are less costly than traditional remittance services and products.
- Stimulate competition among banks and other nonfinancial institutions by reducing barriers to entry of new remittance service providers, which will help reduce overall transaction fees.

Develop investment and financial products. Finally, to strengthen the links between remittance flows and investment, financial institutions should implement the following innovative strategies:

- Develop financial products that target the Cape Verdean diaspora, including disapora bonds.
- Increase awareness of investment opportunities among the Cape Verdean diaspora in both Europe and the United States.
- Use future remittance flows as collateral to improve long-term capital (through securitization of remittances, trade payments, and investment)—a strategy that has already proven effective in other developing countries such as Ecuador, the Arab Republic of Egypt, and Turkey.

Annex 3.A   Financial Sector Development in Cape Verde

Cape Verde's modern financial sector has developed over the past decade. The central bank, the Central Bank of Cape Verde is responsible for regulation. Four commercial banks are currently the main banking service providers in Cape Verde: Banco Comercial do Atlântico (BCA) (spun off from the central bank in 1995), Caixa Económica de Cabo Verde (CECV), Banco Interatlântico (BIA), and Banco Caboverdiano de Negócios (BCN).[8]

The financial sector is performing well and is exhibiting a relatively high level of financial intermediation. It is also highly liquid, with broad money representing 72.3 percent of GDP by the end of 2004—one of the highest levels in Sub-Saharan Africa. Credit to the private sector and deposits of commercial banks were 34 percent and 60 percent of GDP, respectively, at the end of 2003. This is much higher than in other low-income countries in Africa and comparable to those of other lower- and upper-middle-income countries (average of 12.4 percent) (IMF 2005).

The bankwide nonperforming loan portfolio, although higher than that in developed countries, has gradually decreased from 9.00 percent in 2002 to 6.31 percent (of the total) in 2005 as a result of improved supervision by the central bank and accelerated collection efforts. The returns to equity appear to be higher than global benchmarks and those in other countries from Sub-Saharan Africa (IMF 2005).

The banking sector is highly concentrated[9] and dominates the financial sector, with commercial banks accounting for 87 percent of financial system assets, while the insurance[10] and the stock markets[11] are relatively small. Altogether, seven nonbank financial institutions (two insurance companies, one venture capital firm, two exchange houses, a leasing company, and the Sociedade Interbancária e Sistemas de Pagamento [SISP]) and four offshore banks are operational.[12]

The market infrastructure, which is still developing, includes the payment system and interbank market. In addition to SISP, another institution, Sistema Integrado de Compensação Interbancária e Liquidação, was created to integrate compensation of checks and interbank transfers with 24-hour processing operations. SISP integrates VISA services to support tourism and attract foreign exchange and is expanding in some other islands of Cape Verde.

The interbank market is dominated by two big banks and characterized by a limited number of participants, inelastic interest rates, lack of interbank deposits, and temporary excess liquidity in the banking system. The central bank sets reference rates (including those for lending and borrowing facilities) and may use treasury bills of maturities of up to one year in open-market operations to inject (and absorb) liquidity in the banking sector. However, these instruments have not been used since 1999 because there has been no shortage of liquidity in the banking system (IMF 2005).

Notes

1. See Ratha (2003).
2. Empirical analysis of remittances to Cape Verde shows that the domestic real interest rates were negative in the first part of the 1980s (the inflation rate surpassing the nominal interest rate of 6.5 percent), but after the mid-1990s, returns on deposits increased as special accounts for emigrant remittances were created, yielding 1 to 3 percentage points more than resident deposits (IMF 2008).
3. CECV provided data that included only inward remittances processed through Western Union services. The account-to-account transfers are not included.
4. Based on the annual average exchange rate (2007) of US$1 = CVEsc 80.56.
5. Based on the annual exchange rate (2008) of US$1 = CVEsc 75.27.
6. Based on the annual average exchange rate (2007) of US$1 = CVEsc 80.56.
7. See Gupta, Pattilo and Wagh (2009).
8. BCA and BIA are subsidiaries of the same state-owned bank in Portugal: Caixa Geral de Depósitos. CECV is a subsidiary of two Portuguese banks: Caixa Económica Montepio Geral and Montepio Geral-Assoçiacão Multulista.
9. BCA controlled 66.3 percent of the total deposits and the total assets and 55.6 percent of the total loans of the commercial banks at the end of 2004 (IMF 2005).
10. Car insurance accounts for 55 percent of total insurance premiums, providing very limited long-term capital to the market. Life insurance is underdeveloped, representing only 1.3 percent of insurance premiums.
11. The Bolsa de Valores de Cabo Verde was inaugurated in 2005. Several companies (BCA, Garantia, CECV, and a tobacco company) have already been listed, and the government also placed 44 treasury bonds dating back to 1993 in addition to new treasury bills.
12. Five additional offshore banks have requested licenses.

References

Bourdet, Y., and H. Falck. 2004. "Emigrants' Remittances and Dutch Disease in Cape Verde." *International Economic Journal* (Korean International Economic Association) 20 (3): 267–284.

Gupta S., C. Pattillo, and S. Wagh. 2009. "Impact of Remittances on Poverty and Financial Development in Sub-Saharan Africa." *World Development* 37 (1): 104–15.

IMF (International Monetary Fund). 2005. Cape Verde: Selected Issues and Statistical Appendix. IMF Country Report 05/319, IMF, Washington, DC. http://imf.org/external/pubs/ft/scr/2005/cr05319.pdf.

———. 2008. "Cape Verde: Selected Issues." Country Report 08/243, IMF, Washington, DC. http://www.imf.org/external/pubs/ft/scr/2008/cr08243.pdf.

Maimbo, S., and D. Ratha, eds. 2005. *Remittances: Development Impact and Future Prospects*. Washington DC: World Bank.

Ratha, Dilip. 2003. "Workers' Remittances: An Important and Stable Source of External Development Finance." In *Global Development Finance: Striving for Stability in Development Finance*, 157–175. Washington, DC: World Bank. http://siteresources.worldbank.org/INTRGDF/Resources/GDF2003-Chapter7.pdf.

World Bank. 2006. *Global Economic Prospects 2006: Economic Implications of Remittances and Migration*. Washington, DC: World Bank.

———. 2007. "Cape Verde Investment Climate Assessment." Report of the Africa Regional Program on Enterprise Development, World Bank, Washington, DC. http://siteresources.worldbank.org/INTAFRSUMAFTPS/Resources/Cape _Verde_ICA_March_07_r1.pdf.

———. 2010. "Migrant Remittance Flows: Findings from a Global Survey of Central Banks." Working Paper 194, World Bank, Washington, DC.

———. 2011. *Migration and Remittances Factbook 2011*. Washington, DC: World Bank.

CHAPTER 4

Ethiopia

Alemayehu Geda and Jacqueline Irving

Remittances are an extremely important source of foreign exchange for Ethiopia. Although World Bank data based on the International Monetary Fund's (IMF) Balance of Payments statistics provide a figure of $387 million for remittance inflows in 2010 (World Bank 2011), the figure for officially recorded remittance inflows reported by the National Bank of Ethiopia is more than $600 million (NBE 2010). The actual volume of remittances in Ethiopia, including flows through formal and informal channels, could be in the range of $1 billion to $2 billion annually. This chapter draws on a 2008–09 survey of remittance service providers (RSPs) in Ethiopia and on the Ethiopia-specific findings of a global survey of central banks conducted in mid-2008 to provide a picture of the remittance industry in Ethiopia and discuss, among other issues, competition, the regulatory environment, new technologies, and access to remittances and other financial services.

The volume of remittances that flow into a country depends on several factors, including the following:

- Size of emigrant population (World Bank 2011)
- Facilities for transferring funds (Ratha 2003; Puri and Ritzema 2004)

- Level of economic activity in the migrant-recipient countries
- Rate of inflation in the recipient country (El-Sakka and McNabb 1999).

The views on the role of domestic inflation have been mixed. El-Sakka and McNabb (1999) hold that inflation has a positive relationship to the size of remittance inflow because migrants increase the amount they send in response to inflation in the home country to maintain the consumption of families back home. Elbadawi and Rocha (1992), however argue that a high inflation rate is a sign of economic instability and, thus, may discourage remittances. In Ethiopia, the former argument seems applicable to remittances destined for consumption, while the latter view may relate to the investment-related flows.

Recent Migration Trends

The revolution and unrest that characterized Ethiopia's political climate in the 1970s caused large numbers of Ethiopians to migrate overseas. Most of the people in this first wave of migration to the West came from Ethiopia's urban elite—primarily young and well-educated Ethiopians who, for political reasons, sought refuge in Western countries. In the decades that followed, however, migration gradually became an aspiration of most of Ethiopia's urban people, mainly for economic reasons. Since the mid-1980s, even rural peasants have been migrating in large numbers to the Gulf Cooperation Council and other Middle Eastern countries in search of jobs and better pay. More than 1 million Ethiopians are believed to reside abroad (Aredo 2005) out of a population of 83 million (World Bank 2011).

The country's internal and international migration is based largely on individuals' or families' responses to adverse local socioeconomic, physical, and political environment conditions. In this context, the character, direction, and volume of migration within and from Ethiopia in the past three decades have been shaped by political instability, decline or stagnation in the agricultural sector, and government resettlement programs of the 1980s (Gebre 2001; Ezra 2001; Mberu 2006).

Remittance Sources and Trends

Despite its large migrant population, Ethiopia has not fully tapped its potential, some authors note. Nega and others (2004), cited in Aredo

(2005), indicate that the remittance flow to Ethiopia is only one-sixth of its potential, covering just 8 percent of the nation's budget deficit. These authors indicate that if the potential level of remittances were to materialize, it would exceed the level of official development assistance, which reached $3.3 billion in 2008 (World Bank 2011).

The remittance inflow data for Ethiopia vary by source. The World Bank (2011) reported remittance inflows totaling 1.3 percent of gross domestic product (GDP) in 2009. According to the Bank's latest data, remittance flows grew steadily from $27 million in 1995 to $53 million in 2000 and more than tripled in the subsequent years to reach $387 million by 2010. However, data from the National Bank of Ethiopia (NBE) suggest that the figure could be substantially higher. The NBE reported that net transfers from private individuals reached $661 million in the 2009-10 fiscal year (NBE 2010). Informal remittance flows to Ethiopia also appear to be significant. The *NBE Quarterly Bulletin* reports that of the above individual transfers, $428 million was "underground private transfers" (NBE 2010). If Ethiopian migrants send an estimated $100 to $200 monthly to their relatives back home, applying this amount to the estimated 1 million Ethiopian migrants results in an annual total estimate in the range of $1.2 billion to $2.4 billion in remittance transfers.

The NBE has not yet compiled disaggregated data for cross-border remittance flows to Ethiopia by source country (Irving, Mohapatra, and Ratha 2010).[1] According to recent World Bank data, the largest destinations for Ethiopian migrants among high-income countries in 2010 were the United States, Israel, Saudi Arabia, Canada, and Germany (World Bank 2011). In 2008, based on available information on migration trends, the major source countries for migrant remittances to Ethiopia were the United States and Gulf Cooperation Council countries (notably, the United Arab Emirates, Bahrain, Saudi Arabia, and Kuwait).

As figure 4.1 shows, recorded remittance flows to Ethiopia appeared to have declined by 22 percent in 2009 as a result of the global financial crisis, partially reversing the dramatic growth in the previous decade. According to some Ethiopian commercial banks participating in this study, the volume of migrant remittance inflow transactions they were handling (as of March 2009) had declined since the September 2008 onset of the more severe phase of the global financial crisis because of layoffs in migrant-employing sectors. However, other banks reported increases in transactions because increasing numbers of Ethiopians in the

Figure 4.1   Remittance Flows to Ethiopia, 1990–2009
US$, millions

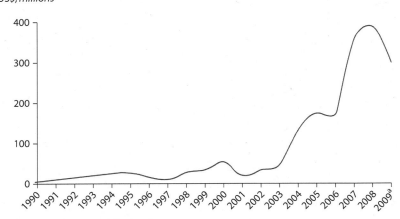

Source: Ratha, Mohapatra, and Silwal 2010.
a. Estimated.

diaspora were opting to invest in the Ethiopian real estate market, primarily in Addis Ababa and large cities in Ethiopia.

Characteristics of the Remittance Industry

The Ethiopian remittance services sector is characterized by the presence
of both state-owned and private sector banks as well as several money
transfer operators (MTOs) and a significant informal sector. However,
compared with African countries such as Ghana or Kenya, the number of
formal RSPs is extremely limited in Ethiopia, partly because of low levels of overall financial development, as box 4.1 describes.

The Formal RSP Sector

Banks and MTOs facilitate the bulk of formal remittance inflows to
Ethiopia. A mid-2008 survey of central banks indicated that six MTOs,
eight private commercial banks, one state-owned commercial bank, and
one state-owned savings bank provided these services in Ethiopia (Irving,
Mohapatra, and Ratha 2010). However, the actual number of RSPs could
be to be higher because of underreporting of remittance service providers
in the survey and entry of new providers since the survey was conducted.[2]

Three MTOs—Western Union, MoneyGram, and Dahabshiil—are
considered the predominant players in the country's RSP market. In

Box 4.1

The Ethiopian Financial Sector

The Ethiopian financial sector is one of the least developed in Sub-Saharan Africa. On a financial liberalization index—which measures banking security and independence from government control on a scale of 10 to 100 (100 being the most liberal)—Ethiopia scores only 20 (Kiyota, Peitsch, and Stern 2007). The sector is characterized by a shallow financial market, a closed nature, and strong government control. The financial infrastructure in rural areas is poor. This low level of financial development also manifests in a relatively low domestic savings rate.

The government implemented several financial reform measures since the 1990s (Alemayehu 2008):

- Liberalizing the private bank and insurance sectors
- Liberalizing the foreign exchange market
- Strengthening domestic competitive capacity before full liberalization
- Strengthening NBE's regulatory and supervisory capacities
- Giving the banks autonomy
- Opening the interbank money market.

The reforms have led to a decline in the dominance of state-owned banks and a rise in the private banks' market share. In 1998, the three state-owned banks (the Commercial Bank of Ethiopia, the Development Bank of Ethiopia, and the Construction and Business Bank) accounted for 94 percent of the assets of Ethiopian banks. By 2006, however, this figure had fallen to 70 percent. Meanwhile, the share of assets held by private banks increased from 6.4 percent in 1998 to 30 percent in 2006. Over the same period, the total assets of the banking sector have doubled (Kiyota, Peitsch, and Stern 2007).

Source: Alemayehu 2008 and authors' elaborations.

Ethiopia, MTOs are legally required to handle foreign exchange transactions through commercial banks, which are required to pay out cash to the recipients in local currency.[3]

State-owned banks tend to have more extensive branch networks outside of the capital city, Addis Ababa, than do private commercial banks. According to the Ethiopian central bank, the National Bank of Ethiopia, as of the mid-2008 RSP survey, the eight private commercial banks providing remittance delivery services had a combined total of 298 bank branches in the country, fewer than half of which were outside of Addis Ababa. However, the two state-owned banks that provide remittance services had a combined total of 232 branches, nearly three-quarters of which were outside of Addis Ababa (Irving, Mohapatra, and Ratha 2010).

Based on a separate survey of RSPs for this study, the five private commercial banks that participated in the survey had an average of 41 branches, as table 4.1 shows, and 38 percent of those branches were in rural areas. The one participating state-owned commercial bank had 205 branches, with just under 80 percent of these branches in rural areas. By contrast, the three MTO participants indicated that they had no branches in rural areas. Annex 4.1 lists the RSP firms that responded to the survey.

The Informal Remittance Sector

The Ethiopian remittance services industry also has a significant informal sector. According to input provided by some RSPs in Ethiopia for this study, a larger percentage of migrants have used formal channels in recent years, particularly through MTOs. A large amount of remittances, however, is still sent through informal channels, mainly because of lower up-front costs and, to some extent, lack of awareness of the formal money transfer options.[4]

Important players in the service sector with the infrastructure to provide remittance services—such as postal service providers, telecommunications service providers, credit unions, and microfinance institutions—still have only a limited presence and role in cross-border remittances.

Table 4.1   Branches of Primary Remittance Service Providers in Ethiopia

RSP type	Number of firms in country	Number of firms interviewed	Average number of branches among interviewed firms
MTOs[a]	6	3	3
Private commercial banks	8	5	41
State-owned commercial bank	1	1	205
State-owned savings and loan institution	1	1	31

Source: RSP survey in Ethiopia and authors' calculations.
a. One MTO, name hidden to protect privacy, despite having no rural branches, has established a presence in 70 branches of Ethiopia's national postal service, which does provide strong rural coverage.

Partnerships and Agreements between Banks and MTOs

All the surveyed RSPs indicated that they have at least one partnership agreement with other RSPs to provide cross-border remittance transfer services. Partnerships between banks and MTOs are currently by far the most common type of partnership in the Ethiopian RSP market. All six commercial banks participating in the survey indicated that they have partnerships with MTOs in providing remittance services to recipients in Ethiopia. Similarly, all three MTO participants indicated that they partner with banks. One innovative MTO has various types of partnership agreements to provide its remittance and remittance-linked services, as described in box 4.2.

In the past few years, NBE has been encouraging banks to form partnerships with microfinance institutions to reach the unbanked, particularly in rural areas. Three of the firms participating in the RSP survey (one MTO, the state-owned commercial bank, and one private commercial bank) indicated that they have recently begun or were planning to form partnerships with microfinance institutions or the national post office. One MTO reported that it has kiosks in some 70 branches of Ethiopia's postal service, with a focus on rural areas. Two microfinance institutions in Ethiopia—the Dedebit Credit and Savings Institution (DECSI) and the Amhara Credit and Savings Institution (ACSI)—are already providing domestic remittance transfer services and are seeking a license from NBE to transfer cross-border remittances.[5]

Prohibition of Exclusive Partnerships

Exclusivity contracts are not legally permissible in Ethiopia under regulations implemented by NBE in August 2006.[6] Since the abolition of exclusivity contracts, banks and other RSPs have clearly begun taking advantage of the more competitive operating environment for the provision of remittance services. Virtually all the banks participating in the RSP survey indicated that they have recently negotiated, or are in the process of negotiating, new partnership agreements with MTOs, particularly with some of the smaller MTOs in the market. Among the RSP survey participants for this study, only one MTO indicated that it continued to operate in partnership with a bank.

How RSPs Benefit from Partnerships

Nearly all (9 out of 10) of the surveyed RSPs in Ethiopia cited commissions on remittance receipts as a benefit of their partnerships with other

Box 4.2

Case Study: Birritu Express

Through innovative partnership agreements, money transfer operator Birritu Express provides a form of health care insurance and real estate investment services to the Ethiopian diaspora and resident Ethiopians. Birritu has established partnerships for money transfer services with Ethiopia's national postal service and the state-owned Commercial Bank of Ethiopia. Birritu's partnership with ICICI Bank in India also enabled it to develop a way for Ethiopian residents to send tuition money to recipients in India to attend school.

In the health care arena, the company has partnership agreements with St. Yared Clinic in Addis Ababa to provide health care services to Ethiopian migrants' families. For $25 per month, an Ethiopian living abroad can provide a designated beneficiary in Ethiopia with access to health care services.

Source: Authors.

RSPs. All six commercial banks and the savings and loan indicated that partnership agreements with other RSPs give them access to foreign exchange and commission-earning opportunities on remittance receipts. There is a shortage of foreign currency in Ethiopia, and the banks can use the foreign exchange from migrant remittance inflows to provide trade financing for other bank clients.

A common arrangement seems to be for each MTO partner of a particular bank to have kiosks or some other form of physical presence on the premises of bank branches, with the bank receiving a share of the commission for providing this service. Two of the five private commercial banks surveyed also cited access to distribution networks as a benefit of their partnerships with other RSPs. According to one of these banks, by working in partnership with the national postal service and savings cooperatives, the bank gains access to a distribution network that serves people in less populated areas; in exchange, these partners gain access to the bank's technology. Another bank indicated that money transfers can be transacted more quickly and at a lower cost when working with MTOs as partners.

Remittance Products and Services

As table 4.2 shows, 70 percent of the RSPs surveyed offer electronic cash transfers. All three participating MTOs and four of five private commercial

Table 4.2   Remittance Instruments in Ethiopia, by RSP Type
number of firms offering each instrument

RSP type	Firms interviewed	Electronic cash transfers	Bank drafts	Acct.-to-acct. transfers	Checks	Money orders	Other
MTOs	3	3		1			
Private commercial banks	5	4	3	4	1	1	5
State-owned commercial bank	1		1	1	1		1
State-owned savings and loan institution	1		1		1	1	1
Total	**10**	**7**	**5**	**6**	**3**	**2**	**7**

Source: RSP survey findings and authors' calculations.

banks offered such transfers for remittance transactions. Among the different types of RSPs in Ethiopia, private commercial banks apparently offer the widest choice of instruments for remittance transfer, including electronic cash transfers, bank drafts, account-to-account transfers, checks, and money orders.

Account-to-account transfer ranks as the second most commonly available remittance-transfer instrument among RSPs in Ethiopia, offered by five of the commercial banks and one MTO. One of the MTOs, name hidden to protect privacy, offers a relatively wider range of instruments for transferring money from the United States to Ethiopia: by Visa or MasterCard, Internet checks, or on a cash-to-cash or cash-to-account basis.

Card-based payment systems in Ethiopia have been growing fast in recent years. Two commercial banks in the country (including the state-owned Commercial Bank of Ethiopia) have introduced wider use of debit or ATM cards. Commercial banks in Ethiopia also cited plans to use new technologies for remittance transfers, including mobile-phone transfers and remittance-linked financial products such as prepaid cards.[7] However, significant challenges to these plans include a lack of adequate financial and telecommunications infrastructure for the new technologies.

Cross-border transfers on a cash-to-cash basis can be nearly instantaneous if sent electronically from overseas to a recipient in Addis Ababa. Using the RSPs' most popular transfer services, remittances can be sent from abroad to urban destinations in Ethiopia in less than one day, according to 5 of the 10 RSP survey respondents (2 of which are MTOs). If remittances are transmitted by electronic or Internet check to a bank account, a recipient typically has access to the funds within two to four business days after the online transaction is completed.

By contrast, none of the surveyed RSPs indicated that they could deliver remittances sent from abroad to rural destinations in Ethiopia in less than one day—although four RSPs indicated that next-day delivery was possible to recipients in rural areas. Further delays in rural deliveries may occur because people often schedule a trip to the remittance-disbursing branch or agent to coincide with other business (for example, waiting until market day). Of the 10 RSP study participants, 2 (both of which are banks) indicated that they had no branches or other physical presence in remote rural areas.

Access to Other Financial Services

The financial services most commonly offered by the surveyed RSPs to remittance recipients are savings deposits and other savings products—cited by five of the 10 firms, of which three were commercial banks. Access to credit for starting or developing a business was cited by 2 firms (a savings and loan institution and state-owned commercial bank), each of which reported offering loans to both small and large businesses that are geared specifically to remittance recipients. Mortgage loans are offered recipients by a savings and loan institution and an MTO, Birritu Express, which provides mortgage loans to Ethiopian migrants in the United States for themselves or family members, as noted in box 4.2. A state-owned bank handles a government-guaranteed corporate bond (issued by the Ethiopian Electric Power Corp.) that targets the Ethiopian diaspora.

Aside from these instances, Ethiopia's banks and other RSPs have not yet made much progress in using remittance transfers as an entry point for formal financial products. According to the RSPs responding to the survey, remittances not used for consumption are often invested in tangible assets, such as real estate, instead of in savings deposits and other financial instruments that generate low or even negative returns in real terms. Thus, most banks and other financial-service providers do not appear to be actively marketing savings instruments and investment vehicles to Ethiopian migrants or their families.

Nevertheless, commercial banks do offer a few different types of accounts geared to the Ethiopian diaspora. Private individuals and companies in the Ethiopian diaspora can typically hold foreign currency in these Ethiopian accounts as U.S. dollars, U.K. pounds sterling, or euros. One impediment to holding more money in local savings accounts is the $50,000 limit imposed on savings held locally in an interest-bearing foreign currency account by Ethiopians in the diaspora, combined with the low interest payable on these accounts, according to some banks responding to the survey.

Nonrepatriable, local-currency-denominated savings accounts that the holder can use for local payment purposes are also available to Ethiopians in the diaspora. This latter type of account pays a significantly higher rate of interest than the minimum savings deposit rate set by NBE, but funds held in this account cannot be transferred abroad and cannot be converted into foreign currency. At least one commercial bank has begun offering a zero-balance account—a new savings product that sets no minimum balance and was launched to encourage unbanked people who come into the bank for remittances to open an account to hold some portion of their remittances. Those eligible for this and other savings accounts at Ethiopian banks include nonresident Ethiopians and nonresident foreign nationals of Ethiopian origin living abroad more than one year; companies owned by such individuals are also eligible.

Although they have not yet begun using new technologies in earnest, banks and other RSPs are considering how they may adopt new technologies in the future to develop remittance-linked financial products such as prepaid debit cards or microfinance loans.

Resolution of Customer Grievances

Most of the remittance service providers in Ethiopia encounter frequent consumer grievances concerning failure of delivery. The responses from the RSPs emphasize the need for a dedicated system to handle such complaints. The RSPs seem to lack the personnel to handle customer grievances, a lack that may reflect the relatively low level of competition in the sector.

The frequency of such failures varies markedly among the operators. Fifty percent of the firms indicated that consumer grievances occur once a week, and 10 percent noted that they occur once every two to three months. Another 10 percent said they receive an average of one grievance per day.

Once grievances are received, the operators also vary widely in the speed with which they address the problems: 20 percent of the firms resolve them within a day, 40 percent within a week, and 10 percent take up to a month.

The Regulatory and Business Environment

The process of obtaining a license from NBE to provide remittance transfer services can be time consuming and lengthy. As of March 2009, it was not unusual for the entire procedure to run up to two years for an MTO, according to interviews with RSPs. Four of seven RSPs (two MTOs and two commercial banks) that provided input about perceived barriers to starting a remittance transfer business in Ethiopia cited the licensing requirements as a main barrier.

Access to financial infrastructure was also cited by four of seven remittance service providers (two MTOs and two commercial banks) as a main barrier to starting a remittance transfer business in Ethiopia. The inability of RSPs in Ethiopia to undertake remittance outflow transactions because of foreign exchange regulations and difficulty obtaining access to capital or financing were each cited by one MTO as a main barrier to starting a remittance transfer business in Ethiopia.

The lack of a modern national payment system and, in particular, the lack of a real-time gross settlement (RTGS) system currently pose a major challenge to RSPs in Ethiopia because it means that there is no effective common clearing and settlement system linking all the banks. In the first quarter of 2009, it could take up to five days to clear a domestic remittance transfer from one bank to another within Ethiopia. Lack of a telecommunications infrastructure in rural areas also makes it difficult for RSPs to offer remittance transfer services in these areas. Because there is no broadband telecommunications system in rural areas and some MTOs require broadband for their "fast money" transfer services, sending money from Addis Ababa to rural areas could take as long as two to three days.

A relatively larger number of firms (8 of 10) participating in the survey cited barriers to providing remittance transfer services, once a business has been launched. The top-cited barrier (mentioned by three RSPs) was lack of access to clearing and settlement systems, cited by two commercial banks and one MTO. A second-ranking (and closely related) barrier, cited by two firms, was the inadequate information and communications technology infrastructure, particularly in rural areas. Capital requirements and anti-money-laundering (AML) requirements were also cited by two RSPs each. Although only one RSP (a commercial bank) cited competition posed by informal providers when queried about barriers to doing business generally, when the participating RSPs were asked specifically and directly about obstacles posed by informal providers, 7 of 10 indicated that it was a major or severe obstacle.

Exchange Controls and AML/CFT Requirements

The U.S. dollar is the most common currency of denomination for cross-border remittances transferred to Ethiopia. However, remittances must always be paid out in local currency when received as cash in Ethiopia, although they can be held locally in foreign currency accounts subject to limitations on maximum- or minimum-balance amounts.

Because of foreign exchange shortages, commercial banks and other RSPs in Ethiopia typically do not handle cross-border migrant remittance outflow transactions. Sending foreign exchange abroad requires documentation of purpose, and migrant remittance outflow transactions are not generally a permissible purpose for obtaining foreign exchange. One MTO's partnership with ICICI Bank in India has enabled it to develop an innovative way for Ethiopian residents to send tuition money to family member recipients who are residing as students in India to finance the costs associated with their studies (described in box 4.2).

Exchange controls were not specifically cited as one of the top barriers to providing remittance transfer services by the RSPs surveyed for the study, with the exception of one MTO. One of the commercial banks and the savings and loan institution consider exchange controls to be a moderate to fairly major barrier, however. To some extent, exchange control regulations governing foreign currency held locally are perceived as a barrier to the provision of remittance-linked financial services in Ethiopia, according to some of the banks, which have cited as too low the $50,000 limit on what any one account holder can hold in a foreign currency account.

AML and combating the financing of terrorism (CFT) requirements, conversely are considered top barriers to doing business in the remittance transfer industry by two of the RSPs participating in the study and were cited as moderate barriers by another three RSPs (two private commercial banks and an MTO).

Remittance Industry Competition in Ethiopia

As discussed earlier, since 2006, MTOs have been forbidden to impose exclusivity contracts when partnering with banks in providing remittance services in Ethiopia, and banks have taken advantage of this regulatory change to forge multiple partnerships with MTOs. Along with the entry of new market entrants in recent years, this has helped to foster improved competitiveness in Ethiopia's remittances transfer industry.

Competition from informal providers remains a major challenge to many RSPs in the formal sector because informal RSPs typically can offer transfer services at lower cost and foreign exchange commissions at a better (black market) rate. Sixty percent of the survey participants cited competition from informal providers as a major obstacle, and another 10 percent consider it a severe obstacle. Two of the 10 RSPs consider it no obstacle at all, however. Although NBE launched an effort to close many informal kiosks that were operating illegally in 2008, many of these informal providers reportedly have since reopened elsewhere.

Remittance Costs

In past years, banks and other RSPs in Ethiopia that provide remittance services have eliminated the service fees previously charged to remittance recipients. The fees and other costs for these transactions are now imposed on the transaction senders only.

Fees payable by the sender opting for formal channels tend to be highest for fast-money (electronic) cash transfer via MTOs. As of October 2009, MTO transfer fees payable by senders in the United States ranged from $7 to $10 for transfer of $200 by the three niche MTOs participating in this study (each of which had a physical presence in at least one U.S. city as well).[8] The MTOs impose various fee structures on senders of remittances from overseas to recipients in Ethiopia. For example, one of the MTOs participating in this study charges a flat fee that decreases in proportion to the amount sent, once a certain threshold was exceeded, and others charge a fee in direct proportion to the amount sent.

For domestic transfers, fees charged by the banks to senders for domestic transfer of $200 varied from the Ethiopian birr equivalent of $0.18 to $1.82, according to the participating commercial banks. These fees are considerably lower than those of MTOs for domestic transfers, although in the latter case (as with cross-border transfers), the sender is charged a premium for quicker transmission.

Ethiopia's central bank operates a webpage[9] that publicly posts information about MTOs that have partnerships with banks in Ethiopia and the associated fees for remittance transfers by MTOs. It obliges RSPs to reveal the following:

- Terms and tariffs applicable to a remittance service, including their correspondent bank, agent fees, and other services they provide
- The estimated time it will take to get the money to the receiver (RSPs are required to transmit remittances to their customers within 24 hours)
- The exchange rate that the RSPs use to convert the foreign currency to domestic currency and vice versa.

Customer Identification Requirements

Driver's licenses and national passports are the most commonly accepted forms of identification from remittance recipients, accepted by all nine participating RSPs providing this information. Eight of the RSPs accept national identification (ID) cards as well. Less commonly accepted forms of ID are verification of employment or a letter from a local or village authority. A few of the commercial banks and one MTO also accept ID cards issued by local or regional authorities, although one of these banks stated that the only acceptable ID for foreign nationals residing in Ethiopia is a national passport. A wider range of ID forms are apparently accepted by the state-owned commercial bank, savings and loan institution, and MTOs.[10]

Private commercial banks had the most limited range of acceptable ID requirements among the participating RSPs, which could impede the ability of the poorest recipients, particularly those dwelling in rural areas, to collect remittances from them. All participating RSPs providing input on this issue accept a national ID card, however.

Among most of the RSPs, there was no difference in ID requirements for account holders or registered customers versus customers without accounts or nonregistered customers, with one exception: the participating savings and loan institution accepts a savings passbook from account holders as a valid ID.

Conclusions and Policy Implications

The importance of the remittance industry for Ethiopia is worth empha-sizing because it contributes at least as much (or more) foreign exchange as the Ethiopian export sector. Despite an increase in the amount of remittance inflows transferred through formal channels in the past decade, the current low level of financial intermediation and the lack of a modern national payments system currently pose major challenges to RSPs. The top-cited barrier to operating a remittance transfer business—among both bank and nonbank RSPs—was lack of access to clearing and settlement systems. There may be beneficial lessons for Ethiopia in ini-tiatives to modernize its payment and settlements system infrastructure (such as introducing an RTGS system), as other developing countries have done in the past few years.

The development of new technologies and products for the delivery of cross-border remittance inflows, such as mobile money transfers and card-based technologies, could further reduce the cost of remittance transfers and further boost competitiveness among RSPs in Ethiopia's remittances services market. The development of prepaid and debit cards and other remittance-linked financial products could eventually also expand access to financial services by unbanked remittance recipients in rural areas. However, the telecommunications infrastructure remains underdeveloped in Ethiopia, and this is a sector that will require further modernization and development.

New types of partnership agreements are emerging in Ethiopia's RSPs market. These include partnerships involving microfinance institutions (MFIs) and the national post office to better serve the unbanked, particularly in rural areas of the country. Ethiopia's postal service has begun linking with some MTOs to provide money transfer services. Granting certain nonbank RSPs such as MFIs and national post offices access to national clearing and settlement systems could more effectively expand rural access, increase competition, and reduce transmission costs (Ratha and Riedberg 2005). Expediting the process for obtaining a license to operate a money transfer business in Ethiopia, by facilitating entry, also could help boost competitiveness of the formal sector for remittance transfers. The cost of remittance transfers tends to decline, and the quality of available services to rise, as the number of market competitors increases (Orozco 2002; Ratha and Riedberg 2005).

Making information on remittance transfer fees publicly available to both potential senders and receivers enhances market transparency among the market's RSPs and can further increase the remittance inflows sent through formal channels. The public posting and frequent updating of information on remittance transfer fees on the NBE website—and providing this information in the destination countries, such as through Ethiopian embassies and migrant associations—would further enhance market transparency.

Ethiopia's banks and other RSPs have not yet made much concrete progress in using remittance transfers as an entry point for formal financial products, partly because of the relatively underdeveloped state of Ethiopia's financial system. The share of remittances not used for consumption is often invested in tangible assets, such as real estate, which has been offering higher returns than savings deposits and other financial instruments.

Striking the right balance in administering AML/CFT requirements will also be important to ensuring that the RSP industry's formal sector will continue to grow and benefit from the dynamism and new technologies that can accompany the entry of new market participants. Half of the respondents to the RSP survey consider AML/CFT requirements to be moderate to major barriers to doing business in the remittance transfer industry in Ethiopia. It will be important, therefore, to ensure that overly onerous AML/CFT requirements do not make it difficult for legitimately registered and operating RSPs to do business—an unintended consequence that could drive more remittances into informal channels if the competitiveness of the formal sector is negatively affected.

Annex 4.1   Banks and MTOs Interviewed for the Study of the Ethiopian Remittance Services Industry

Table 4.A1   Ethiopian RSPs Interviewed

RSP name	RSP type
Commercial Bank of Ethiopia	State-owned bank
Construction and Business Bank	Private commercial bank
Bank of Abyssinia S.C.	Private commercial bank
United Bank	Private commercial bank
Wegagen Bank S.C.	Private commercial bank
Dashen Bank S.C.	Private commercial bank
NIB Iinternational Bank S.C.	Private commercial bank
Dahabshiil	Money transfer operator
Amal Express Money Transfer	Money transfer operator
Birritu Express	Money transfer operator

Notes

1. The National Bank of Ethiopia provided this information in response to a mid-2008 survey of central banks conducted by the World Bank (Irving, Mohapatra, and Ratha 2010).

2. These data are sourced from the National Bank of Ethiopia's responses to a survey of central banks conducted in 2008 by the World Bank's Migration & Remittances team (Irving, Mohapatra, and Ratha 2010).

3. Money can be held locally in foreign currency accounts, however, up to a maximum amount of $50,000.

4. The National Bank of Ethiopia reportedly closed down several informal providers in 2008, but other informal providers seem to be active now.

5. DECSI website, www.decsi.com.et; ACSI website, http://www.acsi.org.et/. One of the commercial banks participating in the study indicated that it has begun working with microfinance institutions in extending microloans, but it does not link (at least not yet) this part of its product and service line with its remittance transfer services.

6. Information on directives available at http://www.NBE.gov.et. See Directive FXD/30/2006, "Provisions of International Remittance Service," accessed June 10, 2008.

7. Some local commercial banks already offer telebanking services, which give Ethiopians living abroad who maintain an account with the bank a personal identification number (PIN), which they can use to contact the bank by telephone and pay money directly to people in Ethiopia.

8. Birritu Express currently charges senders in the United States a fee of $7 for electronic transfer of amounts up to $300 to a recipient in Ethiopia—an amount that increases to $8 for transfer of $301–$500 and $13 for amounts of $501–$800. Dahabshiil charges 5 percent on transaction amounts up to $1,000 from the United States (or $10 for sending $200).

9. See http://www.nbe.gov.et. However, the information in the central bank's website appears to be out of date.

10. The state-owned commercial bank accepts a Kebele ID card, pension card, student ID, and signature verification as acceptable forms of ID for receiving remittances.

References

Alemayehu, Geda. 2008. "The Structure and Performance of Ethiopia's Financial Sector in the Pre and Post Reform Period: With Special Focus on Banking." In *Domestic Resource Mobilization and Financial Development*, ed. George Mavrotas, 163–202. Basingstoke, U.K.: Palgrave Macmillan.

Aredo, Dejene. 2005. "Migrant Remittances, Shocks and Poverty in Urban Ethiopia: An Analysis of Micro-Level Panel Data." Addis Ababa University, Addis Ababa, Ethiopia.

Elbadawi, Ibrahim A., and Roberto Rocha. 1992. "Determinants of Expatriate Workers' Remittances in North Africa and Europe." Working Paper WPS 1038, World Bank, Washington, DC.

El-Sakka, Mohammed I.T., and Robert McNabb. 1999. "The Macroeconomic Determinants of Emigrant Remittances." *World Development* 27 (8): 1493–502.

Ezra, Markos. 2001. "Ecological Degradation, Rural Poverty, and Migration in Ethiopia: A Contextual Analysis." Policy Research Division, Population Council Working Paper 149, Population Council, New York, NY.

Gebre, Ynitso D. 2001. "Population Displacement and Food Insecurity in Ethiopia: Resettlement, Settlers and Hosts." University of Florida, Ph.D. dissertation.

IMF (International Monetary Fund). 1993. *Balance of Payments Manual.* 5th ed. Washington, DC: IMF.

Irving, Jacqueline, Sanket Mohapatra, and Dilip Ratha. 2010. *Migrant Remittance Flows: Findings from a Global Survey of Central Banks.* Working Paper 102, World Bank, Washington, DC.

Kiyota, Kozo, Barbara Peitsch, and Robert M. Stern. 2007. "The Case for Financial Sector Liberalization in Ethiopia." Working Paper 565, Research Seminar in International Economics, University of Michigan.

Mberu, Blessing U. 2006. "Internal Migration and Household Living Conditions in Ethiopia." *Journal of Demographic Research* 14 (21): 509–40.

Nega, B., K. Tadesse, S. Nuru, and Z. Mamma. 2004. "Using Resources from Migrants for Development in Ethiopia." Ethiopean Economic Association/ Ethiopean Economic Policy Research Institute. Report prepared for the International Organization for Migration Addis Ababa.

NBE (National Bank of Ethiopia). 2010. "Quarterly Bulletin." Vol. 25, Quarter 3, Addis Ababa, Ethiopia (available at http://www.nbe.gov.et/publications/ quarterlybulletin.htm).

Orozco, Manuel. 2002. *Attracting Remittances: Market, Money and Reduced Costs.* Report commissioned by the Multilateral Investment Fund of the Inter- American Development Bank, Washington, DC.

Puri, Shivani, and Tineke Ritzema. 2004. "Migrant Worker Remittances, Micro- Finance and Informal Economy: Prospects and Issues." International Labour Organization (ILO) Working Paper 21, ILO, Geneva.

Ratha, Dilip. 2003. "Worker's Remittances: An Important and Stable Source of External Development Finance." In *Global Development Finance: Striving for Stability in Development Finance,* 157–75. Washington, DC: World Bank. http://siteresources.worldbank.org/INTRGDF/Resources/GDF2003- Chapter7.pdf.

Ratha, Dilip, and Jan Reidberg. 2005. "On Reducing Remittance Costs." Unpublished manuscript, World Bank, Washington DC.

Ratha, Dilip, Sanket Mohapatra, and Ani Silwal. 2010. "Outlook for Remittance Flows 2010–11: Remittance Flows to Developing Countries Remained Resilient in 2009, Expected to Recover in 2010–11." Migration and Development Brief 12, World Bank, Washington, DC. http://www.worldbank .org/prospects/migrationandremittances.

Wimaladharma Jan, Douglas Pearce, and David Stanton. 2004. "Remittances: The New Development Finance?" *Small Enterprise Development* 15 (1): 12–19.

World Bank. 2006. *Global Economic Prospects: Economic Implications of Remittances and Migration.* Washington, DC: World Bank.

———. 2011. *Migration and Remittances Factbook 2011.* Washington, DC: World Bank.

CHAPTER 5

Ghana

Peter Quartey

Migrant remittances have become a stable source of income for most developing countries, proving to be more stable flow than official development assistance (ODA) and other private capital flows (Maimbo 2003; Sander 2003). Global remittance flows currently exceed $420 billion, about $317 billion of which goes to developing countries—more than three times the ODA these countries now receive and more than 10 times the $2.98 billion in remittances they received in 1975 (World Bank 2009).

Studies analyzing the impact of remittances show that these flows are beneficial at all levels—individual, household, community, and national. This trend is no different in Ghana, where migrant remittances increased from about $449 million in 1999 to $1.8 billion in 2008, far exceeding ODA (Bank of Ghana 2008). The World Bank figures on migration and remittances show a smaller increase in remittances to Ghana, from $31 million in 1999 to $128 million in 2008 (World Bank 2009).[1]

Remittance and Migration Trends

The rapid growth in migrant remittance volumes and the proliferation of money transfer institutions (both formal and informal) have boosted the contribution of remittances to the development and growth of the Ghanaian economy. They have helped many households get through income disruptions and have financed education, real estate, and small businesses. Partially offsetting these positive contributions, however, is the exodus of skilled workers from Ghana to developed countries such as the United Kingdom and the United States—a migration with a major impact on the country's economic and social sectors.

A large portion of remittances to Ghana are transferred through informal channels, and this method reduces the potential contribution of remittances to development—through financial sector deepening, credit multiplier effects, savings, and investment. Remittance flows outside the formal financial sector also raise issues of money laundering and other financial crimes.

Apart from cash transfers through the formal financial system, the fourth Ghana Living Standards Survey (GLSS 4), conducted in 1999, estimated that cash remittances accounted for 20 percent of total private inward remittances (Quartey 2006). Therefore, it is reasonable to conclude that a considerable amount of remittances are sent through informal means such as home associations and friends or illegally through nonbank financial intermediaries. According to at least one survey, as figure 5.1 shows, an estimated 64 percent of remittance inflows may be sent through a friend, relative, or other intermediary of the sender.

Remittances have an impact on the Ghanaian economy through investment in housing, which has spinoff effects on a large number of businesses (Mazzucato, van den Boom, and Nsowah-Nuamah 2004). The GLSS 3 and 4 also reported that remittances significantly improved household welfare.[2] The bulk of remittances, however, are reserved for private consumption and recurrent expenditures, including living expenses, school fees, hospital bills, weddings and other social activities, funerals, repayment of debt, and the costs of migrating abroad.

According to the figures in table 5.1, an estimated 17–25 percent of remittances are used for small businesses, housing development, and other uses (Black, King, and Tiemoko 2003; Asiedu 2005; Quartey 2006).[3] Thus, migrant remittances enhance the growth of the private sector through their impact on the financing of small- and medium-scale enterprises.

The analysis in this chapter is based also on a 2008 survey of remittance service providers (RSPs) in Ghana for the policy-oriented research project on Migration, Remittances and Development, undertaken jointly by the World Bank and the African Development Bank (AfDB). The findings are expected to provide a better understanding of the RSP market and to help national policy makers in Sub-Saharan Africa to enhance the RSPs' impact on development.

Figure 5.1   Remittance Transmission Channels in Ghana
% respondents selecting each option as primary choice

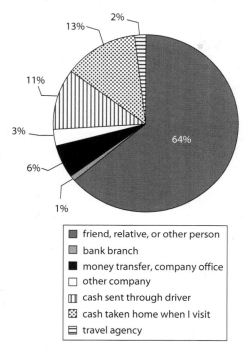

- ▨ friend, relative, or other person
- ▧ bank branch
- ■ money transfer, company office
- ☐ other company
- ▥ cash sent through driver
- ▨ cash taken home when I visit
- ▤ travel agency

Source: Survey of remittance senders (Orozco and others 2005).

Table 5.1   Uses of Migrant Remittances in Ghana

Uses	Respondents	Share of all uses (%)
Living expenses	79	47.59
School fees	45	27.11
Working capital	6	3.61
Investment for sender	22	13.25
Funeral expenses	2	1.20
Social activities	5	3.01
Other	7	4.22
Total	**166**	**100**

Source: Quartey 2006.

Destinations of Migrants

The changing trends in technology and the interdependency among regions of the world have resulted in the migration of both professionals and nonprofessionals either to other places in their home countries or to other parts of the world. The migrants' reasons vary from a need to practice their trade to a desire for particular training or education. Other reasons such as tourism and national missions cause people to migrate to other countries. While away from home, migrants maintain their family and business ties as well as the flow of communication, which encourages them to send money home for consumption or investment.

Ghana has a long history of migration dating back to antiquity, and the internal movement of people from one town to another has been an integral part of the culture and economy. There has also been a long history of migration from Ghana to the West African subregion and the rest of the continent. This trend changed with time, however, and migrant destinations eventually expanded to include Europe, North America, the Middle East, and Asia, as figure 5.2 illustrates. Migration to the West African subregion, especially to Côte d'Ivoire and Nigeria, has continued. Migrants were initially skilled workers and professionals, but in the early 1980s, many unskilled workers also migrated (Anarfi and others 2003).

Complete, reliable migration data about the numbers of Ghanaian emigrants are difficult to obtain. Institutions in Ghana have not made such data consistently available, and various estimates may have been based

Figure 5.2   Destinations of Ghanaian Emigrants

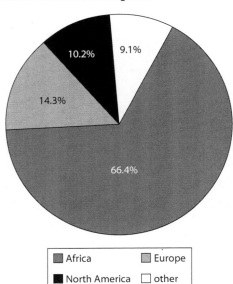

on differing definitions, assumptions, and time periods. The varying estimates have included the following:

- In 2000, an estimated total of 906,698 Ghanaians (4.56 percent of the country's population) lived outside Ghana (World Bank 2006).[4]
- In 2006, an estimated 189,461 Ghanaians resided in the 33 Organisation for Economic Co-operation and Development member countries, representing less than 1 percent of the estimated total population of 22.1 million (EU 2006).[5]
- According to data from the various country embassies in Ghana, an estimated 461,549 Ghanaians live in Europe and North America, and 1 million more Ghanaians live in other African countries. On this basis, Twum-Baah (2005) concluded that approximately 1.5 million Ghanaians live outside the country—not 3 million, as some publications reported. However, this estimate excludes Ghanaians in the Gulf States and Asia.
- Both the Ghana Statistical Service and the Ghana Immigration Service lack data about Ghanaians living abroad. Recent data from the Ministry of Foreign Affairs indicate that 107,487 Ghanaians were registered with Ghana missions in 33 countries, but the ministry estimates that this number exceeds half a million.[6]

Internal Migration

Some authors have described Ghanaians as migratory (Caldwell 1969). Indeed, internal and cross-border migration has long been a significant livelihood strategy for Ghanaians (Kabki 2007). From all indications, internal migration began before independence (in 1957) and has continued ever since. The trend is notably a rural-to-urban shift, and internal migrants represented 13 percent and 17 percent of the total population in 1960 and 1970, respectively. As of 2000, 27.4 percent of Ghana's 18.9 million people lived outside their places of birth. Intra- and interregional migrants were 9.9 percent and 17.5 percent of the total population, respectively.[7]

North-south migration has been prevalent in the country, in part because of the different ecological zones. In view of the heavy dependence on small-scale agriculture, usually for subsistence, the long dry season constitutes a lean farming season and provides an opportunity for many people in the north to move southward to work instead of remaining idle in their localities. They return at the beginning of the rainy season to resume their farming. This type of migration is temporal, cyclical, and dominated by males.

The types of internal migration observed in Ghana include rural-to-urban, intrarural, urban-to-rural, and intraurban.[8] The volume and intensity of these movements keep changing and are influenced by the social and economic factors that shape migrants' aspirations. The GLSS 4 results showed that rural areas receive more than 60 percent of internal migrants; intrarural migration, 32 percent; urban-to-rural migration, 35 percent; interurban migration, 23 percent; and rural-to-urban, 10 percent.[9]

Internal migrants maintain links with their hometowns. Even when they are away, they contribute to the development of their indigenous communities through the payment of levies and transfers. Caldwell (1969) observed that migration may lead to a decline in family ties, but it rarely removes migrants from their communities, and few Ghanaians would desire that. These hometown connections are fostered through visits during funerals, festivals, and marriage ceremonies. There is a view that if one migrates and does not return, then he or she is "aimless." Thus, the purpose of migration is to acquire wealth and experience to benefit the hometown.

Remittance Sources

Most of the remittances to Ghana are sent by Ghanaian migrants living outside the African continent, primarily from the United States and Canada (Quartey and Blankson 2004). In 2004, remittances received through money transfer institutions amounted to almost $970 million—$665.7 million of which came from those two countries. The United Kingdom is the third-largest source, with $163.3 million; followed by the European Union, with $96.8 million; and other countries, which accounted for $25.1 million. The United Kingdom and European Union account for 18 percent and 14.6 percent of remittances to Ghana, respectively.

The Economic Community of West African States (ECOWAS) and the rest of Africa accounted for $11.7 million and $7.5 million, respectively (Bank of Ghana 2004). Data from the central bank show that the United States and Canada accounted for a combined 76 percent in 2005, 63 percent in 2006, and 59 percent in 2007.[10] The amount of money sent from the United States and Canada has been decreasing over the three-year period, while figures from other regions are on the rise. Remittances from the United States may have declined because of stricter laws regarding the transfer of money.

Characteristics of the Remittance Industry

For the purpose of the 2008 RSP survey in Ghana,[11] remittances were broadly defined as "person-to-person" transfers of resources, whether

Figure 5.3   Sources of Remittance Inflows to Ghana through Banks, 2007
% of remittance inflows

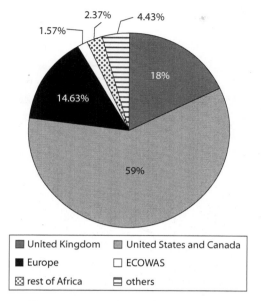

Source: Bank of Ghana Annual Report 2008.
Note: The data apply only to remittances sent through the banking sector and exclude noncash remittances and remittances sent through informal means. ECOWAS = Economic Community of West African States.

cross-border or within the country. The survey therefore captured only transfers sent by migrants and received by relatives. It included RSPs both in the formal sector (including commercial banks, money transfer operators [MTOs] and in the Ghanian postal service [Ghana Post]) and the informal sector (nonfinancial institutions such as retail shops and travel agencies).

Methodological Issues

The RSP survey questionnaire and a cover letter were sent to the head offices of all the formal financial institutions (banks and nonbank financial institutions), all of which are based in the capital city, Accra.[12]

Informal RSPs (in view of the illegal nature of their business) were suspicious of interviewers when initially contacted.[13] To get responses from this sector, a discussion guide was developed from the original questionnaire. The guide focused on all the key areas of the questionnaire: the regulatory and business environment; remittance costs; access and identification requirements; and remittance volumes, sources, and destinations.

The definition of migrant remittances (as previously stated, person-to-person transfers of resources cross-border or within-country) was a bit problematic because it was difficult for almost all the RSPs to disaggregate their migrant remittances from certain other capital flows; hence, they provided the bulk volumes. In addition, most of the RSPs lacked specific remittance units or departments where data could be compiled and easily accessed. The gathering of data and other information from RSPs in Ghana often required contacting various departments separately because the RSPs lacked internal coordination on remittances, and this contributed to delays in completing the questionnaire.

Although the introduction of universal banking in Ghana has enabled all the banks to engage in remittance services, the traditional commercial banks have the advantage of extensive branch networks and, therefore, more coverage. At the time of the survey, 22 banks and 4 nonbank financial institutions were authorized to process inward remittances. The nonbank financial institutions include MTOs and Ghana Post. Some of these institutions are also authorized to process outward remittances. Various informal businesses also offer remittance services. Nine banking institutions and two nonbank financial institutions responded to the questionnaire and are included in the survey—a response rate of about 50 percent.

Types and Coverage of Remittance Firms

Private commercial banks made up 73 percent of the responding RSPs. A state-owned bank, Ghana Post, and an MTO each accounted for about 9 percent of the responding RSPs, as figure 5.4 depicts.

All of the firms engage in international remittances, and about 20 percent also exchange currencies for RSPs and for domestic and international messaging services. About 36 percent of the firms receive domestic remittances, provide domestic settlement services, and send international remittances. Slightly fewer than 30 percent of the firms send domestic remittances and provide cross-border settlement services. Currency exchanges are not allowed to operate remittance services, but they do so informally because they have access to large amounts of currency and can easily provide the services to their known clients.

Partnerships and Agreements with Money Transfer Operators

About 82 percent of the RSP firms, comprising mainly private commercial banks and Ghana Post, operate in partnership with MTOs such as Western Union, Vigo Money Transfer, and MoneyGram. However,

Figure 5.4   RSP Types in Ghana
% of RSP firms

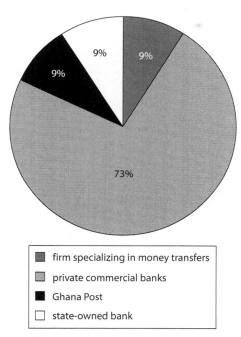

9%
9%
9%
9%
73%

- firm specializing in money transfers
- private commercial banks
- Ghana Post
- state-owned bank

Source: Author's compilation from 2008 RSP survey in Ghana.
Note: Percentages derived from the 11 formal sector RSPs that responded to the survey.

partnerships between MTOs and mobile phone companies or other telecommunications service providers are virtually nonexistent in Ghana.

All the firms indicated that these partnerships are not exclusive and that they were free to engage in other arrangements. Although all of the firms in partnerships have access to the remittance payment infrastructure through the MTO partner (for example, Western Union or Vigo), they do not all have access to the distribution network and currency exchange.

Most of the financial sector RSPs are in major urban areas. The ARB Apex Bank caters to the rural population through the rural banking network and collaborates with some of the nonbank financial institutions such as the MTO Express Funds International, which has a market share of 34 percent. Because Express Funds International has six main branches in the country, its partnership with ARB Apex Bank is important to reach most of the rural population. However, most of the private commercial banks also have branches in the rural areas.

Ghana Post offers remittance services in partnership with Western Union. Its core business enables it to provide wide coverage through about 96 branches in the urban and rural areas.

Firms in partnership with Western Union receive 20 percent of the commission on remittances, although this percentage varies depending on the source country. Firms partnering with MoneyGram receive about 13 percent of the pretax profit plus 3.5 percent of the commission on remittances.

Remittance Instruments

Electronic funds transfer is the most popular instrument for remittance transactions and is used by all the RSP firms. The majority (9) receives commissions through partnership arrangements with MTOs (figure 5.5). Most of the surveyed financial institutions also use account-to-account transfers, bank (floats or loans), and checks.

Few institutions use prepaid debit cards or money orders (figure 5.6). The use of money transfers through mobile phones and prepaid cards for use at designated retailers remains a gray area, and none of the firms reported using those instruments. Even though there is widespread access to mobile phones, people generally use them for calls; banking-by-phone use is limited, possibly because the technology is not trusted and customers need more time to get accustomed to it.

Figure 5.5   Partnership Benefits to RSP Firms

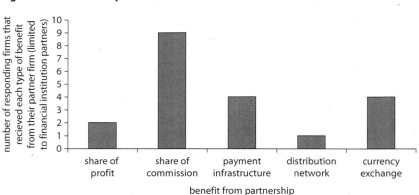

Source: Author's compilation from 2008 RSP survey in Ghana.
Note: "RSP Firms" denotes only formal RSPs.

Figure 5.6   RSP Remittance Instruments

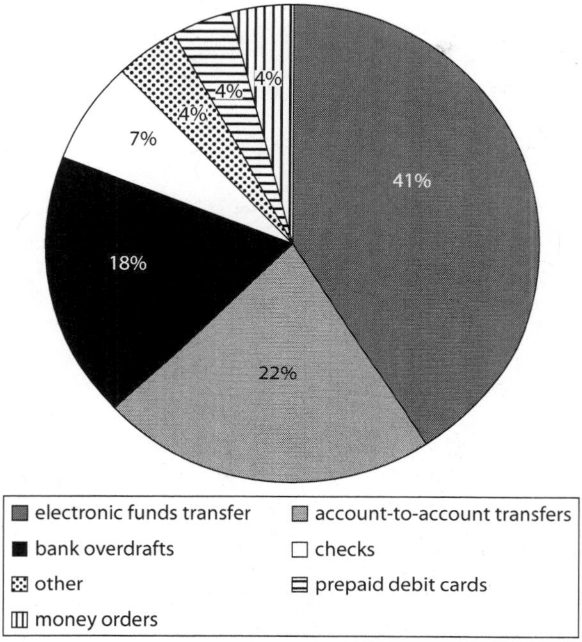

Source: Author's compilation from 2008 RSP survey in Ghana.

Most financial institutions also do not use Internet transfers because Ghana has a low Internet penetration rate. However, completion of the fiber-optic backbone will reduce the cost associated with the Internet, and this model might become more common in the future.

As for the informal RSPs, the case study in box 5.1 illustrates the nature of the informal remittance business, which is illegal in Ghana, and the difficulty of tracking activities in that sector.

Access to Other Financial Services

The banking institutions use remittance transfers as an opportunity to sell formal banking products to customers. The survey revealed that banks offer deposits and savings products to both senders and recipients of remittances. This practice is to be expected because banks usually want more customers, and they believe that convincing customers to

Box 5.1

Informal RSP Case Study: A Shoe Seller at Madina Market, Accra

The RSP survey interviewed two informal RSPs: a shoe seller and a pharmacy operator. The shoe seller, permanently based in Ghana, sells men's shoes and clothes, which he usually imports from Italy with the help of a relative who lives in Italy. He never goes to Italy himself. The relative buys and ships the goods to Ghana, and the shop owner marks up the prices of the goods before selling them. The relative in Italy is more interested in the repayment of the sum invested in buying and shipping the goods than in the profits. To ensure the security of his investment (in terms of repayment and devaluation effects), the migrant (the person staying in Italy) collects money from friends and close relations who want to remit money to Ghana and instructs his partner in Ghana to disburse the amount collected in the local currency, Ghanian cedis (¢).

According to the shop owner, no commission is paid on the transaction. A form of identification is typically required, and the payment is usually made in the retail shop, but it is sometimes sent to the houses of the recipients, who normally reside in Accra and its environs. On average, remittances of up to ¢4,000 ($1=¢1.2) could be received in a month.

The shop owner revealed that he sometimes pays people before a settlement is made to his partner in Italy. He began the remittance business about six years ago and it is growing, but although business is good, he is not ready to venture into full-time money transfer services.

Source: RSP survey 2008.

open a savings or other current account is easier than advising them to obtain a loan or buy insurance products.

Some nonbank financial institutions, in addition to remittance services, also provide deposit and savings products geared toward remittance receivers and senders, including low-end insurance and credit facilities for consumption purposes. Of the banks and other financial institutions surveyed, only the state-owned banks reported using revenue from selling other financial products to subsidize their remittance services.

Express Funds International noted that it helps both senders and recipients of remittances gain access to investment opportunities by providing advice on Treasury bill and mutual fund rates. The company also offers its customers a service package called "MyMorgan Services," which allows a sender to allocate remittance funds to a specific purpose in Ghana—such as purchasing real estate or paying hospital bills or school fees—on behalf of a designated beneficiary and even to invest in financial instruments such as Treasury bills, mutual funds, and certificates of deposit. This product is popular among Ghanaian migrants in the United Kingdom.

The Regulatory and Business Environment

The Ghanian financial institutions reported that the country's current laws and regulations present no major challenges to their business activities, specifically in remittance transmission. Of the surveyed RSPs, 55 percent of the firms perceived these laws as a minor obstacle and 45 percent as no obstacle. Financial sector reforms, described in box 5.2, have made it easier for institutions to engage in remittance services if they meet the regulatory requirements.

Of all the financial institutions surveyed, most of the firms (89 percent)—including the private commercial banks and the state-owned banks—indicated that they pay no fee to conduct cross-border money transfers. Ghana Post, by its articles of incorporation, is permitted to provide money transfer services, but because it is not a bank, it pays a $10,000 annual fee to conduct cross-border money transfers.

Ghana Post noted that, to fulfill anti-money-laundering (AML) requirements, the central bank limits currency exchange holdings and remittance inflows. This may also account for why some banks cited AML laws as a significant obstacle to their remittance service businesses. By central bank directive, no cash exceeding $10,000 can be brought into the country. More than 90 percent of the RSP firms confirmed that they must also file currency transaction reports with the central bank and that the reports are required for any amount. More than 90 percent of the firms indicated that they report suspicious activities to the central bank as the regulatory authority.

Entry Barriers

The primary regulatory burden for any RSP firm is the central bank's ¢7 million minimum capital requirement. Most of the survey respondents consider access to financial infrastructure, a distribution network, and capital as barriers to starting a remittance service business. Because these requirements are all within the service provider's domain, any provider that can satisfy them would not find obtaining a license to be difficult. The RSP survey respondents ranked AML laws, licensing regulations, and

Box 5.2

The Financial Sector in Ghana

Ghana has been pursuing financial sector reforms to enhance financial development since 1983. To facilitate the reform process, the country passed laws such as the P.N.D.C. Law 225 in 1989 and later the Banking Act (Act 673) in 2004. The reform also liberalized controls on interest rates and bank credit. As part of the process of liberalization, the Bank of Ghana introduced "universal banking" in the first quarter of 2003. Universal banking allows banks to undertake commercial, development, investment, or merchant banking without the need for separate licenses. The enactment of these laws added depth and diversity to the financial system (Gockel 2003).

To further deepen the financial system, the country enacted the Foreign Exchange Act (Act 723) in December 2006. This Act, which replaced the Exchange Control Act of 1961, partially liberalized the capital account. Among its provisions, it allowed for the repatriation of funds from Ghana without prior central bank approval and allowed nonresidents and foreigners to open currency exchange accounts in Ghana. The Act also regulates currency exchange businesses and provides for related matters.

To reduce overdependence on cash-based transactions, the Bank of Ghana also is undertaking reforms in the legal, institutional, and infrastructural framework of the payments system to make the Ghanaian financial system modern and competitive. As part of this process, the bank has implemented the real-time gross settlement (RTGS) system for high-value payments. The RTGS has helped create an environment for safe, sound, secure, and timely payments. It has also reduced systemic payment and settlement risks because payment orders are settled almost instantaneously.

To complement the RGTS, the Bank of Ghana introduced a paper-based credit clearing system to facilitate the settlement of low-value payments. The bank plans to migrate these settlements to an electronic platform in the near future. The bank also established a National Switch (E-Zwich) payment platform and ATM network to establish a common platform for all payment transactions within the country. This common platform would result in the integration of all existing bank switches and allow banks without switches (such as ARB Apex Bank) to join the common switch at low cost. It would also enable the interoperability of all ATMs and the settlement of payment transactions by customers of different banks at points of sale. The introduction of these technological advancements in the financial system would make remittance transfers much more flexible and encourage the use of technology by senders and recipients.

Source: Bank of Ghana 2008.

capital requirements as the most significant barriers to entering the remittance business, as shown in table 5.2.

Most of the survey respondents did not perceive exchange control requirements to be a significant barrier, but the few who did ranked it as a major obstacle. In addition, firms are not typically required to charge taxes on remittance services, rendering tax policy a relatively low entry barrier as well.

Competitive Factors

Most survey respondents perceived competition from informal RSPs to be a significant (major, moderate, or minor) obstacle to their business activities, as figure 5.7 shows. Eleven percent considered informal RSPs to be "no obstacle." Although half of the respondents reported that access to financing is an obstacle in doing business, it is unclear whether that is why informal RSPs pose such a challenge. On the contrary, when asked to identify their major competitors, most of the financial institutions named banks and nonbank financial institutions.

Remittance Fees and Identification Requirements

As noted above, Ghana's laws and regulations governing remittance services are progressive and, in general, do not present significant barriers to the RSPs' business operations. However, formal sector remittance fees and identification requirements may create a preference among migrants for informal RSPs.

Informal RSPs typically know their clients personally and are thus more likely to waive identification requirements. Exchange rate volatility

Table 5.2   RSP Perceptions of Laws and Regulations as Entry Barriers
number of RSP firms rating each regulation type as a barrier

	High barriers			Low barriers	
Rating	Licensing requirements	Capital requirement	AML laws	Clearing and settlement systems	Tax policy
1	1	0	3	0	0
2	0	3	1	0	0
3	3	0	0	0	0
4	0	1	1	1	1
5	1	1	0	2	2

Source: Author's compilation from 2008 RSP survey in Ghana.
Note: In the survey ratings, 1 = high barrier, 5 = low barrier.

Figure 5.7   Perceptions of Competition from Informal RSPs

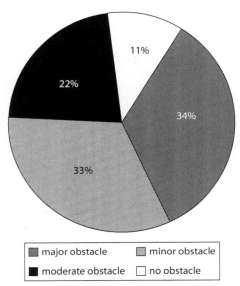

Source: Author's compilation from 2008 RSP survey in Ghana.
Note: RSP firms were asked, "Is competition from informal remittance service providers an obstacle for your firm when doing business?"

also might increase customers' preference for informal channels. Because remittances that pass through formal channels are always paid to the recipients in the local currency (Ghanian cedis), some recipients believe they lose money in the conversion because the MTOs use lower exchange rates than the prevailing market rate. The informal channels sometimes pay their clients in dollars because the money is sometimes sent through someone traveling to the country.

Remittance service fees. The RSP survey indicated that remittance fees are normally paid by the senders if funds are received in Ghanian cedis. Money transfer charges, however, depend on the RSP. Most of the surveyed providers refused to disclose their transfer fees for strategic reasons, but according to a Bank of Ghana study in 2004, transfers through smaller (national) companies cost between $1.50 and $3.00 for every $100.00 sent. The study also revealed that sending fees are 1.5–2.5 percent of the amount sent if transmitted through a commercial bank and 2.0–3.5 percent of the amount sent through nonbank operators such as Western Union. However, Express Funds International notes that for every $200 sent from the United Kingdom or the United States, the average fees are 4 percent and 5–6 percent, respectively.

Within the informal sector, remittance service fees are difficult to quantify and depend on the agreement between the sender and the agent bringing the money into the country. There are typically no commission charges.

Identification requirements. The financial institutions offering remittance services always require identification documents—a requirement that prevents poor households from using the formal sector. People with little means can afford neither the time nor expense to obtain a passport or a drivers' license. However, the Electoral Commission of Ghana opened the voters' register for the December 2008 elections, and the turnout was high. Henceforth, most recipients will be able to use the voter's identification card that was issued as a form of identification when receiving a transfer.

Conclusions and Recommendations

The introduction of universal banking, as a result of the financial sector reforms in Ghana, has favored banks in the remittance business. According to the 2008 RSP survey, remittance flows through the banks increased from 2005 through 2007, with the banks increasing their collective market share of the private remittance business. Remittances through nonbank financial institutions decreased from 2005 through 2007, perhaps because people have more confidence in the banks or because the banks have added rural branches. In addition, many of the nonbank financial institutions have relatively few branches and thus have to partner with the banks to transfer money to customers in the rural areas.

The Remittance Instrument Outlook

In general, the remittance industry uses traditional instruments such as electronic funds transfers, account-to-account transfers, and checks. Money orders and prepaid debit cards are used but are not popular among the firms. The use of mobile phones for money transfers has not been introduced on any significant scale in Ghana even though mobile phone penetration is relatively high.

Nor are Internet transfers prevalent among most financial institutions, partly because the Internet penetration rate in the country is still low. However, customers may be more inclined to use online instruments when the fiber-optic backbone is completed and costs are reduced. In addition, the Bank of Ghana recently introduced National Switch (E-Zwich) to allow the establishment of a common platform for all payment transactions in the country. This would integrate all bank switches and allow banks without switches to join the common switch at significantly reduced costs. With the introduction of the E-Zwich card, financial institutions are expected to launch a product that will enable remittance recipients to access money transfers through the card.

The Regulatory Outlook

The RSP survey respondents generally believe that the regulatory environment affecting remittance services is effective and that the current laws and regulations present no major challenges to business operations. Recent financial sector reforms have made it easier for institutions to provide remittance services if they meet the regulatory requirements. The formal RSPs' requirement for a reliable form of identification, however, creates business for informal RSPs that do not require such identification because they know their clients on a personal level.

The Remittance Fee Outlook

The survey also revealed that remittance senders usually pay the fees if funds are received in Ghanian cedis, but the transfer charges vary by RSP. The survey could not gather enough specific information about the commissions and charges paid by remittance senders, but a 2004 Bank of Ghana study found the charges to be high. Further study of the senders' transaction costs may provide a clearer picture.

The Remittance Source Outlook

Remittance volumes from the United States and Canada have been decreasing since 2005, while those from other regions of the world are on the rise. U.S. remittances may be declining because of more stringent money transfer laws. That constraint notwithstanding, the increase in remittances from all the other regions presents potentially interesting opportunities for RSPs and policy makers.

Recommendations

RSPs provide valuable services in Ghana, significantly increasing the volume of funds sent by migrants. However, high transfer fees and restrictions on payment to recipients in foreign currencies are challenges to the MTOs and have allowed informal transfer businesses to thrive. It is therefore important that the monetary authorities provide incentives for people to receive transfers in any currency of their choice.

In addition, outward remittances through MTOs such as Western Union are outlawed in Ghana. This prohibition is a major limitation to migrants who invest in Ghana and would like to transfer funds to their destination countries for emergency financial needs. A timely review of this policy will be beneficial, especially considering the effects of the global financial crisis on migrants.

Notes

1. The two sources' widely differing figures have not been reconciled. Whereas the Bank of Ghana bases its estimate on survey data from remittance service providers in Ghana, the World Bank and International Monetary Fund use Balance of Payments estimates.

2. GSS (Ghana Statistical Service) 2000 Population and Housing Census Report. http://www.statsghana.gov.gh/surveys/CENSUS2000/survey0/index.html.

3. The upper end of the range (25 percent) would comprise all uses listed in table 5.1 except for living expenses and school fees.

4. The total is based on United Nations Development Programme 2000 population data.

5. This migration figure excludes an estimated 22,847 Ghanaians living in Germany during the same period, according to the Organisation for Economic Co-operation and Development Continuous Reporting System of Migration.

6. Compilation of data on Ghanaians abroad is ongoing, and the recent data were obtained in September 2008.

7. GSS (Ghana Statistical Service) 2000 Population and Housing Census Report. http://www.statsghana.gov.gh/surveys/CENSUS2000/survey0/index.html.

8. GSS (Ghana Statistical Service) Ghana Living Standards Survey Round 4, 1998–99. http://www.statsghana.gov.gh/surveys/GLSS1998/survey0/index.html.

9. GSS (Ghana Statistical Service) Core Welfare Indicator Questionnaire Report, 2003. http://www.statsghana.gov.gh/surveys/CWIQ2003/survey0/index.html.

10. The data apply only to remittances sent through the banking sector and exclude noncash remittances and remittances sent through informal means.

11. The Ghana survey began on May 28, 2008, and was completed on August 9, 2008. Follow-up surveys were conducted until November 2008 to supplement the information already gathered.

12. Follow-up telephone calls (mostly to the offices of the chief executives and managing directors) were made to ask whether the questionnaire had been received and was being completed. In most cases, the questionnaires were sent to the remittances, treasury, or research and strategic planning departments. Appointments were booked to meet officials charged with completing the questionnaire and to explain the importance of the survey. Because the completion of the questionnaire was not part of the officials' regular duties, at least three phone calls had to be made weekly to remind respondents about the urgency of the questionnaire. In addition to the phone calls, weekly visits were made to the respondents' offices. Another strategy was to use personal contacts at some of the banks to encourage officials to complete the questionnaire. Because of some major gaps in the data gathered from the survey, follow-up questionnaires were sent to most of the surveyed RSPs to fill in the gaps.

13. In Ghana, all informal RSPs are illegal because they are not licensed by the Bank of Ghana to perform remittance services.

References

Anarfi, J., S. Kwankye, O-M Ababio, and R. Tiemoko. 2003. "Migration from and to Ghana: A Background Paper." Working Paper C4, Development Research Centre on Migration, Globalisation and Poverty, University of Sussex, Brighton, England. http://www.migrationdrc.org/publications/working_papers/WP-C4.pdf.

Asiedu, A. 2005. "Some Benefits of Migrants' Return Visits to Ghana." *Population, Space and Place* 11 (1): 1–11. http://www.geog.sussex.ac.uk/transrede/work shop/IWMP7.pdf.

Bank of Ghana. 2004. "Annual Report 2004." Bank of Ghana, Accra.

———. 2008. "Annual Report 2008." Bank of Ghana, Accra.

Black, R., R. King, and R. Tiemoko. 2003. "Migration, Return, and Small Enterprise Development in Ghana: A Route Out of Poverty?" Working Paper 9, Sussex Centre for Migration Research, University of Sussex, Brighton, England. http://www.sussex.ac.uk/migration/documents/mwp9.pdf.

Caldwell, J. C. 1969. *African Rural-Urban Migration: The Movement to Ghana's Towns.* New York: Columbia University Press.

EU (European Union). 2005. The Cotonou Agreement, EU, Brussels.

Gockel, A. F. 2003. "Managing the Constraints to Development Finance: Is Universal Banking the Solution?" Discussant's comments at the 4th ISSER (Institute of Statistical, Social and Economic Research)-Merchant Bank Annual Economic Lectures, Accra, November 24.

Kabki, M. 2007. "Transnational Networks and Economic Principles in Rural Communities of Origin of Ghanaian Migrants in the Netherlands." Vrije Universiteit, Amsterdam.

Maimbo, S. 2003. "The Money Exchange Dealers of Kabul: A Study of the Hawala System in Afghanistan." Working Paper 13, World Bank, Washington, DC.

Mazzucato, V., B. van den Boom, and N. N. N. Nsowah-Nuamah. 2004. "The Impact of International Remittances on Local Living Standards: Evidence for Households and Rural Communities in Ghana." Paper presented at the "Conference on Migration and Development in Ghana," Accra, September 14–16.

Orozco, M., M. Bump, R. Fedewa, and K. Sienkiewicz. 2005. "Diasporas, Development and Transnational Integration: Ghanaians in U.S., U.K. and Germany." Report commissioned by Citizen International through the U.S. Agency for International Development, Institute for the Study of International Migration and Inter-American Dialogue, Washington, DC. http://www.thedialogue.org/PublicationFiles/Ghanaian%20transnationalism.pdf.

Quartey, P. 2006. "The Impact of Migrant Remittances on Household Welfare in Ghana." AERC Research Paper 158, African Economic Consortium, Nairobi.

Quartey, P., and T. Blankson. 2004. "Do Migrant Remittances Reduce the Impact of Macro-Volatility on Poor Households in Ghana?" Final report to the Global Development Network, International Monetary Fund, Washington, DC. http://cloud2.gdnet.org/cms.php?id=research_paper_abstract&research_paper_id=9035.

Sander, C. 2003. "Capturing a Market Share? Migrant Remittance Transfers & Commercialisation of Microfinance in Africa." Paper prepared for "Current Issues in Microfinance" conference, Johannesburg, August 12–14. http://www.dai.com/pdf/Capturing_a_Market_Share.pdf.

Twum-Baah, K. 2005. "Volume and Characteristics of International Ghanaian Migration." In *At Home in the World? International Migration and Development in Contemporary Ghana and West Africa*, ed. T. Manuh, 55–77. Accra: Sub-Saharan Publishers.

World Bank. 2006. *Global Economic Prospects*. Washington, DC: World Bank.

———. 2008. *Migration and Remittances Factbook*. Washington, DC: World Bank.

CHAPTER 6

Kenya

Rose W. Ngugi

Cross-border remittance inflows are an increasingly significant source of development finance in Kenya. In 2009, recorded remittance inflows equaled 5 percent of gross domestic product (GDP)—more than the private sector raised in capital markets for the corresponding period (World Bank 2011).

Numerous studies have shown a correlation between remittances and poverty reduction (for example, Gupta, Pattillo, and Wagh 2007; Orozco and Fedewa 2006; Lucas 2004; Adams and Page 2003). Remittance inflows also correlate positively to human capital formation (Hanson and Woodruff 2003; Edwards and Ureta 2003). Because remittances enable households to access formal financial services, including savings products and credit facilities, they promote financial deepening (Gupta, Pattillo, and Wagh 2007). However, remittances also can distort the functions of the formal capital and foreign exchange markets (Chimhowu, Piesse, and Pinder 2003).

One analysis of the remittance service provider (RSP) market in Kenya found service gaps, inefficiencies, and unmet demand, especially among low-income groups and micro- and small-business community members (Kabbucho, Sander, and Mukwana 2003). Similarly, most rural residents were being served by the informal sector. Few of them enjoyed formal banking services—a trend that worsened following the rationalization of bank branches in the mid-1990s, when many banks closed their rural branches (FinScope Kenya 2007).

However, a follow-up study (FinScope Kenya 2007) found that the mobile-phone money transfer service M-PESA—which entered the domestic remittance market in 2007—had become the most popular mode of money transfer in the domestic market. This branchless banking service was developed for mobile telecom company Vodafone and is now the largest mobile-phone money transfer operator in Africa. M-PESA offers domestic money transfer services in Kenya and is currently working with Western Union to kick off cross-border money transfer services. In 2009, mobile telecommunications provider Zain also entered the market by offering mobile-phone money transfer services.

This chapter examines the money transfer services in Kenya, covering the type and scope of services offered; the networking arrangements; the competitive factors affecting the RSPs; and the opportunities to further improve remittance services. The chapter also explores the possibility of enhancing financial service access in the course of providing remittance services. Although remittances could be classified as person-to-person or business-to-business transactions, this analysis does not do so because the RSPs report remittances as total money transfers. The RSPs survey upon which this study is based was carried out in 2008; since then, developments have included the expansion of M-PESA services and the entry of Zain.

Remittance and Migration Trends

The major findings from this study highlight the following remittance industry trends:

- *Data collection.* Remittance data collection in Kenya is not a well-developed process. Only recently (in 2006) were banks requested by the central bank to collect remittance-flow data.
- *RSP types.* A diverse range of formal and informal providers offer remittance services. Among the new entrants, M-PESA and Zain are revolutionizing the domestic and international money transfer markets with popular mobile-phone money transfer services.
- *Partnerships.* RSP networks and partnerships are based on complementary functions. Except for the community-based and transport-company RSPs, all providers have links to the banking sector. More recently (since 2008), however, banks have become more integrated with M-PESA and Zain by extending their financial services.

- *Remittance costs.* Directmoney transfer costs vary but are significantly high across the board. To send US$200, providers charged 8 to 18 percent for international transfers and 0.4 to 12.5 percent for domestic transfers.
- *Access to financial services.* High costs and unavailability constrain many remittance clients' access to other financial services. For example, account maintenance is too expensive to expand demand for other services. However, since 2008, M-PESA users have been able to enjoy more banking services, including bank account management, by mobile phone. Most RSPs use brochures to give remittance customers information about their other services.
- *RSP regulation.* Formal RSPs are regulated. The central bank defines the limits on single transactions for banks and foreign exchange bureaus and also indicates the threshold amounts for reporting to the central bank. The formal RSPs must also report suspicious situations, such as attempts to split large transfers to stay within the threshold. The central bank also asks banks and foreign exchange bureaus to require identification of the senders and recipients.

Remittance Volumes

Kenya receives, on average, 60 percent of remittances to East Africa and an average of 10 percent of all remittances to the Sub-Saharan region. In 2009, inward remittances to Kenya stood at US$1.7 billion, representing 5.4 percent of GDP (World Bank 2011).[1]

Table 6.1 reports remittance data from the Central Bank of Kenya. Because the central bank captures only inward remittances transmitted through the banking institutions, the level of reported remittances seems on average lower—an average of 40 percent of the total remittances reported by the World Bank in the period between 2004 and 2009. However, the two data sets show similar increasing trends in remittance inflows.

Table 6.1   Remittance Inflows to Kenya

	2004	2005	2006	2007	2008	2009
Volume (US$, millions)	338.3	382.2	407.6	573.6	611.2	609.2
Remittance source, by region (%)						
North America	61	59	57	50	50	52
Europe	26	27	28	34	32	26
Other	12	14	15	15	18	22

Source: Central Bank of Kenya.
Note: Figures are estimated at 40 percent of total international remittance inflows to Kenya reported by World Bank.

Destinations of Migrants

As of 2005, the number of emigrants from Kenya stood at 427,324, or 1.2 percent of Kenya's population (Ratha and Xu 2008). Their primary destinations include (in descending order) the United Kingdom (33.7 percent), Tanzania (25.6 percent), the United States (11.3 percent), Uganda (7.7 percent), Canada (5.2 percent), Germany (1.7 percent), and Australia (1.6 percent).

Migration to the United Kingdom has a historical link, given that Kenya is a former British colony. Kenyan migrants to Tanzania and Uganda are taking advantage of the opportunities in those two neighboring economies. Economic links between Kenya and these other East African Community[2] members are extensive; for example, about 25 percent of foreign direct investment in Tanzania and Uganda originates in Kenya.

Internal migration is driven largely by the need for business or employment opportunities, resources such as land, or a peaceful environment during times of insecurity. In Kenya, 19 percent of domestic migrants seek employment opportunities, 9.4 percent seek business ventures, and 7 percent seek land (KIHBS 2005).

Migrants seeking work have migrated to industrial or urban areas such as Nairobi, Mombasa, and Nakuru. The Rift Valley region in Kenya is a major destination in the search for land. Migrants who find formal sector employment elsewhere in the country often use the formal sector RSPs such as banks and nonbank financial institutions to send money to their families, mainly for upkeep and settlement of school tuition. Migrants who find work in the informal sector are more likely to send money home via taxi and bus companies, or with traveling relatives and friends, or to carry it themselves when they return home to visit their families.

Characteristics of the Remittance Industry

This research involved collecting primary and secondary data (where possible) from providers of remittances and also conducting specific case studies for M-PESA, the transport industry, and the community-based Hawala. The sample was selected to represent all the segments of the market, but without a clear picture of the population, especially of the informal sector, the sample was selected purposively. The sample included, banks, foreign currency exchanges, savings and credit cooperative organizations (SACCOs), microfinance institutions (MFIs), the Kenya Post Office Savings Bank (Postbank), the Postal Corporation of

Kenya (Posta Kenya), transport services, mobile-telephone money transfer providers, and community-based service providers.

The study targeted only the service providers, not users. Table 6.2 shows the survey sample distribution. Three case studies also were conducted to obtain more, albeit anecdotal, insight into the remittance mechanisms and channels used by the semi-informal and informal sector RSPs.

RSP Types and Coverage

This section examines RSPs' structures and community presence. Borrowing from Orozco and Fedewa (2006), the analysis focuses on institutional ability to provide remittance transfers, offer low-cost remittance services, and complement transfer services with other financial services. In general, RSPs can be categorized into three primary groups, according to transmission method:

- *Financial institutions* that provide remittance transmission services include the banks, currency exchanges, Postbank, MFIs, and SACCOs. Except for Postbank, these financial institutions partner with banks to facilitate transmissions.
- *Money transfer operators* (MTOs) include both local and international operators. In Kenya, the mobile-phone money transfer operator M-PESA operates as a local MTO. The international MTOs include Western Union and MoneyGram. MTOs have elaborate transmission systems that enable them reach out widely, but they do not offer other financial services. They offer their services in collaboration with banks and currency exchanges.

Table 6.2   Kenyan RSP Survey Sample Distribution

RSP, by type	Identified RSPs	Responding RSPs
Banks	26	12
Currency exchanges	10	4
MFIs	6	3
SACCOs	12	8
Posta	1	1
Postbank	1	1
Mobile-phone money transfer providers	3	3
Transport services	15	6
Somali community services	2	1
Total	**76**	**39**

Source: RSP Survey data.
Note: RSP = remittance service provider. MFI = microfinance institution. SACCO = savings and credit cooperative organization. Posta = Postal Corporation of Kenya. Postbank = Kenya Post Office Savings Bank.

- *Community-based systems* are based on social networks that generally use physical money transfers or systems that "float" funds without an elaborate transmission procedures (as some transport companies offer). They offer both domestic and international transfer services but tend not to offer other financial services. Examples of community-based systems include friends, relatives, village members, transport services owned by community members, and traditional Somali community-based systems.

Financial institutions. Although a diverse array of firms provide remittance services, the RSP survey indicates that the banking sector dominates the market, handling more than 80 percent of the volumes, especially because banks conduct international transfers. In the local money transfers services, though, banks face competition from other financial institutions—MFIs, SACCOs, currency exchanges, and Postbank—and the mobile-phone MTO, M-PESA.

The international banks, because of their reach, dominate the remittance services market. The largest five international banks account for more than 30 percent of the remittance flow into Kenya, whereas the top five local banks have a 10 percent share of the market.

Postbank was set up with a key objective to help alleviate poverty by encouraging thrift among the small savers. Its close partnership with Posta enables it to penetrate deeply into rural areas. Postbank also is the main agent for Western Union. Cooperative Bank of Kenya (including the SACCOs) partners with the MoneyGram and has a market share of about 8 percent.

The distribution of banking activities, detailed in table 6.3, shows concentration in major towns and minimal outreach into the rural areas,. In Kenya, despite the rapid expansion of bank branches—from 512 in 2003 to 740 in 2007—the distribution is highly skewed geographically. Nairobi Province has both the highest number of bank branches and the highest percentage of the population with bank accounts. North Eastern Province has the most limited financial services. Therefore, even for local transfers, many clients have limited choices because only a few can use facilities that require bank accounts. Banks' inaccessibility to rural populations may have led clients there to rely heavily on the informal sector (including the community-based and transport systems) for money transfers.

MTOs. The MTOs work in partnership with banks, currency exchanges, and Postbank. Thus, their distribution is proportional to the availability of

Table 6.3   Financial Services Coverage in Kenya, 2007

Province	Branch network as of 2007 (% of all branches)	Population with bank accounts (% per province)	Cooperative Bank of Kenya[a] (% of total)
Nairobi	42	38	27
Rift Valley	14	20	5
Central	14	24	15
Coast	13	15	5
Eastern	6	15	17
Nyanza	7	12	15
Western	3	11	15
North Eastern	1	—	..
Total	**100**	**n.a.**	**100**

Sources: Central Bank, FSD Kenya 2007, Safaricom M-PESA brochure, and Cooperative Bank of Kenya website (http://www.co-opbank.co.ke).
Note: — = negligible.
a. Cooperative Bank of Kenya is a major agent of MoneyGram and a bank for SACCOs.

banking services. M-PESA, the mobile-phone money transfer service, does not necessarily work in partnership with the banking institutions; it may also function as a freestanding RSP. However, the ability to receive communication signals, the extent of mobile phone ownership, and population size are major factors that influence the overall number of MTOs in the various regions.

Posta services are also widespread, with a significant rural network of 900 branches. In 2005, Posta introduced an electronic fund transfer service. PostaPay sends and receives money instantly from various destinations and can be accessed in more than 300 outlets countrywide. However, it receives heavy competition from the mobile-phone money transfer service, M-PESA.

With the 2007 introduction of M-PESA by Safaricom, the leading mobile telecommunications provider in Kenya, access to partial financial services has improved, especially for the unbanked. M-PESA has made it easy to send money domestically at low cost. It is also becoming a major challenge to the banking institutions that have long dominated the local market because it is improving the money transfer technology while also reducing money transfer charges. This is an important innovation, especially for those who cannot access traditional banking services. As box 6.1 describes in more detail, M-PESA has provided a domestic remittance channel throughout Kenya that competes, among the unbanked, not only with the semi-formal and informal sector but also with the financial institutions. M-PESA has about 14,000 agents spread all over the country, 60 percent of whom serve rural areas.

Box 6.1

The M-PESA Money Transfer System

Kenya is the first country in Africa to use M-PESA—a Safaricom service (in partnership with Vodafone) that provides a fast, safe, and affordable way to transfer money by mobile phone. Through M-PESA, one can deposit, withdraw, or transfer (send) money; buy Safaricom prepaid airtime; or pay utility bills. The high number of Safaricom airtime subscribers gives M-PESA a wide network, with more than 14,000 agents countrywide and 10 million customers. M-PESA is a domestic money transfer system operating only within Kenya. Customers choose M-PESA because it is convenient, efficient, fast, and cheap and provides a 100 percent guarantee that the money will be delivered. M-PESA customers can transfer money to any other network and can send money to or receive money from (unlike other means of money transfer) any part of the country 24 hours a day. They can also keep money in their phones and withdraw it, send it, or pay bills at their convenience.

An explanation of M-PESA operations must begin with its national network of about 14,000 agents, who register customers and process cash deposits and withdrawals on their behalf.[a] All agents have an existing business—for example, selling groceries, Safaricom airtime, or fuel—so they already deal in cash. They purchase a mobile money (e-money) float from M-PESA with a cash deposit. They also maintain a real cash float.

As cash-in/cash-out points, from the customer's standpoint, the agents function much like human automated teller machines (ATMs). As they buy and sell this e-money, they earn a commission for each customer transaction. M-PESA customers can send up to K Sh 35,000 per transaction and keep up to K Sh 50,000 in a virtual account. There is no minimum balance required, no monthly fees, and no hidden charges. The maximum account balance is 50,000 K Sh, and the maximum daily transaction is 70,000 K Sh.

An M-PESA money transfer involves these basic steps:

1. If not already registered, a customer can register for free at any M-PESA agent. Nonregistered customers may receive but cannot send money unless the agents allow them to use their account; MPESA is only for Safaricom customers at the moment. Although customers may deposit funds in an M-PESA account for free, registered customers pay lower withdrawal fees. All one needs to register is a Safaricom SIM card, a mobile telephone, and an original ID or passport.

2. The sender hands funds to an attendant at an M-PESA agent (including either Safaricom dealers or other registered businesses such as gas stations,

(continued)

Box 6.1 *(continued)*

supermarkets, and retail outlets), who converts the funds into mobile money (e-money).

3. The agent transfers the e-money by text to the recipient.

4. The recipient withdraws the funds as cash at another M-PESA agent's location.

The transfer of money through the phone in Kenya is not regulated at all. After assessing the operations of the Safaricom and Zain communication companies, the Central Bank of Kenya found that there is little or no risk involved and issued them a "letter of no objection" to operate. There is the danger of sending cash to the wrong number and the recipient redeeming it straight away. However, disputes have been rare except in the case of network problems; when they occur, Safaricom has sorted out the matter directly with customers.

The future of M-PESA is bright because the service is convenient; customers can send money from any point within Kenya at any time. M-PESA is moving toward e-banking whereby money can be moved from bank accounts to the M-PESA virtual account. The growth in M-PESA use implies there is a huge market. Furthermore, it is affordable to low-income customers, who are the majority of the population.

Source: RSP Survey.

a. The Safaricom M-PESA website provides greater detail about its operations. http://www.safaricom.co.ke/index.php?id=747.

Community-based systems. The transport system emerged because various groups of the society found themselves without access to financial services. Thus, transport services came in to fill a gap, particularly where communication is a challenge and banking services are thin. Although transport services are licensed specifically for package and parcel delivery and not for funds transfer, the social networks on which they are based have facilitated their emergence, as box 6.2 describes.

Kenya has another community-based system, especially among the Somali community, that evolved because of the breakdown of law and order that led Somalis to emigrate to various parts of the world. This elaborate system for maintaining ties with their relatives back home is called *hawala*. Box 6.3 explains how hawala remittances work.

Partnerships and Agreement with MTOs

Almost all of the RSPs network with banks. Local banks establish partnerships with foreign corresponding banks to cover international transfer

Box 6.2

Transport Industry and Money Transfer Services in Kenya

People have sent and received money through the Kenyan transport system for a long time. During the colonial period and after independence, many Kenyans moved from rural to urban areas to seek work, leaving their families behind. Given the lack of banking infrastructure in the rural areas, the only options for sending money home were buses, *matatus* (Kenyan public transportation), and traveling friends and relatives. Businesspeople send money this way to relatives in the urban areas who, in turn, buy business merchandise and send it back as luggage. Parents also use the transport system to send pocket money and fees to their children in schools and colleges.

Customers view this method as convenient because the transactions are less cumbersome than in the formal sector; no bank accounts or long, complicated forms are required. Survey respondents believe that this system uniquely reaches most of the poor, who live in underdeveloped areas with poor roads, communications, and banking infrastructure. By contrast, the transport system is efficient and more personalized. The vehicle operators are generally well-known villagers whom customers trust with money parcels. However, the entry of long-distance route operators into the business has made it possible for migrants throughout Kenya to use transport services for money transfers, and this expansion is weakening the role of personal relationships and increasing the need for a well-defined market operation.

The particulars of money transfers through the transport system differ from one region to another. In some areas, the locals make arrangements with the vehicle drivers who ply their major routes. The drivers receive money from relatives in the urban areas and deliver it to the rural recipients. This option is favored mostly by people who live in the country's interior, where the banking or mobile phone networks are poor or nonexistent. Senders enclose the money in an envelope, confirm the amount with the driver, and pay the driver a commission of K Sh 100, called a "stamp." No identification is required because this system is used by parties who know and trust each other. No inventories are kept.

A high risk of robbery and thefts on the roads, however, has caused other transport companies to introduce a new money transfer method in which the paying clerks on either end of the route keep an inventory, called a "float," to pay recipients even before the actual money has been received. The sending office gives the sender a receipt and directs the receiving office, by phone, to pay the recipient. The sender typically makes the transfer, and pays the fee (typically,

(continued)

Box 6.2 *(continued)*

10 percent of the amount sent), through the driver or conductor. The amount charged also covers the risk, because if the money gets lost, the accumulated fees cover compensation. (Those companies that transfer money purely on the basis of trust do not provide compensation; in such cases, the sender incurs the loss.) To receive the money, the recipient can produce a national identity card, a passport, or a driver's license to the paying clerk for identification.

Money transfer through the transport system is unregulated. Most transport companies register with the Communication Commission of Kenya to operate as couriers (of parcels only) and join the money transport business behind the scenes. However, the survey respondents agreed that the informal sector could be regulated if the government were to develop adequate road, communication, and banking infrastructure that would make the process affordable and efficient to most Kenyans.

Source: RSP Survey.

Box 6.3

Hawala: The Somali Community-Based Remittance System

The indigenous Somali community-based money transfer system started many years ago, but it expanded in the 1980s after many Somalis fled to seek asylum in other countries.

Until recently, with the introduction of Muslim banks, the Somali community opposed traditional banking because Islamic law prohibits the payment or acceptance of interest. *Hawala* offers the advantages of convenience (operating in close proximity to the Muslim community); trust (embedded in the Muslim belief that people do not steal); and unregulated, tax-free status.

Anyone can send money through the *hawala* system, and the business in Kenya is thriving—especially in the Eastleigh suburb of Nairobi, where about 90 percent of the residents are of Somali origin. The major *hawala* agencies include Dahabshiil (goldmine), Barowaaqo, Frontier, and AMAL Express. Al-Barakat was the biggest company operating globally, but after the U.S. Embassy bombing on August 7, 1998, its accounts were frozen, immobilizing its activities. Several entrepreneurs own these agencies, whose branch networks extend to Australia; France; Germany; Hong Kong SAR, China; Indonesia; Malaysia; the Middle East;

(continued)

Box 6.3 *(continued)*

the Netherlands; the Republic of Korea; Scandinavia; South Africa; Uganda; and the United Kingdom, in addition to the major towns and cities in Kenya.

Because government laws and regulations govern the formal remittance industry, the Somali money transfer dealers have opened currency exchanges as front offices to conduct legal money transactions; behind the scenes, however, a lot of money transfers use the community-based systems. Thus currency exchanges then operate as central points for other small *hawala* agencies. They communicate by radio (in the remote parts of northeastern Africa and Somalia), fax, mobile phones, e-mail, and the Internet. Most of the *hawala* agencies have different branches in different parts of the world and, in the case of money transfer, the person in charge of the agency on the other end is authorized to pay the recipient. The sending agency calls the receiving agency and provides the recipient's transaction number and telephone number and the amount being transferred. The receiving agent calls the recipient and tells him or her where to collect the money. The recipient must produce identification; however, a third party may receive money on behalf of the recipient if there is a witness, especially an elder. The sender pays the fee, which depends on the amount of money sent. For every US$100 (K Sh 6,300) sent, the sender must pay US$6 (K Sh 378) as commission. As the amount increases, the average commission rate decreases. The recipient is paid in Kenya shillings (K Sh), the local currency.

These businesses are usually located near large Somali populations. Remittances are paid in cash, in total confidence, and there is no complex documentation. The agency owner keeps a simple ledger, and customer service is adequate. Liquidity to the Somali money transfer agencies is not a problem because they always have money with them. Sometimes, the agencies transport huge sums by bus. They are accountable only to themselves, and if there is a crackdown on the business, everyone loses—both dealer and sender—with no means of compensation. If a remittance is issued with fake currencies, Somalis resolve the issue by traditional means, resolving disputes internally to keep the matter from leaking out to the authorities.

These agencies compete among themselves. At the moment, several of them are mushrooming in number because the business is so lucrative. Without any formal framework, neither do regulations govern this sector—and whether the Somali agents would want it regulated is uncertain.

Source: RSP Survey.

corridors. Generally the SACCOs work with the Cooperative Bank of Kenya. The banks also work with MTOs such as Western Union, MoneyGram, Mastrex International, XpressMoney, Instant Cash, and American Express.

For their part, the international MTOs collaborate with local banks and currency exchanges. For example, Western Union's major agent in Kenya is Postbank, and it also works with other banks and currency exchanges. MoneyGram's main agents in Kenya include the Cooperative Bank and Diamond Trust Bank.

The range of services that RSPs can offer in Kenya depends on their networks and access to payment systems—the latter of which are limited to members of the Kenya Bankers Association. Nonmembers—which do not have access to the payment systems—include the MFIs, Postbank, SACCOs, currency exchanges, and MTOs. Although the central bank can easily monitor the payment system, remittance industry regulations may be weakened if the designated authorities fail to enforce them and if the transactions are conducted outside of the national payment system. For example, the central bank expects the dealer banks to ensure that the currency exchanges comply with statutory limits. However, because the exchanges collaborate with the MTOs, which do not fall under central bank statutory management, compliance is difficult to monitor. Furthermore, because the transactions are not centralized, clients are free to use alternative institutions to make their desired transfers.

Banks located in the local market have international correspondent banks and Society for Worldwide Interbank Financial Telecommunication (SWIFT) membership. As such, they can offer remittance services abroad and cross-border settlement services. Thus, if banks had adequate branch networks throughout the country, all clients could access international remittance services more easily.

Posta and Postbank offer more services than the courier and transport companies, SACCOs, MFIs, and M-PESA. For example, Posta's PostaPay system can offer instant international remittance services and settlement services. Posta Kenya's partnership with Posta Tanzania and Posta Uganda, through the Universal Postal Union network, enabled Posta to serve a wider remittance corridor. Postbank works closely with Western Union, enabling its participation in the international remittance services. Postbank is not a member of the national payment system and therefore cannot provide settlement services. Similarly, the Somali community-based (*hawala*) services offer both cross-border and domestic remittance services. However, MFIs, M-PESA, SACCOs, and transport systems provide only domestic remittance transfer services. Only banks, Posta, and Postbank operate in more than 10 remittance corridors. However, some banks operate in fewer than five remittance corridors.

The MTOs that have direct contractual obligations with financial and nonbank financial institutions benefit in several ways, as figure 6.1 indicates, including marketing and advertising, access to payment systems, and access to relevant financial information. However, it is important to note that the remittance transfer process usually involves several levels of institutions or persons, including a financial institution, nonbank financial institution, or currency exchange that acts as an agent of the MTOs. This therefore suggests that there are some interrelationships between the formal and informal channels in the provision of remittance services.

Remittance Products

Several remittance products are offered in Kenya, including electronic funds transfers, prepaid cards for use at selected retailers, bank drafts, checks or demand drafts, and money orders. Other remittance instruments include account-to-account transfers, money transfers through mobile phones, and prepaid debit cards. Figure 6.2 summarizes the instruments that the surveyed RSPs use.

Electronic Funds Transfer. Electronic funds transfer (EFT) is the most widely used remittance product, offered by more than 54 percent of the

Figure 6.1   RSP Partnership Benefits

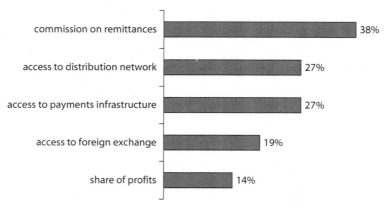

Source: RSP Survey data.
Note: Percentages indicate all surveyed RSPs that said each listed benefit was one they enjoyed because of partnerships with other RSPs.

Figure 6.2   Remittance Instruments Used by RSPs

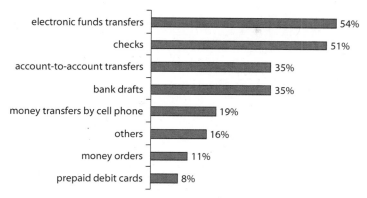

Source: RSP Survey data.
Note: The percentages indicate responding RSPs that use each instrument.

financial and nonfinancial institutions under review. Because the central bank must clear all money sent by EFT and clears the local transfers only twice a day (at 10 a.m. and noon), the transfers are not instantaneous, as they are through M-PESA. In addition, in Kenya, 34 banks are members of the SWIFT network. The central bank encourages banks to join SWIFT because of its robust network.

Checks. Checks are offered by 51 percent of the RSPs. In Kenya, checks are cleared between one and three days after the transaction in most parts of the country, depending on the value of the check. Checks from remote centers are typically cleared in 10 days as opposed to immediate (real-time) settlement. On a gross-basis principle through a Real Time Gross Settlement (RTGS) system, transfers would be effected within 30 minutes (the transfer is done almost immediately), with clearing done at the central bank on the same day. However, a major shortcoming in the current Kenyan payment system is the lack of a real-time interbank exchange. Furthermore, anti-money-laundering legislation has not yet been passed to facilitate dealing with cases of checks that bounce.

Bank drafts. One of the major constraints in using bank drafts is that they are expensive—with charges of K Sh 100–K Sh 600 (US$1.40–US$8.60)—and are not cleared instantaneously. Each bank charges a fixed amount regardless of the amount sent. Transfers by bank draft also require that the receiver have a bank account where the draft is deposited.

Account-to-account transfers. Most banks (35 percent of all responding RSPs) also offer account-to-account money transfers, although this instrument requires both the sender and the receiver to have access to a bank and the receiver to have a bank account. It also requires that a bank be able to network with all its branches, a feat made easier by technological development. Although banks do not charge to deposit funds in another personal account, the Know-Your-Customer (KYC) policy requires the sender to declare the sender and recipient names and contact information. Some banks can finalize the transaction instantly; others the following day. With the entry of M-PESA into the market, competitive pressures have pushed the banks to speed up their account-to-account transfers.

Direct debit. The Kenya Bankers Association introduced direct debit as a means of payment in 2003. However, few RSPs indicated they use this tool for remittance transfers. Direct debits are used primarily to pay insurance premiums, purchase installments, utility bills, and mortgage payments.

Money orders. Posta, the only RSP that issues money orders for remittances, uses postal orders; interstate orders (tailored for use in Kenya, Tanzania, and Uganda); and international money orders (currently available for transfers only between Kenya and South Africa). Ordinary money orders identify the recipient and can be cashed only at specified post offices. They can be drawn for any amount up to K Sh 35,000 (US$500) per order. Telegraphic money orders guarantee customers same-day value, while a postal order is a bearer instrument that can be cashed at any post office. Posta is one of the most accessible RSPs, given its large distribution network that reaches almost every village in the country.

Mobile-phone money transfers. As described in box 6.1, the mobile-phone money transfer facility M-PESA currently offers domestic services based on virtual (e-money) accounts to facilitate transactions between two parties. Plans are under way to enter the international market as well.

Access to Other Financial Services

Both banks and nonbank financial institutions provide several services geared specifically toward the senders and receivers of remittances (box 6.4). The most widely offered services include deposits, other savings products, and credit facilities for consumers and small and large

Box 6.4

The Financial Sector in Kenya

Kenya's diversified financial sector includes commercial banks, MFIs, SACCOs, the post office, savings banks, insurance companies, capital markets, and pension funds. There are also building societies, development finance institutions (DFIs), and informal financial services such as Rotating Savings and Credit Associations (ROSCAs).

The country's 42 commercial banks have 800 branches and handle 6 million accounts. In addition, an estimated 4,900 active SACCOs offer savings and credit services to more than 2.1 million Kenyans—almost three-fourths of whom are salaried workers and only one-fourth of whom are rural residents. SACCOs started mushrooming in 1997 when the banking sector adopted a development strategy favoring branch rationalization, which forced many rural bank branches to close and left many people without financial services. SACCOs stepped in and opened their own branches in some of these same rural areas. About 200 SACCOs are beginning to raise additional, voluntary but more liquid, savings deposits from members and even some nonmembers through Front Office Savings Activity (FOSAs) accounts. It is this facility that enables the SACCOs to offer remittance services to nonmembers.

Islamic banking, introduced in Kenya in December 2005, took the form of deposit products in conformity with Sharia principles. As of this report, two full-fledged Islamic banks have been licensed, and two other traditional banks are offering Islamic banking services.

In addition, two deposit-taking MFIs were licensed in 2008, providing a wide range of products to the financial service clients.

Source: RSP Survey.

businesses. Other financial services include education and vehicle loans. However, the financial institutions that offer these services to remittance senders and recipients indicate that remittance services are auxiliary to their core functions, such as deposit taking and intermediating. Further, currency exchanges—which play an active role in the remittances market—do not offer any additional financial or nonfinancial services to remittance senders and recipients.

Although there are indications that some remittance senders and receivers are enjoying these additional financial services, knowledge of the same among non-account holders would define their use of such services.

For example, over 60 percent of the financial and nonfinancial institutions surveyed indicate that the remittance transfer recipient must be an account holder of the institution. Most of the providers offer financial literacy materials, including brochures, magazines, pamphlets, and posters. It would be interesting to find out how aware senders and receivers are of these other services and how much they use them.

These additional financial services have associated costs for remittance customers. For example, the charges for maintaining a deposit account include maintenance of a minimum balance, the ledger fee, withdrawal charges, and statements. For instance, the average monthly charges for maintaining an account with banks in Kenya range between K Sh 30 and K Sh 300 (US$0.40–US$4.30) for withdrawals and K Sh 100 and K Sh 2,000 (US$1.40–US$29.00) for monthly ledger fees if the account balance goes below a designated minimum, which varies by institution between K Sh 3,000 and K Sh 50,000 (US$42–US$714).

The Regulatory and Business Environment

Market regulation incorporates self-regulation, which guides members' operations. Statutory regulation is expected to protect the customer by spelling out the rules of the game

The central bank regulates banks, deposit-taking MFIs, and currency exchanges. However, MTOs, SACCOs, non-deposit-taking MFIs, transport services, and mobile-telephone transfers are not under central bank or any other statutory regulation. The challenge in the market, therefore, is monitoring the activities of those providers that operate outside any statutory regulatory framework, especially to ensure that clients are protected. Although no serious issues have been reported with these services, considering the increasing size of market share they are commanding, it is important to ensure that activities in the remittance market have a centralized point of authority that facilitates monitoring and ensures that set guidelines are followed without circumvention by unregulated providers.

The enactment of the MFI Act (2006) and the entry into the market of deposit-taking MFIs will extend the regulatory power of the central bank to such institutions. SACCOs are governed by the Co-operative Societies Act (2004), but a proposed SACCOs bill is yet to be passed. That bill is expected to spell out the regulatory framework for the SACCOs. The current challenge is that the SACCOs are operating FOSAs with nonmembers, which makes the SACCOs deposit-taking institutions outside the central bank's regulatory framework.

As authorized dealers, currency exchanges conduct business and are regulated under provisions of the central bank. Their sole activity is to conduct foreign exchange transactions, including the sale and purchase of currencies, traveler's checks, and products as licensed and approved by central bank.

M-PESA operates under a self-regulation framework, and the transport companies are under no regulatory framework. The Communication Commission of Kenya (CCK) issues a parcel license to transport companies operating in Kenya, but the license does not allow the courier companies to transfer or transport money. Posta is the only organization that, under CCK authority, can transfer money through the Postal Financial Services.

Entry Requirements

Given that most institutions offer remittance services, the entry and licensing requirements are defined by their core businesses, as follows:

- *Banks* apply to the Ministry of Finance through the central bank, which is responsible for ensuring that the banking institutions perform their role. Banks are granted the license upon meeting the minimum requirement of K Sh 50 million (US$3.6 million) and licensing fee of K Sh 400,000 (US$570). For branches, the fee ranges between K Sh 30,000 (US$450) to K Sh 150,000 (US$650) between urban councils and municipalities.
- *Currency exchanges* in Kenya pay a nonrefundable application fee and a license fee and satisfy minimum core capital noninterest bearing deposit requirements with the central bank. Exchanges must also hold foreign exchange accounts (a maximum of two) with authorized dealer banks where they also maintain minimum balance requirements.
- *MFIs* in Kenya currently pay a license fee of K Sh 40,000 (US$570). However, under the MFI Act (2006), a deposit-taking MFI satisfies varying minimum capital requirements, depending on the tier it wants to operate in. This minimum capital requirement may cause remittance costs to increase.
- *Courier companies* must pay a license fee, depending on the area of operations. They must also pay a one-time application fee. The other requirements are that 20 percent of the company shares must be held by Kenyans (it can be 100 percent Kenyan-owned) and that the company be tax compliant, pay a value added tax (VAT), file a form with the CCK director, and show a certificate of registration.

Guiding Rules

RSPs are expected to uphold the KYC policy and guard against unacceptable transactions by observing thresholds on the amounts remitted and reporting suspicious cases. However, the ability to enforce some of these rules depends on the strength of the surveillance system and, even more, on the ability to share information across the RSPs at the settlement level. For example, although there are limits on the amounts per transaction, a sender could either use more than one provider to transfer funds at the same time or split the amount and send at different times.

In Kenya, the current currency exchange guidelines prohibit (1) the processing of transactions that are, or appear to have been, deliberately split into small amounts of US$10,000 or less to avoid the documentation requirement or (2) the purchase of foreign currency in excess of or equal to US$10,000. Identification documents such as passports and national IDs also must be requested; transactions in excess of or equal to US$10,000 per customer per day must be reported; and all remittances should be made through the authorized dealer banks (maximum of two), which must ensure all the requirements are followed. When acting as agents for MTOs such as Western Union or MoneyGram, currency exchanges are expected to seek registration from the central bank by sending the signed contract.

Banks in Kenya are expected to keep up to 25 percent of core capital as foreign exchange holdings. Anything above this amount is up to the individual banks to decide. In contrast, the net open position in foreign currencies or in any specified foreign currency for financial institutions in Kenya cannot exceed 25 percent of the core capital of the institution. For banks, the threshold for reporting to the central bank is US$50,000, and US$100,000 for any suspicious activities. Postbank is not under the banking act requirement, and it has a transaction limit of US$7,500.

RSP Perspectives on the Regulations and Requirements

The study asked RSPs how they perceive the laws and regulations as obstacles to doing business. The survey results indicate that most of the RSPs do not consider laws and regulations to pose an obstacle. However, currency exchanges in Kenya view the central bank as applying double standards in its disclosure requirements. The exchange owners also felt that providing remittance services is time consuming for them because they have to work with dealer banks and do not send money directly. However, it is important that they understand that disclosure rules are important in reducing information asymmetry and enabling operational efficiency.

Most RSPs surveyed felt that access to capital or finance did constitute a major barrier to entry in providing remittance services. In Kenya, banks ranked access to distribution networks as a barrier, while government corruption was considered the least of obstacles.

Among the currency exchanges, SACCOs, and the transport sector, the primary perceived problem was access to capital or finance. For the MFIs, it was access to financial infrastructure. For Postbank, it was the licensing requirements, and for the M-PESA agencies, the main barrier is the minimum capital requirement.

Currency exchanges also felt that the central bank took too long to respond to their application, thereby making it impossible to commence business activities in a timely manner. Regarding the operational barriers, the currency exchanges especially indicated license and capital requirements as significant obstacles to business. Lack of access to clearing and settlement systems, anti-money-laundering requirements, and the central bank's reporting requirements are the other impediments to conducting a remittances-related business.

Competitive Forces

It is not possible to measure the level of competition because the various providers seem to provide services to complementary groups of clients. However, the entry of M-PESA has heightened competition among RSPs because it not only serves the unbanked but also receives customers looking for cheap and quick service. As a result, other RSPs are reexamining their fees and transfer times.

The RSP survey asked the providers to mention the institutions they felt were their major competitors and also to provide their views on various competitors. All providers viewed MTOs such as MoneyGram and Western Union as key competitors, while the nonbanking institutions viewed the banks as their key competitors.

Given the high level of partnership among the RSPs, however, the level of competition may be described as a mutual interdependence rather than as rivalry. Nonetheless, banks have a variety of products and access to a wide transfer system, and their growing branch networks are putting them in a more competitive position. The informal market operates only domestically, and therefore informal providers are viewed as threats only by those operating in the same geographic corridor.

In Kenya, the transport companies indicated that M-PESA was a major competitor, especially because of M-PESA's remittance-transfer speed. To maintain market share, the transport sector must change its current mode of processing the transfers to effectively compete with M-PESA. Among the ongoing initiatives in the transport sector are the float system—which eliminates the need for physical movement of money, as is the case with M-PESA—and the Somali community-based services. However, the transport companies still have a market niche, particularly where communication is still problematic. Rationalizing the cost of transfers is another aspect that should be considered by the transport sector if it is to remain in business.

Remittance Costs

RSPs gather information from the users of remittance services. For those under a statutory framework, the regulator dictates the kind of information to be gathered. The consequent extra time needed to finalize transactions may have implications on customers' choice of service. Customers prefer immediate settlement of the transaction. For example, some banks indicated that because of the speed with which M-PESA was completing transactions, they also had to reduce the time taken for account-to-account transfers from next-day delivery to same-day delivery. Some of the informal players also have changed their strategy of handling transfers; instead of the traditional physical transfers, they now operate with a float system.

The RSPs vary in their remittance service charges for the same amount and even for the same destination. However, a particular RSP could charge the same amount, regardless of the destination, and distinguish only between local and international transfers. Charges are generally flat rates that vary across different ranges of payments. These form the RSPs' main sources of revenue. Some of the institutions, though, felt that remittance services operate on very narrow profit margins.

In Kenya, banks offer the lowest minimum charge while Postbank, which works in partnership with Western Union, has the highest maximum charge for remittances abroad (table 6.4). M-PESA is the less expensive means of sending money domestically. In the past three years, rates have not changed. The expectation is that with the new entrants to the market, especially the mobile-phone money transfer services, the rates will go down.

The central bank has embarked on a deliberate effort to persuade the banks not to charge recipients for remittance services. Although formal RSPs are not required to charge taxes such as VAT on financial transactions,

Table 6.4   Remittance Charges in Kenya, by RSP Type

based on average cost to send US$200 internationally by RSP type's most popular service

RSP type	No. of RSP firms interviewed	No. of firms providing cost information	Ave. fee (as % of transfer)	Min. total fee (as % of transfer)	Max. total fee (as % of transfer)
Commercial banks	10	9	9.80	8.3	16.7
State-owned banks	2	1	0.25	—	—
Postbank	1	1	14.00	14.0	14.0
Currency exchanges	4	2	11.00	10.0	12.5
Credit unions	6	6	0.25	—	—
Posta	1	—	0.25	—	—

Source: RSP Survey data.

Note: RSP = remittance service provider. MFI = microfinance institution. — = not available.

including remittance services, the transfer fees are higher for these institutions than they are for informal providers. This could partly be attributed to the need to meet certain minimum capital standards, reporting requirements, and the high operational costs for these institutions, such as renting office space in prime locations. Informal sector RSPs, on the other hand, in addition to not being subject to any minimum standards, have the option of using retail outlets to offer remittance services. Informal RSPs also usually operate in locations farther away from central business districts, where operational costs could be lower. The lower transfer charges offered by the latter have the potential to compensate for the risks associated with money transfers via the informal sector, consequently creating a preference for these RSPs, especially among remitters of small amounts.

Identification Requirements

Most of the RSPs gather customer information, and for some, this is a statutory requirement. All institutions involved in international remittances indicated that they ask for a form of identification, which can include national passports, national identification cards, proof of residence, and in some cases, a the driver's license. This requirement applies to both the account holders and non-account holders. However, the use of any of these documents for identification has implications for the monitoring of transactions because there is no centralized system of matching the identifications. For example, a customer can move from one provider to another using a different form of identification. Furthermore, the personal identification is not fed to the payment system and is therefore not matched to the transaction. Thus the chances of money laundering are high. Some banks insist that the money transfer service be used by account holders only.

Some of the institutions (62 percent), especially the banks interviewed and Postbank, typically inquire about the purpose of the money being transferred. Although it is not possible to verify the final use of the transfers, intended uses mentioned include the purchase of housing, land, food, medicine, fuel, and utilities. A big proportion of the firms (more than 75 percent) indicated that the remittances are used for the purchase of land and housing. The settlement of medical expenses was indicated by 45 percent of firms in Kenya. The "other" category includes construction of housing; purchase of supplies, equipment, and business stock; importation of telecommunication equipment and motor vehicles; and loan repayments.

Addressing Grievances

All RSPs indicated they have a system of dealing with grievances, although some firms indicated that they rarely receive grievances, and others said they never have. Nonetheless, transfers may fail to reach the intended recipients, either because the sender provided incorrect information or because the details were suspicious.

In most cases of grievances (more than 80 percent), the institutions verify the details with the sender. They also talk to the receiver for the same purpose. In such a case, the money is not necessarily returned but held until the details are clarified. Only when the case is suspicious would the institutions talk to the local authorities.

Regarding the length of time it takes to address the grievances, most RSPs indicated that the grievance is resolved immediately after the issue is raised if the issue is not complex and if information is provided immediately. About 50 percent indicated that it takes about a week to address the issue. The firms have a dedicated staff (most indicated two staff members) to deal with grievances or, alternatively, use all staff members involved in the transfer of money. It is rare that remittances remain unclaimed.

Conclusions and Recommendations

The remittance services market in Kenya is thriving in terms of both remittance volume and the diversity of the providers, both internationally and domestically. As the industry evolves, it is capturing more segments of the society and extending its reach to traditionally underserved populations, especially in rural areas. This expansion provides access for some unbanked community members to financial services. As this chapter has explored the RSP market, it has focused on the attributes of good money transfer products and services—including accessibility, reliability, a sizable service network (including external major urban centers), and affordability. The observations below are especially noteworthy:

- *Data collection process on the flow of remittances is not well developed*. There is a growing volume of migrant remittances to Kenya, which correlates positively to the stock of migrants. For example, Kenyan migrants' main destination is the United Kingdom and neighboring countries, and similarly these are the primary sources of inward remittances. Currently, the Central Bank of Kenya's data cover only remittance inflows through the banking institutions. Banks do not categorize their money transfer items and instead treat remittances as part of the money transfer. This is important in understanding the dynamics of the market.

- *Remittance service providers are diverse, but some do not treat remittance services as a core service*. Accessibility to remittance services is facilitated by a wide range of institutions that provide transfer services. However, except for MTOs and mobile-phone money transfer agencies (such as M-PESA), which consider remittance service to be their core service, other RSPs treat remittances as an auxiliary service. The entry of nonbanking services responded to emerging gaps in the provision of financial services. Currently, mobile-phone money transfer is gaining the entry of an additional provider while at the same time trying to explore international services. This is expected to revolutionize the domestic and international money transfer services.

- *RSPs' networks and partnerships reflect significant complementarity*. Except for the community-based and transport remittance service providers, all the RSPs have a link to the banking sector because of its elaborate payment system, which enables them to reach a wider (domestic and international) market.

- *Participation in the formal remittance market is limited to a proportion of clients*. The distribution of RSPs indicates limited access to formal remittance transfer services by potential clients in various parts of the economy. Results show that most of the services are provided in the major urban centers. The rural areas have a lower concentration of the formal providers. The informal market continues to take a significant proportion of the remittance transfers, and this is generally attributable to accessibility of the services and the cost of transfer.

- *Direct costs of remittance transfers are significantly high across the various providers*. To send US$200, the charge ranges between 8.0 percent and 18.0 percent for international transfers and between 0.4 percent and 12.5 percent for domestic transfers. The transfer fee covers processing charges, inventory costs, and delivery costs. When there is a partnership in the use of some transfer facilities, the transfer fee is shared in agreed-to proportions to cover the various costs.

- *Access to a wide range of financial services is constrained by financial costs and availability*. Most of the RSPs indicated that they offer a wide range of products to remittance clients among their core services. However, the costs for such products, like the cost of maintaining a bank account, may be prohibitive in expanding the demand for other financial services. Furthermore, M-PESA may find it difficult to widen the scope of financial services provided its clients if banks do not offer such services where the M-PESA agents operate.

- *Formal RSPs operate under a statutory regulatory system.* The central bank defines the limits on single transactions for banks and foreign exchange bureaus and also indicates the threshold amounts for reporting to the central bank. RSPs are also expected to take note of situations where the client seems to be splitting the transfers and any other suspicious situations. The central bank also asks the banks and currency exchanges to gather information from the customers by asking for the identification of the senders and recipients.

To ensure that the remittance services provided are accessible, reliable, and affordable, one must focus on the networking and partnerships among the providers, technological development, regulatory systems, and data collection. The study makes the following recommendations:

- *Establish an elaborate system for remittance data collection.* This could include period surveys and a reporting system from the formal RSPs. Distinguishing the money transfers handled by the service providers will be useful in accurately depicting migrant remittances. Information on the costs of transfer should be shared publicly so that the client is aware and can choose across the providers. As this increases competition among the providers, the costs of the services will potentially decrease.

- *Treat money transfer as a core service and build its capacity.* Mobile-phone money transfer is revolutionizing the money transfer industry with its accessible and affordable services. Clients' positive response to this technological development indicates that money transfer is a significant financial service that has taken time to receive significant attention. A challenge to the banking sector is to elevate the service from an auxiliary category and to adopt new technologies to facilitate quick and cheaper service.

- *Banks and mobile-phone money transfer agents can make their services more complementary.* Mobile-phone money transfer requires the development of the telecommunication system; it does not require the presence of banks in a particular locality. However, to expose the community being served to additional financial services, banking institutions would need to penetrate the locality with their services and capture the money transfer clients. The model of establishing banking services will depend on the size of the targeted community.

- *Develop the national payments system.* The national payments system is a crucial structure in the remittance market. The speed of service delivery and the costs imposed depend on the level of sophistication of the system. Ensuring that the system adapts quickly to technological development will reduce transaction costs. Membership in international systems is costly, especially at the individual institution level, and such costs are included in the charges on money transfers. In the domestic market, a supportive regulatory system must be established to deal with money-laundering cases and other statutory and regulatory violations.

- *Educate remittance service clients about financial products.* Financial education is crucial for the remittance service clients to understand the financial products available to them. Similarly, banks can develop products that are specific to the remittance clients.

- *Ensure that the regulatory system keeps up with technological development.* While the mobile-phone money transfer facility is not currently at risk, it is important that the operational rules are fully enforced. However, as these services go global, the regulatory framework must be able to address the regulatory challenges that may be envisioned.

Notes

1. The corresponding GDP percentages for all developing countries and Sub-Saharan Africa during the same period were 1.9 percent and 1.6 percent, respectively.
2. The East African Community—headquartered in Arusha, Tanzania—is the regional intergovernmental organization of Burundi, Kenya, Rwanda, Tanzania, and Uganda. http://www.eac.int/.

References

Adams, R. H., and J. Page. 2003. "International Migration, Remittances, and Poverty in Developing Countries." Policy Research Working Paper 3179, World Bank, Washington, DC.

Chimhowu, C., J. Piesse, and C. Pinder. 2003. "Assessing the Impact of Migrant Workers' Remittances on Poverty," presented at the EDIAS Conference on New Directions in Impact Assessment for Development Methods and Practice, November 24–25.

Edwards, A., and M. Ureta. 2003. "International Migration, Remittances, and Schooling: Evidence from El Salvador." *Journal of Development Economics* 72 (2): 429–61.

FinScope Kenya. 2007. "Results of a National Survey on Access to Financial Services in Kenya." Prepared for DFID's (U.K. Department for International Development) Financial Sector Deepening (FSD) Kenya Project. http://www.fsdkenya.org/finaccess/.

Gupta, S., C. Pattillo, and S. Wagh 2007. "Impact of Remittances on Poverty and Financial Development in Sub-Saharan Africa." Working Paper 07/38, International Monetary Fund, Washington, DC.

Hanson, G., and C. Woodruff. 2003. "Emigration and Educational attainment in Mexico." Working Paper, University of California.

Kabbucho, K., C. Sander, and P. Mukwana. 2003. "Passing the Buck. Money Transfer Systems: The Practice and Potential for Products in Kenya." Study for MicroSave-Africa, Nairobi. http://www.dai.com/pdf/Passing_the_Buck.pdf.

KIHBS. 2005. "Kenya Integrated Household Budget Survey 2005/06." Kenya National Bureau of Statistics, Ministry of Planning and National Development, Government of Kenya.

Lucas, R. 2004. "International Migration Regimes and Economic Development." Paper prepared for the Expert Group Meeting on Development Issues, Stockholm, May 13.

Orozco, M., and R. Fedewa. 2006. "Leveraging Efforts on Remittances and Financial Intermediation." Working Paper 24, Institute for the Integration of Latin America and the Caribbean and the Integration, Trade and Hemispheric Issues Division, Inter-American Development Bank, Washington, DC. http://www.nalacc.org/fileadmin/Documents/Biblioteca_recursos/INCID ENCIA_TRANSNACIONAL/DESARROLLO_ECON/Financial_Intermedia tion_and_Remittances_Orozco.pdf.

Ratha, D., and Z. Xu. 2008. *Migration and Remittances Factbook 2008*. Washington, DC: World Bank.

World Bank. 2006. *Global Economic Prospects: Economic Implications of Remittances and Migration*. Washington, DC: World Bank.

———. 2011. *Migration and Remittances Factbook*. Washington, DC: World Bank.

CHAPTER 7

Nigeria

Chukwuma Agu

Nigeria receives the highest amount of remittances in Africa. At an estimated $18 billion in formal flows in 2007 (CBN 2007), remittances have outpaced foreign direct investment (FDI), official development assistance (ODA), and other inflows into the country. They currently rank second to oil receipts as a foreign exchange earner. World Bank estimates are much lower (figure 7.1) but still indicate higher inflows of remittances than other forms of development finance. However, remittance services and the remittance market are poorly regulated, disparate, and little studied.

This chapter sheds more light on the potentials of and impediments to the remittance industry in Nigeria. It examines remittance instruments and the relationships among the diverse players in the industry and identifies opportunities for improving the operational environment and regulation of remittance services, particularly as they relate to improving competition, reducing costs, improving access, and enhancing the use of remittance proceeds.[1]

For a long time, attention has focused disproportionately on traditional sources of funds such as ODA and FDI. Although migrant remittances have been acknowledged as increasingly important to developing countries' efforts to mobilize development resources, the remittance process, incentives, and markets have hardly been analyzed or constructively

Figure 7.1   Foreign Direct Investment and Remittances in Nigeria, 2005–09

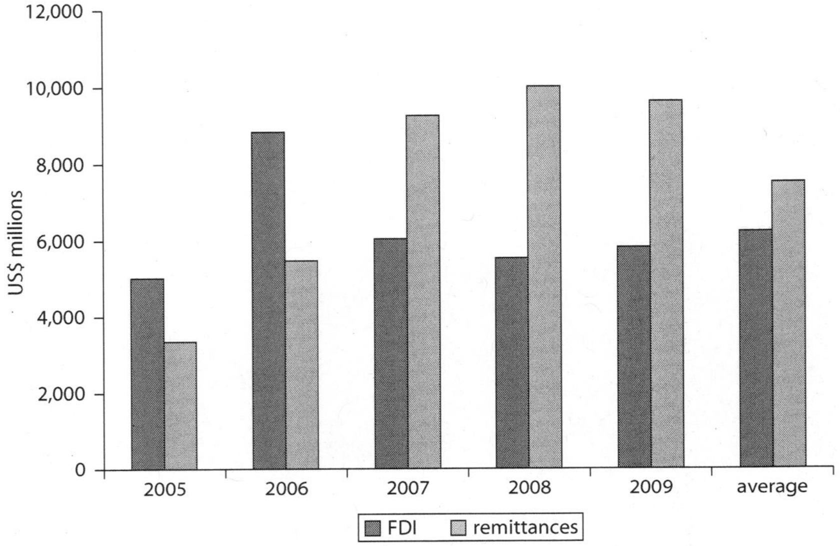

Source: CBN 2007.

tapped (Ratha, Mohapatra, and Plaza 2008). Some researchers have recently studied particular remittance corridors (Hernández-Coss and Bun 2007; Orozco and Millis 2008). The Central Bank of Nigeria also initiated a survey of the remittance environment (CBN 2007).

Although these previous works estimate the size of the remittance market in Nigeria, there is much more to the market than what can be gleaned from official data.[2] Policy makers need help to understand the market if they are to institute relevant policies to use remittance proceeds to catalyze economic growth. This chapter, based on a 2008 survey of the remittance market in Nigeria, aims to contribute to that understanding by analyzing the key bottlenecks and opportunities in the industry.

A few things have changed since the survey, but most of the findings and recommendations of this study remain valid. For example, the central bank in 2009 granted an operating license to MoneyBox Africa, a mobile-banking operating firm, and is considering granting similar licenses to other mobile-network operators. The central bank has also outlawed exclusive partnerships among remittance service providers (RSPs). However, the impact of these measures on the money transfer industry remains to be seen.

Remittance and Emigration Trends

As previously noted, remittances have become Nigeria's second most significant source of foreign exchange. Their volume exceeds all non-oil receipts in the country, including ODA, FDI (as figure 7.1 depicts), portfolio inflows, and non-oil exports.

Volume of Remittances

An estimated 65 percent of total official remittance flows to Sub-Saharan Africa and 2 percent of the global formal remittance flows go to Nigeria (Orozco 2003; Hernández-Coss and Bun 2007). From a relatively meager $1.18 billion in 1999, remittance inflows to the country increased to an estimated $9.98 billion by 2008—second only to oil receipts as the country's prime foreign exchange earner. As a share of gross domestic product (GDP), migrant remittances grew steadily from 0.4 percent in 1996 to about 7.5 percent in 2006 (CBN 2007). The Central Bank estimates that, as of the end of 2007, total remittance flows to Nigeria stood at about $17.95 billion, about 70 percent higher than the 2006 total of $10.58 billion. The dramatic one-year increase may have reflected, in part, improved data collection and measurement techniques rather than actual increases in the remittances.[3] Possibly, the estimates include other private flows. Probably also as a result, World Bank estimates are more modest but still show significant jumps in the size and share of remittances in overall flows. According to Wold Bank data, remittances tripled in the three years between 2005 and 2008, rising from US$3.3 billion to US$9.9 billion. Despite sharp increase in foreign direct investment between 2005 and 2006 from US$4.9 billion to US$8.8 billion, remittances over the five-year period between 2005 and 2009 still outpaced FDI on the average.

Destinations of Migrants

Following the collapse of oil prices and the austerity measures adopted by successive Nigerian governments to correct the macroeconomic imbalances of the late 1970s and early 1980s, economic conditions deteriorated for a large proportion of the population. What followed was massive emigration of Nigerians, driven by the prospect of higher wages elsewhere (Bamoul and Blinder 1998; Kómoláfé 2002; Tomori and Adebiyi 2007).

Most of the emigrants eventually settled outside the country permanently. As of 2006, an estimated 3.4 million Nigerians were living as migrants with different residence statuses across the world, up from

1.9 million in 2004 (Nwajiuba 2005; Tomori and Adebiyi 2007). The prime destinations, in addition to the West and Southern African countries (particularly Benin, Ghana, and South Africa), included North America and English-speaking European countries—primarily the United Kingdom and the United States, followed by Italy, Spain, Germany, and Holland (Nwajiuba 2005) (box 7.1). More remittances come to Nigeria from the United States than from any other single country (CBN 2007). Other destinations include Brazil, Japan, the Republic of Korea, and Saudi Arabia.

Nigeria has a relatively large network of urban centers scattered across all regions of the country (Oluwasola 2007). From 1952 to 2006, the proportion of the Nigerian population living in urban centers grew from just 11 percent to an estimated 46 percent—approximately 65 million of its 140 million people (Oluwasola 2007; UN DESA 2008).

Despite the extent of migration within Nigeria, little to no data exist about the aggregate volume of internal migration or remittances—what

---

Box 7.1

Geographic Nuances of Nigerian Migration and Remittances

Nigeria's geographic and ethnic diversity plays out in most national issues—including migration and remittances. For example, within their broader Nigerian immigrant communities, Ireland has attracted a particularly strong community from southwest Nigeria, and the United States a large contingent from southeast Nigeria.

Northern Nigerians' affinity for Islam affects those migrants' destinations. Consequently, there are vibrant Nigerian communities in, and remittance flows from, Saudi Arabia, its neighbors, and other parts of North and West Africa to northern states in Nigeria.

Remittance flows mirror these differences in both the numbers and spatial distribution of migrants. Interviews with RSPs in Nigeria suggest that remittance flows to the south are far greater than flows to the north. When Hernández-Coss and Bun (2007) mapped inflows from the UK corridor, they found about eight major remittance destinations in Nigeria, spread along four major axes or areas: Lagos-Ibadan (southwest), Enugu-Owerri (southeast), Benin and Port Harcourt (south-south), and the Abuja Federal Capital Territory (FCT).

Source: Hernández-Coss and Bun 2007.

Nwokocha (2008) termed "the burden of migration in a nonregulatory system." Most of those who move out of the rural communities maintain strong links to their places of origin. Consequently, a network of massive income transfer spans Nigeria from the urban to rural areas, particularly among relatives (Adepoju 1987; Mberu 2005; Nwokocha 2008).

Remittance Currencies and Seasonality

For many years, remittance payouts were wholly in the local currency, the naira. However, after the banking consolidation, the central bank permitted the money transfer operators (MTOs) and banks to give the remittance patrons the option of receiving their payment in U.S. dollars. Currently, remittances are received in both U.S. dollars and the Nigerian naira.

Remittance flows are seasonal, whether through formal or informal channels. The highest inflows are recorded in March, September, and December, which correspond to key festive seasons in the country: Easter in March, Mothering Week and New Yam festivals in September, and Christmas in December. The December inflows are consistently larger than those in other months. Consistent with the data from secondary sources, most of the RSP survey respondents confirmed that remittances often peak during the festive seasons, particularly in March (for Easter) and in December for Christmas, as figure 7.2 illustrates.

Figure 7.2   Peak Remittance Periods in Nigeria

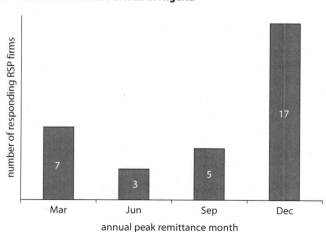

Source: Author's compilation from 2008 RSP survey in Nigeria.

Characteristics of the Remittance Industry

The findings in subsequent sections of this chapter are based on the author's 2008 survey of RSPs in Nigeria. The survey covered RSPs in three major cities—Enugu, Lagos, and Abuja (the capital)—representing three major geopolitical regions in the country (southeast, southwest, and north, respectively).

Survey Methodology

In all, 30 firms were surveyed: 11 each from Lagos and Abuja and the remaining 8 from Enugu. Given the structure of the financial system in Nigeria, banks handle a large proportion of remittances (particularly formal transactions involving contact with the outside world).

Responses came either directly from the firms' management or, in the case of the 16 banks in the survey, from employees. Responses were also obtained from the Nigerian Postal Service (NIPOST), the sole public sector postal agency, and from Peace Mass Transit (a private transport and courier service).

Types and Coverage of Remittance Firms

The remittance service industry in Nigeria is quite segmented—between a formal sector dominated by a few global MTOs and an informal sector that reflects the social network system of a typical African country. Table 7.1 below shows the firm types that are involved in remittances.

Other players in the formal remittance service in Nigeria include NIPOST, the national postal carrier, which has a collaborative arrangement with Cash4Africa to provide remittance services. In the early 1990s, NIPOST introduced initiatives such as remittance transfers to improve and extend the range of its customer services. However, it faces stiff competition from the private sector, whose services are better known and more efficient.

After telecommunications operators became licensed in 2001, many of them also provided indirect remittance instruments for consumers. Recharge cards quickly became instruments for funds transfers among family members and acquaintances, as box 7.2 explains. However, the outreach and depth of these institutions remain meager, especially relative to the banks' and MTOs' operations. The current challenge is that recharge cards are always resold at significant discounts—sometimes losing as much as 30 to 40 percent of their face value. This depreciation can be quite discouraging and often makes people use recharge card transfers and resale only when they have no feasible, immediate funds-transfer alternative.

Table 7.1   Branches and Coverage of Primary RSPs in Nigeria

RSP type	Number of firms in country	Number of firms interviewed	Average number of branches[a]	Average number of rural branches[a]	Percentage of rural branches[a]
Firms specializing in money transfers	5	0	—	—	—
Currency exchanges	610	—	—	—	—
Private commercial banks	24	16	262	92	35.1
NIPOST	1	1	3,955	3,000	75.9
Mobile-phone or telecom providers	6	0	n.a.	n.a.	n.a.
Courier, bus, and other transport services	—	1	15	5	33.3
Microfinance institutions	744	—	—	—	—
Total	1,390	18	4,232	3,097	48.1

Source: Author's compilation from 2008 RSP survey in Nigeria.
Note: — = not available, n.a. = not applicable.
a. Among interviewed firms. Estimates of banks' rural coverage may be overstated because the classification of urban and rural areas, particularly in some states in the south, is somewhat subjective.

Partnerships and Agreements with Money Transfer Operators

Partnerships are the most common operational framework for RSPs in Nigeria. Because a few global MTOs control the franchise and infrastructure for remittance transfers, local Nigerian institutions are left with little option than to form alliances with these MTOs.

Most Nigerian banks are involved in the remittance service industry but only as agents of the global MTOs, the most prominent of which are Western Union, MoneyGram, Travelex, Vigo, and Cash4Africa. Among these, Western Union and MoneyGram dominate transactions in the industry.

About 59 percent of deposit money banks (DMBs) have working relationships with Western Union, and another 18 percent are allied with MoneyGram. The rest of the MTOs, including Travelex and Vigo, account for the balance of market share (Hernández-Coss and Bun 2007; Orozco and Millis 2008). As agents, the DMBs provide fund-transfer desks for the MTOs, while the MTOs design the transfer instruments and set the rules, including identification procedures for remittance recipients.

Nigeria has 24 DMBs and several other classes of financial institutions, as described in box 7.3. In their capacity as fully licensed financial institutions, the commercial banks also offer account-to-account transfers using domiciliary accounts for international transfers. Such within-bank

Box 7.2

Recharge Cards for Domestic and International Remittances: The MTN Model

Following the liberalization of the telecommunications sector, three firms were originally licensed to operate as global system for mobile communications (GSM) telecommunications operators: Econet, MTN, and MTEL. The first two were foreign owned, and MTEL was the property of Nigeria's sole public telephone operator, Nigerian Telecommunications Limited (NITEL). After a few months in operation, MTN clearly established itself as the leading network in Nigeria, while Econet and MTEL struggled with diverse management and operational challenges. Later, Globacom and Etisalat were licensed. Econet, meanwhile, has changed hands three times and currently is owned and operated by the Zain network.

MTN's telecom market share in Nigeria is estimated to exceed 60 percent. After observing the high volume of purchase and transfer of card numbers across the network by customers to remit funds, MTN introduced some innovative products. Although some of the cards are used to make calls, for example, a large proportion is resold at relatively high discounts to retailers in exchange for cash. MTN therefore introduced its "share-and-sell" facility, which allows a customer to define the amount that he or she would like to transfer into the phone of a relative. After MTN introduced share-and-sell, it observed that some miscreants used the service to transfer credit from unsuspecting victims' phones without their knowledge. To remedy the problem, MTN started requiring the owner of the phone to enter a personal identification number (PIN) code. Share-and-sell has become a major channel of internal funds remittance among friends and family members.

MTN is also part of the international remittance market through a top-up facility, which allows an emigrant to Europe or North America to purchase an MTN card and text the number to a relative in Nigeria, who can resell or use the card. This top-up service is much more convenient than money transfer services, particularly for those with little or no means of self-identification. In addition, the text message comes directly to the recipient's phone, eliminating transport costs, queuing, and other hassles associated with formal remittance claims. However, many recipients of these cards resell them either directly as cards or by using the share-and-sell facility, often at a substantial discount (5 to 30 percent). This cost is borne entirely by the recipient of the remittance service—a direct contrast to the formal banking remittance service provision borne by the sender.

Source: Author.

Box 7.3

The Financial System in Nigeria

Nigeria has a dual financial sector—a formal sector (including deposit money banks (DMBs)) coexisting with an informal sector. The formal system provides services to the established formal institutions, informal businesses, and individuals, while the informal system attends to the needs of the less-organized, less-recognized microagents and institutions. These informal institutions generate microdeposits, keep few records, and conduct cash-dominated transactions anchored on personal recognition with higher interest rates.

For many years, governments in Nigeria tried different policies and programs to improve informal and small businesses' access to financing. In the mid-1980s, following the adoption of the structural adjustment program (SAP), the Ibrahim Babangida administration established both the People's Bank and the community banking system with the mandate to provide banking to rural and underserved areas. This policy allowed communities and groups to pool funds to establish a bank where individuals from the community could access funds with little or no collateral. Commercial banks were also required to open branches in rural areas. However, most of these efforts yielded little in terms of establishing banks nearer the rural areas or improving the informal sector's access to banking services.

Because of poor capitalization, poor management, and weak internal governance systems, many of the community banks were not viable and could not provide the services for which they were instituted. In 2005, therefore, the central bank commissioned a study that resulted in a microfinance policy. With the approval of the policy, all community banks were to become microfinance banks, while new microfinance banks were licensed. Most of the microfinance banks are still concentrated in the urban areas where market potentials are much higher.

Following liberalization in the late 1980s and the introduction of universal banking in 2001, the financial system grew rapidly. Total branch networks of commercial and merchant banks rose from 1,323 in 1985 to 3,492 in 2004. However, the sector remained fairly oligopolistic, with about 12 percent of banks controlling more than 50 percent of total assets and deposit liabilities as well as about 43 percent of total credit. In 2004, the central bank responded to this anomaly by announcing far-reaching reforms in the sector, anchored on bank consolidation and capital base restructuring. The 2004 and subsequent reforms rationalized the financial system, leaving 1,558 financial institutions: 24 banks

(continued)

Box 7.3 *(continued)*

(with about 3,535 branches), 610 currency exchanges (from innumerable small operators), 76 finance companies, 93 primary mortgage institutions, 744 micro-finance institutions, 5 discount houses, and 6 development finance institutions.

Even though the microfinancing and other deposit mobilization and funds-transfer institutions are being strengthened, the bulk of financial transactions—including the sending and receiving of migrant remittances in the country—go through the DMBs in the formal sector. The electronic card payment system has grown significantly in recent years, but as with other aspects of the financial sector, competition in the provision of electronic card payments is still weak. For example, the local horizon is dominated by InterSwitch, while foreign (mainly dollar-denominated) payment is dominated by MasterCard.

Sources: Central Bank of Nigeria Annual Report and Statement of Account, various issues.

transfers are operated either in partnership with foreign banks or through foreign branches of the local transferring bank. The commercial banks also offer other financial services such as foreign exchange, money transfer, credit, and loans alongside their traditional roles. Many also have specialized subsidiaries engaged in insurance, mortgage loans, and stock trading. In effect, a number of the country's banks serve as financial one-stop shops. Many of the interviewed banks have designated foreign exchange desks that render the same services as licensed currency exchanges.

For international in-bound transfers, DMBs are the principal agents for the MTOs. However, institutions such as NIPOST also work with some MTOs to provide remittance services. Most of the DMBs admit to working through international partnerships, mainly with the global MTOs (for example, Western Union, MoneyGram, and Cash4Africa). Most of the Nigerian banks, which have little or no external infrastructure for collecting remittances, serve as distribution points for global MTOs in return for commissions from fees and access to foreign exchange. In such partnerships, the global MTO collects the remittances while the local bank provides the distribution outlet in Nigeria. The sender can use any of the MTO agents in the country where he or she resides. The recipient, upon notification of a transfer, can go to any bank in Nigeria that has a working relationship with the particular MTO. The central bank does not permit outward remittances through the MTOs, so banks rely on other means, including checks, drafts, and account-to-account transfers (domiciliary accounts) for all forms of outward remittances.

Nearly 90 percent of the RSP firms interviewed noted that they use some form of partnership to provide remittance services. In addition to partnerships with MTOs, there are partnerships with banks (60 percent of respondents), with mobile phone companies (about 23 percent of respondents), and between banks and retail stores and supermarkets. The convenient partnership arrangements between banks and global MTOs also enable banks to cover multiple remittance corridors. Nearly 50 percent of respondents indicated that their institutions cover more than 10 remittance corridors.

A potentially problematic aspect of the partnerships among Nigerian RSP firms is the exclusivity clause. (As noted earlier, the Nigerian central bank has outlawed exclusive partnerships between RSPs, although 64 percent of the 2008 RSP survey respondents indicated that they had exclusive partnerships.) In the struggle for market share and the reduction of potential attribution conflicts, most of the MTOs ostensibly had exclusive arrangements with the banks. Consequently, it is now common to associate particular banks with particular MTOs (for example, the United Bank for Africa with MoneyGram or the First Bank of Nigeria with Western Union).

NIPOST has a partnership arrangement with Cash4Africa, but it is not exclusive. In addition to that arrangement, NIPOST operates a NetPost[4] program with Western Union through Oceanic Bank. NIPOST's operations are relatively recent and have low market penetration compared with that of the DMBs. As such, its overall remittance operations are a minuscule part of transactions in the industry.

Informal Remittances

Remittances through informal channels are sent not only as cash, but also in the form of valuables such as jewelry, electronics, cars, and clothing—usually carried by traveling individuals. These travelers may be acquaintances of the senders, receivers, or both. Alternatively, they might be either private merchants who also provide remittance services or just good Samaritans.

The benefits of remittances through informal channels include reduced fees for senders and favorable exchange rates for recipients (Osili 2004). But whatever the means used to send informal remittances, the associated risks (and sometimes costs) can be substantial. Among the disadvantages, Osili notes, are the risk of losing the money, a reliance on informal contracts, and the search costs to find someone to take the money abroad. Ultimately, many informal transactions do not cost less than the formal ones. For example, merchant RSPs charge rates that could be as high as 20 percent of the value of the funds or materials being sent (Osili 2004).

Remittance Instruments

Banks dominate inward international remittance transfers, and their principal transaction instrument is electronic funds transfer. The MTO with which the bank has a contract usually notifies the bank whenever a transfer is made, providing details of the transfer, the necessary codes, and the required identification for the recipient. The bank then pays the recipient and debits its account with the MTO. Physical identification is required for the recipient (such as a passport or identity card), but nearly every other aspect of the process of transfer and collection is electronic.

Domestic fund transfers are at least as significant, if not more significant, than international transfers in Nigeria. Both bank and nonbank RSPs have designed a host of instruments and products for domestic transfers. Indeed, there is stiff competition among RSPs, particularly banks, to offer innovative domestic funds transfer products.

For example, to widen the customer base for funds transfers and to increase their market shares, most banks have, since the consolidation of the banking sector, expanded their efforts to ensure that remittance and funds transfer services are not limited to current account holders. Bank drafts and account-to-account transfers, therefore, are now among the most prominent remittance instruments. Because almost all Nigerian banks now have integrated banking facilities, they can charge little or nothing for account-to-account transfers within the same bank (including between different branches).

In addition, products are designed for remitting funds in the same mode as international remittances by many banks. Several banks currently have fairly convenient, online, real-time funds transfer products that enable the recipient to identify oneself with a given code or other means and to collect remittance funds even without an account with the bank. NIPOST also offers prepaid cards (as box 7.4 notes), and the telecom firms offer recharge cards. MTN, as previously noted, has developed its own card instruments for remittances.

Outward remittance services are both more closely regulated and less widespread (Nigeria being generally considered an inward remittance

Box 7.4

NIPOST's Potential to Revolutionize the Nigerian Remittance Market

NIPOST is a potentially powerful institution for the remittance industry. For many years, it held sway as the principal institution, with massive infrastructure, for mail delivery (about 955 post offices and 3,000 postal agencies) across the country. However, with a weak incentive structure and a lackadaisical, poorly motivated workforce, it got enmeshed in corruption. While management embezzled funds allocated for the institution, the workforce regularly tampered with and stole from mail entrusted to their care. Turnaround time for mail delivery in NIPOST became one of the longest in the world and, before long, the general public lost confidence in the institution.

As NIPOST reeled under the combined burden of these institutional challenges, the postal system was liberalized, private courier firms were licensed, and the Internet (and e-mail) emerged to deliver real-time mail services. It became clear that NIPOST's fate was sealed, and its future was in a cruel balance. For many years, NIPOST remained no more than a hollow national carrier, and patronage was left to only those who could not afford any of the numerous alternatives.

During the mid-1990s, NIPOST was reinvigorated and its service delivery tied to market indicators. The management adopted a zero-tolerance policy concerning corruption, making the institution relevant again. With its old delivery infrastructure still intact—a substantial portion of which is in rural areas—the institution doubtless still holds great potential as a significant player in the remittance market. It has taken some steps such as instituting partnerships with Cash4Africa and Oceanic Bank. However, the firm's share of the market is still infinitesimal, with payments made only in local currency.

Despite having initiated a number of remittance products, the institution is still plagued by numerous challenges. In 2006, total remittance disbursement by NIPOST was less than $4,000, with recorded patronage in only three cities: Abuja, Oyo, and Edo. While it is true that the general public has yet to shake the old tag of inefficient, slow, and corrupt NIPOST from their minds, a critical challenge for NIPOST's remittance business has to do with publicity, efficiency, and information technology. In the course of the survey, field officers were surprised to find that NIPOST actually offers effective remittance services, with designated remittance products, but little is known about these NIPOST products. Equally important, NIPOST's electronic payments infrastructure is weak and unreliable, suffering from

(continued)

Box 7.4 *(continued)*

incessant breakdowns. Consequently, its capacity to pay out remittances effectively is limited.

NIPOST has the capacity to design and deliver remittance services through numerous instruments. Nigeria has been designated the hub for West African postal service by the United Nations Universal Postal Union, which ensures that mail to other West African countries passes through NIPOST. As a result, NIPOST can position itself as a principal RSP for other countries in West Africa, collaborating with other postal services globally to deliver quick, efficient, and reliable remittance services to numerous Nigerians abroad. It can also design payment cards (in the same way that it currently gives identity cards to its customers) for remittance senders and recipients, boosting its activity and income spectrum to go beyond regular mail delivery.

NIPOST's existing and new infrastructural facilities could make it the solution to rural remittance bottlenecks and even force down the price of remittance services. But this approach requires attention to its payment system and interconnectivity; innovation in the design of relevant products for its clients; and massive media packaging and investment in image-making, both for itself as an institution and for the products and reach that it offers to its customers. To this end, the institution needs help, particularly from regulatory and funding authorities. It is strictly an understatement to say that NIPOST is worth intensive reexamination if the remittance industry in Nigeria is to have a facelift.

Source: Author.

corridor). The two major instruments for outward remittances are bank drafts and account-to-account transfers (in this case, domiciliary accounts). Some banks provide prepaid debit cards, in collaboration with prepaid card service institutions such as MasterCard and InterSwitch, that can be used for both inward and outward transactions. However, these have limited use for fund transfers, given the preponderance of cash-based transactions.

Bank drafts are important instruments for outbound fund transfers, offered in collaboration with foreign banks, but the drafts are often relatively expensive for low-value transfers. For transfers using bank drafts, there is a fixed cost and a variable cost. When the amount is less than $50, the combination of such fixed and variable costs can exceed 50 percent of the total value of the transfer. This high cost of drafts reduces their appeal to bank customers.

Access to Other Financial Services

In Nigeria, remittance services are nearly entirely independent of other financial services in the formal banking sector. Most banks have a remittance service desk solely to administer the contract between the bank and its partner MTO. Such desks deal with all issues relating to remittances from outside the country through the MTOs. Consequently, many remittance recipients do not use other formal banking services except where they are already customers, in part because it is generally not a requirement to be an account holder to receive remittance services. Once in a while, banks go out of their way to convert a remittance service recipient to an account holder, but this is the exception rather than the rule, and usually, only high net-worth remittance recipients are so targeted.

Although the banks have exclusive commitments to certain MTOs, a remittance recipient can walk into any other bank with the logo of the same MTO to cash funds. Consequently, banks do not feel obliged to give any special treatment to remittance recipients, particularly in the case of small flows. In effect, remittance services are not designed in any way to help patrons become long-term users of the formal banking system for credit and savings purposes. What many RSP survey respondents reported as services available to remittance service patrons are identical to the products available to all other customers—and only if they become bank customers. They are not specifically marketed to either remittance senders or recipients.

The Regulatory and Business Environment

Improved regulations and policies have fostered the growth of the Nigerian financial system, but little of that improvement has been applied to the remittance market. Because of a sharp rise in bank branches over the past decade, however, RSPs now serve nearly all major cities in the country.

The Central Bank of Nigeria is the principal institution for financial (and consequently remittance) service regulation. Nearly every remittance-providing firm (about 96 percent of the respondents in the RSP survey, excluding NIPOST) must be registered with the Central Bank of Nigeria. For NIPOST and the courier companies, the Ministry of Information and Communication makes the rules, with occasional inputs from the Ministry of Finance and the central bank. For other service providers in the informal sector, however, regulation is almost, if not wholly, nonexistent.

Remittances in Nigeria have grown in value in spite of, rather than because of, appropriate policies specific to the industry. Aside from the registration and licensing requirements, no policies or incentives currently encourage sending or guide the specific use of remittances. The central bank guidelines regarding electronic banking and funds transfer cover the following areas:

- Authorization to undertake electronic transfers
- Classes of persons who can receive funds-transfer services
- Currency of transfers
- Security and anti-money-laundering matters
- Periodic control and evaluation of switch systems
- Personnel, security, and disaster control procedures

There are few specific guidelines for the huge remittance market. Even Form MTR 202, which the central bank uses to obtain remittance data from DMBs, is poorly designed. The form does not include such critical information as country of origin of remittance, number of transactions, and uses of remittance funds—omissions that limit the usefulness of the form-generated data. Overall, then, the central bank has given the industry little policy input, and the RSP survey responses reflect that lack of involvement: Most of the industry players do not consider laws and regulations to constitute a major or severe obstacle to conducting remittance business, as figure 7.3 indicates. Poor initiatives and policy makers' weak appreciation of the remittance industry's potential and options are definitely problems.

Entry Barriers

The general rules guiding the provision of financial services extend to remittance services by default. Among those rules, the most important inhibition to starting a remittance business is the banking license, closely linked to minimum capital base requirements. Before 2004, a banking license was not difficult to obtain given the low minimum capital requirement. After the capital requirement increased more than tenfold, however, the number of Nigerian banks has steadily declined. The few that remain are expanding—thus increasing the stakes for potential new entrants—because most of the MTOs would rather work with established banks that already have the necessary distribution infrastructure.

Many of the items noted in the RSP survey concerning entry barriers (including access to a distribution network, access to a financial infrastructure, and access to capital and finance) are perceived as moderate barriers by operators because many of them are taken as a given by those who can meet the NGN25 billion (about $166.7 million) minimum capital base

Figure 7.3   RSP Perceptions of Laws and Regulations as Obstacles to Remittance Business

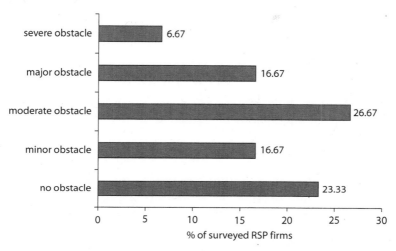

Source: Author's compilation from 2008 RSP survey in Nigeria.

requirement for banks. The only other significant barrier to entry, the respondents noted, is corruption in government circles. This seems easy to understand in the Nigerian context, where corruption always ranks among the top business impediments, but the specific mechanism in relation to remittance business licensing could not be established in the course of this study.

A number of the guidelines for electronic transfers and other financial transactions apply to remittances. For example, the central bank guidelines on electronic banking came into force in August 2003. They stipulate, in part, that only authorized financial institutions can undertake electronic funds transfers on behalf of customers and that the products and services can be offered only to residents with a specific residency designation. The rest are to use automatic teller machines, point-of-sale terminals, and other channels. The guidelines also state that the naira should be the only currency for such operations and that foreign currency should be used only for domiciliary account transactions.

In addition to complying with minimum capital base requirements, every firm is also required to report any suspicious activity or transactions that are above the authorized minimum (in most cases, NGN1 million for individual transactions and NGN5 million for corporate transactions). This requirement generally ties entry into the remittance business to becoming a financial services institution, with all the applicable requirements.

The situation is slightly different when operational barriers are considered with respect not only to the service provider, but also to the service user. At that level, in addition to licensing and capital requirements (which many industry players still think are critical), RSPs give weighty consideration to the following matters:

- Reporting requirements
- Exchange controls
- Anti-money-laundering (AML) and combating the financing of terrorism (CFT) requirements
- Government tax policies (concerning value added taxes, operational taxes, and other levies)

In fact, with respect to remittance service operations, more respondents give greater weight to AML requirements than to capital and licensing requirements, as figure 7.4 shows.

Figure 7.4   RSP Perceptions of Barriers to Remittance Business, by Type

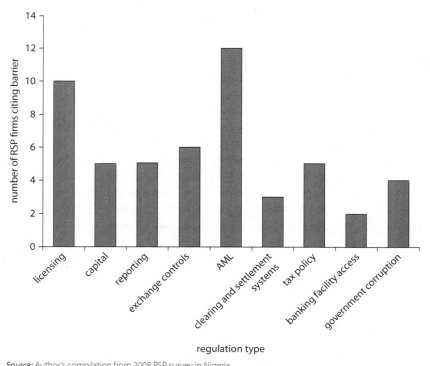

regulation type

Source: Author's compilation from 2008 RSP survey in Nigeria.

Among the RSPs surveyed, exchange controls and tax policy ranked second to licensing requirements as an operational barrier. In part, this reflects the volume of paperwork and care that each RSP firm must exercise to avoid a conflict with the myriad laws guiding international transfers. Following Nigeria's attempt and eventual success at being delisted from the Financial Action Task Force (FATF) list in 2004,[5] the country has particularly pursued AML laws with renewed vigor. The next section examines this issue more closely.

Exchange Controls and Other Reporting Requirements

The central bank requires and receives regular financial reports from all financial institutions, particularly the banks. Such notifications are necessary to keep track of suspicious financial transactions. At least 93 percent of all respondents to the RSP survey said they are required to file currency transactions with one or more regulators regularly. About 90 percent indicated they must report all suspicious transactions to the central bank. In addition, 46 percent of the respondents stated that the central bank limits RSPs' foreign exchange holdings.

Nevertheless, capital controls in Nigeria are, relatively speaking, not too strict. The guidelines for electronic transfers outlined in the previous section are more or less generic provisions to ensure orderliness and effective recording of financial transactions and are hardly specific to the remittance industry. Although limits are applicable in some cases, they are not so much limits on transfers as they are limits concerning notification about such transactions. When such limits are reached or exceeded, the bank does not have to stop the transaction but must simply notify the central bank for possible follow-up actions such as investigations when needed. Sometimes, such follow-up actions do not happen—a fact that some industry players conveniently exploit.

AML, CFT, and know-your-customer (KYC) requirements. To improve its image, Nigeria has exerted more than average efforts to rid its financial system of systemic corruption, distortions, and loopholes. Since 1995, it has amended its Money Laundering Act several times. The 2003 Anti-Money Laundering Act, for example, extended the scope of the 1995 Act to cover all financial crimes.

The 1991 Banks and Other Financial Institutions Decree (BOFID) was equally amended to cover stock and foreign currency exchange transactions. Under BOFID, the central bank gained greater power to issue, deny, and withdraw bank licenses and to freeze suspicious accounts.

The country also enacted an Economic and Financial Crimes Act, which criminalized terrorist financing and established the Economic and Financial Crimes Commission (EFCC) to investigate and prosecute violations. Suspicious transactions are statutorily reported to both the central bank and the EFCC.

Many of the operational guidelines for electronic transfers aim to ensure a safe and sound electronic funds transfer network-switching environment, with adequate internal controls to discourage fraud and provide an adequate audit trail.

Electronic banking products must also be in compliance with AML and KYC rules. The operational burden that this compliance places on operators is not insignificant. Banks routinely photocopy every foreign bill they pay out and must complete a number of forms for transactions involving foreign exchange before payouts. Other forms of recording, including microfilming, are also regularly used to counteract loopholes that may arise from improper completion of forms. Many of these laws are applicable even for domiciliary account holders who ordinarily may be excused on the ground that they are also regular customers of the banks.

Exchange controls. In addition, there is a ban on the sale of foreign exchange by banks except to traveling individuals, for whom attempts are made to confirm every detail, including possession of a travel visa (where applicable) and air ticket. Even with this documentation, there is a limit of no more than $5,000 per individual traveler, and the bank is required to transmit regular reports to the central bank on all such transactions.

All of these documentation and reporting requirements represent attempts to limit opportunities for money laundering and terrorist financing. Eventually, these laws tighten exchange controls, even when they may not have been intended for such purposes.

Competitive Factors

The remittance industry in Nigeria is oligopolistic, dominated by a few MTOs and a small number of banks. In particular, the capital requirements for banking licenses and permission to engage in international funds transfers restrict entry for many individuals and institutions. Regarding remittances, where franchise and infrastructure requirements are heavy, even the banks must collaborate among themselves and with the MTOs to participate. The fees are determined almost exclusively by the MTOs (with little provision for the banks to add tax-related and other charges of their own without authorization). In the RSP survey interviews, some of the nonbank operators (at least 40 percent) also indicated a need to partner with the banks to operate remittance services. In this respect, the industry might be considered oligopolistic and controlled by a few institutions.

However, the banks compete among themselves. Communications that many of the banks claimed provided financial literacy to their customers were no more than flyers advertising their remittance products. Banks engage in extensive advertising and branding of their individual remittance products, even though the competing banks generally have the same MTO partners and provide the same products and services. Except within relationships involving explicit understanding and collaboration, most of the banks see themselves in competition with each other to attract customers and earn commissions. Some of the larger banks, in addition to generating fees and commissions, have other goals such as global visibility, which the remittance contracts help them to achieve. Because the MTOs are fewer in number than the banks and have different operating rules, the banks do not see the MTOs as a threat.

The Nigerian government taxes remittances the same way it taxes other financial transactions. There is no tax on the amount remitted because it is considered the principal. Rather, a value added tax is levied on the income of banks from remittance services. The banks, in turn, incorporate this tax into their user fees. Among the survey respondents, 77 percent admitted that they must tax remittance services, while 17 percent noted that they are not so required.

On casual assessment, one would imagine that the informal sector, particularly given its size, constitutes a competition to the banks and other formal RSPs. However, most of the survey respondents reported this is not the case. A combined 83 percent of the respondents indicated that informal participants are either no obstacle at all or constitute only a minor or moderate obstacle. Only 6 percent perceive them as either a major or severe obstacle to conducting business in the remittance industry; the remaining RSPs did not respond to the question (figure 7.5).

It is easy to understand why this is so. For most industry players, the effective competition comes from other banks, which, as agents of the MTOs, must share the customer base.

However, the informal sector serves a different clientele. Bank officials do not recognize most of the people who use informal means, so it is difficult to even see them as potential customers. Aside from cash sent through relatives and friends, many remittance items in the informal

Figure 7.5   Perceptions of Informal RSPs as Competitors

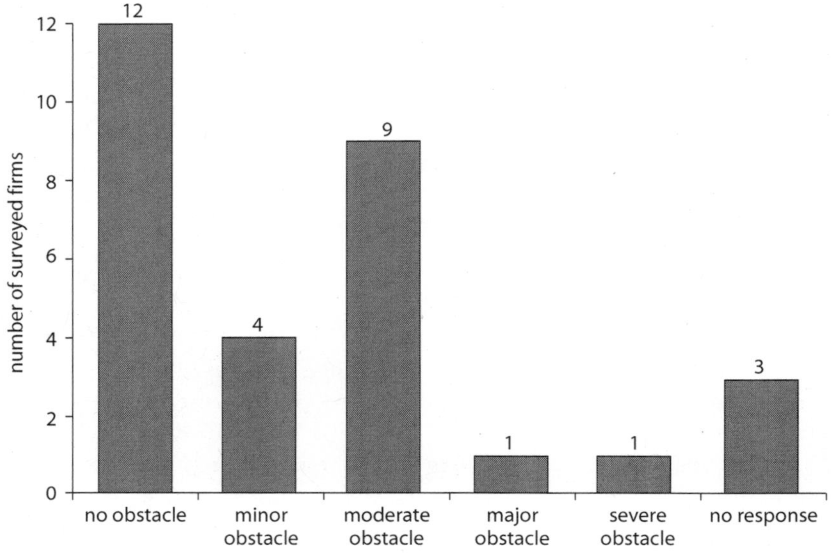

Source: Author's compilation from 2008 RSP survey in Nigeria.
Note: RSP = remittance service provider.

sector are tangible gift remittances handled through the seaports, airports, individual travelers, and courier companies. These remittances are outside the realm of activities covered by banks and so cannot be effectively classified as competition.

Remittance Fees, Customer Protection, and Identification Requirements

Nigeria is primarily an inward remittance corridor; outward remittances using the MTOs are prohibited by monetary authorities. Thus, for remittance inflows from outside the country, the fees are usually determined and paid outside the country by remittance senders. In 22 out of the 26 survey responses on the matter, remittance fees were reported to be the exclusive responsibility of the sender.

Informal discussions with DMB operators indicated that the charges vary among MTOs and depend on the country of origin, but the DMBs could not specify how much the remittance fees were per country. Recipients in Nigeria merely receive the net amount remitted after the MTO has deducted all charges at the point of sending.

In the other 4 out of 26 responses—mainly from domestic remittance operations (including transportation and courier companies) or involving international remittances passing through domestically held domiciliary accounts—there are charges on both ends of the transaction. The market for local courier and transportation firms is semiformal, and the rules are firm specific but often involve variable payments by both the sender and the recipient of remittances. In domiciliary accounts, the account holder pays a specific percentage of the total value of the transfer in addition to any other charges that may be specific to the bank in relation to such service.

Remittance transactions within Nigeria that are conducted within or among banks can be quite expensive. Among the survey respondents, 77 percent indicated that they charge fees to remittance senders within the country. The amount charged for in-country remittances depends on the amount sent and the account status of the sender. However, some banks recently introduced cost-free, within-bank, account-to-account transfers. These services provide for transfers of funds between two or more customers within the same bank without charges. At the forefront of this service are the new-generation banks, including Zenith Bank and Guaranty Trust Bank. However, most potential remittance receivers do not have such account services and have to rely on other means of transfers.

When the sending bank is different from the recipient's bank, the sender (and sometimes the receiver) bears varying charges. Some of these fees are fixed, regardless of the amount being transferred. Table 7.2

Table 7.2   Average Fees for Domestic Remittances in Nigeria
average cost to send $200 or equivalent

RSP type	Number of firms interviewed	Number of firms providing cost information	Average fee as percentage of transfer (a)	Average foreign exchange commission as percentage of transfer (b)	Average total fee (a) + (b) (%)
Private commercial banks	28	13	4.4	—	4.4
Courier, bus, and other transport services	1	1	5.4	—	5.4
Total (firms) or Average (fees)	29	14	4.9	—	4.9

Source: Author's compilation from 2008 RSP survey in Nigeria.
Note: — = not available.

summarizes the average fees obtained from the respondents, disaggregated between banks and courier services. (NIPOST did not provide figures in response to this question.) The average bank fee for transfers was 4.4 percent. The only transport company that responded to the question approximated its own average at 5.4 percent.

For outward international remittances, the charges differ significantly and depend on a number of factors, including the bank handling the transaction, country of destination, nature of relationship between the transferor and the bank (including whether the transferor has a domiciliary account), and availability of corresponding banks in the country of destination. Table 7.3 summarizes the average sums and proportions obtained from the survey responses about charges for outbound remittance services.

Many banks charge fixed fees irrespective of the transfer amount. For many banks, a proportion of the funds being transferred is also charged as fee—and, as some respondents indicated, such proportions could be as high as 10 percent. Charges vary significantly among the key operators for this service. As shown in table 7.3 (reflecting the banks' survey responses), fixed fees remained flat at about $15 between 2007 and 2008, while the proportion of the amount being transferred decreased from 7.45 percent to 5.6 percent.

As such, the highest proportional charges are borne by those who are remitting small amounts. These charges are in addition to whatever other operational and routine charges are levied on the domiciliary account. Some banks provide the alternative of using drafts issued by the remitting bank from Nigeria, but that option is fraught with several challenges, such as delays in draft preparation, and little, if any, guarantee that the foreign

Table 7.3   Bank Fees for Outward International Remittances in Nigeria, 2007–08
average cost to send $200 or equivalent

	Number of respondents	Number of firms providing cost information	Average fixed fee (US$)	Average fee as percentage of transfer (a)	Average foreign exchange commission as percentage of transfer (b)	Average total fee as percentage of transfer (a) + (b)	Minimum total fee as percentage of transfer	Maximum total fee as percentage of transfer
2008	28	9	15.28	5.6	0.63	6.23	7.64	13.87
2007	28	9	15.33	7.45	0.38	7.83	7.67	15.49

Source: Author's compilation from 2008 RSP survey in Nigeria.
Note: Data are from responses of nine bank respondents.

bank to which it is being issued will honor it. For many banks, the draft option does not exist at all.

Customer grievance procedures. Some of the regulatory loopholes in the remittance industry are found in the RSPs' customer grievance resolution system. Official policies to address customer grievances are largely non-existent. Given the relatively high efficiency of electronic transfer systems, though, customer satisfaction is fairly high, and the RSP survey respondents noted relatively low frequency of complaints.

Many RSPs have help desks (almost all respondents said they had a system for dealing with customer grievances)—usually the same customer service unit that caters to the rest of the bank's customers and clients. When an MTO agent receives notification of a problem, it simply takes the complaint to the MTO. In some cases, depending on the urgency the MTO attaches to the issue, the customer has to call the bank repeatedly, to no avail, because the bank cannot pay out or resolve a problem without the MTO's approval.

In sum, there is no established mechanism for handling customer grievances within Nigeria. All powers for conflict resolution are vested in the MTO, and the banks have to take instructions from them or take any additional action at their own risk. So conflict resolution is only as efficient as the invisible hand of the market; there is as yet no formal mechanism for regulatory intervention into conflict and grievance resolution in the remittance industry in Nigeria.

Identification requirements. Remittance recipients do not usually need to hold an account or be registered with an RSP to receive remittances. Individual banks work hard to increase market share and establish a strong presence in remittances. Consequently, most do not require remittance recipients to have an account with them. Only 6 out of the 30 survey respondents indicated this is a requirement.

But paying banks need to secure the integrity of remittance services and check impersonation during collection of remittances. Therefore, they accept only selected means of identification such as the international passport, national driver's license, or national identity card for paying out remittances. For collections in the bank for which a recipient holds an account, the bank can use the photo attached to an account for identification.

With a few exceptions, banks routinely reject employee identity cards and other plastic identity cards as forms of identification. In some cases, the banks ask for additional identification items such as utility (electricity, water, or accommodation) bills to supplement the standard requirements or when potential remittance recipients present dubious identification documents. Banks also seek information about the remittance sender and recipient, country of origin of funds, amount sent, and a secret code (expected to have been sent to the recipient by the remittance sender at the point of notification of sending funds).

These identification requirements lead to the exclusion of some segments of the Nigerian society from formal remittance services. For example, only a small proportion of Nigerians own international passports or driver's licenses. A national ID card project was undertaken by the Ministry of Internal Affairs in early 2000, but a significant proportion of Nigerians have yet to get their identity cards.

For those so excluded, the options are few. Even in cases where employee identity cards could be accepted, most people in this category are either self-employed with no official identity cards or are employed by small businesses in the informal sector that do not give official identity cards to employees. Another excluded group are those casually employed with formal firms who are not entitled to identity cards. Proof-of-residence documents and utility bills do not hold any respite because many of these either do not display clearly designated and identifiable residences, or people share utility bills with others, making presentation of such in their own names impossible.

Moreover, the ability to complete the forms also poses a threat to some of these excluded groups. Typically, many low-income persons who could not afford the identification requirements prefer to use third-party go-betweens in whose name the remittances would be sent from the outset. Sometimes such arrangements are made on the strength of social capital; at other times, the go-betweens must be paid to claim transferred funds, making poor people especially vulnerable to fraud—which, as box 7.5 explains, affects Nigerians using both formal and informal remittance channels.

Conclusions and Recommendations

The remittance market in Nigeria is large but not yet well managed, and there is substantial room for growth and change. To summarize, the status quo is as follows:

- Global MTOs remain the major players, employing the banks as intermediaries.

Box 7.5

The Plague of Fraud in Remittance and Other Electronic Fund Transfers

A major impediment to robust development of the remittance industry in Nigeria is fraud. Electronic communication is critical to the remittance industry. Mobile telephone networks, e-mail, and the Internet have come to play central roles in moving funds across borders or within countries—whether between MTOs and banks, between banks and recipients, or between senders and recipients. Transfer times, identification processes, and payment modalities have all been greatly enhanced by electronic communication.

In Nigeria, fraudsters, through varied means, exploit every loophole in the system to impersonate unsuspecting persons or defraud them of their entitlements. For example, in a situation where the communication flows mostly from the remittance sender, they can tell the recipient about a remittance in cash or in kind (say, a car) that may require small counterpart payments by the recipient (for example, for clearing at the wharf), to be deposited with a designated friend assigned the task of finishing the work. It is also not uncommon to receive notifications of a large sum of money through an MTO (sometimes Western Union) and be asked to visit a particular Web site (designed for that purpose) for necessary confirmations.

Interception of text and e-mail messages and presentation of false identification to receive a remittance in the stead of the rightful owner is also common. Another regular means of laying hands on the personal electronic payment infrastructure of individuals—one for which many have fallen—are phony notifications by "Interswitch" of changes to a customer's personal identification number (PIN), with a requirement to register old cards and PIN numbers at a particular Web site or send the information to a particular e-mail address.

Fraud is one of the greatest threats to the effective development of electronic transfers of remittances (and, indeed, of all funds). Individual and corporate businesses around the world are continually targeted by fraudsters. The system can sometimes be extremely organized. For example, as the EFCC tries to combat the use of cyber cafés for fraudulent activities, the fraudsters have had to resort to installing their own Internet servers. They are mostly young men who use amazing personal initiative to explore new means of keeping ahead of the law and exploiting loopholes in the payment system. So far, the EFCC has been only marginally successful in stopping them. A few of the bigger names have been nabbed in the past. However, most of the smaller operators in the business are still at large, keeping senders and recipients on their toes.

Source: Author.

- Nigerian banks compete among themselves but not in a way that changes the market.
- There is an informal sector, but it seems to work for a different set of consumers.
- NIPOST has struggled to break into the industry but faces challenges.
- The remittance market in Nigeria has few transfer instruments beyond cash-to-cash transfers, and they are expensive, with charges as high as 20 percent for inward-bound remittances.
- Telecom firms offer recharge cards, which are regularly used to send and receive remittances.
- Remittance services are seldom linked to regular bank services in a way that improves either the use of remittance funds or access to other financial services.
- Outward remittances are highly regulated, with limits placed on transactions, and the fees to send internal remittances can be exorbitant except for account-to-account transfers within the same bank.
- The regulatory framework for inbound remittances is weak. Financial reforms have regularized currency exchange activities, but the exchanges are not allowed to handle remittance transactions.

Recorded remittances in Sub-Saharan Africa are relatively small mainly because of inaccurate data (Grabel 2008). Therefore, before proceeding to the recommendations below, it is important to note that incentives to improve the Nigerian remittance market, its size, or its use cannot be effective without a meaningful database (CBN 2007). An overarching concern is the need for a remittance industry database and ombudsman. Some (arguably disparate) studies of Nigerian RSPs and the remittance market are linked only weakly, and there is a near-absence of structured takeoff points for market analyses.[6] Neither the Central Bank of Nigeria's Form MTR 202 nor data returns from banks are comprehensive, and a remittance ombudsman who collaborates with the EFCC could help not only to resolve conflicts, but also to share information about potential sources of confidence-weakening fraud.

The remaining recommendations fall within three areas: (a) increasing competition to reduce remittance service costs, (b) improving access to remittance services, and (c) enhancing the use of remittance proceeds.

Increase Competition to Reduce Remittance Service Costs

As in many other financial transactions, the fees to send and receive remittances should not exceed 2 percent of the amount sent. In Nigeria, formal RSPs currently charge more than 10 percent, and the fees vary (but are often even higher) through informal channels. Increased competition is one prerequisite for reducing these costs.

Enact and enforce regulation to expunge exclusivity from RSP contracts. In line with the Central Bank of Nigeria's recent initiative to outlaw exclusivity in remittance service partnerships with MTOs, regulation to set maximum charges for international transfers could be useful (Hernández-Coss and Bun 2007; Orozco and Millis 2008; Watson and Fortescue 2008).

Increase the number of industry players. To increase competition, banks (for example, through targeted incentives from the central bank) should be encouraged to open remittance outlets in source countries.[7] In addition to the regular services offered by MTOs, patronage of these outlets should automatically qualify the remittance sender and receiver to be account holders in the bank.

In addition, selected currency exchanges and microfinance institutions (MFIs) should be accredited and licensed to partner with other foreign and local MTOs and banks to provide remittance services.[8] The minimum conditions to license currency exchanges and MFIs as independent RSPs could include their ability to arrange adequate partnerships or increase institutional infrastructure to set up remittance outlets outside the country as well as proposals to ensure minimal costs, high efficiency, and reliability.[9]

Exchange rate–related costs also must stabilize to reduce costs to the sender, recipient, and service provider. Despite significant progress in closing the gap between the parallel and official exchange rates in recent years, exchange rates remain highly variable, imposing substantial search and information costs on operators.

An examination of the settlement rates and practices of banks and MTOs in remittance-related transactions may also prove useful.

Improve Access to Remittance Services

The effective deployment of NIPOST's infrastructure across the entire country can go a long way toward improving rural access to remittance services. NIPOST should be empowered, through initial funding and logistical support, to fully compete as an RSP. Because most of NIPOST's services are affordable to rural dwellers, its growth as an RSP also could exert downward pressure on tariffs industrywide.

To the extent that the informal sector fills gaps in access to formal remittance services, it also complicates data capture and policy transmission.[10] Most formal RSPs do not consider the informal sector to be a formidable competitor, but informal players are serving a large market share of cost-conscious remittance patrons who cannot meet formal RSPs' identification requirements for various reasons. It is difficult to simplify the identification process to deal with informal flows without compromising the AML and KYC rules, so a one-off identification of the sort needed for account opening (entitling the recipient of remittances to an account and subsequent rights of an account holder) can help to resolve the dilemma. The system needn't treat every remittance transaction as a one-off event, but it should encourage and reward the regular use of formal banking services in remittance transactions.

Licensing MFIs can help to increase rural outlets for remittance services given that some of the most regular remittance recipients are rural residents. In addition, the central bank can provide incentives (for example, tax waivers) to encourage RSPs and banks to establish remittance disbursement points (not necessarily bank branches) near remote villages.

Enhance the Use of Remittance Proceeds

Related to the access issues are challenges involving Nigeria's cash-based payment system in which remittance services are primarily cash-to-cash transfers. Strengthening the card and credit system and promoting their use in remittance transfers will go a long way toward increasing remittance volume, reducing remittance costs, and using remittance proceeds with greater effect on national growth and development.

Without question, remittances are a potential source of development capital for the continent. For example, the Nigerian stock market has been a major destination of remittances in recent years (Agu 2010). Therefore, the Nigerian government, the central bank, and RSPs must explore these ways of ensuring that remittances benefit the entire country:

- *Provide incentives and otherwise urge banks to package remittance-specific instruments exclusively for remittance patrons*, not just for regular bank customers. For example, in response to Obasanjo's Nigerians in Diaspora Organization (NIDO),[11] the United Bank for Africa designed a "nonresident Nigerian" banking service, offering products such as local account maintenance, loan facilities for real estate development, asset management products, and private equity facilities (Kimani-Lucas 2007).

- *Develop financial literacy programs and allied money and capital market instruments for remittance patrons* that go beyond mere advertising of alliances with Western Union or MoneyGram. After making remittance recipients account holders, advising them on effective use of remittance funds, and linking them to products to securitize those funds, banks should follow up by offering specific bank-designed instruments that will encourage savings and investment.
- *Offer specialized loan packages that are tied to remittance receipts,* in alliance with mortgage firms and, if possible, linked to the National Housing Fund. This alone can boost the housing investment significantly.
- *Harness the power of remittances to fuel growth by offering incentives to the untapped communities and clusters of remittance senders and recipients.* In southeast Nigeria, for example, remittance funds support a significant number of self-help community development projects.[12] Specialized products designed for and marketed to these clusters—emphasizing specific aspects of development such as mortgages, stocks, community electrification projects, road construction, and small and mid-size enterprises—will redirect a substantial share of remittance funds away from consumption and toward investment and development. The central bank can aid banks and mortgage firms in this effort by directly providing (or coordinating with relevant government institutions to provide) matching funds through options such as diaspora bonds and repatriable foreign exchange accounts (Adenuga and Bala-keffi 2005; Ratha, Mohapatra, and Plaza 2008).

The literature is replete with findings that both human and physical capital investments increase (or at least should increase) along with remittances (for example, Glytsos 2002 on six countries in the Mediterranean; Adams 2006 on Guatemala). It is the central bank's job to ensure that RSPs, particularly banks, have incentives to think in this direction.

Remittances in Nigeria hold great promise—to benefit the remittance senders and receivers (microagents) as well as to achieve the larger macroeconomic goal of mobilizing development resources for improved growth. These microagents are already doing their best to affect the economy, given the constraints of maximizing personal utility within the business environment under which they operate.

Making remittances more useful—both economically and socially—is the responsibility of industry operators and macroeconomic policy makers. Although the efforts to meet this challenge have so far been minimal, those who have achieved many other recent positive developments in Nigeria can attest that success is not impossible.

Notes

1. The author is most grateful to Uchenna Amaeze, Ositadinma Uba, Nath Urama, and Gold Nwokeocha for research assistance at various levels of this work.
2. Several studies have estimated that informal-sector remittance transfers to developing countries make up between 40 and 75 percent of total remittances. A big task ahead is to design methods of capturing these informal flows and putting policies in place to formalize or at least boost them.
3. In addition to disaggregating remittance flows from other aspects of the capital account, the Central Bank of Nigeria Research Department designed Form MTR 202 to elicit information from financial institutions about specific flows of remittances as opposed to other flows.
4. NetPost Nigeria Ltd. is a joint venture partnership between NIPOST and two private sector companies. See http://www.netpostnig.com/.
5. See Financial Action Task Force, http://www.fatf-gafi.org/.
6. The central bank's first major work on remittances is yet to be published.
7. Such targeted incentives can come in different forms. For example, the Central Bank of Nigeria can work with the relevant authorities in the partner countries to enhance the registration process for a Nigerian RSP. This is consistent with the recommendation for increased partnership between Nigeria and its partners in working out a better environment for remittance services (Hernández-Coss and Bun 2007).
8. The experience with the conversion of informal money changers into licensed currency exchanges in 2005 shows the potential that can be harnessed through this kind of formalization policy. Previously, the Nigerian foreign exchange system had been littered with informal, unregistered players, making foreign exchange policy transmission nearly impossible and creating significant premiums on foreign exchange transactions arising from information asymmetry and uncoordinated activities. In 2005, however, the central bank designed minimum criteria for currency exchange operations and forced these operators to formally register. Ever since, foreign exchange policies in Nigeria have stabilized, and the exchange rate was relatively stable until late 2008.
9. Orozco and Millis (2008) recognize five conditions as necessary to demonstrate capacity for remittance payments: (a) compliance with international regulatory norms on money transfers (AML, KYC, and so on), (b) minimum cash flow equivalent to four daily remittance payments, (c) trained staff able to perform retail payments in foreign currency, and (d) technological systems

and hardware to adopt or adapt the payment platform. MFIs and currency exchanges would find the cash flow requirement to be the main challenge. To meet it may entail "further consolidation" in the industry, which for competence purposes would benefit the entire economy even more.

10. The distinction between formal and informal segments of the remittance service industry could be misleading (World Bank 2007). Without going into the details of Nigeria's informal remittance service industry, we simply note that the use of "informal sector" here is meant to include illegal providers that are not licensed to provide remittance services as well as small and unincorporated institutional and individual players.

11. The erstwhile president of Nigeria, Olusegun Obasanjo, instituted a process for Nigerians abroad to contribute more closely to the development of the country. NIDO was the umbrella organization that worked to bring this vision to reality.

12. Osili (2004) also reports a substantial number of personal and community housing projects supported by remittances.

References

Adams, Richard H., Jr., 2006. "Remittances, Poverty and Investment in Guatemala." In *International Migration, Remittances and the Brain Drain*, ed. Caglar Ozden and Maurice Schiff, 53–80. Washington, DC: World Bank and Palgrave Macmillan.

Adenuga, A. O., and L. Bala-keffi. 2005. "Inward Remittances and Economic Development in Nigeria: Issues and Policy Options." *Journal of Banking and Finance* 7 (2). Financial Institutions Training Centre, Lagos.

Adepoju, A. 1987. "Demographic Aspects of Internal Migration Politics in Nigeria." In *Population et développement en Afrique*, ed. Hedi Jemai, 353–89. Dakar: Conseil pour le Développement de la Recherche Économique et Sociale en Afrique.

Agu, C., 2010. "Nigeria's Market Crisis, Fundamentals, and Stock Pricing: A Review for Africa." Paper presented at the International Academy of Business and Economics 2010 Summer Conference, Pattaya, Thailand, June 4–6.

Baumol, W. J., and A. S. Blinder. 1998. "Recent Developments in the U.S. Labour Market." In *Economics: Principles and Policy*, ed. W. J. Baumol, 398–99. New York: Dryden Press.

CBN (Central Bank of Nigeria). 2007. "The Remittance Environment in Nigeria." Unpublished study by the Research and Statistics Department, CBN, Abuja, Nigeria.

Glytsos, Nicholas P. 2002. "A Macroeconometric Model of the Effects of Migrant Remittances in Mediterranean Countries." In *Human Capital: Population*

Economics in the Middle East, ed. Ismail Abdel-Hamid Sirageldin, 299–349. London: I.B. Tauris; Cairo: American University of Cairo Press.

Grabel, Ilene. 2008. "The Political Economy of Remittances: What Do We Know? What Do We Need to Know?" Working Paper 184, Political Economy Research Institute, University of Massachusetts, Amherst.

Hernández-Coss, Raúl, and Chinyere Egwuagu Bun. 2007. "The UK–Nigeria Remittance Corridor: Challenges of Embracing Formal Transfer Systems in a Dual Financial Environment." Working Paper 92, World Bank, Washington, DC.

Kimani-Lucas. M. 2007. "Harnessing African Diaspora Remittances and Skills to Drive Growth in Africa." Paper for CAPAfrique. http://www.capafrique.org/pdf/20071711NMaureenKimani.pdf.

Kómoláfé, J. 2002. "Searching for Fortune: The Geographical Process of Nigerian Migration to Dublin, Ireland." *Irinkerindo: A Journal of African Migration* Issue 1, September. http://www. africamigration.com/archive_01/j_komolafe _searching.htm.

Mberu, Blessing U. 2005. "Who Moves and Who Stays? Rural Out-migration in Nigeria." *Journal of Population Research* (Brown University) 22 (2): 141–61.

Nwajiuba, C. 2005. "International Migration and Livelihood in Southeastern Nigeria." *Global Migration Perspectives* 50, Global Commission on International Migration.

Nwokocha, Ezebunwa E. 2008. "Engaging the Burden of Rural-Urban Migration in a Nonregulatory System: The Case of Nigeria." Unpublished paper, Department of Sociology, University of Ibadan, Nigeria. http://www.irmgard-coninx-stiftung.de/fileadmin/user_upload/pdf/urbanplanet/Nwokocha.pdf.

Oluwasola, Oluwemimo. 2007. "Social Systems, Institutions, and Structures: Urbanization, Poverty, and Changing Quality of Life." Paper presented at training session of the Foundation for Environmental Development and Education in Nigeria, Obafemi Awolowo University, Ile-Ife, Nigeria, February 22.

Orozco, M. 2003. "Worker Remittances: An International Comparison." Working paper commissioned by the Multilateral Investment Fund of the Inter-American Development Bank, Washington, DC.

Orozco, Manuel, and Bryanna Millis. 2008. "Remittances, Competition, and Fair Financial Access Opportunities in Nigeria." USAID AMAP MicroReport 86, U.S. Agency for International Development, Washington, DC.

Osili, U. O. 2004. "Migrants and Housing Investments: Theory and Evidence from Nigeria." *Economic Development and Cultural Change* 52 (4): 821–49.

Ratha, Dilip, Sanket Mohapatra, and Sonia Plaza. 2008. "Beyond Aid: New Sources and Innovative Mechanisms for Financing Development in Sub-Saharan Africa." Policy Research Working Paper 4609, Development Prospects Group, World Bank, Washington, DC.

Tomori, S., and M. A. Adebiyi. 2007. "Migrants' Remittances and the Economy: Theoretical and Impact Issues." In *Toward Africa's Renewal*, ed. J. C. Senghor and N. K. Poku, 295–319. London: Ashgate.

UN DESA (United Nations Department of Economic and Social Affairs). 2008. "An Overview of Urbanization, Internal Migration, Population Distribution and Development in the World." Paper UN/POP/EGM-URB/2008/01 for the UN Expert Group Meeting on Population Distribution, Urbanization, Internal Migration, and Development, New York, January 21–23.

Watson, Gregory, and Seymour Fortescue. 2008. "International Remittance Market Reforms in Nigeria." Presentation by World Bank Payment Systems and Remittances Team Mission in Nigeria, February.

World Bank. 2007. "General Principles for International Remittance Services." Report for the Committee on Payment and Settlement Systems and the World Bank, Washington, DC. http://www.bis.org/publ/cpss76.pdf.

CHAPTER 8

Senegal

Fatou Cisse

Remittances from migrants abroad have become a viable means for developing countries to finance their development and reduce poverty.[1] Remittance transfers to developing countries amounted to approximately US$325 billion in 2010—four times greater than in 2000 (World Bank 2011). Overall, remittances have become more significant than official development assistance (ODA) and, in certain developing countries, have outstripped foreign direct investment (FDI). This increase in remittances has led many authors to view them as potentially beneficial for development (Kapur 2004). The transfer of foreign currency through remittances also has a positive effect on national income, savings, and investment; by helping to finance imports, remittances reduce imbalances and thus similarly affect private and public capital flows (Russell 1986).

This chapter analyzes migrant remittances in Senegal, specifically their volume, methods of transfer, regulatory framework, environment, and operating procedures and costs. The study methodology included both primary sources (particularly, a survey of remittance service providers [RSPs]) and secondary sources (consultation of relevant documents).

The author wishes to thank Gaye Daffe for his contribution and useful comments.

Remittance Trends and Their Economic Significance

Remittances have become an important and growing source of external financing for Senegal, although the total amount is unknown because many of these flows are transferred through unidentifiable informal channels. The World Bank (2010) estimates that remittances sent through formal channels increased from US$344 million in 2002 to US$1,288 million in 2008—and that official remittances tripled in six years, as figure 8.1 illustrates. The remittance flows fell to US$1,191 million in 2009, registering an 8 percent decline between 2008 and 2009. The decline in remittances during the global financial crisis was modest compared to a 71 percent decline in FDI and an 11 percent decline in exports of goods and services between 2008 and 2009 (figure 8.1). Moreover, remittances accounted for 9 percent of gross domestic product (GDP) in 2009, compared to 6 percent in 2001 (figure 8.2).

This growth raised Senegal to fourth place among recipient countries in Sub-Saharan Africa (after Nigeria, Sudan, and Kenya) in the total volume of remittances and to fifth place (after Lesotho, Togo, Cape Verde, and Guinea-Bissau) in remittances as a percentage of GDP.

Figure 8.1   Volume of Migrant Workers' Remittances to Senegal, 2001–10

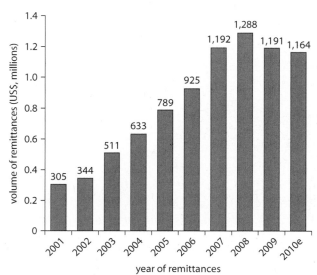

Sources: World Bank 2010, 2011.
Note: e = estimated. Figures do not include remittance flows through informal channels.

Figure 8.2   Share of GDP from Migrant Workers' Remittances, 2001–09

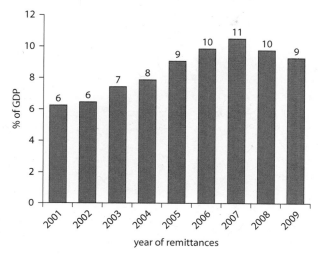

Sources: World Bank 2010, 2011.
Note: Figures do not include remittance flows through informal channels.

The total volume of migrant remittances is difficult to estimate because a large proportion does not pass through the official channels. To avoid the high costs, complexity, and red tape involved when sending money through formal channels, many migrants use the informal circuit—carrying cash themselves, sending it through intermediaries, or transferring funds using new techniques such as telephone or fax transfers.

When informal transfers are considered, however, the estimated totals soar even higher. A 2007 survey by the African Development Bank (AfDB), which covered both formal and informal transfers, estimated that remittances to Senegal totaled CFAF 823 billion in 2005 (or 19 percent of GDP). This figure included formal remittances of CFAF 444 billion (54 percent of the total) and informal remittances of CFAF 379 billion (46 percent of the total).

The AfDB estimate corresponds to an average annual transfer of more than CFAF 960,000 per migrant and more than CFAF 1.9 million per recipient household—exceeding per capita GDP (CFAF 397,000 in 2005) and per capita consumption (CFAF 365,000 in 2005). According to some studies, such payments may represent 90 percent of the household budget in certain villages of Senegal (Ammassari 2004).

Even if one considers only those remittances flowing through the formal sector, several factors could explain the sharp increase in remittances to Senegal over the past decade (Shaw 2007):

- The 50 percent devaluation of the CFA franc against the French franc automatically doubled the value of all remittances made in foreign currencies.
- The emergence of new money transfer operators (MTOs) provided migrants with safer, faster, and more reliable channels.
- The new regulations imposed on the remittance service industry after the September 11, 2001, terrorist attacks in the United States also contributed to the development of the transfer process.

Economic Impact

Remittances have become the principal source of external financing for the Senegalese economy, far exceeding FDI; external borrowing; and, above all, ODA, which had long been the most reliable and stable source of financing.

The transfers thus hold a significant place in the satisfaction of the various needs for households. They are mainly assigned to the daily consumer expenditure of the recipient households (58.5 percent), followed by the expenditure of health and education (13.2 percent together) (table 8.1). The payment of the rent ranks third (12.6 percent).

The results from the second Senegalese Household Survey (ESAM II, July 2004) showed that remittances increased the average per capita expenditure of recipient households by almost 60 percent, thereby reducing nationwide poverty by almost one-third (30.7 percent) (DPEE

Table 8.1   Remittance Transfers by Use in Senegal, 2008
% share of all transfers

Use of remittances	Number of households reporting
Consumption	58.51
Health	9.43
Education	3.59
Rent	12.57
Clothes	2.49
Car	0.15
Business	1.29
Others	11.98
Total	100.00

Source: World Bank and CRES 2011.

2008) (table 8.2). The European Union has the highest contribution to the transfers (52 percent) with Italy at the first place, follow to Spain and France. The West African Economic and Monetary Union contribution is marginal (7 percent), less than that of the United States (7.7 percent) (table 8.3).

A comparison with traditional financial flows from abroad gives an idea of the overall contribution of remittances to the national economy. Figure 8.3 shows the trends in exports, workers' remittances, ODA, and FDI from 1995 through 2009. Of all these flows, migrant remittances have shown the most stable growth. In 2008, they were 2 and 1.22 times greater than FDI and ODA, respectively.

Table 8.2   Impact of Remittances on Poverty Rates, by Location
(percent)

Location	Without remittances	With remittances	Poverty rate change
National	52.4	36.3	−30.7
Dakar	20.5	22.6	+10.0
Other towns	64.0	25.6	−60.0
Rural areas	71.8	52.7	−26.7

Source: World Bank 2011.

Table 8.3   Sources of Remittances to Senegal, 2008, by Location

Source	2007	
	CFAF (millions)	% of total
WAEMU	**37,817**	**7**
Benin	3,149	0.6
Burkina Faso	1,827	0.3
Côte d'Ivoire	21,029	3.9
Guinea-Bissau	1,583	0.3
Mali	8,051	1.5
Niger	771	0.1
Togo	1,408	0.3
EU	**281,793**	**51.8**
France	64,749	11.9
Spain	69,728	12.8
Italy	142,763	26.2
United States	42,028	7.7
China	243	0
Other	182,044	33.5
TOTAL	**543,925**	**100**

Source: BCEAO 2008.
Note: WAEMU = West African Economic and Monetary Union. EU = European Union.

Figure 8.3   Comparison of Remittance Flows to Senegal, 1995–2010, by Source

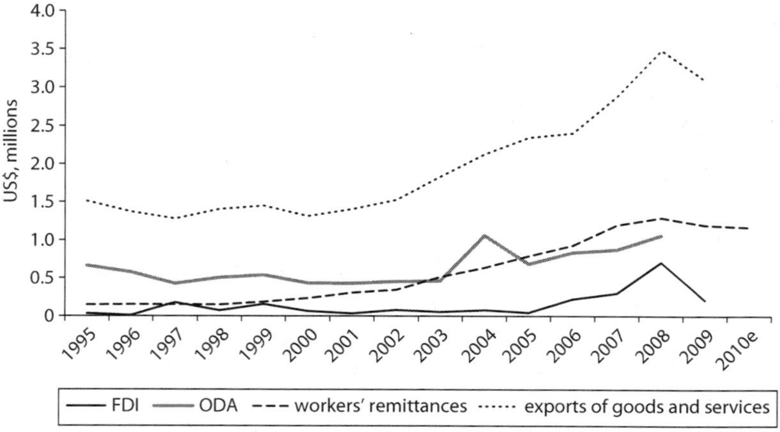

Source: World Bank 2010.
Note: e = estimated.

Moreover, the steady increase in the ratio of remittances to export earnings (from 10 percent in 1995 to 39 percent in 2009) illustrates the growing contribution of remittances to the national account balance. Similar trends have been observed in practically all developing countries (Ratha 2003; Ratha, Mohapatra, and Plaza 2008).

Destinations of Migrants

Senegal has long traditions of both immigration and emigration. For the past three decades, it has been losing ground as a host country and is becoming a country of origin. This trend, which dates back to the West African countries' accession to independence, became more apparent in the early 1980s (Bruzzone and others 2006). However, Senegal remains one of the few countries in the region with stable immigration. According to the 2002 general census, international migrants totaled 276,454, or 3 percent of the total population. Almost 95 percent of these immigrants, most of whom live in the Dakar region, come from other West African countries, particularly Guinea. Only 3 percent come from non-African countries.

Since the colonial period, Senegalese emigration has been characterized by periods of both continuity and fluctuation. Long before the country achieved independence in 1960, some Senegalese emigrants settled in French-speaking West African countries. Others went to central and southern Africa (to what is now the Democratic Republic of Congo or Zambia), where they joined the gem mining and marketing industry.

Indeed, the success of these migrants resulted in major investments within Senegal in real estate and trade. This trend probably occurred when large-scale remittances from Senegalese emigrants were initially recorded in 1960–70 (Daffé 2008).

Although the West African countries still attract a large majority of Senegalese migrants, France's labor needs (for reconstruction and industrialization) established it as the main migration destination for Senegalese workers during the 1950s and 1960s. However, immigration restrictions imposed by France in the mid-1970s resulted in a shift to new destinations (table 8.3) such as Italy and Spain. Migration flows to the United States also showed a marked increase. The steady increase in Senegalese emigration can be attributed to several factors. Largely because of financial difficulties and the crisis of the groundnut, the center of international emigration moved from the Senegal River valley to the Groundnut Basin and involved groups that previously had no reason to emigrate, such as the large Sufi Islamic order—the Mouride brotherhood.

After initially focusing on France and the former French African colonies, Senegalese migration has since expanded in scope, occurring in three successive waves:

(1) Colonial migration linked to the need for construction workers in the other French colonies in Africa (Congo [now the Republic of Congo], Côte-d'Ivoire, Gabon, and Guinea)
(2) Migration to meet the demand for specialized workers in France after the World War II
(3) Modern migration, for economic reasons, to Italy, Spain, and other European destinations, as shown in table 8.3.

However, stricter border control, restrictions on movement, and national immigration laws have constrained official migration and increased the use of clandestine migration networks. The total estimated number of Senegalese emigrants varies from source to source. The attempts to document migration have not been helped by the emergence of illegal routes. According to the World Bank (2011), Senegalese emigrants numbered just over 636,200 in 2010 (5 percent of the total population). This is twice the average rate throughout Sub-Saharan Africa (2.5 percent).

West African countries remain the principal destinations for Senegalese migrants, attracting 53.4 percent of departures (table 8.4). However, France is still the preferred European country. According to

Table 8.4   Principal Destinations of Senegalese International Migrants, 2008

Countries of destination	Number of migrants	Percent
Africa	**339,984.98**	**53.40**
Gambia, The	177,306.41	27.85
Mauritania	64,556.94	10.14
Côte d'Ivoire	33,250.24	5.22
Gabon	21,959.42	3.45
Mali	11,895.00	1.87
Guinea Bissau	9,806.73	1.54
Other Africa	21,210.24	3.33
OECD	**255,463.39**	**40.13**
France	91,446.44	14.36
Italy	81,423.63	12.79
Spain	51,671.57	8.12
United States	16,745.31	2.63
Other OECD	14,176.45	2.23
Other	**41,184.79**	**6.47**

Source: World Bank and CRES 2011.
Note: OECD = Organisation for Economic Co-operation and Development.

official statistics,[2] France had almost 91,446 Senegalese immigrants in 2010—36 percent the population of Senegalese migrants in the Organization for Economic Cooperation and Development (OECD) countries.

Senegalese migrants choose their destinations no longer based only on economic, historic, or linguistic factors but also on the immigration policies of the host countries. Since the 1980s, the migrants' regions of origin have also become more diverse, with the Dakar and Diourbel regions well represented (31 percent and 19 percent, respectively) and the Senegal River valley (historically, the main departure region) no longer dominant (Saint-Louis 4.7 percent).

The Senegalese Migration and Remittances Survey (World Bank and CRES 2010) showed that in more than half out of the households (52 percent), at least one member had emigrated.

Internal Migration and Remittances

The third general population and housing census (Recensement General de la Population et de l'Habitat, RGPH-III 2002) conducted by the National Agency of Statistics and Demography described internal migration in Senegal as the most important form of migration because the exodus from rural to urban areas causes interregional imbalances. The census showed that 1.3 million (13 percent) of Senegal's 9.9 million citizens live outside their birth regions. Between 1998 and 2002, internal migration increased by an annual average of 2.1 percent.

The Dakar region was the principal destination for most of these migrants (47 percent). It was followed by the Diourbel (13 percent) and Thiès (12 percent) regions. People migrate primarily to the regions of Dakar, Thiès, and Diourbel for economic development and employment opportunities. Others move because of a shortage of food in the rural areas or because of climatic reasons, such as inadequate rainfall.

However, relatives cannot continue to rely on migrants for help, and for many rural inhabitants, migration to urban areas is only a stop-gap solution. Interviews with residents revealed that 78 percent of the heads of household had received no assistance from their relatives who migrated to other towns. The few transfers received in the village were typically sent by the younger relatives, particularly girls employed in domestic service in urban centers (Bruzzone and others 2006). As the crisis in rural areas worsens, there is increased migration to urban areas as people search for work and additional income.

Characteristics of the Remittance Industry in Senegal

In Senegal, remittances can be transferred either through formal money transfer services—such as the post office and banks—or through informal channels where the transfers are made directly by migrants or are sent through relatives, friends, or other intermediaries (Bruzzone and others 2006; AfDB 2007). The new money transfer models, whether formal or informal, have enhanced their operations through information and communication technologies.

The Formal Market

The most common formal channels are banks, MTOs, the post office, and microfinance institutions (MFIs). MTOs transfer money through consortiums with the other three.

Banks. The bancarization rate in Senegal's remittance service industry is estimated to be only about 6 percent (Sander and Barro 2007).[3] Transfers through the banking channels accounted for 10 percent of the total volume of remittances, or about CFAF 82 billion, as table 8.5 shows (AfDB 2007).

Table 8.5   Volume and Market Share of Remittance Transfers in Senegal, by Method

	Banks	MTOs	Postal money orders	Informal (cash)	Other informal methods (fax)
Volume					
(CFAF, billions)	82	296	66	312	66
Market share	10%	36%	8%	38%	8%

Source: AfDB 2007.

The small market share of remittance transfers for banks can be attributed to a number of factors other than cost, including the following:

- Distance of bank branches from residential areas (especially in rural areas)
- Long delays in the delivery of services
- Long wait times at branches
- Sometimes unexpected and arbitrary commission charges upon receipt.

As of December 31, 2008, Senegal had 17 banks, with a network of 214 branches, most of which (68 percent) were concentrated in the Dakar region, as figure 8.4 illustrates. The others can be found in medium-size towns such as Saint-Louis (9 percent), Thiès (7 percent), and Diourbel (6 percent). Rural areas have hardly any bank coverage.

MTOs. Partnerships between banks and MTOs are responsible for most of the international money transfers. MTOs became widespread in Africa in the mid-1990s, and they have been the principal beneficiaries of the growth in formal transfers over the past 10 years. They have also contributed to the decline in the number of informal channels by customizing their services to meet the needs of immigrants while ensuring proximity, speed, and safety in the context of low bancarization. Although they account for 36 percent of the remittance market, MTOs can afford to keep their costs high because of their monopoly status.

The MTO market in Senegal is dominated by Western Union, which accounted for 73 percent of remittance transfers between 2006 and 2007, as shown in figure 8.5. MoneyGram, which is relatively new in Africa, had a 22 percent share of the market. The others operate in very specific corridors, such as intra-African transfers or transfers with Arab countries, and they are Money Express, Telegiros, Ria Envia, Travelex and

Figure 8.4   Regional Coverage of Bank Branches in Senegal, 2009

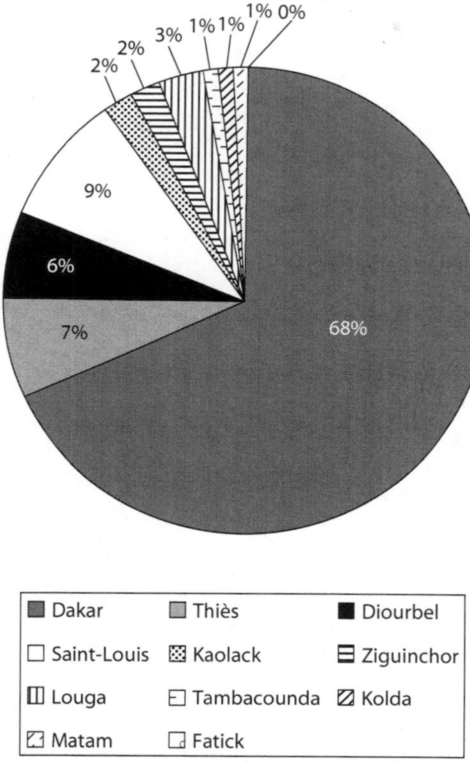

■ Dakar	▤ Thiès	■ Diourbel
□ Saint-Louis	⊠ Kaolack	⊟ Ziguinchor
⊞ Louga	⊟ Tambacounda	⊡ Kolda
⊡ Matam	⊡ Fatick	

Source: DMC/MEF 2009.

Choice Money Transfer. However, these operators are limited by the high prices they charge.

Post Office. The post office has a market share of 8 percent of the remittance market in Senegal. This channel is highly competitive by virtue of its long-standing network and presence in rural areas with low bancarization. The post office uses its traditional products, particularly postal money orders, for local transfers. For international transfers, the post office uses the products of specialized operators such as Western Union.

MFIs. MFIs have become increasingly involved in the provision of remittance services. These institutions have been thriving since the early 1990s because of the restructuring in the banking and financial sector (Sander

Figure 8.5   MTO Remittance Market Shares in Senegal, 2009

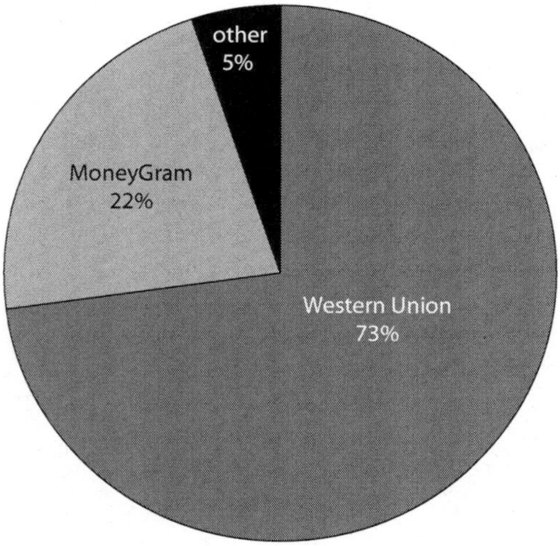

Source: DMC/MEF 2009 (statistics from bank records of rapid money transfers).

and Barro 2007). Between 1988 and 2000, the number of MFIs quadrupled from 30 to 121, and the total number of service points increased from 233 to 324 (a 39 percent increase). These MFIs serve as intermediaries between the MTOs and the recipients, and they also have a share of 8 percent of the total market.

The Informal Market

Although informal channels are still prevalent, their share of remittance transfers has declined by comparison with the formal MTOs, which quadrupled their share of international transfers in the past five years. There were 14 informal channels in the Dakar region alone: 6 in public markets, 5 in offices, and 3 in individual homes (Bruzzone and others 2006).

The prevalence of informal channels makes it difficult to evaluate the actual amount of migrant remittances they facilitate into Senegal. However, AfDB estimated that, collectively, informal transfers accounted for an estimated CFAF 379 billion, or 46 percent of all remittances to Senegal in 2005 (AfDB 2007).

The informal sector developed because of strict banking regulations and offers many advantages, such as immediate delivery, simplicity, proximity to recipients, accessibility (especially for the uneducated), and low costs. For customers who do not meet formal-sector identification requirements or cannot provide proof of residence, the informal channel is often the only option. The reasons for use of informal channels include exchange rate fluctuations, bank branch inaccessibility, national coverage, time spent at branches, cost, safety, low rate of bancarization, and the number of unauthorized foreign residents (AfDB 2007).

Partnerships and Exclusivity Contract Issues

As specified in Article 2 of the regulations that guide the external financial relations of member states of the West African Economic and Monetary Union (WAEMU), money transfer services may be conducted only through the BCEAO (Banque Centrale des Etats de l'Afrique de l'Ouest), the postal administration, and licensed intermediaries—banks established in a WAEMU-member state that are licensed to engage in foreign exchange operations.[4] To comply with this regulation, the remittance market in Senegal is therefore characterized by partnerships, either between MTOs and banks or between banks and MFIs.

To ply their trade, MTOs must rely on a licensed intermediary with whom they must sign a contract and confer on the intermediary status of agent or subagent.

MFIs operating under the Project for the Regulation of Credit Unions (Projet d'Appui à la Réglementation sur les Mutuelles d'Épargne et de Crédit, or PARMEC) law may also engage in money transfer operations. However, they must first obtain a license from the Ministry of Finance (through the unit that provides technical assistance for popular savings and credit banks) by submitting an application, stating their reasons, and providing supporting documentation. Banks also use MFIs to expand their coverage, by issuing a memorandum of understanding that confers the status of subagent on the MFI.

As the leading MTO in Senegal, Western Union established exclusive contracts with the banks, as did the other MTOs established later. The post office, however, avoided exclusivity contracts; as a result, it has been able to work with both Western Union and MoneyGram.

At one time, these contracts posed an entry barrier for new RSPs in view of the relatively small banking system. The resulting monopoly situation hindered competition and kept transfer costs high. Although the arrival of new banks changed the landscape, the increased competitiveness was short-lived because the issue of exclusivity contracts arose again as the Senegalese remittance market developed. The

Minister of Economy and Finance and the Currency and Credit Directorate eventually informed all licensed intermediaries that exclusivity contracts were no longer permitted under the existing rules. This directive was issued via a circular letter from the Minister of Economy and Finance addressed to managing directors of banks.

Remittance Products

In Senegal, remittances are transferred through several service providers that employ different types of products or instruments. MTOs, the post office, and banks provide formal transfers as well as payments to intermediaries for informal transfers. New information and communications technologies have spurred development of new money transfer methods in both the formal and the informal sectors, including the following:

- *International postal money orders.* This system is widely used, although it is often slow and sometimes expensive. The post office uses its own products in addition to the new products offered by the MTOs.
- *Account-to-account transfers.* A migrant with a bank account abroad can transfer money from that account to any other account in the home country through electronic transfers such as SWIFT or telexes. Such transfers are safe but not immediate. This method is also relatively expensive, particularly when the transactions involve two currency zones.
- *Transfers of funds via MTO networks.* These are reliable and fast but also expensive.

The post office is the medium for most domestic transfers, which are made via faxed money orders or traditional money orders. The RSP survey in Senegal shows that electronic money transfer is the main instrument used by almost all the formal operators. In addition to electronic transfers, commercial banks use other instruments such as prepaid usable cards, bank drafts, account-to-account transfers, and transfers by check. Only one of the seven banks interviewed reported using prepaid debit cards. Cell-phone transfers have not yet been introduced in Senegal.

The post office also provides a variety of financial products, particularly for domestic transfers. In addition to postal money orders, it offers electronic fund transfers, and users can also open savings, or "giro," accounts. MFIs use only electronic fund transfers.

For their part, informal operators provide a variety of nonfinancial services in addition to in-person fund transfers. Informal RSPs in Senegal use three main products (AfDB 2007):

- *Transfer by courier,* which accounts for between 60 and 70 percent of the informal market, involves entrusting the remittances collected from a migrant community to a single carrier. This medium relies on strong social ties, and the transfer is made either by a member of the community traveling home on vacation or through specialized couriers, who can transport over €10,000 in cash.

- *Transfer by fax* accounts for 30 percent of the informal market. It is a popular option and involves the collection of transfers at a collection point (usually a tradesperson or a center). A tradesperson then distributes the sum almost instantaneously to the recipients back home. This system is similar to that used by MTOs and is less expensive, but it is riskier because the transactions are not documented.

- *Transfer in kind through a tradesperson* represents less than 5 percent of the informal market. It is particularly popular in rural areas and involves an agreement between the migrant and a tradesperson whereby the latter agrees to give credit to one or more recipients for staple goods (such as rice, sugar, or oil). This system was created by migrants who were concerned about misuse of their remittances.

Access to Other Financial Services

In addition to remittance services, financial institutions also offer financial and nonfinancial products to both senders and recipients of funds. Of the surveyed RSPs, 42 percent of the firms reported that they provided additional services such as deposits and savings options to senders and recipients of funds (RSPs survey 2009). They also offer consumer loans; business loans; credit cards; auto loans;[5] and, more recently, insurance products, mortgages, and education loans. On average, 14 percent of operators indicated that they offered these products in addition to their range of services.

The Regulatory and Business Environment

The RSP industry is strictly governed by laws and regulations. These regulations restrict the emergence of new operators and limit the operational capacities of existing ones. Regulations preventing the establishment of private nonbank operators lead to an increase in the use of intermediaries, raise costs, and foster competition from the informal networks.

Entry Barriers to the Remittance Service Business and Impediments to Remittance Operations

Good governance plays a crucial role in the development process (World Bank 2005). The poor implementation and inconsistent enforcement of regulations have a considerable impact on RSP firms' activity.

Figure 8.6 shows the percentage of RSP firms that perceive the laws and regulations to be a barrier to the exercise of their activity. More than half of the MTOs (57 percent) perceive the laws and regulations governing the transfer of funds in Senegal to be an obstruction to the exercise of money transfer activities: 14 percent as a major constraint and 43 percent as a moderate barrier. Another 43 percent did not think regulations were a barrier to the exercise of their activity.

The constraints perceived by MTOs differed depending on their status. Most banks agreed that the regulatory framework is not a major constraint, but 14 percent mentioned licensing as a major constraint. Another 14 percent perceived the minimum capital requirement imposed on banks as a constraint. MFIs perceived exchange controls and lack of access to clearing and settlement systems as major barriers to the exercise of their activities.

Laws and Regulations that Encourage Use of the Informal Sector

The regulations restricting the establishment of nonbank private operators result in the establishment of more bank partnerships. The fact that such operations are restricted to banking institutions—which are few—

Figure 8.6   RSP Firms' Perceptions of Laws and Regulations as Obstacles to Providing Remittance Services in Senegal

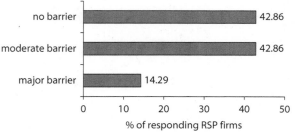

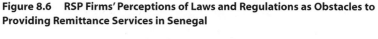

Source: Remittance Service Provider Survey.

increases costs because such institutions are forced to supplement their networks with subagents with whom they share commissions (Sander and Barro 2007).

In addition, the ceilings on transfers and the minimum capital requirement encourage the use of informal networks, which are more difficult to monitor. Naturally, such informal transfers are not monitored by the central bank, and transfers are therefore not guaranteed. Even in cases where these requirements pose no problem for senders, particularly for domestic and WAEMU transfers, MTOs still perceive the ceiling on transfers outside the zone to be a problem. Migrants also consider the ceiling too low because they sometimes have to make large transfers to friends or partners living outside the WAEMU zone and are thus forced by the system to split the transfers to stay below the ceiling. This can be very costly.

The expansion of remittance services to meet demand has changed the relationship that customers have with their banks. Almost all MTOs (86 percent) have established branches to serve more customers. Any delay in the receipt of remittances is reported to the customer service department, and the time taken to resolve customer grievances is quite short—usually not more than one week (RSP survey).

Formal RSPs face competition from the informal operators because the informal sector has many advantages—proximity to recipients, simplicity of operations, lack of overhead, and freedom from regulatory constraints—and offers low-cost products. Of the firms interviewed, 29 percent acknowledged that competition from informal operators is a major obstacle.

Remittance Costs and Identification Requirements

Fund transfers through formal networks (banks or specialized agents) are fast, reliable, and convenient. For example, a transfer sent by Western Union can take as little as 10 minutes to reach the recipient. In addition, neither the recipient nor the sender has to open a bank account to transfer money, and the sender does not need to provide identification, which could be an advantage for illegal immigrants who would rather remain anonymous (Sander and Barro 2007).

However, these services are expensive. The RSP survey revealed that the commission charged on an international transfer of US$200 is 13 percent by banks and 15 percent by the post office. The commission charged by Western Union on a domestic transfer of US$96 is 9.75 percent, the commission charged on a transfer of US$435 within the

WAEMU subregion is 7.36 percent, and the commission charged on an international transfer of US\$483 is 10 percent (Sander and Barro 2007).

MTOs require both senders and recipients to provide proof of identification. Commonly accepted documents are the national identity card, national passport, and driver's license. Business cards and certificates of residence are not an acceptable form of identification.

The study makes specific recommendations on data collection, regulation of the market remittances services, and the cost of remittances.

To improve data collection on remittance flows, it recommends establishing an elaborate system for formal remittance data collection; designing a regular study on informal remittance flows to improve understanding of informal remittance networks; and designing period household surveys on migration and remittances.

To facilitate the access to the market of transfer of money, it recommends reducing the constraints of the regulation of the IMF in such areas as minimum capital requirements and the ceiling of transfers.

To lower transaction costs, it recommends stimulating competition among banks and other nonfinancial institutions to help reduce overall transaction fees, as well as increasing the usage of new technologies for money transfer.

Conclusion

According to this analysis of migrant remittances, some conclusions can be drawn:

- The remittance market in Senegal consists of both formal and informal operators, providing a wide range of services in the various partnership arrangements.
- Of the many diversified origin countries of remittances, the European Union ranks highest, with more than half of the total amount of transfers.
- The remittance flows received by Senegal have increased considerably in the past five years, becoming the principal source of external financing for the Senegalese economy—far exceeding FDI, external borrowing, and, above all, ODA.
- As the principal source of external financing, remittances help in adjusting the current account balance and play an important role in the financing of household budgets and poverty reduction.

- Informal remittances occupy an important place in the remittance market and have many advantages for the population, particularly the poor, because of the proximity to recipients, simplicity of operations, lack of overhead costs, freedom from regulatory constraints, and low-cost products.

Notes

1. The International Monetary Fund *Balance of Payments Manual* (which covers only official channels) defines and measures remittances as the total of "workers' remittances" abroad, "compensation of employees," and "migrants' transfers" (World Bank 2008). "Workers' remittances" are transfers by migrants considered to be residents (for at least one year) in the host country. "Compensation of employees" includes all earnings of migrants who have been in the host country for less than one year. "Migrants' transfers" correspond to the net value of migrants' assets transferred from the host country to the country of origin.

2. World Bank 2011.

3. Bancarization is defined as the proportion of the population with a bank account. It is measured by an index called the rate of bancarization.

4. See R09/98/CM/UEMOA of December 20, 1998.

5. Twenty-nine percent of operators interviewed offer auto loans.

References

AfDB (African Development Bank). 2007. "Les transferts de fonds des migrants, un enjeu de développement: Les Comores, Mali, Maroc, Sénégal." Rapport provisoire, AfDB, Abidjan, Côte d'Ivoire. http://www.afdb.org.

ANSD (Agence Nationale de la Statistique et de la Démographie) du Sénégal. 2002. Troisième Recensement de la Population et de l'Habita (RGPH-III). Rapport National. République du Sénégal, Ministère de l'Economie et des Finances.

———. 2004. Enquête Sénégalaise Auprès des Ménages (ESAM II). Rapport national. République du Sénégal, Ministère de l'Economie et des Finances.

Ammassari, S. 2004. "Gestion des migrations et politiques de développement: Optimiser les bénéfices de la migration internationale en Afrique de l'Ouest." *Cahiers des migrations internationales*, 72 F, Genève, BIT.

BCEAO (Banque Centrale des Etats de l'Afrique de l'Ouest). Various years. Database.

———. 2008.

Bruzzone T. P., D. Fall, M. Tall, C. Gueye. 2006. "Le milieu sénégalais et l'action transnationale des migrants." Working paper, Rome.

CESPI (CentroStudidiPoliticaInternazionale). http://www.cespi.it.

Daffé, G. 2008. "Les transferts d'argent des migrants sénégalais entre espoir et risques de dépendance." In *Le Sénégal des migrations: mobilités, identités et sociétés*, ed. M. C. Diop, 105–32. Paris/Dakar: Research Center on Social Policy (CREPOS)/Karthala–ONU Habitat.

DMC (Direction de Monnaie et du Crédit)/MEF (Ministère de l'Economie et des Finances) du Sénégal. 2009. Database.

DPEE (Department of Forecasting and Economic Studies, Senegal Ministry of Economy and Finance). 2008. "Impact des transferts des migrants sur la pauvreté au Sénégal." Working Paper 7, DPEE, Dakar.

Kapur D. 2004. "Remittances, the New Development Mantra?" G-24 Discussion Paper Series, United Nations, New York and Geneva.

Ratha D. 2003. "Workers' Remittances: An Important and Stable Source of External Development Finance." In *Global Development Finance: Striving for Stability in Development Finance*. Washington, DC: World Bank.

Ratha D., S. Mohapatra, and S. Plaza. 2008. "Beyond Aid: New Sources and Innovative Mechanisms for Financing Development in Sub-Saharan Africa." Development Prospects Group, World Bank, Washington, DC.

Remittance Service Provider Survey. 2009.

République du Sénégal/Communauté Européenne. 2007. "Migration et développement: Opportunités et défis s'offrant aux décideurs." Document de stratégie pays et programme indicatif national pour la période 2008–2013.

Russell, S. S. 1986. "Remittances from International Migration: A Review in Perspective." *World Development*, 14 (6): 677–96.

Sander, C., and I. Barro. 2007. "Étude sut le transfert d'argent des émigrés au Sénégal et les services de transfert en microfinance." Document de travail 40, Bureau International du Travail, Social Finance Program, Geneva.

Shaw W. 2007. "Migration in Africa: A Review of the Economic Literature on International Migration in 10 Countries." Development Prospects Group, World Bank, Washington, DC.

World Bank. 2005. "Enquête Climat des Investissements au Sénégal." Report 37174 SE World Bank, Washington, DC.

———. 2008. "Recueil de statistiques 2008 sur les migrations et les envois de fonds." World Bank, Washington, DC. http://www.worldbank.org/prospects/migrationandremittances.

————. 2010. *World Development Indicators 2010*. Washington, DC: World Bank. http://data.worldbank.org/data-catalog/world-development-indicators/wdi-2010.

————. 2011. *Migration and Remittances Factbook 2011*. Washington, DC: World Bank. http://go.worldbank.org/QGUCPJTOR0.

World Bank and CRES. 2011. "Migration and Remittances Survey in Senegal–2009." Survey Report. World Bank and CRES, Washington, DC.

CHAPTER 9

Uganda

Rose W. Ngugi And Edward Sennoga

Migrant remittances are increasingly becoming a significant source of development finance in Uganda, which had a recorded amount of remittances equivalent to 5 percent of gross domestic product (GDP) in 2009 (World Bank 2011). Users of money transfer services in Uganda include individuals, traders, firms, nongovernmental organizations (NGOs), and other users; however, research shows that the market for money transfer services in Uganda is underserviced (Sander, Mukwana, and Millinga 2001). As the government becomes more decentralized and as the middle class, which supports families in villages and builds houses up-country, continues to grow, the demand for domestic money transfer services is expected to continue increasing.

This chapter explores the remittance service provider (RSP) market in Uganda and focuses on various aspects of money transfer products or services, including accessibility, reliability, service networks, competition, and affordability.[1] The chapter explores the chances of enhancing access to financial services by providing remittance services. A survey of RSPs in Uganda was carried out in the second half of 2008, and it covered both formal and informal RSPs.

Some of the key conclusions of this chapter include the following:

- Data collection on the flows of remittances at the domestic-market level is not well institutionalized. Even commercial banks do not have an elaborate system for reporting remittances.
- Remittance service providers are diverse, including formal and non-formal providers. Banks remain the core institutions in the money transfer market, because they work in partnership with all other formal RSP providers (for both domestic and international remittances). Networking and partnership are common among the providers of remittance services, reflecting a significant level of complementarity. However, money-transfer clients are constrained by high transaction costs in accessing additional financial services from the banking sector.
- Direct costs of remittance transfers are significantly high among the various providers. The cost for sending US$200 is between 10 percent and 17 percent for international transfers and between 0.4 percent and 12.5 percent for domestic transfers.
- Informal services, such as community-based firms and transport firms, have evolved to fill the gaps left by banks, including the high costs, limited accessibility, minimal coverage, and slow speed of transfers.
- Mobile money transfer services, such as Simba Cash and MTN Mobile Money are gaining entry but they are well below the rate of adoption seen in neighboring Kenya.
- Formal RSPs are under a regulatory mechanism of the central bank. The central bank requests that the banks and foreign exchange bureaus gather information from the customers by asking for the identification of the senders and recipients. In brochures, the RSPs also provide information to the customers on the type of services offered, including other services.

The rest of the chapter is organized as follows. The first section discusses trends and uses of remittances, the second section covers the characteristics of the remittance industry, the third section addresses the regulatory and business environment, the fourth section highlights the costs and identification requirements for remittances, the fifth section explores remittance sources and destinations, and the sixth section concludes.

Trends and Uses of Remittances

Uganda receives about 4 percent of remittances to Sub-Saharan Africa. In the period 2000–10, Uganda experienced a significant growth in remittances from US$299 in 2003 to US$773 (World Bank 2011). This increase is mainly attributed to the growing number of Ugandans working abroad, loosening of the foreign exchange regulatory regime, and the adoption of new remittance technologies that helped to reduce transfer costs and increase competition in the market. Outward remittances from Uganda also increased during the same period from US$182 million in 2003 to US$463 million in 2009 (see table 9.1). Inward remittance volumes depicted a marked decline in 2009, possibly because of the fragile labor markets, global financial crisis, and the increased scrutinyof migrants without proper documentation in destination countries.[2]

The Uganda National Household Survey 2005/2006 (Uganda Bureau of Statistics 2006) shows that only 2 percent of Ugandans receive remittances from abroad, with the highest proportion of remittances going to Kampala. However, the 2007 FinScope Uganda study revealed that a significantly larger percentage, 12 percent, of the Ugandan population receives money from abroad. Our survey data indicates that 42 percent of all inward international remittances to Uganda originated from North America. Overall, the United Kingdom tops the list of remittance senders to Uganda, followed by the United

Table 9.1   Remittance Trends in Uganda

Flows (US$ millions)	2003	2004	2005	2006	2007	2008	2009	2010e
Inward remittance flows	299	311	322	411	452	724	694	773
of which								
Workers' remittances	299	311	322	411	452	724	750	—
Compensation of employees	—	—	—	—	—	—	—	—
Migrants' transfer	—	—	—	—	—	—	—	—
Outward remittance flows	182	194	197	206	236	381	463	—
of which								
Workers' remittances	134	140	145	185	203	324	378	—
Compensation of employees	47	54	52	21	33	57	86	—
Migrants' transfer	—	—	—	—	—	—	—	—

Source: World Bank 2011.
Note: — = not available.
e = estimate.

States, Australia, Canada, and Kenya. Remittances are mainly used for consumption (65 percent), education (31 percent), and health (29 percent) (note that the categories are not mutually exclusive and add up to more than 100 percent) (FinScope Uganda 2007). The Uganda National Household Survey 2005/2006 also reports similar findings that half of recipients spent remittances on consumption, while 26 percent used remittances for education. Furthermore, the Bank of Uganda (2008) revealed that remittances were used for consumption, education, investment, and health. The main investment expenditure types include acquisition of property (such as land and buildings), start-up businesses, and farming.

In Sub-Saharan Africa, the Democratic Republic of Congo, Kenya, South Africa, and Tanzania are the major remittance source countries to Uganda. A sizeable population of students from Kenya and Tanzania attend universities and colleges in Uganda. Consequently, the observed remittance inflows could be transfers to offset tuition and related expenses, including general upkeep. South Africa is a major destination for Ugandan workers seeking "greener" pastures within the African continent. Inflows from South Africa could be transfers from immigrants to their families and acquaintances in Uganda. Uganda is also a base for United Nations operations (such as the United Nations Organization Mission in the Democratic Republic of Congo, or MONUC) in the great lakes region. Consequently, several Ugandan expatriates and businessmen are working and doing business with their counterparts in the Democratic Republic of Congo DRC. Thus, money transfers from the Democratic Republic of Congo could comprise both migrant remittances and payments in business settlements and business-related transactions.

As of 2010, the number of emigrants from Uganda was 757,500, or 2.2 percent of Uganda's population (World Bank 2011). The top destinations were Kenya, the United Kingdom, Tanzania, the United States, Rwanda, Canada, Sweden, and Australia. It is important to note that emigration from Uganda to the United Kingdom has a historical basis given that Uganda was a British colony.

According to the survey of RSPs, the main destination of remittances from Uganda in 2007 was Kenya, followed by India, the United States, Tanzania, the Democratic Republic of Congo, South Africa, and the United Kingdom.

It is important to note that the top 25 percent of foreign direct investment (FDI) firms in Uganda are of Kenyan origin. One limitation of our

RSP survey data is the inability to distinguish between remittances and other money transfers such as repatriation of profits, loan repayments, dividends, and royalties. As mentioned earlier, because of the vibrant trade, especially between Uganda and the Southeast Asian countries, most of the money transfers to these countries could be for purchasing of merchandise and for other business-related purposes.

Results of the survey of RSPs are comparable to the results of the 2005/2006 Uganda National Household Survey, which showed that the mean monthly values received varied among regions, with Kampala registering the highest value (U Sh 130,500, or US$75). The FinScope Uganda study (2007) found that almost 50 percent of remittance recipients received US$200 or less, while only 13 percent received more than US$500.

Migrants in search of employment tend to move to industrial towns or urban centers such as Mbale, Jinja, and Kampala to work in factories, on plantations, and on exotic flower farms. Migrants who find employment in the formal sector often use the formal sector RSPs, such as banks and nonbank financial institutions (box 9.1), to transfer money to their families mainly for upkeep and settlement of school fees. In contrast, migrants in the informal sector transfer money using casual means such as taxis and bus companies, family members, and friends, or migrants transfer money themselves whenever they return to their region of origin. In addition, business people who move from one region to another in search of merchandise and agricultural products also provide informal money transfer services. This transfer method usually requires a very informal arrangement, largely based on trust, between the money remitter and the businessperson; there is no guarantee of transfer or "insurance coverage" for the money involved. Remittance volumes in Uganda range from small amounts such as U Sh 50,000 for upkeep to millions of Ugandan shillings for purchasing merchandise and agricultural products such as coffee and farm inputs. Therefore, remittance flows tend to peak at the beginning of a new school trimester and at harvest season, especially for agricultural produce.

Characteristics of the Remittance Industry

The entry of new RSPs into the market reflects a response to existing market gaps. Differences among the scope of services, products provided, and product costs exist. Sander, Mukwana, and Millinga (2001) underscore five key attributes for a good money-transfer product or

Box 9.1

Financial Institutions in Uganda

Financial institutions in Uganda are categorized under four tiers: (1) commercial banks, (2) credit institutions, (3) microfinance deposit-taking institutions (MDIs), and (4) institutions involved in microfinance that do not qualify under tiers 1, 2, and 3. Uganda's financial sector comprises 19 licensed commercial banks (of which 16 are operational), 8 microdepository institutions, and 84 foreign exchange bureaus (of which 22 are licensed to offer remittance services). Credit institutions (tier 2) include the Capital Finance Corporation, Commercial Microfinance, Mercantile Credit Bank, and PostBank Uganda. MDIs (tier 3) accept deposits from the public and use the deposits to make short-term loans to small or microenterprises and low-income households. MDIs include the Foundation for International Community Assistance (FINCA), Pride Microfinance Limited, Uganda Finance Trust Limited, and Uganda Microfinance Limited. Membership-based savings and credit cooperative organizations and most MFIs (between 500 and 700) are considered tier 4 institutions and are allowed to accept only compulsory savings from clients. However, those savings cannot be used for credit operations (except for institutions registered as cooperatives). These tier 4 institutions are not regulated or supervised by the Bank of Uganda.

Source: Authors.

service: accessibility, efficiency and timeliness, reliability, presence of a sizeable service network that includes external urban centers, and affordability.

Participants in the Remittance Market

A recent study by the Bank of Uganda (2008) reveals that there are various channels for remittance transfers, including formal service providers such as banks; money transfer operators (MTOs) such as Western Union, MoneyGram, Coinstar, Xpress Money, and the post office; and foreign exchange bureaus. Informal channels include friends and acquaintances such as traders, especially for thosewith inadequate financial services and for those who find the remittance service costs in the formal sector too high. Financial institutions in Uganda are concentrated mostly in urban areas; therefore, formal service providers are largely used when a remittance transaction originates from an urban center. Formal financial institutions are preferred because of the guaranteed security and safety of the remittances, while informal channels appeal to customers who send or receive money in areas that are underserved by financial institutions. The informal sector's ease of access and flexibility in identification and cost requirements also attracts clients.

A purposive sample of 31 providers was selected to represent all the segments of the remittance market in Uganda (see table 9.2). The sample included 16 banks, 19 foreign exchange bureaus, 8 savings and credit cooperative organizations (SACCOs), 16 microfinance institutions (MFIs), 2 transport services, 1 mobile telephone money transfer provider, PostBank, and the post office (Posta). The survey also included community-based RSPs. The study targeted only the providers of the services and not the users.

The most popular remittance channels are friends and acquaintances (27.8 percent), commercial banks (24.5 percent), and MTOs such as Western Union and MoneyGram (25.4 percent). According to the survey, those channels account for a combined share of 78 percent of total

Table 9.2   Participation of RSPs and Services Provided by RSPs in Uganda, 2008

	Banks	Foreign exchange bureau	MDIs	PostBank	Posta	SACCOs	Transport Sector
Exchanging currencies for remittance providers	X	X					
Providing domestic messaging services	X						
Providing international messaging services	X						
Providing settlement services (cross-border)	X				X		
Providing settlement services (domestic)	X						
Receiving domestic remittances	X	X	X	X	X	X	X
Receiving international remittances	X	X		X	X		
Sending domestic remittances	X	X	X	X	X	X	X
Sending international remittances	X	X		X	X		

Source: Authors' based on survey of RSPs in Uganda.

remittances received in 2006. Other channels reported include foreign exchange bureaus, the post office, traders, and MFIs. Informal money transfer services such as relatives or self-transfers are still the most commonly used methods, especially for small transfer amounts, although semi-formal providers such as bus and courier companies are making substantial headway into a largely untapped domestic remittance market. MTN, a telecom service provider in Uganda, began a pilot service known as MTN mobile money transfer service. This service allows customers to transfer money between phones on the MTN network.

The most common international money transfer agencies include Western Union, MoneyGram, and Express Money, and they operate with both banks and foreign exchange bureaus in Uganda. Transfers through these agencies can be collected instantly at any location worldwide. These agencies offer an online tracking facility for transfers, and senders and recipients do not have to be account holders with the financial institution facilitating the transfer. The sender usually pays the transfer fees, and the recipient is usually required to present an acceptable form of identification and to answer a security question before receiving the money.

The formal, semi-formal, and informal financial and nonfinancial sectors in Uganda play significant and diverse roles in international and domestic remittances. International remittances are largely conducted through the formal sector and community-based systems (friends and relatives), while the semi-formal and informal sector providers play a sizable role in the provision of domestic remittances. However, an accurate estimate of the actual size of the formal sector vis-à-vis the informal sector is hampered by the increased sophistication with which remittances are transmitted in Uganda. In several instances, money received through formal financial institutions is transferred from large banks to smaller financial institutions, including those in the informal sector such as MFIs and SACCOs, which have more intricate branch networks. Attributing and reconciling remittance amounts handled by any one of the four tiers (see Appendix II) often leads to double counting and gross misrepresentation.

In Uganda, RSPs have a wide network across the country, but the those in major urban centers dominate because of the large number of outlets and the mix of providers. Thirty-six percent of bank branches and 32 percent of the PostBank branches are located in Kampala, the capital city. The nonbank financial institutions are quite evenly distributed between urban and rural areas, with 26 percent of the branches in Kampala and Entebbe, 22 percent in the eastern region, and 25 percent in the western region. All 22 licensed money-remitting foreign exchange bureaus and their branches are located in Kampala. Other RSPs in the formal sector include the post office, as well as Simba Telecom, which offers remittance services through MTN Uganda's telecommunications network. Over 76 percent of Posta Uganda operations (Uganda's postal system) are located in rural areas, making it the most widely distributed remittance service provider in Uganda. The key semi-formal and informal sector players in this industry include MFIs, SACCOs, bus companies, commuter taxis, money lenders, and prominent businesspersons. The Association of Microfinance Institutions of Uganda and the Uganda Cooperative Savings and Credit Union—the two major bodies that oversee the operations of MFIs and SACCOs, respectively—estimated the number of registered MFIs and SACCOs at more than 1,000 countrywide. However, most of these tier 4 institutions are location specific with limited or no branch networks.

Simba Cash, a subsidiary of Simba Telecom Uganda Limited, is one of the more recent additions to the money remittance industry in Uganda. Simba Cash provides remittance services in partnership with MTN Uganda and Nokia Uganda. Money remitted by any one of the 60 Simba Telecom shops across the country is available for pick-up within minutes of completing the remittance transaction. Point-of-sale machines in the various shops are connected by server through Generic Packet Radio Service (GPRS) lines to the head office shop in Kampala. Currently, only domestic money transfer services are provided. Simba Cash also offers currency exchange services to remittance senders and recipients. The sender communicates details such as remittance amounts, passwords, and payout locations to the recipient through the telephone.

Informal sector remittance providers such as bus companies and SACCOs also employ diverse modes of business operations. For instance, one of the SACCOs surveyed indicated that it uses partnerships with commercial banks (for example, Stanbic Bank and Centenary Bank) to provide remittance services to its members. Another bus company revealed that it uses its own network of office locations in various cities and countries to offer remittance services. The transport system has emerged as a mode of money transfer in response to unmet demand, particularly among the unbanked population. Thus, transport services fill the void in areas where communication and access to banking services is limited. Although the parcel licenses that transport industries hold do not allow them to transfer funds, social networking helped to facilitate the transport sector's entry into the remittance market.

The transport sector's role in facilitating trade and commerce by linking communities through enhanced communication is both historical and significant, especially before the advent of mobile phones. In the past, individuals with families, friends, or business partners heading to the recipient's area would negotiate with the driver or other attendant to deliver a piece of mail or a parcel to a specified destination for a fee. Often, these parcels contained low-value items; thus, the sender was not particularly concerned about the risks associated with this mode of transfer, including the loss of luggage. The financial sector's slow growth, coupled with the concentration of financial institutions in urban centers, has contributed to the emergence of the transport sector as a key provider of money transfer services in Uganda. This sector offers access to reliable, affordable, and risk-free money transfer services to some of the remote regions of the country. Transfer charges can also be negotiated. Given the extensive coverage of buses and commuter taxis in Uganda, the transport sector is easily the most widespread remittance service provider. The transport sector caters to various clients, particularly those in regions with limited or no access to financial services. Hence, the defining characteristic of clients served by the transport sector is that they are mainly from regions underserved by financial service providers, especially money-transfer service providers.

Business Models

There are significant partnerships among the RSPs in Uganda. Local banks work in partnership with foreign corresponding banks to reach out to various remittance transfer corridors. International money transfer agencies work in collaboration with local banks and foreign exchange bureaus. Almost all the RSPs work closely with banking institutions. All but one of the financial and nonbank financial institutions surveyed indicated that they work with both international and domestic partners in the provision of remittance services. These partnerships are mostly in the form of correspondent or participating financial institutions in the remittance source and destination countries.

For instance, Posta Uganda works in partnership with Posta Kenya and Posta Tanzania through the Universal Postal Union network. Posta Uganda operates an electronic funds transfer (EFT) service Speedie in partnership with PostBank Uganda. This service is accessible from any one of PostBank's 22 branches in Uganda and can be used to send and receive both domestic and international remittances.

Formal sector RSPs also revealed that they operate with agents of Western Union, MoneyGram, Coinstar, and Xpress Money transfer services. In turn, Western Union works with Barclays Bank, Standard

Chartered Bank, and Centenary Bank in Uganda. Western Union also works with a number of foreign exchange bureaus. MoneyGram's main agents include Stanbic Bank in Uganda. The financial and nonbank financial institutions that have direct contractual obligations with the money transfer agents benefit in several ways, including through the provision of marketing and advertisement, access to payment systems, and access to relevant financial information. However, such partnership agreements are often exclusive, suggesting that a financial or nonbank financial institution can work only in partnership with one money transfer agent. In turn, these institutions sub-contract their rights with an even wider network of nonbank financial institutions with explicit agreements on the sharing of the exchange-rate commission.

SACCOs and MFIs work in collaboration with microfinance deposit-taking institutions (MDIs), such as Commercial Microfinance in Uganda, to provide remittance services (especially when customers are from different SACCOs) (box 9.2). On the whole, SACCOs and MFIs hold accounts with the bank and the nonbank financial institutions that facilitate the remittance transfer process. This method has the advantage of increasing the accessibility of remittance services.

Access to the national payment system is limited for several types of remittance service providers. For example, MFIs, PostBank, SACCOs, foreign exchange bureaus, and money transfer agencies are not members of the national payment systems. The central bank expects the dealer banks to ensure that the limits set on the foreign exchange bureaus are met. However, because RSPs such as foreign exchange bureaus work in collaboration with the money transfer agencies, this measure complicates the situation because the foreign exchange bureaus do not operate under central bank statutory regulations and supervision.

Furthermore, because the transactions are not centralized, clients are at liberty to use alternative institutions to meet their needs. Currently, Simba Cash meets its reporting requirements through an MDI (Commercial Microfinance Limited); hence, Simba Cash's transactions are under the purview of the central bank.

The networking defines the range of remittance services provided by the various institutions. For example, local banks with international corresponding banks with membership in the Society for Worldwide Interbank Financial Telecommunication are able to offer remittance services overseas and provide settlement services across the border. Thus, with an adequate branch network in the country, banks could give the entire population access to international remittance services.

Box 9.2

SACCOs and MFIs as Providers of Domestic and Cross-Border Remittance Services

Savings and credit cooperative organizations (SACCOs) and microfinance institutions (MFIs) are considered tier 4 institutions and are not supervised by Uganda's central bank. SACCOs can accept only member savings, whereas MFIs are allowed to collect only compulsory savings from borrowers. Though not registered money remitters, some SACCOs and MFIs offer remittance services to their members. Unlike commercial banks and other regulated financial institutions that tend to be located in urban and semi-urban areas, SACCOs and MFIs cater to low-income individuals in both urban and rural areas. Remittance flows in this case are both one-way (as is the case with inward international remittances) and two-way (especially with traders and farmers who send and receive money for the settlement of merchandise purchased or goods sold).

SACCOs and MFIs that provide remittance services work with regulated financial institutions, especially those with extensive networks such as Stanbic Bank and Centenary Bank. International inward remittances are deposited into the SACCOs' or MFIs' account in a partner bank. The money is then withdrawn from the corresponding bank by an employee of the SACCO or the MFI and is given to the intended recipient in local currency. Because SACCOs and MFIs act as agents of the financial institution in the provision of remittance services, they are not required to carry any additional licenses to provide these services. Because recipients are members of the SACCO or MFI, the only identification required is a membership identification card (issued by the SACCO or MFI). For domestic remittances, a member wishing to send money "deposits" money into the SACCO and is provided a check payable to the partner bank's branch countrywide. Transfer charges for recipients of remittances also vary across these institutions, with some imposing a 5 percent charge on inward and outward international remittances received, while others not imposing any transfer charges. There are no identification requirements for remittance senders because they are members of the SACCO or MFI. The sender is required to provide only the recipient's details and contact information, including his or her name, contact address, and phone number (where applicable). Remittances are usually received within one to three business days, depending on the intended payout destination.

Source: Authors.

Remittance Products

Several remittance products are offered in Uganda, including electronic cash transfers, pre-paid cards for use at selected retailers, bank drafts, checks or demand drafts, and money orders. Other remittance instruments include account-to-account transfers, money transfers through cellular phones, and pre-paid debit cards. Because of technological developments, a number of instruments are being used that finalize transactions at various speeds.

Electronic money transfer is the most widely available remittance product and is offered by 81 percent of the financial and nonfinancial institutions under review. The EFT has gained popularity in Uganda, especially since the introduction of a U Sh 20 million cap on checks in July 2007. As of July 1, 2008, all government departments and agencies, including local governments, had adopted the EFT as the principal transaction method. According to the Bank of Uganda Clearing House rules, EFT transactions should reach the beneficiary's account within 48 hours and, in the case of any errors or omissions, the payer should be notified within 72 hours.

Checks and bank drafts are offered by 42 percent of all institutions studied. In Uganda, checks are cleared in three days in most parts of the country and one day for high-value checks. Checks from remote centers are cleared in 10 days. The real time gross settlement (RTGS) funds transfer system offers immediate, or "real time", settlement options on a gross-basis principle. Instructions given to transfer money are effective within 30 minutes (the transfer is done almost immediately). The central bank clears the money on the same day, and each transaction is done independently. This system is used mostly for high-value payments that are at least U Sh 10 million. In addition, checks for more than U Sh 20 million must be cleared throughan EFT or an RTGS. There are also issues with bounced checks. One of the major constraints in using a bank draft is that it can be very expensive and is not cleared instantly. The amount charged is usually fixed irrespective of the amount sent. A bank draft also requires the recipient to have a bank account in the country where the bank draft is deposited. In Uganda, bank drafts are used mostly by business people and by parents trying to settle their children's tuition payments.

Account-to-account transfers are offered by 45 percent of all the institutions studied. Banks do not charge for depositing in another person's account. Some banks finalize account-to-account transactions instantly, especially when the deposit is made in cash. When the deposit is by check, the transfer process takes up to four days. The mushrooming of bank branches in rural areas and the ability of banks to provide additional services to the remittance recipients will help to expand access to financial services. However, an account-to-account service requires that recipients have access to a bank account.

Posta uses various types of orders including money orders, postal orders, and interstate orders that are tailored for use in five East African countries (Burundi, Kenya, Rwanda, Tanzania, and Uganda). Ordinary money orders identify the recipient and can be cashed at only specified post offices. Money orders can be drawn for any amount up to U Sh 7 million for interstate transfers and U Sh 3 million for domestic transfers. The telegraphic money order guarantees customers same-day value, while a postal order is a bearer instrument that can be cashed at any post office. Given the post office's large distribution network (276 branches in Uganda) and its ability to reach almost every village in the country, the post office is the most widely accessible RSP.

Emerging Products: Mobile Money Transfers

Emerging products, such as mobile money (for example, Simba Cash and MTN mobile money) and debit and credit cards, are gaining popularity because of their versatility and affordability. Sixteen of the operational financial institutions offer debit cards.[3] In addition, one credit institution (Commercial Microfinance) and one MDI (Uganda Finance Trust) offer debit card services as well. In Uganda, three of the financial institutions studied indicated that they offer prepaid cards that can be used at designated retailers, particularly grocery stores, restaurants, and fuel stations.

The direct-debit mode of payment in Uganda has been used mainly by schools and colleges. Parents sign agreements that allow participating commercial banks to deduct specified amounts from a parent's account on behalf of the school or college to settle school tuition. Credit card use is quite limited in Uganda, with only a few banks offering this payment method. Prepaid store value cards are currently not being offered by any financial institution.[4]

Simba Cash, a subsidiary of Simba Telecom Uganda Limited, is one of the more recent additions to the money remittance industry in Uganda. Simba Cash provides remittance services in partnership with MTN Uganda and Nokia Uganda. Money remitted at any of the Simba Telecom shops across the country is available for pick-up within minutes of completing the remittance transaction. Money transferred through the network of Simba Cash shops involves inventory management (for small transfers) and account-to-account transfers (among the Simba Cash shops) in cases of sizable payouts. The sending agent usually calls the agent at the expected payout location to inquire about the availability of money. In the case of shortages at the expected payout locations, the sending agent initiates an account-to-account transfer to the shop receiving the payout.

Parents use Simba Cash to send money for their children's upkeep and to cover other incidentals, while workers use this medium to send tuition, upkeep money for their families, and other allowances such as payment of farm workers and medical bills. Remittance flows are both one-way (as in the case of parents sending subsistence allowances to students) and two-way (as in the case of worker's remittances).

Simba Cash is not regulated directly by the Bank of Uganda. Commercial Microfinance (CMF) reports remittance transactions that are handled by Simba Cash to the Bank of Uganda. In essence, Simba Cash acts as an agent of CMF in the provision of money transfer services. Furthermore, as a subsidiary of Simba Telecom, operations of Simba Cash are currently regulated by the Companies Act. However, the Companies Act does not contain specific provisions regarding money remittance operations. Hence, there is no insurance coverage for money transferred through Simba Cash's network.

Senders pay between 2 percent and 5 percent of remittance amounts as transfer charges. Small amounts such as U Sh 100,000 require transfer fees of 5 percent, while large amounts (U Sh 1,000,000 and higher) incur lower transfer charges of 2 percent of the remittance amount. Identification requirements for both the sender and the recipient include a driver's license, voter's card, or village identification card. In addition, the recipient is required to provide a test question and answer, as well as the secret code issued to the sender by Simba Cash.

MTN, one of the telecom service providers in Uganda has started a money transfer service also referred to as MTN mobile money transfer service. This service allows customers to transfer money between phones on the MTN network. A typical customer purchases U Sh 50,000 (approximately US$30) worth of mobile money from an agent, and the agent then sets up a transaction indicating that this customer has "deposited" this amount on his or her mobile phone. The customer then receives a short message service SMS to confirm the transaction and is asked to select a personal identification number (PIN). A customer is issued a PIN for every transaction (both to send and to receive money), and both the sender and the recipient must present valid identification to complete the transaction. Though the customer is at liberty to send money to anyone across mobile telecommunication networks, only MTN customers can possess these mobile money accounts.

More than 6 million Ugandans own mobile phones, suggesting that the mobile transfer service will become accessible to 6 million people. This could, in essence, make mobile money transfer the most widely accessible transaction method, particularly for the unbanked population.

Transport Service for Domestic Remittances

Transport companies deliver money physically or by maintaining a float (box 9.3). The vehicle operator receives money from the sender, and it is enclosed in an envelope or packaged for delivery. The driver then delivers the money physically. However, because of the risks of insecurity and

---

Box 9.3

The Transport Sector as a Provider of Remittance Services in Uganda and in East Africa

The concentration of formal financial institutions in urban centers has contributed to the emergence of the transport sector (buses and commuter taxis) as a key provider of reliable, fast, and affordable money transfer services, especially to remote regions of the country with limited or no access to financial services. Clients include parents with students in country-side schools and workers in urban centers with families in the rural areas. Average remittance amounts range from between US$50 and US$200 for school tuition, student upkeep, and general subsistence to U Sh 3 million for purchasing of traders' merchandise. Inward and outward remittances through transport companies tend to peak around November and December and also near the commencement of school terms—usually the beginning of February, May, and September. Money is sent from (and received in) all major towns in Kenya, Tanzania, and Uganda.

Transfer charges are usually very competitive (sometimes 7 percent to 10 percent of the amount sent or a fraction of the fare charged for the journey), but in many cases, charges are subject to negotiation between the remittance sender and the bus driver. To collect the remittance, the recipient is required to present some form of valid identification such as a village identification card, a voter's

(continued next page)

Box 9.3 *(continued)*

card, an employer-issued identification card, or a driver's license. A consignment or transaction number is used as a password between the remittance sender, the recipient, and the company. The sender often communicates the consignment number and other particulars to the recipient by telephone.

Remittances for prominent customers are usually transmitted instantly, and the recipient can pick up the money within minutes of concluding the transaction. This special consideration is typically accorded to traders and students. All other remittances usually take one to three business days. Transport companies manage inventories in several ways. For small payout amounts, branch offices use available cash and are later reimbursed by the head office. For sizable remittances (usually about U Sh 3 million), some transport companies move money from one branch to another through chartered planes, buses, or commercial bank networks.

However, in cases in which the remittance is not delivered, the sender usually has little or no recourse. Transport companies offering remittance services are not regulated by the Bank of Uganda and are not required to file any reports regarding remittance transactions.

Source: Authors.

robberies, transport companies now maintain a float on either end of the route so that money transfer is not dependent on the arrival of the vehicle and the recipient is guaranteed delivery. The sending office issues a receipt to the sender and makes a call to the receiving office, instructing it to make payment. The sender contacts the recipient to indicate the money has been sent and can be collected from the office. This step has made the transfer process quicker. However, the process works only in areas where telecommunication is not an issue.

Remittances and Access to Financial Services

Remittances have been identified as a potential catalyst for financial growth in receiving countries and regions by providing greater access to banking services for migrants' families. Orozco and Fedewa (2006) observe that linking remittances to financial intermediation will harness remittances' influence on development. They concentrate on three factors that define the ability to tap remittances more effectively for development: institutional ability to provide remittance transfers, institutional ability to offer low-cost remittance services, and institutional ability to complement transfer services with other financial services. Ratha (2003) observed that credit unions and microfinance institutions can play a major role in delivering low-cost and convenient remittance services, encouraging more savings and investment.

Financial institutions and nonbank financial institutions in Uganda treat remittance services like auxiliary services; hence, senders and recipients of remittances can also benefit from these institutions' mainstream services such as deposits, savings products, and credit facilities for consumers; small and large business loans; and education and vehicle loans. For international money-transfer institutions, remittance service is the core business and senders and recipients can benefit from other services that their partner banking institutions provide. Foreign exchange bureaus also offer currency exchange services.

However, more than 60 percent of the financial and nonfinancial institutions surveyed in Uganda indicate that the recipient needs to be an account holder in the institution. However, these services come at a cost to remittance customers. For example, there are charges for maintaining of a deposit account, including a minimum balance that must be maintained on the account, ledger fees, withdrawal charges, and, in some cases, statement fees. The average monthly charges for maintaining an account with a bank in Uganda range between U Sh 1,000 and U Sh 3,000 Ush. The minimum balance ranges between U Sh 50,000 and U Sh 100,000. These high fees can limit access to formal remittance services for low-income individuals.

Regulatory and Business Environment

The remittance market in Uganda has some RSPs providing money-transfer services under the purview of the central bank, which observes the statutory regulatory framework. Other RSPs in the transport sector and the community-based institutions either are not under a regulatory framework or are based on a social network. Financial institutions in Uganda operate under various regulatory frameworks. For example, commercial banks (tier 1) and credit institutions (tier 2) are licensed and regulated by the Bank of Uganda under the 2004 Financial Institution Act. MDIs (tier 3) are regulated under the 2003 MDI Act, while all other MFIs and SACCOs (tier 4) are not under the Bank of Uganda's purview and supervision, yet they form the core of the microfinance sector (see Annex 2). Foreign exchange bureaus are regulated and supervised under the 2004 Foreign Exchange Act and the 2006 Foreign Exchange Regulations. SACCOs and MFIs in Uganda operate under three legal regimes: the Cooperative Societies Act, the Companies Act, and the NGO Act. However, tier 4 institutions operate in a supervisory and regulatory vacuum because those legal regimes do not distinguish tier 4 institutions from cooperatives, which do not provide financial services.

For transport companies, there are no additional requirements for establishing this kind of remittance-related business besides obtaining a license to provide transportation and parcel- and luggage-handling services and obtaining an operating license issued by the Registrar of Companies. Though money transfer is one of the services provided, transport companies offering remittance services are not regulated by the Bank of Uganda and are not required to file any reports regarding remittance transactions, volumes, and destinations (see Annex 1).

In Uganda, the Financial Institutions Act (2004) states the minimum capital requirement for banks and nonbank financial institutions as U Sh 4 billion and U Sh 1 billion, respectively. In addition, financial institutions are required to observe minimum and on-going capital requirements, including maintaining a core capital of at least 8 percent of total risk-adjusted assets and a total capital of at least 12 percent of total risk-adjusted assets. This requirement is in addition to an annual license fee of U Sh 1 million. Banks and nonbank financial institutions provide a variety of services; only the mobile transfer and international money-transfer agencies enter the market specifically to engage in money transfer services.

The two regulatory regimes that govern the operations of exchange bureaus issue four types of licenses for money-remitting foreign exchange bureaus. Each type of license allows for a different scope of operation, such as conducting international remittances, and minimum requirements for the licenses vary.

In carrying out remittance business, RSPs are expected to uphold the know-your-customer policy and to prevent unacceptable transactions by observing thresholds on the amounts remitted and reporting suspicious activities. However, the ability to enforce some of these rules depends on the strength of the surveillance system and the ability to share information across the RSPs at the settlement level.

There are no limits on how much money can be sent or received, but average remittance amounts range between US$50 and US$200 for school tuition, student upkeep, and general subsistence, and remittances can be up to about U Sh 3 million for purchasing merchandise from traders. The major source and destination locations include all major towns in Kenya, Tanzania, and Uganda. Remittances for prominent customers are usually transmitted instantly, and the recipient can pick up the money within minutes of the sender concluding the transaction. All other remittances usually take one to three business days, depending on the intended destination.

Regulations and Requirements

The findings indicate that laws and regulations are not an obstacle for most RSPs in Uganda, with only one of the surveyed firms indicating otherwise. Regarding the barriers to entry into the remittance business, most providers felt that access to capital and finance was a major barrier to entry. In Uganda, however, license requirements and capital requirements posed the most significant hindrance to starting a remittance services business. Regarding operational barriers, RSPs indicated license and capital requirements as significant obstacles to businesses. Lack of access to clearing and settlement systems, anti-money-laundering requirements, and reporting requirements imposed by the central bank are other impediments to conducting a remittance business. Firms consider the corruption of government officials and the government's tax policies to be the least significant barriers to providing remittance services.

All RSPs viewed money-transfer agencies such as MoneyGram and Western Union as key competitors, while nonbank institutions felt the banks were key competitors. As indicated earlier, banks and foreign exchange bureaus work closely with money-transfer agencies, while foreign exchange bureaus also work in partnership with local banks. Thus, competition between RSPs and nonbank institutions may be described as interdependence rather than rivalry.

Consequently, Uganda's RSP market can best be described as an oligopolistic market. This description is especially true given that there are relatively few major players in the RSP market—mainly the banks and licensed foreign exchange bureaus—but these market leaders work in partnership with the relatively smaller RSPs, including credit institutions, MDIs SACCOs, MFIs and foreign exchange bureaus without remittance service licenses.

Remittance Costs and Identification Requirements

There are differences in charges for remittance services, for the same volume and even for the same destination, across RSPs (table 9.3). On

Table 9.3   Remittance Charges for Sending U.S. Currency, 2008

		Average cost for sending US$200 or equivalent amount internationally				
	Total number of firms interviewed	Average fee (% of transfer amount)	Average foreign exchange commission (% of transfer amount)	Total average fee (% of transfer amount)	Minimum total fee (% of transfer amount)	Maximum total fee (% of transfer amount)
Foreign exchange bureaus	9	7.0	0.50	7.50	5.8	10.4
MFIs	2	10.0	0.50	10.50	10.5	10.5
Private commercial banks	15	11.6	0.34	11.94	3.9	16.7
Post office	1	1.5	–	1.50	1.5	1.5

Source: Survey of RSPs in Uganda.
Note: Total average fee = Average fee + average foreign exchange commission. Cost data were not available for credit unions and for PostBank.

average in Uganda, fees for sending US$200 range from U Sh 13,000 (approximately US$8 at the prevailing exchange rate at the time of the survey) to U Sh 55,000 (approximately US$33). Transfer charges are the lowest for courier companies and foreign exchange bureaus and the highest for financial institutions. In addition, it is more expensive to send money to the United States, the United Kingdom, and Middle East (particularly the United Arab Emirates) from Uganda, than it is to send money to neighboring countries such as Kenya and Tanzania).

In Uganda, foreign exchange bureaus do not charge a fixed fee for international inward remittances; instead, they charge a foreign exchange commission by offering the remittance recipient an exchange rate that is lower than the market exchange rate. On average, the foreign exchange commission ranges between 0.25 percent and 0.5 percent of the remittance amount. On average, the commission on foreign exchange does not vary widely across remittance corridors. In addition to the fixed transfer charges and foreign exchange commissions, other levies and fees can also be charged. For instance, one foreign exchange bureau reported that a "handling" fee of 0.5 percent is levied on a customer who sends money in U.S. dollars. This "handling" fee is ostensibly imposed given that the RSP cannot, in this case, extract a foreign exchange commission because the sender has already converted the money to U.S. currency.

The cross-border outward remittances market is highly concentrated in the formal sector. The only exceptions are outward remittances to Kenya and Tanzania, which are also transferred through the informal sector, such as bus companies. As mentioned, friends, family members, and acquaintances of the remittance senders are also used to transfer money across the border. One explanation for the dominance of the formal sector RSPs in the outward remittance market is that money is usually sent through a network of financial institutions, particularly banks. RSPs in the informal sector have limited access to the bank network; as a result, sending money would call for expensive transfer charges that render the provision of outward remittance services unfeasible for the informal sector. The minimum charge for sending remittances domestically in Uganda is U Sh 3,000 (approximately US$2), while the maximum charge is U Sh 66,000 (approximately US$40). However, there is significant variability in domestic transfer charges, especially between formal-sector remittance service providers and their informal sector counterparts, with the informal sector industries offering much lower rates, on average, than the formal sector. Banks and foreign exchange bureaus impose charges on receivers that are almost 50 percent of the sending fees. In Uganda, these charges go by various names such as bank charges, ledger fees, or foreign-currency handling fees. They range from U Sh 2,500 to U Sh 33,000, while the foreign exchange commission ranges from 0.25 percent to 5.00 percent of the remittance amount received. The RSPs surveyed also indicated that they charge either a fixed fee or a commission on remittances received.

Though formal RSPs are not required to charge taxes (for example, a value added tax) on financial transactions, including remittance services, transfer fees are higher than for informal RSPs. This higher fee could be partly attributed to the need to meet minimum capital standards, reporting requirements, and high operational costs (such as renting office space in prime locations). Informal sector RSPs, however, in addition to not being subject to any minimum standards, could use a retail outlet to offer remittance services. RSPs in the informal sector also usually operate in locations far away from the central business district where operational costs are lower. The lower transfer charges offered by the informal sector have the potential to more than compensate for the risks associated with transfers made through this sector, consequently creating a preference for informal transactions (especially for small remittance amounts).

RSPs gather information from users of remittance services. All the institutions involved in international remittances indicated that they ask for various types of identification, including national passports, national identification cards, verifications of residence, and driver's licenses. Additional acceptable types of identifications include voter registration cards and any other form of photo identification. Identification requirements apply to both account and nonaccount holders, though the requirements are not so stringent for account holders. Some banks insist that only account holders use money-transfer services. Some institutions, especially banks and PostBank, ask the sender to indicate the purpose of the money being transferred.

In urban areas, most international inward remittances reach the intended recipients in a day, as indicated by 58 percent of firms interviewed in Uganda. However, 23 percent report a next-day delivery. No firm reported a delivery period of more than five days. The trend slightly differs in rural areas, with 31 percent reporting that inward remittances reach the intended recipients in one day. As with deliveries in urban areas, no firm reported a delivery period of more than five days. Banks indicated that international inward transfers could be paid out in both local and foreign currency. However, Western Union payments are made in the local currency, and Western Union tells the sender the foreign-currency equivalent. There is a limit on the amount of money that customers can receive. For example, banks have a US$10,000 limit, and the same limit applies to the PostBank and Posta.

All providers indicated they have a system for dealing with grievances. Some of the firms indicated that they rarely receive grievances, and some indicated they have not received grievances. Transfer may fail to reach the intended recipient either because the information given was not correct or because the details were suspicious. When sending the money, the company dealing with the sender can indicate the time it will take to reach the recipient. In most cases (more than 80 percent), the institutions ask the sender and the recipient to verify the details to prevent discrepancies. In the case of a discrepancy, the money is not necessarily returned, but it is held until the details are clarified. Only when the transaction is suspicious would the institutions involve the local authorities. Regarding the length of time to address grievances, most firms indicated that concerns are dealt with as soon as they are raised. A small fraction of the firms indicated that it takes about a week to address grievances. The firms typically have dedicated staff members (two members in most firms) to deal with grievances, but firms can dedicate all staff members in the money-transfer section if the need arises. Only on very rare occasions are remittances not claimed.

Conclusion

The remittance market in Uganda is experiencing significant growth in terms of the volume and the diversity of the providers, in both international and domestic remittance markets. The following observations are noteworthy.

Data collection for remittance flows is not well developed. A growing number of migrant remittances is flowing to Uganda, which is positively correlated with increasing migration. However, data on migrant remittances is not collected regularly. Our RSP survey data do not allow for a fine disaggregation of remittances and other capital inflows as RSPs do not distinguish the various types of money transfers for which they provide services in their reporting to the central bank.

Participation in the formal remittance market is limited to a small proportion of remittance clients. The distribution of RSPs indicates limited access to formal-remittance transfer services by potential clients in various parts of the country. Results show that most services are provided in the major urban centers. Rural areas have a lower concentration of providers. The informal market continues to take a significant proportion of the remittance transfers, which can be attributed to the accessibility of informal services and the low cost of transfer.

Most remittance service providers do not treat remittance services as a core service. Except for money-transfer agencies, providers treat remittance services as auxiliary services.

Partnerships reflect a significant level of complementarity across remittance service providers. Except for community-based and transport-sector remittance service providers, all providers have a link to the banking sector because of its elaborate payment system that enables providers to reach a wider market both domestically and internationally.

Direct costs of remittance transfers are significantly high across the various providers. For sending US$200, the international transfer charge ranges between 10 percent and 17 percent, and the domestic transfer charge ranges between 0.4 percent and 12.5 percent for the domestic transfers. The fee covers processing charges, inventory costs, and delivery costs. In the case of a partnership, the transfer fee is shared in the agreed proportions to cover the various costs.

Access to a wide range of financial services is constrained by financial costs and availability. Most of the remittance providers indicated that they have a wide range of products in the menu of their core services to offer to remittance clients. However, the costs for such products (for example, the cost of maintaining an account) may be prohibitive for other financial services for remittance clients. Furthermore, Simba Cash may find it difficult to widen the scope of financial services provided to its clients if banks do not offer core services in localities where Simba Cash operates.

Mobile money transfer services are entering the Ugandan market. The entry of nonbanking services was a response to emerging gaps in the provision of financial services. Currently, mobile money transfer is gaining entry into the market and gaining ground in domestic remittances.

The regulatory system is substantially developed but must catch up with the technological developments. The central bank regulates only a small proportion of remittance service providers in Uganda. However, the regulation of mobile-phone money transfer has yet to evolve.

Recommendations

For assurance that remittance services provided are accessible, reliable and affordable, it is important to focus on the network and partnership among the providers, the technological developments, the regulatory system, and the data collection.

Designing and improving collection of remittance data could include administering periodic surveys and developing a reporting system for formal RSPs. Categorizing money transfers handled by service providers will be useful in accurately depicting migrant remittances.

Mobile-phone money transfer is revolutionizing the money transfer industry by providing accessible and affordable services. Client response to this technological development indicates that money transfer is a significant financial service that has taken time to receive proper attention. This developing industry challenges the banking sector to elevate remittance services from auxiliary services to core services and to adopt new technologies that will facilitate quick and cheaper transactions.

The speed of service delivery and the costs imposed depend on the national payment system's level of development. Thus, ensuring that the system adapts quickly to technological development will help to reduce the cost of transactions.

Information on the costs of remittance transfer should be shared publically so that clients are aware of charges and are able to choose their service provider wisely. Providing more information encourages competition among providers, decreasing the costs of the services.

To facilitate access to financial services, remittance clients should be given financial education because it is crucial for the remittance clients to understand the products that are available. Similarly, banks can develop products specifically for remittance clients.

Although the mobile-phone money transfer facility is currently not at risk, it is important that the operational rules are fully enforced. However, as these services become global, the regulatory framework must be able to address the challenges that may arise.

Notes

1. Although remittances can be person-to-person and business-to-business, this book does not distinguish between the users of the services; analysis is from the providers' perspective.
2. The Bank of Uganda (2008) records show that gross remittance receipts for 2006 were estimated at U Sh 277.3 billion (approximately US$148.5 million), with urban households accounting for 73 percent of those receipts. This amount is significantly lower compared to World Bank data that estimate total remittances for the same year to be US$411 million (World Bank 2009).
3. Debit card services provided by United Bank of Africa, which started operations early 2011, are yet to be tested as of April 2008.
4. The Advantage Card, a prepaid store value card issued by Standard Chartered Bank Uganda for use at Total Uganda Limited fuel stations, was withdrawn from the market.

References

Bank of Uganda. 2008. "Survey on Workers' Remittances to Uganda." Unpublished report, Bank of Uganda, Kampala.

FinScope Uganda. 2007. "Results of a National Survey on Access to Financial Services." In *Access to Financial Services in Uganda*, Department for International Development's Financial Sector Deepening Project: Kampala.

Orozco, Manuel, and Rachel Fedewa. 2006. "Leveraging Efforts on Remittances and Financial Intermediation." Working Paper, Inter-American Development Bank, Washington DC.

Ratha, Dilip. 2003. "Workers' Remittances: An Important and Stable Source of External Development Finance." Chapter 7 in Global Development Finance 2003, World Bank, Washington, DC, 157–75.

Sander, Cerstin, Peter Mukwana, and Altemius Millinga. 2001. "Money Transfer Systems: The Practice and Potential for Products in Tanzania and Uganda."

MicroSave Africa. http://www.microsave.org/research_paper/passing-the-buck-money-transfer-systems-the-practice-and-potential-for-products-in-ta.

Uganda Bureau of Statistics. 2006. *Uganda National Household Survey 2005/2006*. Uganda Bureau of Statistics, Kampala.

World Bank. 2011. *Migration and Remittances Factbook 2011*, World Bank, Washington, DC.

PART III

Remittance Markets in Remittance-Source Countries

CHAPTER 10

France

Frederic Ponsot

In 1962, only 20,000 immigrants from Sub-Saharan Africa were living in France. This number increased to more than 580,000 by 2005. In just six years, from 1999 to 2005, the number of migrants to France from Sub-Saharan Africa increased by more than 50 percent. Despite this rapid growth, however, Sub-Saharan immigrants remain a minority, representing only 12 percent of the immigrant population in France. As of 2005, the number of immigrants to France from Sub-Saharan Africa was approximately three times less than the number from European or North African countries, as figure 10.1 illustrates.

Remittance and Migration Trends

Money transfers from France increased by about 6 percent a year on average from 1999–2007, balance of payment data show. However, remittance volumes may have declined over the past two to three years because of the global economic crisis since 2009. The crisis has affected the labor market in France, much as it has in the United States and the rest of Europe, although its effect on immigration has not been well documented. An impact on African migrant workers is likely, however, because they are widely employed in the building and other industries within the most vulnerable sectors of the French economy.

Figure 10.1   Migrants in France, 2007, by Region of Origin

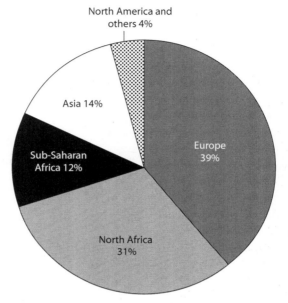

Source: INSEE 2007; INED database: http://www.ined.fr/fr/pop_chiffres/france/immigres_etrangers/pays
_naissance_1999/.
Note: North Africa = Algeria, Morocco, and Tunisia.

Anecdotal evidence indicates that potential immigrants from Senegal are delaying emigration to Europe because of the crisis. However, migration flows from neighboring Mali (particularly from the Kayes and Yelimene regions, where migration flows are part of the risk mitigation strategy and embedded in the culture and because Bamako, the capital, is becoming another migration center for international flows) are not likely to diminish over the medium to long term. Nor is migration expected to slow appreciably through other corridors where flows are due to poverty and political instability.

As the crisis affects the labor market, migrants' savings capacities and the amounts they send home (including savings at home) could decrease in the medium term (figure 10.2). Interviews with migrants in France suggest that they are concentrating their help on basic family needs and are postponing their own long-term projects.[1] Remittance declines could have long-term negative effects on developing countries. For example, as migrants' ability to invest and save diminishes, the urban real estate and banking sectors could suffer. However, once the post-election troubles

Figure 10.2   Migrant Remittance Outflows from France, 1999–2007

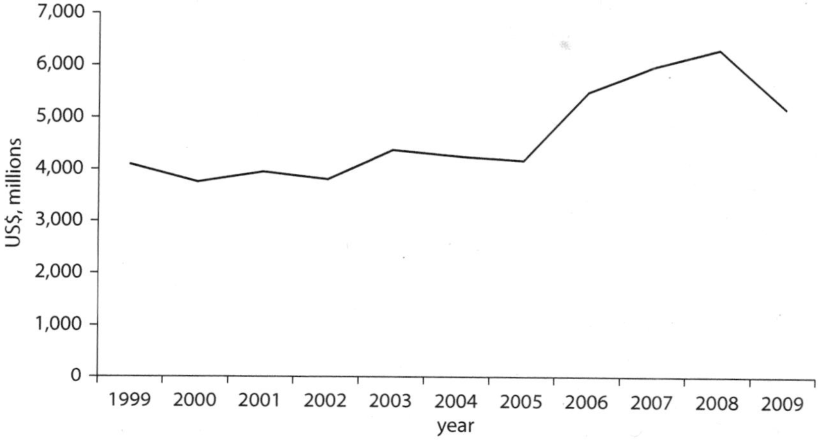

Source: World Bank 2011.

end, economic stabilization in Côte d'Ivoire could have a positive impact on the western region.

The French social-welfare model, given its social shock absorbers,[2] should help to limit return migration (French statistics do not measure return migration from France). The French government's investment in unemployment benefits, universal health care, and a proportional tax system should help low-income earners to maintain consumption in the short term. After favorable fiscal and public policies begin to relieve economic pressures, long-term growth and a surge in immigration can be expected, especially from neighboring European countries. In the long term, demographic changes in France,[3] with an aging population, might be another driver of migration because the country will require migration flows (including workers from Sub-Saharan Africa) to ensure economic growth. Overall, the number of African migrants should continue to increase in the medium term, but their living and working conditions will be harder than in the past in the short term. Remittances could decrease in the short term but can be expected to increase in the long term as the migrants' stock increases.

Sources of Migrants

This chapter considers those who send money or goods home to family or friends regularly, using the official categories in the census and annual surveys conducted by the French National Institute for Statistics and Economic Studies (Institut National de la Statistique et des Études Économiques, or INSEE).[4]

INSEE defines *immigrants* as people born abroad who currently live in France. The category does not include people who may have family members abroad but are of French nationality (binationals), nor does it include second and subsequent generations who may still send money home.[5] The definition also excludes illegal immigrants because they are not well documented in any sources. Table 10.1 shows the growth rate in the number of immigrants from each region.

In addition to the immigrant population totals shown in table 10.1, the French government estimates that the country has 400,000 illegal migrants from all origins. In 1999, 30,000 illegal immigrants obtained a residence permit (*permis de séjour*) out of an estimated 42,000 who applied.[6] If 12 percent of the entire migrant population is from Sub-Saharan Africa, the number of illegal immigrants from that region would be 48,000— clearly an underestimation.

Volume of Remittance Outflows

The Sub-Saharan remitters market includes at least the official estimate of 631,654 immigrants living in France (INSEE 2007), and the market expands greatly if the count also includes binationals. Lacking information about the number of illegal immigrants, we can assume that the official data underestimate the size of the remittance market.[7]

The ratio of the official estimated number of immigrants (INSEE 2005) to the sum of immigrants and binationals from Sub-Saharan Africa varies

Table 10.1   Growth of Immigrant Population in France, 1999–2005, by Region of Origin

Region of origin	1999 (thousands)	2007 (thousands)	Growth rate (%)
Sub-Saharan Africa	376	632	68
Maghreb*	1,298	1,578	22
Europe	1,935	2,013	4
Asia and Pacific	554	696	26
America	127	187	47
Total	**4,290**	**5,106**	19

Source: INSEE census surveys 1999, 2007; http://www.insee.fr/fr/bases-de-donnees/default.asp?page=recensements.htm.
Note: These numbers exclude illegal immigrants.
* = Algeria, Morocco, Tunisia.

between 21 percent (for Côte d'Ivoire) and 51 percent (for Madagascar) (table 10.2). Consequently, if the number of immigrants who are potentially sending money home is two to five times more than the number of immigrants as defined by INSEE, the remittance market is much larger than the INSEE estimates suggest (figure 10.3). Adding binationals and illegal immigrants would bring the market of potential remitters to Sub-Saharan Africa to about 1 million. We will use this hypothesis to estimate the size of the remittance market in the next section.

Table 10.2   Remittance Market from France to Selected North African and Sub-Saharan Countries
thousands

Remittance destination	Immigrants (a)[a]	Immigrants + binationals (b)[b]	Remitters, extrapolated from AfDB study 2007[c]	Ratio of immigrants to size of remittance market (a/b)
North Africa				
Algeria	679	1,500	—	45%
Morocco	625	1,100	1,219	57%
Tunisia	222	550	—	40%
Total North Africa	**1,526**	**3,150**		
Sub-Saharan Africa				
Cameroon	50	100	—	50%
Côte d'Ivoire	52	250	—	21%
Comoros	250[d]	—	57	n.a.
Congo, Dem. Rep., + Congo, Rep.	93	—	—	n.a.
Madagascar	41	80	—	51%
Mali	54	—	154	n.a.
Mauritius	30	—	—	n.a.
Senegal	67	300	307	22%
Other Africa	195	—	—	n.a.
Total Sub-Saharan Africa	**582**	**730**		

Sources: INSEE 2005 (all but Comoros); AfDB 2007 (Morocco, Senegal, Mali, Comoros); embassies and chambers of commerce (Algeria, Morocco, Tunisia, Senegal, Ivory Coast, Cameroon, Madagascar).
Note: Figures exclude illegal immigrants for lack of data.
a. Immigrants are people born abroad who live in France (INSEE 2005).
b. Binationals are people of French nationality with family members abroad and another nationality, registered in their embassy in France.
c. Estimates of the people sending money home using the following equation: Total flows divided by the average amount sent from France to the designated country's remittance corridor (AfDB 2007).
d. *Source:* Central Bank of Comoros.
— = not available.
n.a. = not applicable.

Figure 10.3   Comparisons of 2005 GDP Per Capita, by Region

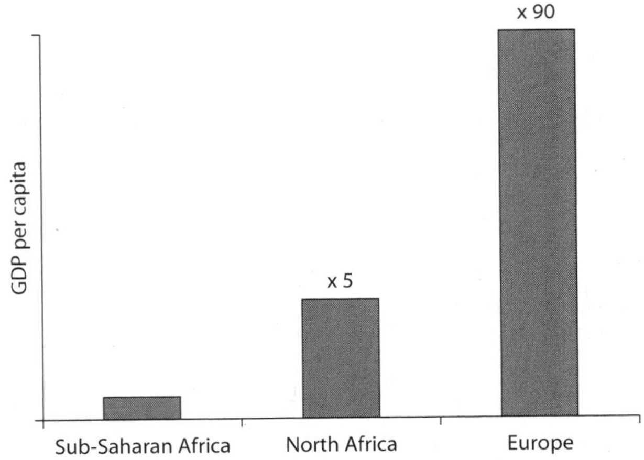

Source: INSEE 2005.
Note: GDP = gross domestic product. North Africa = Maghreb = Algeria, Morocco, Tunisia

Characteristics of the Remittance Industry

This section reviews the different groups of remittance service providers (RSPs) and, for each, provides insights on their payment structures, instruments, and mechanism and business models. The analysis is based largely on a survey of RSPs in France. From a catalog of more than 60 RSPs (primarily banks), 18 were interviewed, covering the full spectrum of RSP types. Some potential RSPs—such as domestic Internet person-to-person services or domestic mobile-phone payment pilots—were excluded because they were not considered relevant to this study. The survey questionnaires were administered in face-to-face interviews, except for a few conducted by phone and one done electronically. The questionnaire for the informal RSPs was customized to capture specific aspects of the informal sector and to ensure accuracy of data. For more specific information about the survey sample and the informal RSP questionnaire, see annex 10.1.

Methodological Issues

The methodological issues encountered during this process included the unwillingness of some of the key players, such as Western Union and MoneyGram, along with the other money transfer operators (MTOs), to disclose their figures (even with a confidentiality agreement). The informal

RSPs were more likely to disclose business information, although they were also harder to identify.

Informal flows dominate the remittance market but are not quantifiable on the basis of only a small sample of RSPs. The leaders of the migrant associations are far from the grassroots members or were reluctant to risk their reputation or that of their intermediaries by sharing their knowledge of the sector or of the main informal RSPs.

Moreover, major money transfer operators and certain banks cannot, by law, publicly disclose their figures because of the confidentiality clauses in their contracts with their partners. And specific details on flows, amounts by corridors, and very small amounts are not captured in the balance of payments of the central bank.

Types and Coverage of Remittance Firms

About 50 percent of the formal sector RSPs was interviewed, including the primary MTOs and some newcomers (figure 10.4). Informal channels were found mostly in the Burkina Faso, Côte d'Ivoire, Guinea, Mali, Mauritania, and Senegal corridors.

The industry is shaped by a bank-led model with a narrow array of services, with MTOs registered as financial institutions leading the cash-to-cash market and retail banks providing cash-to-account or account-to-account services. The sector has been evolving recently, thanks to a global awareness of the potential market by an increasing number of actors (notably the retail banks already covering mature migrant markets like Morocco) as well as regulatory evolution toward greater flexibility and a new type of financial intermediary: the payment establishment (PE) operator, described in more detail in the "Regulatory and Business Environment" section.

In terms of penetration and outward remittance flows, the market is dominated by the Société Financière de Paiement (SFDP), a product of the consortium between La Banque Postale and Western Union. On the receiving side, the corridors in Africa are marked by a weak financial infrastructure,[8] although the emergence of microfinance institutions (MFIs) and retail card-based payment systems (with the help of monetary authorities and international donors) has brought improvements.

At the end of the Sub-Saharan corridors (the receiving side), formal remittances have conquered substantial shares of the informal market, thanks to MTOs' partnerships with banks and MFIs as their subagents, which enlarged the network in the suburbs and secondary rural towns.

Figure 10.4   Distribution of Interviewed RSPs, by Type

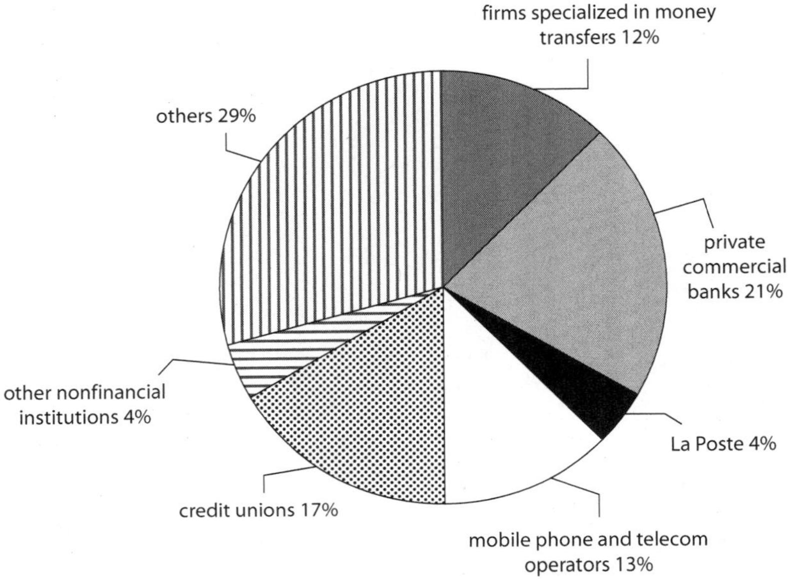

firms specialized in money transfers 12%

others 29%

private commercial banks 21%

other nonfinancial institutions 4%

La Poste 4%

credit unions 17%

mobile phone and telecom operators 13%

Source: Survey of RSPs 2009.

MNOs (mobile network operators) launched mobile-banking pilots in the domestic market, and leapfrogging technologies are addressing cross-border niche markets through an experimental project. With national spread networks, notably in rural areas, the postal service (La Poste) affiliated networks are, nevertheless, not working efficiently in every African countries.

The informal sector dominates the market in rural areas and is strong in urban areas as well, making it the main channel for several corridors from France to Africa and opening doors for innovative, technology-based business models to cover some segments of the market.

Table 10.3 lists the primary remittance channels, formal and informal, used by Senegalese migrants in France and shows that channels used vary according to the characteristics of migrants, especially the age and the home town location.

The predominance of the informal channels in Africa for international remittances is also revealed by the study led by the African Development Bank (AfDB 2007) (table 10.4).

Table 10.3   Remittance Channels Used by Senegalese Migrants in France

| | Categories | | | Area of origin/ family settlement | |
| | Young generations <35 years old | Older generations | | | |
Channel		Graduates (high school and higher)	Nongraduates	Urban	Rural
Formal					
Western Union	+++	++++	++	++++	+
MoneyGram	+++	+++		+++	
Other MTOs	+++			++	+
Banks	+	+++			
Informal					
Carriers (professional carrying money home with suitcase)	++		+++		++++
Wholesalers merchants (compensation)			++++	+++	++
Vacations (individuals bringing money home when they return for vacations)	+++		++++	++	++++
In form of goods sent from abroad	++			++	

Source: Survey interview. Informal commercial RSP based in Paris and sending money home to the Kaolack region of Senegal. The manager rated the preference of its clients and nonclients as well, on the basis of knowledge of the Senegalese community.
+ marginally used
++ sometimes used
+++ mainly used
++++ most preferred
Note: RSP = remittance service provider. MTO = money transfer operator.

Table 10.4   Transfer Channels from France to Mali, Senegal, and Comoros

percentage of transfers, by RSP type

	Informal	Banks	MTOs	Post	Total
Comoros	82	1	16	1	100
Mali	73	10	16	1	100
Senegal	46	10	36	8	100

Source: AfDB 2007.
Note: RSP = remittance service provider. MTO = money transfer operator.

Formal sector RSPs and partnerships. The formal French remittance industry is led by financial intermediaries registered as bank or financial establishments providing cash-to-cash services for international MTOs, cash-to-account services for African banks registered in France or partnering with French banks, and account-to-account for French banks with African subsidiaries. The retail French banks with African subsidiaries have a client-focused approach and are reluctant to serve nonclients, especially in cash operations. The segmentation and the small size of the Sub-Saharan African migrant markets are another hindrance to the establishment of French retail banks, and partnerships seem to be the only alternative for those with no subsidiaries in African countries and vice versa for the African banks (box 10.1).

Société Générale (SG), one of the leading retail banks in France with subsidiaries in Africa, developed its own package of products[9] and has dedicated three agencies to African migrants. Even though this package

---

Box 10.1

French Banks and Sub-Saharan Migrants

As a whole, French banks are beginning to consider the migrants as a mass market. For instance, low-cost transfers and a package of services for Moroccans are now close to being standard offerings, and partnerships between French banks and Moroccan banks are becoming ever more frequent.

For Sub-Saharan migrants, however, the market is not yet mature, and French banks still face constraints such as the following:

- A migrant remittance market that is segmented among several countries, each with its own specific financial regulation, infrastructure, and culture
- Reluctance to communicate aggressively like MTOs to capture migrant clients
- Desire to avoid the "reputation risk" of being considered by existing customers as the "bank of the migrants" (migrants still perceived as being poor in France)
- Migrants' preference for cash operations and a convivial atmosphere (staff speaking their language)
- Migrants' high illiteracy rates and a poor banking culture, which limits their understanding of the benefit of using formal services
- The existence of a population of undocumented migrants not registered by a French administration.

Source: Author, based on AfDB 2007.

is available at all SG branches in France, the potential market is not completely tapped into.

The anti-money-laundering (AML) regulations and regulations combating the financing of terrorism (CFT) impose additional constraints on the occasional client who wants to deal in cash, especially when the immigrant's identity is not formally established with French administration identifying papers, which is the standard of identification usually required by banks. Money-laundering risks are also perceived to be higher with cash transactions. As a result, instruments offered to immigrants are mainly traditional wire transfers from an open account in the bank books. SG is the only French bank that offers a low-cost transfer product for small transactions within its own large network, which includes subsidiaries in Africa.

Banque d'Escompte (BdE), with only a few branches in France, developed a commission-based money transfer business model, thanks to partnerships with African banks and regional MTOs. This bank is unique in the formal sector because it has developed a money transfer instrument especially for migrants, called "BdE Cash" (box 10.2). BdE also seeks to develop loyalty among the remitters and add value to its remittances services by linking remittances services to financial products offered by its African partners, including savings accounts and mortgages loans. Caisse d'Epargne Ile-de-France also recently launched a new, low-cost money transfer service in partnership with Ecobank.

Box 10.2

The BdE Experience: Developing Agent Networks

BdE recently introduced an automatic cash transfer machine (collecting cash) for direct transfers and is developing a program to hire 50 agents in France. Through the program, agents in migrant communities can be provided with a cash transfer machine and a specific identification and fidelization process providing the migrants an identification smart card to facilitate its transfers. With its card, a migrant can designate up to three preferred beneficiaries, and the money (up to €3,000) deposited at a cash machine or by debit card is transferred directly into a selected beneficiary's account or remit in cash. Migrants must be registered by the BdE but do not need bank accounts with BdE.

Source: Author.

Among the MTOs, which offer only cash-to-cash instruments, Western Union is the market leader because of its partnership with La Banque Postale, which has more than 6,600 branches.[10] The French postal service, La Poste, exclusively delivers its own electronic money transfer products (Mandat Express and Mandat Express International) as well as Western Union's product. Western Union's network of 50 branches includes SFDP[11] and other partnerships, notably since the PE directive transposition with change operators and callshops.[12]

Other MTOs' networks are small by comparison. MoneyGram now has only 47 branches since its partnership with Caisse d'Epargne Rhones-Alpes ended, and its main partner is a financial subsidiary of Carrefour (the leading supermarket company), which has 17 branches. Crédit Agricole du Nord Est and MoneyGram are working on a pilot branch. Coinstar has 16 branches throughout France and is partnering with African MTOs such as Money Express. Ria Money Transfer has even fewer branches (six), and they are concentrated in Paris although its payment partners are mainly MFIs in Africa. Ria (especially) developed its agent networks thanks to the new PE directive and a more aggressive strategy to address African corridors.

Regional MTOs—relatively minor players in this market—operate by forming partnerships with Coinstar and BdE. They include Money Express (which partners are La Banque Postale in Côte d'Ivoire and Senegal, MFIs, La Poste, and several other small banks throughout francophone Africa) and Express Union (a leader in Cameroon that is also established in other Economic and Monetary Community of Central African States [Communauté Économique et Monétaire de l'Afrique Centrale, or CEMAC] countries).

African banks, despite their limited number of branches, are more integrated into the market than are the French banks with African subsidiaries because of the simplicity of their products and because they accept foreign identity papers from their clients. Some African banks have representative offices in France—either under the umbrella of a French partner bank (such as CBIP) with capital from the African bank or by establishing their own bank in France (for example, Attijariwafa Bank and the Bank of Africa [BOA]). Through these representative offices, migrants can open accounts in their home countries and deposit funds into them from France. CBIP's African partners usually pay a yearly fee and share a part of the commissions. Long-term or stable resources are the banks' main objective, and a presence in Paris is a decisive factor in creating a relationship with migrants and international wholesalers from the home country. Certain Moroccan banks have a global strategy that encompasses the migrant market, with subsidiaries in France and throughout the African markets. (Attijariwafa Bank has subsidiaries in Africa, and Banque Marocaine du Commerce Extérieur recently established subsidiaries in France by investing in the BOA group.) In particular, Attijariwafa bank bought the Senegalese Compagnie Bancaire de l'Afrique Occidentale (CBAO)—CBIP's main stake-holder—as well as the Banque Internationale pour le Mali (BIM), the second-largest bank in Mali, with a presence in eight Sub-Saharan African countries.[13]

Informal sector RSPs. The informal sector includes diverse providers and individuals for whom money transfer is not necessarily the main activity. Three types of models dominate, often in combination or even including formal channels for efficiency:

- Individual (carrying money and goods on trips home)
- Community-based
- Business-oriented.

In the individual model, when a migrant worker returns home on vacation, he or she carries remittance money, not only for his or her own family but also on behalf of fellow migrants or close friends. The name of the sender, the receiver, and the amount are pasted on the bank notes. Costs are not formally fixed, but senders typically pay to the transportation carrier 3 to 10 percent of the amount carried.

The community-based model involves a group of individuals (typically 15 to 20 people) living in the same village or the same building who create an "association" (formal or not) to send money home and manage a small shop in the village.[14] This model is particularly prevalent among migrants from rural areas, where community ties are still strong. The money is collected within a small and close community group, and goods are purchased in France or from wholesalers in the home countries. Retail orders for individual money transfers or goods purchases (for the family) are made daily by mobile phone or fax (if the village has a regular phone connection). The group must ensure that it can always finance the collective village shop's cash flow to remit money to relatives in the village and to buy goods for the community shop in bulk. The migrants' regular visits to the village guarantee this minimum cash flow. Alternatively, bank wire transfers or cash advances from wholesalers in the home country can help to finance the cash flow. In turn, the revenue from sales and commissions also pay the group's shopkeeper, a collector in charge of gathering funds in France and routing them to their destination by its own means or by identifying a migrant going home, and accountant in France.[15] Yearly remittances through these means could total €50,000 and require a monthly cash flow of about €4,500. Table 10.5 summarizes each actor's role in a community-based informal RSP.

The business-oriented model is a variant of the community-based model, the main difference being that the money transfer activities are conducted by business-oriented individuals (such as wholesalers, retailers, or hostel collectors) instead of by the migrants themselves. Generally, these individuals have family members running the business in France, in the home country, or in other countries. The scale of operation (mostly informal but including formal elements) depends on the strength of the relationship between the partners (typically family members) and the ability to finance cash flows in a timely manner at different points of payment simultaneously. In the remittance recipient country, retailers are often found in the capital city and secondary towns. In France, funds are gathered through designated collectors or directly in retail shops or at wholesalers. The biggest retail players act as clearinghouses serving various small networks and can provide currencies for wholesalers. They have a strong reputation with the other players and help to ensure the viability of the system. Monthly cash flows can amount to more than €30,000, and annual flows can add up to €500,000 for 150 to 200 clients in one informal RSP. In the case of flexible exchange rates, speculation could affect revenue.[16]

Profit maximization is not the sole objective of business-oriented informal providers. They are also interested in putting their capital to best use and increasing their business volume by building international networks of correspondents. Commissions and fees are flexible and do not always reflect the true costs of the transaction. (For example, the informal RSP generally does not pay the agent's travel costs but compensates the traveler in other ways.)[17] Desirable features of this kind of informal service include confidence, discretion, immediate delivery of cash, advance transfers for regular clients, and lower commissions if problems arise. Compared with the formal channels, this channel's accessibility and cordiality are also big advantages—and often considered even more important than costs (which are sometimes not competitive with the formal sector's, especially for transfers of small amounts).

Some of the interviewed providers cited embezzlement, robbery, or loss as risks of the business-oriented model.[18] In such cases, there is no

Table 10.5 Community-Based RSP Chain of Operations and Main Actors, by Role

Actor	Originating and funding transfer orders	Clearing transfer orders	Receiving transfer orders	Changing money	Paying transfer orders
Migrant	Brings remittances to collector Calls family to confirm transfer			May bring money personally from France	Remits money to beneficiaries (individuals and retailers)
Small-scale collector	Collects funds and originates transfers for migrant group by phone, fax, or Internet	Maintains retail shop's cash flow with cash advances from wholesalers and formal channels	Identifies migrants to carry money		
Master of networks	Receives "gross" transfer orders in euros from wholesalers Mobilizes funds through collectors Identifies migrants to carry money	Ensures settlement of transfers among stakeholders on time, arranges players, and guarantees efficiency		Provides euros for wholesalers for international purchases	

(continued)

Table 10.5 *(continued)*

Actor	*Originating and funding transfer orders*	*Clearing transfer orders*	*Receiving transfer orders*	*Changing money*	*Paying transfer orders*
Wholesaler in urban centers			Receives transfer orders from master of networks	Provides CFA francs in exchange for euros	Pays master agents, small retailers, or migrant families
Master agents in capital cities			Receive transfer orders from master of networks		Remit money to families
Village shopkeeper or retailer			Receives transfer orders from collectors or migrants		Remits money to families

Source: Survey data.

attempt to recompense for the loss of one's money. Specific operations could be formalized, especially the collection and transfer of funds, to avoid these risks. Payments made through mobile phones at a low cost per transaction could also be a convenient means of avoiding frequent calls or the use of fax machines. Some RSPs interviewed are interested in formalizing certain operations with the new PE regulations in mind, but they are concerned about potential fiscal losses from their inability to compete in a technologically advanced environment. Another constraint is posed by some wholesalers who have a strong interest in having access to cash currencies to finance their international purchases. User preference, origin of migrants, and financial literacy are strong determinants in the choice of channels and mechanisms used.[19]

Remittance Volumes, Sources, and Destinations

Several hypotheses were used to estimate the size of the French remittance market. The formal flows were then separated from the data gathered through primary and secondary sources. Two scenarios were modeled for the entire market on the basis of estimated population of migrants. The data from the study were then aggregated to estimate the total formal market.

Model 1 was based on the average amount sent and the propensity to send. The model estimated a population of 1 million migrants, the propensity (62 percent of migrants) to send money home, and an average monthly transfer per capita. The estimate based on Model 1 is shown in table 10.6.

Model 2 was based on an African Development Bank (AfDB) study from 2007, from which partial data were extrapolated. The estimate based on Model 1 is shown in table 10.7.

Based on the estimates derived from both models, as shown in tables 10.6 and 10.7, the size of the French remittance market for Sub-Saharan Africa is between €1 billion (low hypothesis) and €1.8 billion.

Formal market estimates. The global formal market from the sample was extrapolated by use of several hypotheses and complementary sources, including the following:

- 2006 data from La Banque Postale (from an official source), which is the backbone of the market[20]
- Flows generated by MTOs, extrapolated from the volume of transactions of a typical Western Union branch

Table 10.6   Estimate of Total French Remittance Market from Average Transfer and Propensity Data (Model 1)

Migrant population	1 million
Propensity to send money	62%
Average monthly transfer[a]	€150
Average annual amount sent[b]	€1,650
Total remittances	**€1.02 billion**

Sources: Milhaud 2006.
Note:
a. Average generally observed for African migrants in France (AfDB 2007; CFSI 2004).
b. Based on 11 monthly transfers a year.

Table 10.7   Estimate of the French Remittance Market from AfDB Country Data (Model 2)

Country	Transfers from formal + informal RSPs (€ millions)	Transfers through informal RSPs (%)	Migrants from country/total migrants from SSA (%)
Mali	295	73	15
Senegal	449	46	30
Comoros	70	82	1
Total	**814**		**46**
Market estimation (100% migrants Sub-Saharan Africa)	1,770		

Source: AfDB 2007.
Note: SSA = Sub-Saharan Africa.

- The global amount extrapolated from SG's number of active clients, by corridor, considering an annual amount sent of €1,500 (a conservative hypothesis).

Finally, these extrapolated flows were added to the sample data using an assigned weight that corresponds to the size of the sample plus La Banque Postale's figures (shown in table 10.A.1). The data are not fully homogeneous because they do not use the same year of reference (2008 for the sample and 2006 for La Banque Postale).

By this analysis, as table 10.8 shows, the overall formal remittance market is estimated at €800 million, which is consistent with the higher estimate above for the global (informal + formal) market given that informal flows represent at least 50 percent of total flows (Freund and Spatafora 2005).

Table 10.8   Remittances from France to Selected Sub-Saharan African Countries

Country	Total remittances (€)
Senegal	248,511,040
Côte d'Ivoire	134,373,400
Mali	129,001,777
Cameroon	116,329,621
Madagascar	39,006,497
Congo, Dem. Rep.	35,514,547
Congo, Rep.	31,853,565
Benin	28,745,029
Togo	26,991,495
Comoros[b]	8,012,361
Ghana	2,693,515
Total	**801,032,847**

Source: Author's calculations.

The core remittance corridors are Cameroon, Côte d'Ivoire, Mali, and Senegal, with more than €100 million for each. The most important formal remittance channels are the MTOs, followed by the La Poste mandats and the banks, as figure 10.5 illustrates.

Unfortunately, the 2007 and 2008 data are insufficient to assess the impact of, and examine the trends set in motion by, the global financial crisis. The only variable available is the number of transactions, which has been stable although the amounts have somewhat declined.[21] For the main CBIP partners in Mali and Senegal, the flows decreased between 2007 and 2008 by 10 percent (BIM) and 7.7 percent (CBAO), respectively. Informal RSPs confirmed an overall decrease in flows.

New business models and remittance products. Newcomers from the communications and technology sectors have developed new business models in France. In so doing, these providers have introduced instruments such as branchless banking, Internet-based services, cashless micropayment technology, and mobile-phone money transfer systems.

- *Branchless banking models.* These are card-based or multichannel MTOs. Flouss.com[22] is an intermediary for Banque Accord (a bank with few branches, held by the supermarket Auchan group), which uses prepaid cards. Flouss is currently operating and has acquired a

Figure 10.5   Distribution of Formal Remittance Flows, by Channel

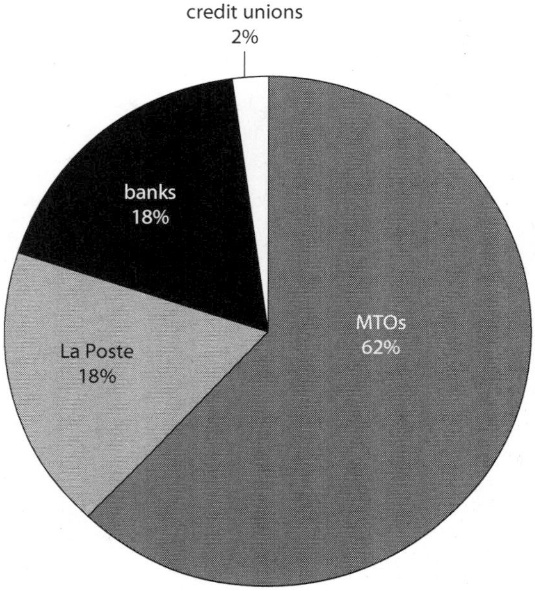

Source: Author's calculations.

small share of the market since it started in 2008. Transcash, a Visa prepaid card, began its operations in late 2009. Transcash introduced three main innovations: no bank account required, reloadable tickets that are available at bars and retail shops, and acceptance of a national passport as identification.[23] Two others (Woo-Group[24] and MAÂTCARD[25]) have raised capital on the stock exchange but have not yet begun operations. These models are limited to migrants whose families are close to point-of-sale (POS) or automated teller machine (ATM) networks and are familiar with electronic banking.

- *Internet-based services.* Another telecommunications company, Telemedia,[26] offers a set of services for migrants (such as calling family, managing village shops from France, sending money, and prepaying for health services) through the Internet and prepaid arrangements. The model, described further in box 10.4, targets the migrant village associations to develop economies of scale and cover the connection fees

Box 10.3

Loro/Nostro Accounts Enable African Banks to Collect Deposits in France

French banking law does not allow the representative offices of African banks to collect cash deposits in France. To address this limitation, these banks have signed partnership agreements with some French banks to have their representative offices considered legally as partner branches of the French banks, which are thus able to collect deposits.

Under this arrangement, migrants' deposits fund CFA franc accounts opened on their behalf on the African bank's books. In turn, the African bank also opens a specific account, called a *loro*, that goes on the French bank's books. This loro can be cleared through an international wire transfer or used by the African bank to fund its trade operations in euros.

Source: Rouchy and Gourvez 2006.

in the village. It has a pilot in two rural villages in the Kayes region of Mali, which is partly financed with a €227,000 contribution from the French Ministry of National Identity, Immigration, Integration, and Development.

- *Micropayment operators.* Tagattitude[27] has developed a technology that uses existing analog (voice) technology, as further described in box 10.4. Its pilot project in Mali, supported by the World Bank, involves a micropayment cashless system (for transactions of less than €150) built on an Internet platform that sells prepaid units to be transferred by mobile phone from France to Mali, where 25 Bamako retailers currently accept it. Tagattitude is not registered to operate as a payment establishment or as a bank; therefore, the money has to be spent only in shops or pharmacies (for example, as a gift transfer).

- *Orange.* One of the big three licensed telecommunications firms in France, Orange is considering the international remittance market. Cross-border transfers are complex from a regulatory point of view; however, through its BNP Paribas subsidiaries in Africa, the company launched a pilot for national money transfer by mobile (Orange Money) in Côte d'Ivoire and Senegal.[28] Sending prepaid airtime from

Box 10.4

Telemedia and Tagattitude: New Channels for Micropayments to Mali

Two telecommunications firms, Telemedia and Tagattitude, are testing innovative channels to support Internet-based services for migrants and micropayments through mobile phones and are working together to market their solutions to Malian migrants' associations in France.

Telemedia is testing an approach that puts migrant associations at the center. In the business case set for migrants, Telemedia call shops managed by migrants deliver a package of services that may include any or all of the following: international calling by a VoIP channel; videoconferencing with family; microtransfers or payments; retail shop management; and individual prepaid accounts for family purchases, health care, and other needs. The model requires an existing Internet connection in the village, and migrants would pay the recurrent connection costs. The infrastructure would require a partnership with the public or private sector as well as the contribution of the migrants' association.

Tagattitude has developed a secure protocol to transfer information between mobile phones and an Internet platform that uses the Global System for Mobile Communications (GSM) network without requiring a specific mobile chip mechanism called NSDT™ (Near Sound Data Transfer). Prepaid units can be loaded (cashed in) on mobile phones either with cash or from a bank card through Tagattitude's Internet platform, called TagPay, and transferred by phone. Prepaid money can then be spent within a private network of "merchant acceptors." Retailers can accept the m-payment thanks to a simple communication with the foreign platform through the channel of their mobile phone. Compensation is made daily in their bank accounts in Mali.

Source: Author.

France to Africa and within Africa is already feasible, but Orange is also testing contactless payment in France.

- *Suncard Family.* Suncard Family is a telecommunications firm in the French Caribbean that has developed a subsidiary allowing the purchase and delivery of food to families of the Haitian diaspora.[29] The company also recently set up a firm in France to cover the markets in Côte d'Ivoire, Mali, and Senegal. In addition to the purchase and delivery of goods, Suncard plans to offer money transfers and to establish partnerships with MTOs.

Other new remittance products have emerged from innovative diaspora initiatives. Hope Finance, an MFI, is developing a set of services (money transfer services, payment for goods, and payment for health care) dedicated to the African diaspora and their families.[30] Formerly in partnership with Money Express, Hope Finance now has developed its own software for electronic cash-to-cash transfers, to be implemented throughout its proprietary network of MFIs in Africa. These money transfer services are used to attract migrants to other services, mainly health care programs.

La Mutuelle d'Epargne et de Crédit des Sénégalais de France (MECSEF) plans to offer money transfer services to Senegalese migrants. MECSEF has entered into a partnership with Poste Finance in Senegal, where it complies with the microfinance laws. Both institutions, however, need to meet additional requirements to develop their payment operations from France.

On the payment system side, there have been no solutions among major operators (Visa, MasterCard, and SWIFT) for microtransfers to Africa. However, Caisse d'Epargne is discussing plans to issue Visa cards with an African bank that has a large network in several African countries. MasterCard launched Money Send in the Asian corridors and could transpose it to the African corridors if there is market demand. Initiatives not yet linked to major card issuers in France include the Interbank Electronic Banking Group of the Economic and Monetary Union of West Africa.[31] Integration of French banks in the Single Euro Payments Area (SEPA)[32] remains slow, and it is too early to examine opportunities for microtransfers in this area.

The Regulatory and Business Environment

In France, only financial institutions (*établissement de crédit*) can engage in services involving means of payment, such as settlement of international person-to-person money transfers.[33] The minimum capital requirement for creating a financial institution is €2.2 million—a constraint for MTOs that want to open branches in France, whether they are mobilizing funds to create the institution or maintaining the required capital after the institution is established. Alternatively, MTOs can partner with financial institutions to deliver person-to-person transfer products. Nonbank institutions (intermediary bank operations, or *intermédiaire en operations de banque*) can also manage means of payment on behalf of financial institutions by offering card-to-card money transfers.

With a New Payment Services Directive, New Operators

A new type of financial intermediary, called a payment establishment, is now allowed to implement means of payment within the SEPA countries.[34] The new PE operators could become players in the African remittance market because operations outside SEPA are permitted and because the minimum capital requirement will be reduced to €20,000 for basic operations. This new regulatory environment will also bring some flexibility to the agent role because anyone can be a PE agent who complies with the required procedures.

Several RSPs interviewed during the study (Flouss.com, Telemedia, and Suncard Family) are considering becoming PEs, and some informal RSPs are interested in either creating a PE or becoming an agent for a PE or an existing MTO. African banks, African MFIs, and regional MTOs could also be interested in either creating PEs or collaborating with one as an alternative to the major MTOs and La Banque Postale (because of the latter's exclusivity contract with Western Union and its own products).

Among the implications of the new payment services law are the following:

• It could present an opportunity for regional MTOs or African banks and MFIs to enter the market directly or through partnerships with the new PEs.
• It could allow newcomers such as mobile-phone or Internet-based niche market operators to create their own PEs and add money transfer operations to their core business services.
• It could enlarge the network of agents, especially through the establishment of more retail shops and associations of migrants.

However, the delivery of new agreements could be gradual. With the introduction of new types of operators in the market and greater competition in terms of remittance instruments and technologies, new types of risks may also emerge. However, points of sale and innovative alliances among nonbank operators should increase and will cover a wider array of specific needs (table 10.9).

Entry and Coverage Limitations

As previously mentioned, banks are reluctant to handle cash operations, especially for nonregistered clients. This aversion limits the coverage of basic electronic transfer services through their branch infrastructures.

Table 10.9 Main RSP Types and Coverage of Selected Remittance Corridors

Remittance corridor	Potential no. of remitters	Global MTOs[a]	Regional MTOs[b]	French banks with African subsidiaries[c]	African banks[d]	Alternative operators[e]	Card-based operators[f]
Senegal	300,000	WU, MG	Money Express	SG	CBIP (BHS*)	Suncard Family*	Flouss.com, TransCash
Côte d'Ivoire	250,000	WU, MG	Money Express	SG	(Bq Atlantique*, BHCI)	—	Flouss.com, TransCash
Mali	153,646	WU, MG	Money Express	—	BOA (BIM, BDM, BHM,* Bq Atlantique)	Telemedia, Tagattitude, Suncard Family*	Flouss.com, TransCash
Cameroon	100,000	WU, MG	Express Union	SG	(Afriland First Bank)	—	Flouss.com, TransCash
Congo, Dem. Rep.	93,000	WU, MG	Express Union	—	(BIAC)	—	Flouss.com, TransCash

Source: Author's compilation.

Note: RSP = remittance service provider. MTO = money transfer operator. BdE = Banque d'Escompte. WU = Western Union. MG = MoneyGram. SG = Société Générale. CBIP = Compagnie de Banques Internationales de Paris. BHS = Banque de l'Habitat du Sénégal. BOA = Bank of Africa. BIM = Banque Internationale pour le Mali. BDM = Banque de Développement du Mali. BHM = Banque de l'Habitat du Mali. BHCI = Banque de l'Habitat de Côte d'Ivoire. BIAC = Banque Internationale pour l'Afrique au Congo. ATM = automated teller machine.

a. Cash-to-cash providers.

b. BdE or Coinstar partners; cash-to-cash providers.

c. Double account and €10 transfers, burial and repatriation insurance, transnational mortgages, and insurance to maintain remittances.

d. CBIP or BdE partners; mainly deposits; *mortgage, prepaid card.

e. Potential to address rural areas.

f. Depends on Visa's (TransCash) and MasterCard's (Flouss.com) ATM infrastructure in receiving countries.

— = negligible.

* = mortgage only.

For niche market operators like Telemedia, the major barriers are lack of broadband access, high energy costs, and local telecom monopolies. Telecom regulators need to provide open access to their networks because licenses are expensive for firms that serve migrants from remote rural communities. It is particularly difficult for smaller e-payment providers that lack their own telecom infrastructures. Wi-Max can be an alternative means of connectivity for the small subregions from which migrants originate, but there is little infrastructure to support this model. For example, energy costs for batteries can be up to 60 percent of the total cost of operating a dispensary and call shop. The lack of access to national telecom networks means the provider has to build its own infrastructure.

During the RSP survey interviews, many of both the formal and informal RSPs know their customers and their preferences but lack adequate information to help them better penetrate their markets because the ability to offer money transfer services depends on transaction volume and sufficient investment to build secure branches.[35] In addition, retail banks with large networks seem unable to monitor small amounts of transfers in each corridor.[36]

Ever since the launch of the Send Money Web site (http://www .envoidargent.fr), which lists money transfer charges, overall public policy has shifted toward reducing the cost of sending money home. This represents an important evolution from the original approach, which focused mainly on helping migrants leverage their savings toward development by investing in collective initiatives or local development and establishing small enterprises in their home countries. However, codevelopment—a strategy by which migrants contribute toward the development of their countries of origin—remains an important public policy issue. Supporting financial innovation and the migrants' efforts to invest in their home countries or involving migrants in implementing social services (including education, capacity building, health, and access to water) is at the forefront of the French public strategy.

Remittance Costs

The cost to send €150 varies from €5 in the informal sector to €20 in the banking (formal) sector. This does not include the costs of receiving the transfer for the banks.

For both informal RSPs and MTOs, the fee to send money decreases as the amount sent increases, in percentage. In the informal sector, the fee is under €5 for any amount less than €150, increasing to €10 for any amount beyond that. Informal RSPs do not include the cost of international travel when the cash is carried in luggage. The lowest fee to send money through Western Union is €8.[37] The other MTOs (including informal RSPs) have kept their charges slightly above Western Union's. In the banking sector, fees to send money are generally fixed and vary from €10 to €20.

The banks offer three general types of services and pricing:

- *French banks with African subsidiaries:* Transfers are done within the network, costs are lower and transparent, and the receiver bears no costs.
- *African bank representatives in France:* The average deposit fee is between €8 and €10, and the average withdrawal fee is €20.
- *Banks with correspondent agents:* Each transaction costs about €20, but the receiving banks' fees were not disclosed (estimated to be also about €20).

Card-based providers generally charge three types of fees:

- *Registration:* €19
- *Loading a prepaid card:* €3 plus an additional 1.5 percent of the amount
- *Withdrawals:* €5.

Although the sender's costs are not fully transparent (because of the different prepaid card solutions), this solution could be more competitive and produce greater economies of scale if the withdrawal fees in Africa were much lower. Similar services cost much less in Morocco because of a higher volume of transactions and revenue from better liquidity management.[38] Overall, client preferences must be considered when comparing costs. Indeed, small cash-to-cash transfers through all channels remain the most used and the most expensive instrument,[39] but alternative channels still exist. The banking channels[40] are the most effective, charging a flat commission rate, considering the average amount sent, as shown in table 10.10.

Micropayment by mobile phone remains the dominant means of payment in rural remote areas. It is one of the cheapest instruments, and it holds potential for frequent microtransactions, even in remote areas, if there is a retailer and a GSM network. Prepaid cards are another convenient instrument because they allow the recipient to withdraw money at any time of the day. However, they require a large and efficient payment infrastructure, making this model expensive and unusual, especially

Table 10.10   Remittance Charges of African CBIP Partners, 2009
costs to send €150

Destination	Commission	% of amount sent
Senegal	15	10
Comoros	8	5
Mali, Côte d'Ivoire	8–10	5–7

among unbanked people. Finally, in-person delivery can be a viable instrument for migrants who want more control over the effective use of their money.

Commission sharing among partners can increase the charges to clients. Hope Finance, an unpartnered MFI, charges the least—5 percent of the amount sent—and it can afford to, its commercial manager said. Because Hope Finance has its own branches in receiving countries, it has been able to develop its own platform. GCE Payment, the payments subsidiary of Caisse d'Epargne, charges €5 (or €16 in case an anomaly occurs). However, Caisse d'Epargne charges between €20 and €30 for each transfer—unappealing for sending small sums. Most of the transfers are sent to African countries that have fixed exchange rates and currencies that are backed by the euro. Foreign exchange fees are rarely imposed compared with other corridors.[41] Table 10.11 displays a range of fees charged by selected RSPs in France.

Data from the most popular MTOs (Western Union and MoneyGram) show that charges for remittance transfers from France are quite high relative to other countries. Table 10.12 displays some sample differences in MTO charges to send €150.

Identification Requirements

To ensure against fraud and to comply with AML-CFT reporting regulations, RSPs (particularly in the formal sector) usually require identification from senders and receivers of funds. The accepted forms of identification vary by RSP type but typically include the following:

- MTOs require an identification document with a picture and the name of the receiver. In the receiving country, the recipient usually must present an official document. On-site visits revealed that driver's licenses are no longer accepted. French papers (*permis de séjour*), national ID cards, or passports are preferred.[42]

Table 10.11   Charges to Send €150 through Selected RSPs

RSP	RSP type	Cost (€)	(% of remittance)
Flouss.com	prepaid-card RSP	13	8.7
Telemedia	micropayment RSP	9	6.0
Hope Finance	semiformal MTO	8	5.0
BIM	CBIP partner	10	6.7
BDM	CBIP partner	10	6.7
BHM	CBIP partner	8	5.3
BOA	CBIP partner	8	5.3
CBIP	CBIP partner	10	6.7
Coinstar	MTO	11	7.3
Western Union	MTO	15	10.0
MoneyGram	MTO	10	6.7
Caisse d'Epargne PAC	cooperative bank	20	13.3
Caisse d'Epargne IDF	cooperative bank	30	20.0
BdE	bank	12	8.0
SG	bank	10	6.7
Crédit Agricole du Nord Est	bank	16	10.7
Banque postale	MTO	15	10.3

Source: Author's calculations.
Note: RSP = remittance service provider. MTO = money transfer operator. CBIP = Compagnie de Banques Internationales de Paris. BIM = Banque Internationale pour le Mali. BDM = Banque de Développement du Mali. BHM = Banque de l'Habitat du Mali. BOA = Bank of Africa. BdE = Banque d'Escompte. IDF = Ile de France. PAC = Provence-Alps-Côte d'Azur. SG = Société Générale.

Table 10.12   MTO Charges to Send €150 from Selected Countries

MTO	Italy % of amount sent	Italy Charge (€)	France % of amount sent	France Charge (€)	Spain % of amount sent	Spain Charge (€)
Western Union	8	11.50	10	15.00	12	18.00
MoneyGram	7	11.00	7	10.00	9	13.90

Source: RSP survey Western Union and MoneyGram website, December 2009.
Note: MTO = money transfer operator.

- *French banks* require the senders to present, at least, proof of legal status and proof of residence in France. National papers from the country of origin, such as passports, are generally not accepted, although La Banque Postale and the Caisse d'Epargne sometimes make exceptions.[43]
- *African banks' representative offices* in France require senders to present national identity cards and national passports from the home country.

- *Card-based operators* have the same requirements as the banks, except for TransCash, which accepts passports. The recipient, however, does not need any form of identification.
- *Informal RSPs* do not require identification papers from the senders. RSPs sometimes assign a code for first-time recipients, and this is to be presented along with other forms of identification.[44]

Some RSPs impose a ceiling on the amount transferred to avoid money laundering. Box 10.5 lists several examples of these remittance limits.

Conclusions and Recommendations

The recommendations fall under three categories: statistics and data, regulation, and policy (for the French government, banks, migrants and other clients, and global initiatives).

Box 10.5

RSP Remittance Ceilings

The ceilings are particularly restrictive for collective transfers and informal remittances. Informal RSPs admit they use banks to remit money and would like to use this secure channel more. Banks sometimes authorize representatives such as moral persons—registered associations—or association leaders (of informal community-based RSPs) to provide a comprehensive lists of group members or remitters, with addresses and phone numbers. However, the migrant association leaders are often reluctant to provide members' names because some of them are illegal immigrants.

Informal RSPs prefer not to handle amounts of more than €1,000 from an individual, and they seek information to check whether the remitters are part of a social network and whether the amounts sent are consistent with the levels of incomes of the remitters.

MTOs have no official ceilings, but MTOs do require bills, proof of payment, justification of the origin of funds from €8,000 sent yearly or quarterly, and proof of identity of both the sender and the receiver.

Banks are particularly vigilant since amounts of €3,000 in one day and have specific policies to detect or declare suspicious operations.

Source: Author's compilation.

Statistics and Data

Statistics are the entry point for policy makers as well as market operators. Knowing the amount of remittances by corridor is a prerequisite to leveraging their impact on development and encouraging formal operators to enter the market with lower costs than major MTOs when affordable. Remittances are a key resource for African countries that are partners with France and can help to expand migrants' access to finance. The following data and research activities would help policy makers better understand migrants' preferences and remittance behaviors:

- Data on such should be reported by financial intermediaries to the Ministry of Economy, Industry, and Employment (which regularly meets with its peers from the French-speaking African countries) on a confidential basis. The aggregated figures should be disclosed by corridor, by channel, and by instrument used.
- A comprehensive survey also should be undertaken to assess and better understand the informal market, which is just as important as the formal market in certain corridors.
- Because formalizing flows is also a prerequisite to formulating policies, it may help policy makers to compare the repartition between formal and informal figures, in addition to the costs of sending money home with those from other European countries, and to assess the efforts to formalize the informal flows and to cut costs.
- Increased demographic and anthropologic research on migration and remittance patterns, by generation, could yield better understanding of migrants' specific needs (if any) involving remittances to their families or their ability to invest in their countries of origin.
- Access to existing demographic data is currently not available from the National Commission for Informatics and Liberties (Commission Nationale de l'Informatique et des Libertés, or CNIL), but the release of such data could help complete the market picture for financial intermediaries that are studying their own client bases.
- The national Send Money Web site (http://www.envoidargent.fr) could be another viable informational resource for migrants, regulators, policy makers, market operators, and organizations that support money transfers from France. It should help to address relevant migrant issues by providing information on the costs charged by the leading RSPs. Migrants' preferences and each instrument's features should be highlighted as well as the services migrants could access from supporting organizations. The list of operators should include

African banks' representative offices in France (those that have an important share of the market), and semestrial notes should be provided to mention the progress toward the objective to reduce costs.

Regulation

The introduction of the payment establishment in the financial landscape, and especially in the remittances industry, is a major innovation that will encourage diversification and competition. Remittance benchmarks, including the level of costs, the range of institutional status for RSPs and the diversity of channels and instruments, could be undertaken in countries where African diasporas are important, such as France, Italy, Spain, and the United Kingdom. They should be analyzed now that the regulatory framework is harmonized to find a balance between flexibility and risk control. In addition, the following steps would advance the development of a reliable, safe, and competitive remittance industry:

- A dialogue among central banks in France and Africa should be held regularly to encourage the development of services in a secure environment for both RSPs and clients.
- The entry of new players should be explored, and adherence to regulations should be enforced.
- Certain MFIs (with strong enough solvability ratios, supervised by the banking committee of their respective central banks) should be able to make cash-to-account, international money transfers directly without partnering with local banks and MTOs as subagents. This will help to increase competition, reduce costs, and contribute to the expansion of the payment infrastructure as a result of their branch networks. Furthermore, it would leverage the potential for the biggest MFIs in countries with high international migration profiles to link remittances with savings, loans, or insurance products in a development perspective.
- The regulations governing telecom operators that are already offering mobile banking in the domestic market but want to offer cross-border money transfers should be clarified.
- The contracts of MTOs in Africa should be scrutinized to assess and ensure their conformity with all the legal requirements, notably the competitive issues. In particular, exclusivity clauses should be canceled to ensure a safe competitive market environment.
- Communication and, when relevant, coordination among central banks should be improved to assure French financial intermediaries

that their African peers respect prudential measures, AML-CFT procedures, and consumer protection standards.
- In Africa, the central banks' capacity to monitor financial intermediaries (especially the biggest MFIs) and to gather harmonized data on
remittances should be improved.

Policy

Recommendations for the French government. Increasing the level of
information among policy makers in both France and Africa is a core
issue. Working groups that include policy makers and representatives in
the private sector and diaspora should be set up with a concerted agenda.
Key players from France and Africa also should be brought together for
peer-to-peer meetings, where lessons from success stories such as
Morocco could increase policy makers' knowledge.

The enlargement and diversification of the infrastructure for remittance
collection in cash (cash being the main instrument used for remittances)
are the primary means of reducing costs in France. Implementation of the
following proposals would start to improve the remittance infrastructure:

- The exclusivity contract between La Banque Postale and Western
Union (which is not reciprocal; Western Union has other partners in
France) should be canceled so that La Banque Postale (whose capital
is mainly public) can open its remittance services to other brands.
- Overall, promotion of the PEs and multibrand MTOs also should be
encouraged to help to increase the points of payment, volume of transactions, and finally competition among global and regional MTOs—
ultimately reducing the fixed costs and commissions that clients pay.
- Incentives should be offered to migrants' associations to open bank accounts—for instance, through systematic, facilitated access to public
resources to finance collective projects and related technical support,
leveraging migrant resources.

Recommendations for banks. Policy makers should consider the following recommendations:

- From a banking perspective, migrant associations' collective transfers
could be better handled using electronic banking devices (at points of
sale or by mobile phone) and formal agent managing identification issues, thus avoiding in-cash operations at branches or the need for informal collectors as agents for the bank.

- Partnerships between banks and information technology firms providing smart card, mobile banking, or Internet-based services that would enable migrants to send money home using convenient instruments and channels going to a non-bank-agent outlet (grocery, callshop) without having to go to a bank branch with cash should be encouraged (branchless banking approach).
- Banks wanting to increase their market share with migrants could be involved in financial education campaigns for migrants to promote and explain their own products.

Recommendations for migrants and clients. Both migrants and clients would benefit from these recommendations:

- The new PE perspective is a pragmatic tool for motivating informal providers to increase their awareness of the regulatory and fiscal environment. Training modules could be conceived thanks to focus groups of informal RSPs, emphasizing regulation and technological innovations or simply the benefit of formalizing certain activities. Training would also include information about how to create or become an agent of a PE, negotiate commission sharing with banks as a representative agent, and finance individual or collective projects at home for home town associations involved in the informal money transfer business.
- Migrants in general (especially those living in hostels) could receive financial education from formal financial institutions. "Train the trainer" sessions for migrant leaders and major informal RSPs could disseminate information and make evident the advantages of using a formal channel or being a part of one.

Recommendations for global initiatives. Global organizations and other stakeholders also can make important contributions toward greater formalization of the remittance market. They are well positioned to act on the following recommendations:

- Payment infrastructure development—a fundamental challenge in African countries—is necessary to increase access and reduce marginal costs. Development agencies should support private-public partnerships to address the infrastructure challenge by implementing pilot projects in specific corridors (for instance, the France-Mali [Kayes] and France-Comoros corridors) that financial intermediaries cannot fully reach.

- Financial literacy among migrants' families should be enhanced, and access to formal financial services and technologies should be promoted.
- Innovative financing for development, including securitization of future flow receivables, diaspora bonds, and GDP-indexed bonds, should be developed and implemented (Ketkar and Ratha 2008). Addressing migrants' basic financial needs in a competitive and secure environment is a first step toward instilling confidence among the players and achieving the economies of scale that will lay the foundation for that development.

Annex 10.1

Formal Market Sample

The sample of interviewed RSPs was extracted from the initial catalog of 60 RSPs, including a large variety of institutions, such as promising RSPs. This variety is reflected in the sample of the firms interviewed, as shown in figures 10.A.1, 10.A.2 and 10.A.3. Institutions that do not offer money transfer services and those that are not currently operational did not respond to the questionnaire. However, the firms that responded covered all identified RSP types except for some of those in the "nonfinancial" category. The sample of institutions interviewed covered 86 percent of the estimated market. This was possible because most of the market is dominated by a handful of RSPs (MTOs licensed under the bank law, La Poste, and banks) with a few major stakeholders.

Overall, this sample is considered representative because it gives a complete picture of the actual remittance market, and it also gives a good idea of how the landscape could evolve with newcomers.

Figure 10.A.1   Formal Sector RSP Categories Identified in the Catalog

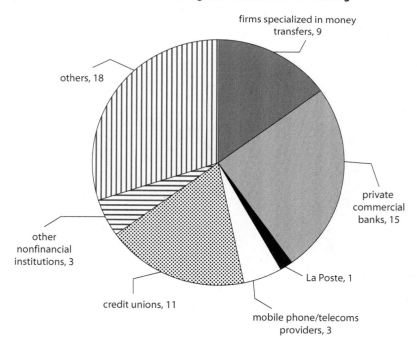

Source: Author's compilation.
Note: "other" includes e-Card issues, online payments or transfers, and online purchases.

Figure 10.A.2   Categories of Formal Sector RSPs Interviewed

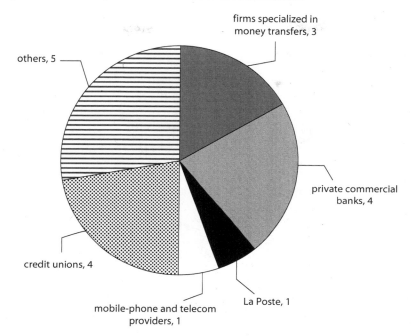

Source: Author's compilation.

Informal Market Sample

The questionnaire was adapted for informal RSPs so that, in addition to providing answers to the key questions of the regular questionnaire, the following issues could be addressed:

- Identification of the most current instruments used in specific corridors
- Identification of the population distribution for each type of instrument
- Assessment of the volume of transactions for each type of operator
- Understanding of the RSP business model
- Assessment of the ability to convert some (or even all) of the operations to the formal model and according to the new regulatory environment.

In addition to targeting the informal RSPs directly, the study contacted intermediaries, such as migrant representatives, entrepreneurs familiar with the informal market, and researchers who understand the dynamics of the informal RSPs. This effort was quite ambitious, but these objectives helped to structure the interviews.

Figure 10.A.3   Formal Sector Market Shares, by RSP Type

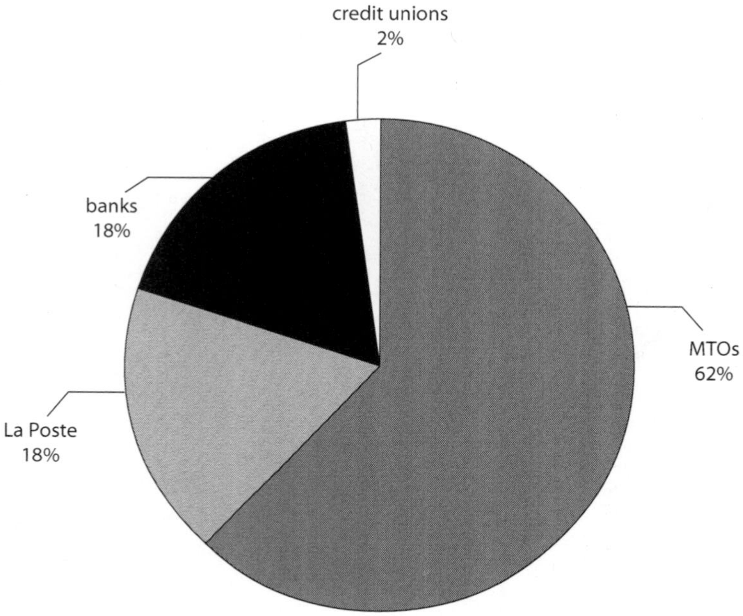

Source: Author's calculations.

Table 10.A.1   Extrapolated Data

MTOs		
Hypothesis, one branch 1 agence =	€2 million	per year
Western Union (y compris travelex)	50	
MoneyGram	47	
Ria Money Transfer	8	
Hope Finance	1	
Total agence	106	
Total flux (1)	**€212 million**	
SG (2)	**€6,142,352**	
Total (1 + 2)	**€218,142,352**	

Source: Survey data.
Note: MTO = money transfer operator. SG = Société Générale.

Acknowledgments

Frederic Ponsot led the survey team and authored the paper. Jean-Yves Rouchy, consultant on the formal RSPs, put to use his strong

Table 10.A.2   Repartition of Extrapolated Data, by Destination Country

Countries	Annual flows	Country share/total extrapolated data
Senegal	€67,676,105	31%
Mali	€35,130,583	16%
RCI	€36,593,418	17%
Comoros	€2,181,977	1%
Cameroon	€31,679,621	15%
Congo, Rep.	€8,674,565	4%
Congo, Dem. Rep.	€9,671,547	4%
Madagascar	€10,622,497	5%
Togo	€7,350,495	3%
Benin	€7,828,029	4%
Ghana	€7,33,515	0.3%

Source: Survey data.

background on the French banking and remittance sectors, based on years of experience working at the Caisse Nationale des Caisses d'Epargne. M. Benoit Hazard, PhD—consultant on the informal RSPs and a researcher at the Centre National de La Recherche Scientifique and formerly at the École des Hautes Études en Sciences Sociales—provided particularly relevant insight on the informal RSP approach, especially the methodology of the questionnaire.

Sanket Mohapatra, Sonia Plaza, and Neil Ruiz from the Development Prospects Group, Migration and Remittances team, of the World Bank provided methodological inputs, constructive discussions, and feedback based on their experiences from other countries.

The author would also like to acknowledge the cooperation of M. Bamadi Sanokho, deputy mayor of the city of Gentilly, just south of Paris, and M. Papa Amadou Sarr, research assistant at the Center for Development at the Organisation for Economic Co-operation and Development, who helped to establish contacts with informal RSPs in the Malian and Senegalese corridors.

Notes

1. Among Senegalese migrants in Italy, the reverse seems to have occurred. Since the crisis, those immigrants have reduced the amounts sent home but continue to seek credit to help finance investments in Senegal, either as alternative revenue sources or to enable them to return.

2. French gross national product was expected to decrease by 3.3 percent in 2009, compared with decreases of 4.1 percent in the European Union and 4 percent in the United States.

3. The French population renewal is quasi-insured with a fertility rate of 2.0 births per woman.

4. For the purposes of this analysis, *remittances* are broadly defined as cross-border or within-country "person-to-person" transfers of resources (including in-kind gifts). Typically they are recurrent payments of small value by migrant workers to their families and friends in their home countries.

5. Even if there is no scientific evidence regarding the behavior of first and subsequent generations of immigrants, empirical analysis tends to demonstrate that connections with family members in their home countries are less strong for second and subsequent generations. Second and subsequent generations' tendency to send money home depends largely on their individual experiences and usually occurs when they are advised to do so by their first-generation parents.

6. Applying a gross regularization rate of 72 percent of the total number of applicants.

7. For instance, although INSEE estimates show that 53,000 immigrants are from Mali, the Compagnie de Banques Internationales de Paris (CBIP) has 100,000 accounts for Malian citizens. According to the CBIP director, 80 percent of the bank's Malian clients are illegal immigrants or registered with national papers (interview, RSP review, 2009).

8. The banked population rate is less than 10 percent in the Sub-Saharan African receiving countries.

9. SG's package of financial products for migrants includes double account and €10 transfers, burial and repatriation insurance, transnational mortgages, and insurance to maintain remittances.

10. Questionnaire response from Western Union, July 27, 2009.

11. Capital is shared as follows: 49 percent for La Banque Postale and 51 percent for Western Union Financial Services Inc.

12. Notably, Travelex (14 branches) and Banque Accord (with one pilot branch in its supermarket subsidiary, Auchan). Some banks also offer Western Union in only one branch: Attijariwafabank (only for registered clients), CBIP, and Crédit Municipal de Marseille. Finally, Western Union has other partnerships with French banks' African subsidiaries.

13. Cameroon, the Republic of Congo, Equatorial Guinea, Gabon, Côte d'Ivoire, Mali, Mauritania, and Senegal.

14. These associations also have other purposes and can participate in other initiatives from the same villages or regions.

15. Other benefits, if any, can be allocated to collective initiatives such as investment in the shop.

16. By 3 percent, in the case of an informal RSP in Mauritania.

17. In Malian associations, for example, the suitcase carrier can be paid from the gains when he sells euros to wholesalers against the CFA francs in Bamako or Kayes. Indeed, banknotes of €200 and more are overvalued by wholesalers. These gains can represent 1 percent of the amount changed.

18. The riskiest operation of the informal remittances chain is the transportation of cash from the home-country airport to the final destination.

19. To get a good picture of the market, one should perform a corridor-by-corridor analysis to account for individual peculiarities and specificities regarding the following characteristics: generations or cohorts by migration waves or cycles; levels of education, financial infrastructure, and literacy in the home country; sectors of employment and nature of contracts; and geographical areas of settlement or origin.

20. These data include Western Union transfers delivered through La Banque Postale branches plus its proprietary Mandat Express service. These remittance channels represent 45 percent of the estimated formal market.

21. Western Union interview, July 24, 2009.

22. See http://www.flouss.com.

23. TransCash cards are distributed by Raphael Bank and MFTEL in France, a leading firm specializing in selling prepaid airtime in supermarkets. TransCash is an American brand that has been particularly successful on the U.S.-Mexico corridor. MFTEL plans to sell 100, 000 packs in 2010. See http://www.trans-cash.fr.

24. See http://www.woo-group.com.

25. See http://www.maatcard.com.

26. See http://www.telemedia.fr. Telemedia is quoted on the market stock exchange.

27. Tagattatitude, created in 2005, is financed by Innovacom, a capital venture vehicle of France Telecom. Tagattitude won an Innovation Award in the "Consumer Application or Services" category at the World GSM de Barcelone in February 2008. It has facilitated domestic and international transfers in more than 25 countries, including South Africa (MobiCash) and Tunisia (CasyCash, which allows withdrawals from cell phones at distributors). It is currently exploring transfers to Pakistan (from the United Kingdom and the United States); to India, through a pilot with a small bank in Delhi; to Bangladesh; and to Kazakhstan. See http://www.tagattitude.fr and http://www.tagpay.fr/.

28. Orange wants to launch such a pilot in Cameroon with SG, but the CEMAC Central Bank requires a specific license. SG also plans to launch a pilot with MTN in Côte d'Ivoire called Mobile Money.

29. See http://www.suncardfamily.com.

30. See http://www.hopefinance.org.

31. The Interbank Electronic Banking Group of the Economic and Monetary Union of West Africa is a regional platform promoted by the Central Bank of the States of West Africa (BCEAO) to support interoperability among banks in the West African Economic and Monetary Union (WAEMU) region using EMV norms at lower costs.

32. SEPA is an integrated retail payment market created in 2009 to enable consumers using the euro "to allow cashless payments throughout the euro area from a single account under the same basic conditions, regardless of location" (ECB 2009). SEPA comprises (a) 32 member states from the European Economic Area and the European Union (EU) in addition to Switzerland and Monaco and (b) several territories and jurisdictions considered to be part of the EU or that use the euro by agreement with the EU.

33. Article L. 311–3, Monetary and Financial Code.

34. The European directive (Directive 2007/64/CE) was introduced in the National Regulatory Framework with the ordonnance n°2009-866 du 15 juillet 2009 relative aux conditions régissant la fourniture de services de paiement et portant création des établissements de paiement and the arrêté du 29 octobre 2009 relatif à la réglementation prudentielle des établissements de paiement («l'arrêté»), publié au JORF N°0253 du 31/10/2009, disponibles sur le site http://www.legifrance.gouv. PEs will be supervised by the central bank and agreed to by the Credit Institutions and Investment Firms Committee (Comité des Établissements de Crédit et des Entreprises d'investissement, or CECEI) under the same prudential regulations that enforce AML-CFT procedures and other reporting requirements.

35. One interviewed RSP mentioned that it needs 450,000 transactions a year, with a fixed cost of €125,000 per branch, to break even.

36. For Caisse d'Epargne, international transfers are handled by GCE Payment, which is part of the Caisse d'Epargne Group. GCE Payment has agreed to make some retreatments by country for the study on the major corridors covered.

37. Western Union's transfer prices are higher in Poste Finance branches. Western Union has also the lowest offer (48-hour delay if the transaction is done over the Internet). Interestingly, commissions are lowest in the Moroccan and Senegalese corridors (December 2009), where competition is higher.

38. At Attijariwafa Bank in Morocco, loading the card costs €2.00, withdrawals cost €0.60, and annual fees are €4.00. Float is a significant source of revenue (interview with Attijariwafa Bank, June 30, 2009).

39. The average transfer amount for the only MTO that volunteered this information is €280. It is €180 for reloading operations with Flouss.com. The

AfDB study and other studies mention an average transfer of around €150 per transaction (among all instruments).

40. This channel is preferred for savings and for collective transfers, notably wholesalers' payments for food purchases (interviews with CBIP and its partners).

41. For informal RSPs covering the Mauritanian corridor, exchange fees are around 3 percent.

42. Cases of fraud have been associated with false driver's licenses in Côte d'Ivoire.

43. The COMOFI (Code Monétaire et Financier) does not require an official paper delivered by an administrative official (but an official paper with a picture from the French administration or another official administration). Because many illegal migrants use papers of others or false papers, banks do not consider foreign papers as reliable enough to identify the client.

44. The person must be introduced by a client well-known to the informal RSP, and the funds must not exceed the imposed limit.

References

AfDB (African Development Bank). 2007. "Annual Report." AfDB, Tunis.

ECB (European Central Bank). 2009. "The Single Euro Payments Area (SEPA): An Integrated Retail Payment Market." Brochure, ECB, Main, Germany. http://www.ecb.int/pub/pdf/other/sepa_brochure_2009en.pdf.

Freund, Caroline, and Nikola Spatafora. 2008. "Remittances, Transaction Costs, and Informality." *Journal of Development Economics* 86: 356–66.

GCE (Caisse d'Epargne Group). 2008. "Annual Report," GCE, Paris.

IMF (International Monetary Fund). 2008. *Balance of Payments Statistics Yearbook*. Washington, DC: IMF.

INSEE (French National Institute for Statistics and Economic Studies). 2005. "Census and Annual Survey." INSEE, Paris.

Ketkar, Suhas, and Dilip K. Ratha, eds. 2008. *Innovative Financing for Development*. Washington, DC: World Bank.

La Banque Postale. 2008. "Annual Report." La Banque Postale, Paris.

Milhaud, Charles. 2006. *L'intégration économique des migrants et la valorisation de leur épargne*.

Official Gazette No. 162 of 2009, Text 12, "Report to the President of the Republic on Ordinance No. 2009–866 on the Conditions Governing the Provision of Payment Services."

Ponsot, Frederic. 2007. *Le rôle des institutions de microfinance dans l'offre de produits financiers spécifiques aux migrants dans leurs pays d'origine.* PRIME, Epargne sans frontière.

Ratha, Dilip. 2003. "Workers' Remittances: An Important and Stable Source of External Development Finance." In *Global Development Finance.* Washington, DC: World Bank.

Rouchy, Jean-Yves, and Jean-Yves Gourvez. 2006. "Étude sur la valorisation de l'épargne des migrants maliens en France."

World Bank. 2011. *Migration and Remittances Factbook 2011.* Washington, DC: World Bank.

CHAPTER 11

United Kingdom

Leon Isaacs

This chapter provides an overview of the U.K. market for sending remittances to Sub-Saharan Africa—part of a wider study of migration and remittances by the African Development Bank and the World Bank. The findings here are based on a survey of U.K. remittance service providers (RSPs) that serve the Sub-Saharan African market conducted in mid-2008.[1] The chapter provides insight into the marketplace from an operator's viewpoint and outlines remittance market characteristics such as competitive factors, barriers to entry, regulatory constraints, and pricing approaches. Although other market surveys from the consumer viewpoint and studies of pricing to specific markets such as Nigeria have been conducted earlier (DMA 2007), this is the first systematic survey of providers in the U.K. market that transmit remittances to a wide range of countries in Africa.

Migration and Remittance Trends

The primary driver of remittances is migration. The United Kingdom has been a major destination for migrants for centuries, and traditionally most migrants to the United Kingdom have originated from countries that were part of the British Empire and are now mostly part of the Commonwealth of Nations. However, this trend has changed in recent years.

Sources of Migrants

The current stock of migrants in the United Kingdom is 7 million people, whose main countries of birth (from largest to smallest number of immigrants) are India, Poland, Pakistan, Ireland, Germany, South Africa, Bangladesh, the United States, Jamaica, and Kenya (World Bank 2011).

In recent years, the composition of immigrants in the United Kingdom has shifted toward Eastern and Central Europe. Since the last census in 2001, the European Union (EU) was enlarged to include countries from Central and Eastern Europe. The United Kingdom was among the few EU countries that did not place barriers to stop migrants from the enlarged Europe from entering and working. As a result, an estimated 1 million or more people from Poland alone moved to the United Kingdom in the past four years, accompanied by large influxes from the Czech Republic, Estonia, Lithuania, and the Slovak Republic. In 2007, the EU was further enlarged with the accession of Bulgaria and Romania. This time, however, the U.K. government made it more difficult for people to move to the United Kingdom, resulting in fewer new arrivals than from the previous accession countries. The growth from Central and Eastern Europe has been accompanied, coincidentally, by a reduction in the number of asylum seekers—in particular, from Africa. As the U.K. migrant profile changes, so also do the remittance destinations.

Initial anecdotal evidence shows that, as a result of the 2008–09 financial crisis, many migrants returned to Eastern Europe, while people from Africa have tended to remain in the United Kingdom. Box 11.1 tells the story of one formal remittance service provider (RSP) that serves several major African remittance corridors in the wake of the economic downturn.

The 2001 census identified 850,000 migrants from Africa living in the United Kingdom. Anecdotal evidence suggests that immigration from most of Sub-Saharan Africa has grown since then. The largest communities currently are from Ghana, Kenya, Nigeria, Somalia, South Africa, Uganda, and Zimbabwe. Significant migrant communities also have come from the Democratic Republic of Congo, Sierra Leone, and Tanzania. Data have not been gathered about how much money these groups remit from the United Kingdom to their home countries, but discussions with these African communities confirm that the immigrants consider the sending of remittances to be an important feature of their life in the United Kingdom.

Although the number of officially recorded new migration from Africa has declined in recent years, there is significant evidence of continued growth from African countries, such as from Somalia and Zimbabwe. In

Box 11.1[2]

Case Study: A Formal Remittance Service Provider Coping with Global Financial Crisis

Mr. A (name not provided to protect privacy) is a director of a West African RSP based in Tottenham, North East London, within the never-ending hive of activity in the heart of one of the capital's most multiethnic areas. It has a large, long-established Afro-Caribbean population; a recent influx from Eastern Europe; and growing diasporas from African countries such as Ghana, Kenya, Nigeria, Sierra Leone, and Somalia.

During an interview in mid-2008, Mr. A says more than once that he is having a really bad business year. Like many other small companies, his is struggling through the global economic downturn that had hit the United Kingdom hard in the preceding months. His revenues over the past financial year are a fraction of what they were the year before, and he recently had to lay off two staff members. With concern and resignation in his voice, he can't help but wonder how his company will survive in such a competitive market if the negative trend continues. The company is a fully registered RSP and a member of the UKMTA (U.K. Money Transmitters Association). It charges a 5 percent commission on any transfer under £1,000, and transmits remittances mainly to Ghana, Nigeria, and Sierra Leone.

Source: Author interview for 2008 U.K. RSP survey.

addition, many informal migrants travel from Sub-Saharan Africa to the United Kingdom through North Africa and Europe. The migrant communities from Ethiopia and from French- and Portuguese-speaking Africa are extremely small and therefore did not feature in the survey results.

Remittance Volume and Destinations

The survey also attempted to quantify (to the extent possible) the volume of transactions sent over the previous three years on both a consolidated basis and a receiving-country basis for the top 10 remittance corridors in Africa. Unfortunately, the analysis was limited because the sample was too small to provide representative information, as the discussion of methodology in the next section explains. Only three U.K. companies provided consolidated data about their volumes; another six provided some information by corridor. In all, therefore, nine companies provided corridor-specific volume information, amounting to approximately 1.1 million transactions over the previous year.

Among the survey respondents, the largest corridors for transactions from the United Kingdom to Africa (in order of largest to smallest volumes) were Nigeria, Ghana, Somalia, and South Africa (figure 11.1). Although remittance market observers had expected those countries to be among the major corridors, they had also expected to see data for Kenya and Zimbabwe, but the respondents did not provide such information.

For purposes of comparison and scale, U.K. Remittances Task Force estimated that about 25 million remittance transactions flow from the United Kingdom each year to all destinations worldwide, amounting to an estimated £4.1 billion in outbound payments.[3]

The money goes primarily to recipients in the following developing regions or countries: South Asia, Eastern Europe, Africa, the Caribbean, and China.[4] The total remittance estimates cannot be precise because there is currently no formal requirement for institutions to submit, or for the government to collect, the relevant data, as the next section further explains. Even projects that have tried to estimate the size of the total market and of specific corridors have produced largely inconsistent results.

Characteristics of the Remittance Industry

This section looks at the fundamental characteristics of the U.K. remittances market, including descriptions of the RSP types, their business models, and some case studies.

Figure 11.1   Average Fees and Foreign Exchange Charges for Remittances to Africa

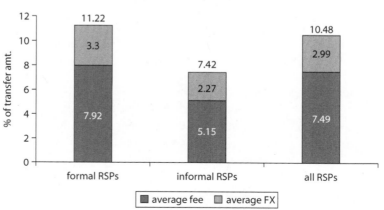

Source: Author's compilation from 2008 U.K. RSP survey.
Note: The remittance sender usually pays all charges. Prices did not change dramatically in the 12 months following the mid-2008 U.K. RSP survey. FX = foreign exchange. RSP = remittance service provider.

Methodology

For the RSP survey, *remittances* were defined broadly as cross-border, "person-to-person" transfers of resources (including in-kind gifts)—typically small, recurrent payments by migrant workers to families and friends in their home countries. An *informal RSP* was defined as a provider unregistered with either the Financial Services Authority (FSA) or Her Majesty's Revenue and Customs (HMRC), the two U.K. bodies that regulate RSP firms.

The primary data were gathered in June and July 2008, and this chapter broadly reflects that data set. However, significant changes that have occurred since the survey have been noted to the extent that they affect the recommendations (for instance, regarding new regulations or price changes).

Although the survey was broadly qualitative, the chapter includes general attempts to provide a quantitative assessment based on the research data. These quantifications should be treated as indicative and not statistically significant.

Objectives. The survey aimed to meet the following objectives:

- Develop a catalog of companies that send money to Sub-Saharan Africa.
- Obtain in-depth, high-quality feedback from a broad range of providers, including both formal and informal money transfer operators (MTOs).
- Develop a coherent market view of the regulatory, competitive, and operational environment within the U.K. market.
- Provide recommendations to help policy makers improve the U.K. remittance market by reducing the costs of remittances to Africa and channeling more of these flows through formal rather than informal channels.

Methodological issues. An unfortunate by-product of an open market, in which RSPs are not required to report remittance transactions, is that it is challenging to obtain data from individual firms. In the United Kingdom, all limited companies must submit accounts annually for public scrutiny. However, these accounts provide no detail about the volume or value of remittance transactions, which are often consolidated with other products. Therefore the reports' value is quite limited. Additionally, many of the formal businesses did not want to release information, even when it was available, because they considered it to be commercially sensitive and saw limited value in providing it.

Types and Coverage of Remittance Firms

Geographically, more than half of the U.K. remittance market[5] is based in London, where some two-thirds of the African immigrants in the United Kingdom live. The other main source cities of African remittances are Birmingham, Liverpool, and Leeds.

A "light touch"[6] regulatory regime makes it is relatively easy for a business to legally provide money transfer services, so a broad range of business types send money to Africa:

- *Money transfer operators.* MTOs such as Western Union and Money-Gram provide remittance services through their own locations, networks of agents, and other methods, including Internet-based remittances.
- *Banks.* Banks can offer a broad range of financial services but provide money transfer services only to their account holders.
- *Nonbank financial institutions.* At these outlets, such as currency exchanges, a consumer can transfer money either through its own money transfer service or as an agent for an RSP.[7]
- *Informal operators.* Individuals or businesses such as transportation companies are not regulated or registered with the authorities but provide a variety of remittance services.

MTOs dominate the market for remittances, which, more often than not, constitute their main business. For example, Western Union is likely to be the single most dominant player for remittances from the United Kingdom to Sub-Saharan Africa based on the prominence of the brand and previous private sector research that showed high awareness for that company (DFID 2005).

Some companies, particularly in the informal sector, offer money transfer services on their business premises, which are often small retail establishments, convenience stores, Internet cafés, or freight forwarding companies (as described in box 11.2). The informal operators do not advertise their services through traditional media but instead rely on word-of-mouth referrals in their communities.

Just over half of the U.K. RSPs both send money and receive money. A much smaller number handle domestic remittances. Foreign exchange and settlement are handled predominantly by the banks. Few MTOs offer such services, suggesting that RSP roles are relatively clearly defined for transactions to Africa from the United Kingdom.

Box 11.2

Case Study: A Shipping Company as Informal RSP

Mr. B (name changed to protect privacy) is the owner of an international shipping company that sends goods to most parts of East and Central Africa. The company also transfers money for individuals.

The business is housed in a typical East London warehouse. Mr. B is relatively open about his remittance operation. Since he could transfer money as efficiently as he transfers goods, he began to send money to East Africa through the same contacts who handle his shipping business. He keeps a record of everything and operates similarly to formal RSPs. He says he has a flexible relationship with his East African partners. Although they usually make pretty straightforward settlements, sometimes he does pay third parties on their behalf.

To avoid red tape and bureaucracy, he does not formally offer remittance services, adding that he wants to focus on his shipping business and provide money transfers only as a favor to his community. Trusted by his community and a savvy businessman, Mr. B has an innate mistrust of bureaucracy and regulators—particularly those in East Africa.

Source: Author interview for 2008 U.K. RSP survey.

Most RSP firms offer their own branded services to consumers and have partnership arrangements in the recipient countries to ensure payout. Few U.K. remittance businesses have branches in Africa because the regulatory environment in most of Africa requires nonbank RSPs to operate in partnership with banks. About one-third of the surveyed companies also send money to regions outside of Africa, which implies that two-thirds specialize in remittances to Africa. U.K. migrant communities from the Democratic Republic of Congo and Somalia tend to have predominantly single-country operators, although there is a preponderance of regional operators that send to East Africa (Kenya, Tanzania, and Uganda) or West Africa (Ghana and Nigeria).

The surveyed RSP companies cover nearly 25,000 locations in their combined networks. Some could not provide data differentiating between urban and rural locations, but the split seems to be three to one in favor of urban areas. Even so, this ratio seems to overstate the rural coverage in the United Kingdom, possibly because the survey included the U.K. Post Office, which has a nationwide network and a large number of rural locations. Moreover, some operators were vague about how they determined their urban-to-rural ratio. Banks and other formal RSPs tend to have large, nationwide networks (such as the RSP described in box 11.3), whereas the informal providers tend to operate from one or two locations in urban areas.

Partnerships and Agreements with Money Transfer Operators

Most RSP firms, whether formal or informal, have formed partnerships to deliver reliable remittance services, increase their distribution networks, and ensure that they earn commissions.

Although banks are among the likeliest partners in these arrangements, the survey showed that the banks are often unaware that other RSPs,

---

Box 11.3

Case Study: An Arab RSP with a Large Branch Network in the United Kingdom

Company C (name changed to protect privacy), an Arab RSP that originated in Dubai, has a strong presence in the United Kingdom, with a nationwide network of more than 60 branches. Its remittance markets are the Middle East and the northern, largely Arab, portion of East Africa. The branch visited for the interview is situated on one of London's longest and busiest streets, the Seven Sisters Road, which stretches across the north of the city and takes in areas as diverse as Turkish Green Lanes and Jewish Stamford Hill. The shop, which also acts as an Internet café, is part of a small Muslim enclave on the Seven Sisters, next door to an Islamic bookshop and opposite a mosque.

Mr. C (name changed to protect privacy), the owner, is polite but in a hurry. During the interview, he is constantly interrupted by acquaintances, customers, or other staff members, whom he berates in heated Arabic. It is a wet Monday night, but the shop is busy—with a healthy stream of comings and goings. The Internet café, in particular, appears to be doing good business.

Company C is a fully registered RSP and a well-known brand in the marketplace. It offers a 6 percent commission on all transfers under £1,000 as well as the margin on the exchange rate. Company C's policy is to send only U.S. dollars, so if a customer has pounds sterling, the money is converted by the company or its bank.

Source: Author interview for 2008 U.K. RSP survey.

especially informal operators, view them as partners because their U.K. provider partners use either their own or a sender's relative's account in Africa as the payout vehicle.

Most companies would not divulge their partnerships, although a small minority (10 percent) mentioned working with MoneyGram. Interestingly, given the significant global opposition to exclusivity clauses in contracts as being anticompetitive, only 10 percent of the RSP firms said they are locked into an exclusive arrangement. Some respondents told researchers that even if their agreements did include an exclusivity clause, they (as sending businesses) were not observing it.

These RSP partnerships enable about half of the surveyed firms to send money to 10 or more countries. An increasing trend in the United Kingdom is for companies to offer their own services to their preferred countries and to partner with another RSP to serve a broader range of countries.

The RSP survey respondents split evenly between those who said their firms needed a partnership with an intermediary to handle foreign exchange deals and those who did not. The split reflects variations between the formal and informal RSP operating models. Nearly all of the nonbank formal companies said they needed to work with a bank to operate in the United Kingdom (although they did not need to operate *from* bank branches). However, nearly all of the informal operators said they did not need such an intermediary (box 11.4).

Of the RSPs needing an intermediary, most needed to work with a bank to buy their foreign exchange for settlement purposes. In other cases—particularly for those sending to Kenya and some smaller operators sending to Ghana and Nigeria—settlement took place by crediting a U.K. bank account in pounds sterling, a process requiring less need for an intermediary bank relationship.

Interestingly, though, many of the informal players allow people to deposit funds into their personal bank accounts to pay for a transaction. Nearly all of the organizations recognize that there is no regulatory limit on the amount of foreign exchange holdings or remittance inflows. A few of the respondents who had operations in receiving markets in some parts of Africa did cite this as a problem in those markets.

Regardless of the form of partnership, the banks and other formal RSPs all tend to follow the same settlement model, in which the bank account of the paying-out institution is credited. Importantly, it is rare for settlement of transactions to Africa to take place in the pay-out currency of the country. For example, although someone in Nigeria may receive a

Box 11.4

Case Study: A Competitive Small Formal RSP

Company D (name changed to protect privacy) is a registered money service business in Finsbury Park, north London—a bustling, ethnically diverse area where one is never far from an MTO. There are numerous agents for Western Union, MoneyGram, and Ria Envia as well as smaller, independent operators such as Company D that survive by knowing their market (and their customers) and by providing competitive rates. The company's premises comprise two small offices above a fast-food shop (also an independent retailer). Its Nigerian owner, Mr. D (name changed to protect privacy), is a forthright but soft-spoken man whose telephone never stops ringing while he works under a mountain of paperwork.

The walls of Mr. D's office are adorned with religious iconography, advertisements for his travel company, and posters for Chequepoint and Ria Envia, for which he acts as an agent for certain remittance corridors. Company D's primary market is the U.K.-to-Nigeria corridor, where it costs £5 plus the exchange-rate margin (about 2 percent) to send £100 to a Nigerian bank account. Although the office's atmosphere is informal, even chaotic, its remittance service is efficient.

Source: Author interview for 2008 U.K. RSP survey.

remittance in Nigerian naira, the RSP's business partner would have received the payment in U.S. dollars or pounds sterling. Settlement almost always occurs in deposits of either pounds sterling or U.S. dollars to an offshore account. Thus, for many African businesses, the attraction of paying out remittances is that they receive hard currency that they can sell to their own clients at a significant profit.

The timing of settlement varies between the same day and seven days—and is usually between one and two days. Some informal operators use the same settlement method as the formal sector. However, others use a "netting" method whereby the money that would have gone to the paying-out entity in the receiving country is instead paid to a third party to settle an outstanding invoice. For example, a Ghanian shoe importer who also serves as a money transfer agent may ask the RSP in the sending country to send the funds to an Italian exporter to pay for a previous shoe shipment.

One or two informal RSPs in the U.K. survey said they paid when their counterparty asked them to do so but that settlement was spasmodic.

One said that it even paid in advance to help the paying-out agent with cash flow.

Remittance Instruments

Remittances are currently sent in a variety of forms: cash to cash, account to account, cash to card, card to card, cash to mobile phone, mobile phone to mobile phone, cash sent through the post, and cash carried by a friend or relative.

As with the market size estimation, no official data are available about the amounts of money sent through each method. Indeed, at least two of the methods would be termed informal and thus are particularly challenging to measure. However, market experience and feedback from the surveyed RSPs leads to the conclusion that most remittances are sent cash to cash. Cash sent through friends and other informal methods make up most of the remainder. The cash-to-account method would be the fourth most-used means of transfer, although it accounts only for an estimated 5 percent or less of the total.

The landscape is changing, however. Interest in remittances has increased as awareness has grown about the global size of the market—estimated at $325 billion sent to developing countries in 2010 (World Bank 2011). This growth, combined with the increased use of new technologies in the financial services arena, means that new approaches to remittance transmissions are being applied.

Not all providers offer a broad range of remittance products to the consumer. Unsurprisingly, the banks offer the widest range of transfer products, including account to account, prepaid debit cards, and bank drafts. The rest of the providers that send remittances to Africa focus on electronic cash transfers, with cash both paid and received in the beneficiary's country.

A reasonable number of nonbank financial institutions offer credit-to-account transfers, although the informal operators generally stick to cash-to-cash payments. Africa has a low bank-account penetration, so most transactions are collected in cash (except for those sent to South Africa, where bank-account penetration is significantly higher). Most banks offer money transfer services only to their own account holders, making it difficult for consumers to shop around for the best deal when looking to credit a bank account.

Some RSPs now offer services through the Internet whereby customers either pay by card or deposit the money directly in the RSP's bank account. Companies such as uTransfer, Global Link, Double

Crown, and Western Union all offer online services. The model is effective and becoming increasingly attractive to consumers, although the receiving markets still use traditional payout methods. Interestingly, except for the banks, few of these Internet providers offer any other financial services.

Around one-third of the survey respondents said their firms allow remittance transmissions for specific purposes, mostly for land and housing payments. One interesting phenomenon was seen in the Zimbabwe corridor. Given the massive political and economic problems present in that market, many firms stopped sending money. With inflation running at over 10 million percent, the value of funds often decreased dramatically between the time of sending and the time of collection. As a result, companies such as Mukuru and Premier 786 arranged for people to collect food, fuel, and phone minutes as alternatives to cash. These organizations sourced the goods through contacts in South Africa and Zimbabwe and made them available to beneficiaries. The senders' costs were relatively low, and the beneficiaries received tangible goods that were worth more than the cash they otherwise would have received. Costs for cash collections were relatively high, with foreign exchange margins of around 10 percent. Since the U.S. dollar and South African rand were declared as legal tender in Zimbabwe in mid-2009, it is likely that the share of cash transactions has increased, and the share sent as goods has become smaller. The extraordinarily high foreign exchange margins charged for conversion to local currency are also have likely to have declined or disappeared altogether.

The use of new technologies for domestic payments has grown within some African countries, most notably in Kenya and South Africa. Surveys also have found that new technology can financially enfranchise migrants in the United Kingdom (DMA 2008). As consumer attitudes change and willingness to adopt new technologies increases, opportunities have arisen to introduce new technological solutions in the U.K.-to-Africa corridors in markets where the appropriate conditions exist. Given that automated teller machine (ATM) and electronic point-of-sale systems are limited in large parts of Africa, mobile-phone-based solutions will be more likely to succeed. Currently, only one active scheme is in place for international payments from the United Kingdom to Africa: a pilot involving M-PESA[8] in Kenya and some remittance-sending operators in selected parts of the United Kingdom. Any development in this area would require an RSP firm to meet the appropriate regulatory approval, as the next section further describes.

The Regulatory and Business Environment

The United Kingdom is commonly considered the easiest European country in which to establish a remittance business because the U.K. regulatory environment for money transfer providers is based on Her Majesty's Treasury's "light-touch" approach. At the time of the survey, two different regulators oversaw the market, depending on the type of business offering money transfer services.

Until 1997, remittance companies—whether individual, location-based operations or global RSPs—had to register with HMRC to become a money service business (MSB). Thus, HMRC had been the main financial authority for remittance providers (primarily MTOs). Since 1997, however, banks have been regulated by the FSA under a more onerous and a much-regimented process.

After the survey was conducted, the EU Payments Services Directive (PSD) came into force, as box 11.5 describes further. The PSD will affect regulation moving forward. The following sections summarize the RSPs' responses regarding regulatory, customer identification, and other reporting requirements as well as the RSP business environment and remittance fee structures. These responses were obtained before the introduction of the PSD—before many PSD-related details were known or understood.

Registration and Licensing Requirements

U.K. regulatory bodies do not set many significant restrictions on remittance providers. Even so, the RSPs' understanding of remittance market regulations in general was not good. Although surveyed providers generally knew that some regulatory requirements existed, their knowledge about specifics showed room for improvement.

Most, but not all, of the surveyed companies knew that some form of registration was required to operate a remittance business. Most of the companies that did *not* know of a registration requirement were from the formal sector, perhaps because they misunderstood the terms "central bank" or "financial authority" as the questionnaire defined them. Those respondents that did know about the registration requirement also knew the appropriate regulatory body. The vast majority of respondents are registered with HMRC, as expected.

The RSP firms also generally lacked understanding about whether they were required to file currency reports with the regulators. In fact, there is no such requirement. Most of the confusion occurred in the

Box 11.5

The EU Payment Services Directive

Since November 1, 2009, RSPs in the United Kingdom have been regulated and approved by the FSA. Under the new EU Payments Services Directive, however, a new category of institutions has been created, called payment institutions (PIs). Among the PIs are two subcategories: authorized PIs and small PIs (also known as registered PIs). The requirements to become an authorized PI are relatively onerous, whereas is the process to become a small PI is relatively straightforward.

All organizations that transact more than €3 million per month must apply for authorization. Those that transfer less have the option to apply for either full authorization or small PI status. The transition period for businesses operating before December 25, 2007, will end on April 30, 2011. An authorized PI can "passport" its license to other European Economic Area (EEA) countries without obtaining separate local licenses in those host countries.

The PSD brings much-needed transparency to the market, albeit only for transactions from one EU country to another. In addition, remittance transactions will come under the U.K. Financial Ombudsman Service for the first time, meaning that a consumer who cannot gain redress for a complaint from the service provider can ask the financial ombudsman to investigate the case. If the case is investigated, the ombudsman's decision is binding. The PSD also gives consumers an incentive to use authorized PIs, which will safeguard the clients' money until the receivers collect it. However, a small PI safeguards funds only if it opts to do so—and it is generally assumed that most will not.

Since November 1, 2010—when the PSD came into force—more than 60 authorized PIs and more than 500 registered PIs (small PIs) have been approved and placed on the register. The introduction has not been without its challenges, and there is a large backlog of applications, although the number of applications is considerably less than the size of the market. The delay is driven by the transition-period provision, which states that all organizations must be either registered or authorized by April 2011, after which they will be operating illegally if they have not been approved. A large increase in applications to the FSA is expected by the end of 2010.

Throughout Europe, most countries have introduced their PSD regulations and have taken a reasonably consistent approach. Only the United Kingdom has introduced the two-tier registration status—of "authorized" and "registered" PIs. All

(continued)

Box 11.5 *(continued)*

other countries have only an authorized status, making it harder for many businesses to gain approval in those countries.

Operators in many countries are using the passporting element of service (whereby an authorized PI can use the same authorization in any EEA member country). Initial feedback is that this is operating as intended in the legislation, but there are concerns that the full implications are not yet understood by the regulatory authorities in every country.

Source: Author.

informal sector. Nearly all the African providers knew they needed to file suspicious transaction reports, but most were hazy about the amount threshold. In fact, there is none; if a cashier is suspicious about a transaction of any amount, a Suspicious Activity Report must be completed.

Most of the surveyed providers knew that there are currently no financial regulatory requirements for operating money transfer businesses, although there are stringent requirements for banks. Even with the introduction of the PSD, companies are still required to register with HMRC for anti-money-laundering (AML) compliance. MSBs must pay a £120 licensing fee (per outlet that operates the service, whether owned by the MSB or operating as an agent). Many of the formal operators knew this (and formal operators across a range of corridors as diverse as Kenya, Nigeria, Somalia, and South Africa all note their MSB licenses on their websites), but most of the informal operators were unaware of both the requirement and the cost. They knew there were some regulatory restrictions but had made no effort to find out what they were. By contrast, nearly every company knew there is no requirement to charge a value added tax on remittances because they are zero-rated products.

The regulatory landscape for new technologies may present some new challenges as well. No additional barriers arise for RSPs that offer money transfers by mobile phone if no value is stored on a device. However, when value is stored, an electronic money license (EML) is required. Obtaining a full license is a complicated process and requires initial capital of €1 million, although this figure will be lowered to €350,000 in 2011. The capital requirement clearly limits the number of businesses that apply for an EML.

Barriers to Entry

Most of the RSP firms (especially banks and informal companies) felt that, in general, the existing regulatory environment was not a barrier to entry. However, more than one-third of the nonbank formal operators, particularly those sending to West African countries such as Nigeria and Sierra Leone, did consider the regulatory environment to be a major barrier. Much of their concern regarded interpretation of the AML regulations rather than the registration aspects.

AML compliance. In fact, all of the formal operators considered AML compliance to be the biggest regulatory barrier to remittance operations, particularly because of the number of new regulations and requirements in this area. (Understandably, the informal operators did not consider it to be a major barrier at all.) Compliance with the U.S. Office of Foreign Assets Control lists, EU lists, the (U.S.) Patriot Act, the AML Directive, and so on consumes extensive resources, causing many RSPs to view the many requirements as major barriers and as disproportionate to the perceived risks of the typical transaction.

Based on general feedback, established businesses view some form of AML regulation as necessary but believe the industry is being made a scapegoat. Because most remittance transactions are of low value, they said, the procedures unduly restrict profitability. Furthermore, as a wide variety of bodies introduce more and more restrictions, it becomes extremely challenging to keep up with all the changes. This concern was mentioned by all companies but particularly by those that send to Ghana, Kenya, and South Africa.

Cross-border registration. All surveyed RSP firms except banks also were concerned about registration in other markets, such as France and Germany, rather than being connected specifically to the United Kingdom. Most companies felt that access to distribution networks (particularly in payout countries) and financial systems (for example, the U.K. clearing system) were big barriers to entry. This seemed to be applicable to all operators who send to a single corridor. Some single-corridor players were also concerned that they could not expand their networks easily in their recipient markets. Providers to Kenya, Nigeria, South Africa, and Uganda mentioned this particularly. No organization mentioned contractual exclusivity clauses as a barrier, however.

Capital and finance access. Access to capital and finance was a reasonably strong concern for the informal companies but not considered an issue by the formal RSPs. Note that this survey was completed before the credit crunch began to affect businesses. However, most well-run RSPs generate a positive cash flow.

Most MSBs have come under intense scrutiny from their banks and cite lack of access to the banking system as a major challenge. Furthermore, when they have explored the possibility of opening accounts at other banks, they found that most do not want to open accounts for MSBs because they are concerned about possible AML violations. This issue was an emotive one for many MSBs, particularly those serving communities from conflict-ridden countries such as Somalia and Zimbabwe.[9] Some of the formal operators said the lack of access to clearing and settlement systems was a major concern, particularly in the paying-out countries, and that this obstacle had stopped their expansion, as highlighted by companies that sent money to South Africa in particular.

Competitive Factors

Most of the firms surveyed did not view informal RSPs as major competitors, although some providers to Cameroon, South Africa, and Zimbabwe did perceive a competitive threat. Most notably, the informal operators themselves did not see other informal RSPs as competitive obstacles because they felt securely positioned within their own community niches and believed it would be hard for other operators to take their markets away from them.

The MTOs interviewed were asked to rate, by provider type, which RSPs they regarded as their primary competitors. Not surprisingly, the main ones listed were Western Union, MoneyGram, Chequepoint,[10] and some corridor-specific players such as Dahabshiil and Kaah Express to Somalia. Some of the banks (particularly those from the migrants' country of origin) and informal providers rounded out the list of competitors. Although the United Kingdom has around 400 credit unions, they generally have small memberships and many do not offer remittances. Therefore, the MTOs did not consider them to be a major competitive threat.

Remittance Fees, Customer Protection, and Identification Requirements

This section discusses the fees and foreign exchange margins applied to remittances to Africa and compares those costs to those cited in previous studies. It also discusses the ways that RSPs address customer grievances and the customer identification requirements for compliance with AML and other regulations.

Remittance service fees. Because only five RSP companies provided financial data for the survey, few conclusions can be drawn as to the size of individual firms' revenues or the remittance volumes they processed. Among the responding firms, however, remittance-related income followed a broadly consistent pattern: Firms sending to Africa earn 65–80 percent of their revenues from fees and 20–35 percent from foreign exchange earnings. Almost without exception, providers neither earn interest nor receive other revenues from remittances.

The current pricing model among RSPs is based on the sender paying all of the fees for a remittance transaction. The only real exceptions are among banks, where it is still typical for the sender and receiver to share the fees for account-to-account transactions.

The U.K. RSP questionnaire asked each provider for the amount it charges to send the equivalent of US$200 to Africa.[11] Each responding company provided the fee levied and the foreign exchange margin charged for each transaction. The organizations were not asked for any other costs because the sender usually pays all costs, so any hidden costs should be quite limited. The survey results are shown in table 11.1 and figure 11.1.

Before these results are discussed in detail, it is useful to compare them with data gathered in April and May 2008 for the Global Remittances Price Benchmarking project.[12] The methodology differed slightly from that used in the 2008 U.K. RSP survey, in that the transaction value was £105 in benchmarking project. In addition, that survey was limited to the top 10 providers for each corridor. For the United Kingdom, 11 corridors were surveyed, of which five were for Africa. Table 11.2 compares these two data collection exercises.

A more detailed comparison of prices can be found in figures 11.2, 11.3, and 11.4, which show the pricing for transactions to 10 different

Table 11.1   Average Fee and Foreign Exchange Charges
percentage of transfer amounts

Survey	Average fee (%)	Average foreign exchange margin (%)	Total (%)
U.K. RSP survey	7.49	2.99	10.48
Global database (Africa only)	6.58	3.11	9.69
Global database (all corridors)	7.09	3.08	10.17

Source: Author's calculations from 2008 U.K. RSP survey and World Bank Remittance Prices database (http://remittanceprices.worldbank.org).

Table 11.2   Fee Comparison for Remittances to Africa, 2008 vs. 2007
percentage of transfer amounts

RSP sector type and year	Average fee (%)	Average foreign exchange margin (%)	Total (%)
Formal, 2008	5.17	3.69	8.86
Formal, 2007	5.50	3.80	9.30
Informal, 2008	4.14	2.30	6.46
Informal, 2007	4.04	3.18	6.22
Total 2008	**4.87**	**3.10**	**7.97**
Total 2007	**4.80**	**3.45**	**8.25**

Source: Author's calculations from 2008 U.K. RSP survey and World Bank Remittance Prices database (http://remittanceprices.worldbank.org).
Note: The data are not consistent with those in table 11.1 because the average costs in table 11.2 were based purely on a figure provided by the companies being surveyed rather than through an independent exercise.

Figure 11.2   Prices to Send £100, by African Corridor

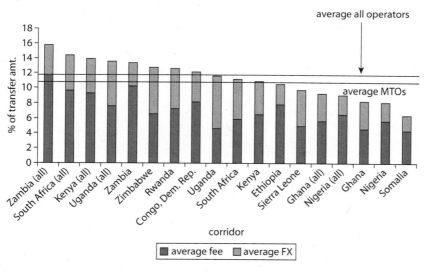

Source: http://www.moneymove.org, accessed September 15, 2008.
Note: Bars labeled "(all)" following a country name designate total average fees for MTOs and banks in that country. Bars labeled with only the country name designate the average total fees charged by MTOs only in that country. MTO = money transfer operator. FX = foreign exchange.

Sub-Saharan markets, obtained from an independent price comparison site (http://www.moneymove.org) on the basis of data obtained by mystery shopping.[13] For some markets, where banks also currently send money, their costs have been identified and included separately because their charges can skew the results.

Figure 11.3   Prices to Send £250, by African Corridor

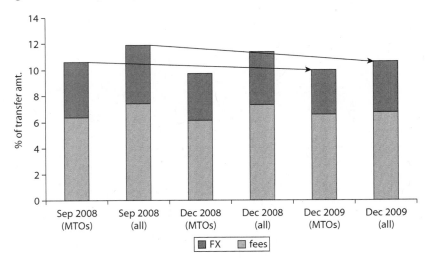

Source: http://www.moneymove.org, accessed September 15, 2008.
Note: Bars labeled "(all)" following a country name designate total average fees for MTOs and banks in that country. Bars labeled with only the country name designate the average total fees charged by MTOs only in that country. MTO = money transfer operator. FX.= foreign exchange.

Figure 11.4   Comparison Remittance Fees to Africa over Three Waves of Data

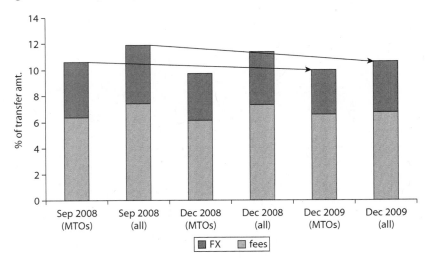

Source: Author's calculations and http://www.moneymove.org, accessed September 15, 2008.
Note: Bars labeled "(all)" following a country name designate total average fees for MTOs and banks in that country. Bars labeled with only the country name designate the average total fees charged by MTOs only in that country. Data represent unweighted averages of all the surveyed RSPs by the remittance price comparison site http://www.moneymove.org for the eight corridors that the site covers, from the United Kingdom to Africa. Data for each wave were based on the same methodology, but there were changes to the number of RSPs surveyed to take account of new entrants to the market. MTO = money transfer operator. FX = foreign exchange.

Annex 11.1 shows the breakdown of data for each of the corridors in more detail. The three surveys, although adopting different methodologies, produced reasonably similar data.[14]

Banks can send remittances to many African countries but tend to impose higher minimum charges, which makes their service seem more expensive at lower levels. In addition, note that these figures represent a simple average of the data that were gathered; they have not been weighted or manipulated in any way. In the absence of accurate market share data, it is not possible to undertake this type of exercise.

From the available data, it is clear that formal remittances are costing consumers around 10 percent when sent from the United Kingdom to Africa. This is a high cost for relatively small sums, but it is broadly in line with the levels charged to send remittances from the United Kingdom to all other destinations (although the global remittance price database shows that pricing for transactions to South Asia is somewhat cheaper than for those sent to Africa).[15]

Prices have decreased significantly during the past two years to the current levels (DMA survey).[16] The fees remained reasonably stable from mid-2008 to early 2009, although foreign exchange margins continue to decline, as figure 11.5 shows. In addition, a further survey using the same methodology in December 2009 showed that prices had declined further, albeit by a small margin. Therefore, a gradual decline in remittance prices occurred over a 15-month period between September 2008 and December 2009.

Figure 11.5   Costs to Send Remittances to Africa and South Asia

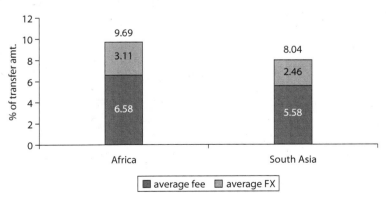

Source: Author's calculations from 2008 U.K. RSP survey and World Bank Remittance Prices database (http://remittanceprices.worldbank.org).
Note: "South Asia" includes Bangladesh, India, Pakistan, and Sri Lanka. FX = foreign exchange. RSP = remittance service provider.

Some banks in the U.K. market offer fee-free remittance services to attract customers in the Indian and Polish communities. Interviews indicate that banks are also planning to do this for some African communities, in particular for Ghanaians and Kenyans.

Informal operators are charging lower fees and foreign exchange margins than formal operators do. On average, the difference is just under 4 percent, or around one-third of the total cost. This price differential helps to explain why informal operators can attract remittance volume. Annex 11.1 shows that, in general, banks charge more for lower-value remittances. For example, it is not uncommon for banks to charge a flat fee of £20 for all transactions from £1 to £2,000. Thus banks are seen as less competitive at the average remittance transaction amounts.

Annex 11.1 also shows that, on a country-specific basis, the more providers a country has, the more competitive the pricing. Ghana and Nigeria provide good examples of competitive pricing structures. In those corridors with fewer formal players, such as Rwanda and Zambia, the pricing is higher. Normal market forces are at work here, and because the Rwandan and Zambian communities in the United Kingdom are much smaller than the Ghanaian and Nigerian communities, this result is not unexpected. However, Zimbabwe also has a large population in the United Kingdom (estimated at over 1 million), and yet few formal companies are serving this market and the pricing is high, largely because of the extreme political and economic instability in Zimbabwe. Measures to improve the situation must be taken in Zimbabwe before more formal companies will enter the market.

The 2008 U.K. survey also asked RSPs whether they had changed their pricing over the previous 12 months. Half the companies responded, as shown previously in table 11.2, that there had been a small drop in overall costs, driven largely by formal sector price cuts.

Customer service and grievance procedures. The significant majority of surveyed RSP firms said they had a system for handling complaints. Indeed, the sending agent is normally the point of contact for complaints, although a reasonable number encouraged the beneficiary to talk to the receiving agent.

Many companies said they did not track the number of complaints received; the few that did respond said the number of complaints ranged between 1 and 10 per month. Most complaints are resolved in less than a week. Just under half of the companies surveyed had dedicated full-time staff to address customer grievances. Many advised that team members shared these duties, which form only a part of each employee's workload. Reassuringly, the companies also responded that few transactions go missing at any stage.

Most of the businesses surveyed stated that they provide financial literacy material to their customers. Upon closer inspection, however, these materials were normally described as leaflets, posters, or brochures. Most of the items, where available, were marketing pieces of limited educational value. African consumers would benefit from greater understanding about how financial products work and the costs associated with them.

Identification requirements. Most of the businesses surveyed said they required identification documents from their customers to be able to transfer money overseas. (Strictly speaking, this is not a necessity for a one-off transaction below €1,000 in value that does not arouse suspicion, so this response was interesting.)

All of the banks and nearly all of the formal operators responded that they require documentation. Surprisingly, one-third of the informal operators said they required identification as well, perhaps because they often operate in partnership with formal organizations in the payout market. This response does, however, question the assumption that the informal sector neither understands nor operates within the AML environment. One-third of the informal operators said they did not require documentation. These companies served a variety of corridors, including Nigeria, Somalia, and Zimbabwe.

When identification is required, the most commonly accepted forms were a passport, followed by a driver's license, national ID, and proof of residency. The companies sending money to South Africa are more likely to accept national ID cards than are operators sending to other countries. Operators did not distinguish between existing customers and new customers (not previously registered with the operator) in terms of the ID that was required.

The United Kingdom does not have a national identity card system, so it is interesting to observe that there is a common approach to the accepted type of ID. In some of the migrant communities—among Somalians, for example—the availability of ID is variable. Although the Somalia-based businesses use the same process as other U.K. operators to identify their customers in the United Kingdom, their approach in Somalia is more localized. There, when individuals lack formal identification, they use community contacts and the clan-based system: A respected clan elder accompanies the receiver on his or her first visit to collect the money, formally identifies the individual, and vouches for him or her—a serious commitment in Somali society.

Conclusions and Recommendations

This section outlines some recommendations that, if implemented, would improve the remittance market from the United Kingdom to Sub-Saharan Africa for operators and consumers.

Africa-Specific Recommendations

- Regulators in African countries should recognize the benefit of introducing regulations that encourage competition. To this end, they should consider broadening the types of business that can provide remittances to include not only banks but also other classes of trade, including nonbank financial service providers and retail businesses.
- Mechanisms to establish a dialogue between remittance industry and the central banks and governments of the origin and destination countries should be developed, which will help to shape regulation and market operations to the benefit of all stakeholders. Such mechanisms can also help to examine how to facilitate the introduction of new services and expand the reach of existing services.
- Research on specific remittance-receiving markets (such as the Africa country studies included in the previous chapters of this volume) could produce more detailed data—about volumes, revenues, and market challenges—that would help policy makers to develop effective action plans. For example, the parallel (informal) market in Nigeria currently may give consumers better value than the formal market, but it also fails to protect consumers, and the government cannot monitor volumes. As circumstances improve in Zimbabwe, there should be efforts to include the Zimbabwean money transfer companies in designing remittance solutions that will work for the community.
- Specific, consumer-oriented financial literacy materials should be produced and promoted—probably through a campaign initiated by the U.K. government and the governments of recipient countries, in conjunction with the remittance industry. Financial literacy efforts should be part of a broader financial inclusion initiative that educates remitters about the optional ways to send money as well as the options available to their families back home about what to do with the money.

General Market Recommendations

- A useful tool for RSPs to form win-win partnerships with organizations in the receiving markets would be the establishment of a communications program including development of a website, conferences, and dissemination of general information. In the customer service arena, although many companies have procedures for addressing complaints, other research has shown that customers are not always aware of the appropriate policies. All remittance service providers should be encouraged to sign up with the U.K. Remittances Customer Charter (see figure 11.6), launched in January 2008, which requires firms to comply with service standards. More than half of the RSP industry already voluntarily complies with the charter, but other organizations should be encouraged to do so. Wherever consumers see the charter displayed, they know they will receive a certain standard of service. The change in regulation brought about by the PSD in November 2009 means that consumers can file complaints with the Financial Ombudsman Service. Because the charter requires signatories to give this information to consumers, signing up by RSPs could be a useful tool to engender further trust in operators.

Regulatory and Business Recommendations

- Many of the informal operators already run their businesses like formal operators but remain unaware of the RSP industry regulations. Regulatory authorities should work with diaspora organizations and community groups to communicate with informal operators about how straightforward it is to comply with the regulations and operate within the law.
- HMRC and UKMTA have made significant efforts to explain the AML regulations and the risk-based approach. However, RSPs still lack clarity about what is and is not acceptable. A continuation of these efforts, together with the establishment of clearer answers wherever possible, would be beneficial.
- Money transfer companies find it difficult to obtain new bank accounts because of some banks' approach to AML concerns. This is particularly true for MTOs from Somalia and Sudan. UKMTA is working closely with the banks, but further input and guidance from the regulatory bodies would help to provide workable guidelines that would make it easier for banks to operate.
- The PSD went into force on November 1, 2009. All businesses that have not applied should be actively encouraged to do so.

Figure 11.6   U.K. Remittances Customer Charter

Remittances Customer Charter

Any organisation that displays this Charter agrees to meet the following standards when sending money abroad (in a foreign currency) for individuals.

Our commitment to you is:

Before agreeing to undertake a transaction we will provide you with:

- ✔ An estimate of the total fee that you, the sender, will be charged by us for the transaction. If we believe that the receiver may also have to pay a fee, then we will tell you
- ✔ An indication of the exchange rate that we will apply to your transaction, if requested. If a further exchange rate may be applied we will tell you to expect this
- ✔ Information on where the receiver should collect the money from and what they have to do
- ✔ An indication of when the funds will be available at the organisation to which you are sending the money
- ✔ Information on cancellation procedures and any charges for cancelling or amending a transaction.

Upon completion of a transaction we will provide you with the following in writing:

- ✔ A transaction reference number that is unique to your payment
- ✔ Confirmation of the exact amount we are sending for you
- ✔ The fees that you have paid to us for this service
- ✔ The estimated amount that the receiver will receive and the currency that the money will be paid/credited in
- ✔ The exchange rate that has been applied to your transaction where this is available. Where this is not available or where additional rates will be used we will tell you how the foreign exchange conversion will be calculated
- ✔ Information on where the receiver collect it or confirmation of the bank to which the money has been sent
- ✔ When the money will be available for the receiver. Whether this timescale is definite or the best estimate that we can make
- ✔ In the case of cash collections, what the receiver has to do in order to collect the money.
- ✔ The procedure to follow if you have a need to query this transaction. We will advise you how long it will take us to provide an answer or an update.

Should you have any queries concerning this charter please contact Seymour Fortescue, Chairman UK Remittances Task Force, c/o Archie Laing, DFID, 1 Palace Street, London SW1E 5HE

Source: U.K. Remittances Task Force.

- Many formal operators are concerned that informal sector competition creates an uneven playing field. The Payment Service Regulations under the PSD should make it easier for the regulators to identify organizations that operate in an unregulated manner. The regulators should proactively and publicly clamp down on informal operators wherever they are identified and enforce the regulations.

- The cost to send £100 is more than 10 percent of face value, which is high for a competitive market. Options to raise consumer awareness include price comparison websites that provide unbiased and current information, such as http://www.moneymove.org and http://remittance prices.worldbank.org. A communication campaign with the African diaspora groups and communities also could be arranged in conjunction with the first regulatory recommendation listed.

Annex 11.1 Country-Specific Pricing Grids

Table 11.A.1.1   Remittance Pricing, by African Corridor

Country	Operation type[a]	No. of operators	To send £100			To send £250		
			Average fee (£)	Average FX (%)	Average total cost (%)	Average fee (£)	Average FX (%)	Average total cost (%)
Congo, Dem. Rep.	MTOs	5	8.18	3.96	12.14	17.18	3.96	11.06
Ethiopia	MTOs	6	7.82	2.67	10.49	16.82	2.67	9.40
Ghana	MTOs	17	4.52	3.76	8.28	10.36	3.76	7.90
Ghana	All	19	5.63	3.62	9.25	10.85	3.77	8.11
Kenya	MTOs	14	6.49	4.45	10.94	11.67	4.45	9.12
Kenya	All	18	9.27	4.62	13.89	13.3	4.62	9.94
Nigeria	MTOs	20	5.64	2.46	8.10	12.99	2.46	7.40
Nigeria	All	22	6.50	2.54	9.03	13.18	2.75	7.76
Rwanda	MTOs	3	7.30	5.28	12.58	13.30	5.28	10.60
Sierra Leone	MTOs	10	4.89	4.86	9.74	10.69	4.86	9.13
Somalia	MTOs	4	4.25	2,15	6.40	11.38	2.15	6.70
South Africa	MTOs	10	5.90	5.23	11.13	7.10	5.23	8.07
South Africa	All	14	9.64	4.78	14.42	10.50	4.78	8.98
Uganda	MTOs	5	4.60	6.93	11.53	9.40	6.93	10.69
Uganda	All	7	7.57	6.05	13.62	11.00	6.05	10.45
Zambia	MTOs	4	10.23	3.11	13.34	18.35	3.11	10.06
Zambia	All	6	11.82	3.86	15.68	17.23	3.86	10.39
Zimbabwe	MTOs	5	6.58	6.19	12.77	12.58	6.19	11.22
Average, Sept 15, 2008	MTOs		6.37	4.25	10.62	12.65	4.25	9.28
Average, Sept. 15, 2008	All		7.4	4.49	11.89	13.36	4.51	9.79
Average, Dec. 4, 2008	MTOs		6.14	3.60	9.53	12.62	3.60	8.31
Average, Dec. 4, 2008	All		7.32	4.00	11.02	13.44	4.00	9.04
Average, Dec. 15, 2009	MTOs		6.55	3.44	9.99	13.20	3.44	8.71
Average, Dec. 15, 2009	All		6.70	3.91	10.2	13.03	3.57	8.77

Source: http://www.moneymove.org, accessed September 15, 2008, December 4, 2008, and December 15, 2009.
Note: MTO = money transfer operator. FX = foreign exchange.
"All" in the "Operation type" column designates total average fees for MTOs and banks. Other entries in the column designate the average total fees charged by MTOs only.

Notes

1. The survey was conducted by Developing Markets Associates Ltd (DMA). (http://www.developingmarkets.com/dma). DMA provides advice and management services to donor agencies, governments, and the wider business community in three areas of expertise: remittances, investment programs, and international development events. Its goal within the remittance market is to encourage greater amounts of funds to be remitted through formal channels at the lowest possible cost and at the greatest possible efficiency.

2. The four case studies in the chapter boxes are based on interviews at businesses visited during the RSP survey. The companies' identities have not been divulged to protect the firms' privacy.

3. The £4.1 billion estimate was included in a statement from Her Majesty's Treasury that was read in the House of Commons.

4. The U.K. Office of National Statistics identifies these other key receiving markets (in order of largest to smallest remittance volumes): Germany, Ireland, the United States, France, and Australia. These countries do receive significant remittance volumes from the United Kingdom but are not considered developing markets.

5. Unless otherwise stated, findings about the RSP market refer to both formal (including banks) and informal providers.

6. "Light touch" is Her Majesty's Treasury's term to describe its regulatory approach.

7. All money service businesses in the United Kingdom—including MTOs, currency exchanges, and other nonbank financial institutions—are registered with HMRC. As of June 2008, there were 1,751 registered money service businesses in the United Kingdom.

8. M-PESA, a mobile-phone money transfer service, has become the most popular mode of money transfer in the Kenyan domestic market. Its branchless banking service was developed for mobile telecom company Vodafone. Now the largest mobile-phone money transfer operator in Africa, M-PESA offers domestic money transfer services in Kenya and is currently working with Western Union to kick off cross-border money transfer services.

9. Subsequent anecdotal discussions with MTOs have shown that they hope the PSD will enable banks to look upon authorized PIs more favorably.

10. Although Chequepoint was a large RSP at the time of the survey, it stopped operating in the United Kingdom in 2009 because of the PSD.

11. The US$200 was assumed to be the equivalent of £100 (at the time of the survey), which, coincidentally, is about the mode for transactions made from the United Kingdom. The average transaction size is estimated to be £275.

12. Base data come from the World Bank Remittance Prices database, http://www.remittanceprices.worldbank.org.

13. Data obtained by DMA, which provides mystery shopping services (see note 1).

14. The global database survey was based on five African corridors. Within that survey, the data for Nigeria distorted the overall findings more than was the case with the U.K. RSP survey conducted by the author. (During the African RSP survey, Nigeria had a negative foreign exchange market because of the parallel market.) In addition, the U.K. RSP survey included banks and informal companies distorted the overall findings more than was the case with the U.K. RSP survey conducted by the author. (During the African RSP survey, Nigeria had a negative foreign exchange market because of the parallel market.) In addition, the U.K. RSP survey included banks and informal companies.

15. Data come from the World Bank Remittance Prices database, http://www.remittanceprices.worldbank.org.

16. DMA market surveys based on historic data are found at http://www.money move.org.

References

DFID (U.K. Department for International Development). 2005. "Sending Money Home? A Survey of Remittance Products and Services in the U.K." London: DFID.

DMA (Developing Markets Associates). 2007. "Mystery Shopping Exercise for Transactions from U.K. to Nigeria." Report to the U.K. Remittances Task Force, DMA, London.

———. 2008. "Migrant Remittances and Linkage to Broader Access to Financial Services." Research for the U.K. Remittances Task Force, DMA, London. http://www.moneymove.org/Images/Documents/ACF1AD2.pdf.

World Bank. 2011. *Migration and Remittances Factbook 2011*. Migration and Remittances Unit. Washington, DC: World Bank.

Contributors

Chukwuma Agu coordinates Research and Publications at the African Institute for Applied Economics in Enugu, Nigeria. His research interests are mainly in openeconomy macroeconomics, international economic coordination and finance, trade and regional integration, and macroeconomic policy reforms. He also has deep interests in and familiarity with tools of macroeconometric and systems modeling and forecasting. Mr. Agu has attended several specialized trainings, including the Cambridge Advanced Programme on Rethinking Development Economics as well as the training program on Financial Programming and Policies of the International Monetary Fund (IMF) He has published several journal articles, and he has coedited and contributed to books in his areas of interest. He has been actively involved in development policy making, being part of the team that developed Nigeria's current economic policy reforms program. Mr. Agu consults for several economic policy groups and serves as external reviewer for a number of international academic and policy journals. He holds a Ph.D. in cconomics from the University of Nigeria.

Yiriyibin Bambio is a Lecturer at the Faculty of Economics and Management, University of Ouagadougou, Burkina Faso. His current research examines the effects of migration and remittances on poverty and inequality in rural Burkina Faso. His research interests include poverty analysis, impact evaluation, and microcredit. He has been involved in many research or development projects, elaborating survey methodologies, and conducting surveys and data analysis. He holds a Ph.D. in Economics from the University of Ouagadougou.

Fatou Cisse is a Lecturer and researcher at the Faculty of Economics and Management at the Cheikh Anta Diop University and Consortium pour la Recherche Économique et Sociale (CRES) in Dakar, Senegal. Her fields of interest are dynamics of poverty, education, labor markets, and migration. She specializes in general equilibrium modeling and microsimulation. She has authored or coauthored several published papers on the implications of regional integration and trade liberalization on poverty and income distribution and on determinants of demand for education.

Alemayehu Geda is Professor of Economics at the Department of Economics, Addis Ababa University. He is also a research associate of the University of London (School of Oriental and African Studies [SOAS], London), the African Economic Research Consortium (Nairobi), and The Kenyan Institute for Public Policy Research and Analysis (KIPPRA), Nairobi. He has worked as a consultant for a number of international organizations including the United Nations Economic Commission for Africa (UNECA), the United Nations Development Programme (UNDP), the World Bank, the Swedish International Development Cooperation Agency (Sida), and the U.K. Department for International Development (DFID), as well as the governments of Ethiopia, Kenya, Tanzania, Uganda, and Zambia. He has taught macroeconomics, macroeconometric modeling, and international economics at the University of London, Addis Ababa University, and the African Economic Research Consortium. He has published widely on African, Kenyan, and Ethiopian economies in major international journals and has authored several books, including *Applied Time Series Econometrics for Africa* (Addis Ababa University and AERC 2006) and *Readings on Ethiopian Economy*.

Jacqueline Irving is a consultant economist in the Development Prospects Group at the World Bank. She has also worked for the World Bank's African Department on local sources of infrastructure finance in Africa and its Development Prospects Group's *Global Development*

Finance report as a coauthor on topics including South-South bank lending and foreign investment in African bond markets. She has participated in operational work and published papers, including for the IMF, on African countries' access to foreign private capital and regional integration of African securities markets. Previous experience includes seven years with the Economist Intelligence Unit (EIU), most recently leading a team of analysts for the country report series, *Financing Foreign Operations*. She has continued to contribute articles on African financial markets to the EIU and has also consulted for the United Nations, including the Development Financing Unit and the UNECA. She has a Master's degree from Columbia University.

Leon Isaacs is a Chief Executive of Developing Markets Associates (DMA), a firm specializing in consultancy services in and around the international remittance market. He is acknowledged as one of the world's leading private-sector experts on remittances. In addition to his position at DMA, he is Managing Director of the International Association of Money Transfer Networks (IAMTN). His role includes liaising with international regulators, technology companies, consumers, and stakeholders who have an interest in the remittance market. He is a member of the Steering Group of the U.K. Remittances Task Force and sits on the Consultative Committee of the World Bank's G8 Public Private Partnership on remittances. Prior to establishing DMA, he worked for 15 years at a senior level for a number of international money transfer companies, including MoneyGram, Travelex Thomas Cook, and Coinstar.

Sanket Mohapatra is an economist with the Development Prospects Group of the World Bank. His research interests include international capital flows, sovereign and subsovereign ratings, corporate financing patterns, poverty, inequality and growth, and the development impact of remittances and migration. He has contributed to various issues of the World Bank's flagship *Global Development Finance* and *Global Economic Prospects* reports. He is a core team member of the Africa regional flagship report, *Leveraging Migration for Africa: Remittances, Skills, and Investments.* He work has been published in peer-reviewed journals and working papers. He holds a Ph.D. in Economics from Columbia University and has a Master's degree from the Delhi School of Economics.

Rose W. Ngugi is an Adviser to the Executive Director for Africa at the International Monetary Fund. She has been a Senior Lecturer at the School of Economics at the University of Nairobi in Kenya. She has also served as member of the Monetary Policy Advisory Committee of the Central Bank of Kenya and participated as a member in the Police Reform Task Force under the Office of the President and the Private Sector Development Strategy Technical Committee under Kenya's Ministry of Trade and Industry. Her research areas are financial sector issues, private-sector development issues, and economic reforms in general. Her research has been published in refereed journals and as working papers and discussion papers. She holds a Ph.D. in Financial Economics from the University of Birmingham.

Frederic Ponsot is an inclusive finance expert and independent consultant based in Paris, with a specialization in microfinance and remittances. He has worked in Africa for CAPAF, a microfinance capacity building Consultative Group to Assist the Poor (CGAP) program based in Dakar, Senegal, and with the GRET in Paris, a French international nongovernmental organization, as a program manager in the Microfinance and Small Enterprise Department in charge of a program aiming to set up housing finance products for Senegalese migrants in Italy with the support of the International Fund for Agricultural Development (IFAD) and the Financial Facility for Remittances. He has led several studies targeting Europe-to-Africa remittance corridors covering West African remittance markets, as well as feasibility studies to set up remittance channels with microfinance institutions in Africa using new technologies, regulatory issues, and financial products for migrants for the World Bank, the African Development Bank, the European Union, the Cooperation of Luxembourg and the French development agency (AFD). Mr. Ponsot has an M.B.A. in macroeconomics and development economics.

Georgiana Pop is an Economist with the Poverty Reduction and Economic Management Network in the Africa Region, World Bank. She joined the World Bank in 2008 and has substantive operational experience with growth, competitiveness, and infrastructure issues in several West African countries. Before joining the World Bank, she specialized in competition and investment policies at the Organisation for Economic Co-operation and Development (OECD) in Paris, the European Commission Delegation in Bucharest, and the Competition Council of Romania. She also has in-depth expertise in economic issues in several emerging markets from Southeast Europe and Central Asia. She has authored papers on growth and competitiveness, export promotion, infrastructure, competition, and investment policies. She holds an M.P.A. in Economic Policy Management from Columbia University and an M.A. in European Economics and International Affairs from the National School of Politics and Public Administration in Bucharest.

Peter Quartey is a Senior Research Fellow at the Institute of Statistical, Social, and Economic Research (ISSER), University of Ghana. He is also the Deputy Head at the Centre for Migration Studies, University of Ghana. His research interests include private sector development, development finance, monetary economics, migration and remittances, and poverty analysis. He is an active member of the African Economic Research Consortium (EARC) and the Global Development Network (GDN). He holds a Ph.D. in Development Economics from the University of Manchester, an M.Sc. in Quantitative Development Economics (University of Warwick), and a M.Phil. and B.A. in Economics from the University of Ghana.

Dilip Ratha is a Lead Economist and Manager of the Migration and Remittances Team in the Development Prospects Group of the World Bank. He is also the CEO of *Migrating Out of Poverty* research consortium and a Visiting Professor of Economics at the University of Sussex. He was a lead author of the World Bank flagship *Global Economic Prospects 2006* and editor of *Remittances: Development Impact and Future Prospects*. He is the lead author of the regional flagship report, *Leveraging Migration for Africa: Remittances, Skills, and Investments*. He has advised many governments and played a role in international and intergovernmental forums, including the Global Forum on Migration and Development, the G8 Global Remittances Working Group, and the World Economic Forum Council on migration. Reflecting his deep interest in financing development in poor countries, he recently edited *Innovative Financing for Development* featuring his work on shadow sovereign rating, diaspora bonds, and future-flow securitization. Prior to joining the World Bank, he worked as a Regional Economist for Asia at Credit Agricole Indosuez; an Assistant Professor of Economics at the Indian Institute of Management, Ahmedabad; and an Economist at the Policy Group, New Delhi.

Edward Sennoga is a country economist at the African Development Bank (AfDB). His research interests are in the fields of public finance, tax policy, economics of developing countries, and applied econometrics. His research has been published in economics journals such as the *Economic Inquiry*, *FinanzArchiv*, and the *National Tax Journal*. He is responsible for the Economic and Sector Work agenda of the Uganda Country Office. Dr. Sennoga has also provided research and technical support to Georgia's Department of Labor, the Georgia Legislature, Uganda's National Planning Authority, the New Partnership for Africa's Development (NEPAD), and the World Bank. He has also taught various courses at both undergraduate and graduate levels, including macroeconomics, microeconomics, public sector economics, and econometrics at the University of North Texas, Georgia State University, and Makerere University. Dr. Sennoga obtained his Ph.D. from Georgia State University in Atlanta, Georgia.